AF720411

Gun Jumping In Merger Control

A Jurisdictional Guide

Foreword by
Prof. Richard Whish

Editors
Catriona Hatton
Andrea Hamilton
Yves Comtois

All rights reserved. No photocopying: copyright licences do not apply. The information provided in this publication is general and may not apply in a specific situation. Legal advice should always be sought before taking any legal action based on the information provided. The publisher accepts no responsibility for any acts or omissions contained herein. Enquiries concerning reproduction should be sent to the Institute of Competition Law, at the address below.

Copyright © 2019 by Institute of Competition Law
106 West 32nd Street, Suite 144 New York, NY, 10001, USA
www.concurrences.com
book@concurrences.com

Printed in the United States

First Printing, September 2019
978-1-939007-10-0 (hardcover)
978-1-939007-08-7 (paperback)
LCCN: 2019946940
Cover: Yves Buliard, www.yvesbuliard.fr

Book Design and Layout implementation: Nordcompo

Contributors

Sakshi Agarwal
Trilegal

Inbal Rosenblum Brand
M. Firon & Co

Logan Breed
Hogan Lovells

Neil Campbell
McMillan LLP

David Cardwell
Baker Botts LLP

Anisha Chand
Khaitan & Co

Cecil Saehoon Chung
Yulchon LLC

Yves Comtois
Baker Botts LLP

Eytan Epstein
M. Firon & Co

Sandhya Foster
Herbert Smith Freehills

Marcos Garrido
Pinheiro Neto Advogados

Gönenç Gürkaynak
ELIG Gürkaynak Attorneys-at-Law

Andrea Hamilton
McDermott Will & Emery LLP

Michael Han
Fangda Partners

Etsuko Hara
Anderson Mori & Tomotsune

Catriona Hatton
Baker Botts LLP

Kristin Heilborn
Roschier

Kristian Hugmark
Roschier

Niko Hukkinen
Frontia

Arshad (Paku) Khan
Khaitan & Co

David Mamane
Schellenberg Wittmer

Mazor Matzkevich
M. Firon & Co

Jean Meijer
Herbert Smith Freehills

Alastair Mordaunt
Freshfields Bruckhaus Deringer

Miranda Noble
MinterEllison

Jens Munk Plum
Kromann Reumert

Amilcar Peredo Rivera
Basham, Ringe y Correa

Paul Schoff
MinterEllison

Christian Steinle
Gleiss Lutz

Didier Théophile
Darrois Villey Maillot Brochier

Anastasia Usova
Redcliffe Partners

Amalie Wijesundera
Schellenberg Wittmer

Atsushi Yamada
Anderson Mori & Tomotsune

Cristianne Zarzur
Pinheiro Neto Advogados

Concurrences Books

Antitrust Liber Amicorum

Eleanor Fox – Liber Amicorum, *Nicolas Charbit, Sonia Ahmad (ed.), 2021*

Richard Whish – Liber Amicorum, *Nicolas Charbit, Sonia Ahmad (ed.), 2020*

Herbert Hovenkamp – Liber Amicorum, *Nicolas Charbit, Sonia Ahmad (ed.), 2020*

Albert Foer – Liber Amicorum, *Nicolas Charbit, Sonia Ahmad (ed.), 2020*

Frédéric Jenny – Standing Up for Convergence and Relevance in Antitrust, Vol. I & II
Nicolas Charbit, Sonia Ahmad (ed.), 2019 & 2020

Douglas H. Ginsburg – An Antitrust Professor on the Bench, Vol. I & II
Nicolas Charbit, Sonia Ahmad (ed.), 2018 & 2020

Wang Xiaoye – The Pioneer of Competition Law in China, *Adrian Emch, Wendy Ng (ed.), 2019*

Ian S. Forrester – A Scot Without Borders, Vol. I & II, *Assimakis Komninos et al. (ed.), 2015*

William E. Kovacic: An Antitrust Tribute, Vol. I & II, *Nicolas Charbit et al. (ed.), 2013 & 2014*

Practical Law

Competition Digest – A Synthesis of EU and National Leading Cases, 4th ed.
Frédéric Jenny (ed.), 2020

Competition Law Inquiries in the EU – A Practitioner's Guide, *Nathalie Jalabert-Doury, 2020*

Competition Women, Vol. I & II, *Kristina Nordlander & Evelina Kurgonaite (ed.), 2019*

Gun-jumping in Merger Control – A Jurisdictional Guide, *Catriona Hatton, Andrea Hamilton & Yves Comtois, 2019*

Choice – A New Standard for Competition Analysis?, *Paul Nihoul et al., 2016*

EU Law and Life Science, *Peter Bogaert, Damien Geradin (ed.), 2014*

PhD Theses

The Role of Media Pluralism in the Enforcement of EU Competition Law, *Konstantina Bania, 2019*

Buyer Power in EU Competition Law, *Ignacio Herrera Anchustegui, 2017*

Conference Proceedings

Antitrust in Emerging and Developing Countries – Vol I & II
Eleanor Fox, Harry First (ed.), 2015 & 2016

Global Antitrust Law – Current Issues in Antitrust Law and Economics
Douglas Ginsburg, Joshua Wright (ed.), 2015

Competition Law on the Global Stage: David Gerber's Global Competition Law in Perspective
David Gerber (ed.), 2014

e-Book versions are available to Concurrences+ subscribers.

FOREWORD

RICHARD WHISH, QC (HON)

Emeritus Professor of Law, King's College London

The majority of merger control regimes in the world today require the parties to a transaction to pre-notify it to the relevant authorities. A standstill obligation then comes into effect which requires them not to begin the process of integration of the two businesses until clearance has been given. There are a few systems, for example in the United Kingdom and Singapore, that do not mandate pre-notification, but these are the exception to the general rule. Penalties can be imposed for infringing the requirements to pre-notify and to refrain from implementation; in some regimes these can be imposed on natural as well as legal persons.

There is nothing particularly new about mandatory pre-notification: for example in the United States, the Hart-Scott-Rodino Antitrust Improvements Act ('HSR'), which created section 7A of the Clayton Act, is now more than 40 years old. The European Union Merger Regulation ('EUMR') required pre-notification of mergers from its inception in 1990. In the US there has been quite a lot of enforcement action under the HSR legislation, and that is where the most helpful decisional practice on the topic of 'gun jumping' will be found. The European Commission has also taken action from time to time against gun-jumping. It did so for the first time in 1997 in the case of *Bertelsmann/Kirch/Premiere*, but without reaching a formal conclusion. Subsequently the Commission imposed fines in a few cases for failure to notify a merger: the first decision was *Samsung* in 1998, in which a fine of €33,000 was imposed. Larger fines, each of €20 million, followed in the cases of *Electrabel/Compagnie National du Rhône* in 2009 and *Marine Harvest* in 2014. The *Marine Harvest* decision was unsuccessfully challenged before the General Court in 2017 and a judgment from the Court of Justice is now awaited in this case. Gun-jumping has also been penalised in various other jurisdictions around the world, for example in Brazil, China, India and Korea.

It follows that the duty to avoid gun jumping, and the risks associated with it, are a reasonably well-known part of the legal landscape. What is interesting, however, is that this is a topic that has not been explored very much in the legal literature, nor on the conference circuit. Little guidance has been provided by competition authorities on what constitutes gun-jumping, one notable exception to this being the *Guidelines for the Analysis of Previous Consummation of Merger Transactions* of the Brazilian Administrative Council for Economic Defence (CADE) published in September 2016.

Four recent cases in Europe have given the subject of gun-jumping much greater prominence. First, the French Competition Authority (*Autorité de la Concurrence*) imposed a fine of €80 million in the case of *Altice/SFR & OTL* in November 2016 for the premature completion of two mergers that had been notified in 2014. Altice was then fined a second time, this time by the European Commission, which imposed a fine of €125 million in the case of *Altice/PT Portugal* in April 2018. Perhaps most interesting of all was the judgment of the Court of Justice in the *Ernst & Young/KPMG Denmark* case in May 2018, in which case Advocate General Wahl pointed out that the issue of gun-jumping had never been considered in the jurisprudence of the Court even though the EUMR had by then been in force for 28 years. More recently the Commission has imposed a fine of €28 million in the case of *Canon/Toshiba Medical* in June 2019.

Increased interest in the subject of gun-jumping led the OECD Competition Committee to hold one of its roundtable discussions on *Gun jumping and suspensory effects of merger notifications* in November 2018. Papers were submitted by 30 national competition authorities, the European Commission and by Business at OECD ('BIAC') containing a great deal of useful information about the decisional practice on gun-jumping around the world and, in the case of BIAC, a discussion of the difficulties for firms in complying with the various provisions on gun-jumping around the world while at the same time planning for the future integration of the businesses to be merged, preserving the value of the assets to be acquired and conducting effective due diligence. The roundtable, in conjunction with the four recent cases referred to above, revealed that a systematic approach needed to be taken to the subject of gun-jumping, both in terms of the substantive law and the practical steps that firms need to take in order to avoid transgressions of that law.

As far as the substantive law is concerned, the *Ernst & Young* case was of particular interest. The EUMR specifically imposes a duty to pre-notify mergers in Article 4(1), and the standstill obligation is to be found in Article 7(1) EUMR. In *Marine Harvest* and *Altice* those firms were fined for imposing both of these provisions. But *Ernst & Young* also made clear that conduct that does *not* fall foul of the standstill obligation may nevertheless amount to an infringement of Article 101 TFEU. It is relatively easy to work out whether and when there is a duty to pre-notify a merger; what is less clear is what constitutes the partial acquisition of control of the target business. Suppose that a would-be acquiror of a business obtains information about the target: is that a 'normal' part of the due diligence process and entirely innocent? Or a breach of the standstill obligation imposed by merger control? Or an independent antitrust infringement subject to Article 101? Given the obvious risks of infringing one or other of these provisions, firms need to know what practical steps need to be taken in order to avoid entanglement with competition authorities and to ensure a smooth and efficient integration of the two business.

These important and complex issues have led to the publication of this excellent work by Concurrences, containing the work product of the Mergers Working Group of the Antitrust Section of the International Bar Association. The book contains the first multi-jurisdictional survey of gun-jumping to have been undertaken, and looks at the decisional practice in 21 major jurisdictions, from Australia to the US via China, India and many other countries. The subject matter is presented in a highly accessible, systematic manner, looking at the substantive legal provisions, including the relationship between the merger-specific rules such as Articles 4 and 7 of the EUMR and antitrust law as such, for example Article 101. The actual decisional practice in various jurisdictions is analysed, and an excellent high-level view is provided in the introductory chapter by Catriona Hatton and Yves Comtois of Baker Botts and Andrea Hamilton of McDermott Will & Emery. Concurrences and the contributors to this project deserve to be congratulated on the production of a highly timely work which will be of immense benefit to firms, their business advisers and to competition authorities around the world.

TABLE OF CONTENTS

TABLE OF CASES

AUSTRALIA

ACCC v Cryosite [2019] FCA 116

ACCC v Pacific National Pty Ltd [2018] FCA 1221

ACCC v Pacific National Pty Ltd (No 2) [2019] FCA 669

Norcast S.àr.L v Bradken Limited (No 2) [2013] FCA 235

BRAZIL

Acquisition by OGX of a 40% share from Petrobras of a concession contract, Concentration Act No. 08700.005775/2013-19

Acquisition of assets by the Enzo Group from the Group Smaff, including inventory and trademark representation, Concentration Act No. 08700.010071/2015-20

Acquisition of assets in at least 6 different transactions from 2012 to 2015 by the SAGA Group, mostly related to car dealers, Concentration Act No. 08700.004924/2015-94

Acquisition of Fratelli Dorazio Investments Ltd, Mataboi Foods Ltd, subsidiary by JBJ Agropecuária Ltda, Concentration Act No. 08700.007612/2016-13

Allpark/Bagattini/CGB, Concentration Act No. 08012.011323/2010-81

Blue Cycle/Shimano Inc, Concentration Act No. 08700.002655/2016-11

Condor/Tigre, Concentration Act No. 08700.009988/2014-09

FIAT SpA and Chrysler Group LLC, Concentration Act No. 08700.002285/2014-41. Settlement agreement approved by the Tribunal on 14 May 2014

GNL Gemini Comercialização e Logística Ltda and Companhia de Gás de Minas Gerais (Gasmig/ Gáslocal), Concentration Act. No. 08700.000137/2015-73. Settlement agreement approved by the Tribunal on 24 June 2015

Goiás Verde Alimentos Ltda, Brasfrigo Alimentos Ltda and Brasfrigo S/A, Concentration Act No. 08700.010394/2014-32. Settlement agreement approved by the Tribunal on 22 April 2015

Hypermarcas SA/Reckitt Benckiser Ltda, Concentration Act No. 08700.003462/201679

JBS SA, Tinto Holding Ltda, Unilav Industrial Ltda, Flora Produtos de Higiene e Limpeza Ltda and Tramonto Alimentos SA, Concentration Act No. 08700.007160/2013-27. Judged by the Tribunal on 17 August 2016

Potióleo SA and UTC Óleo e Gás SA, Concentration Act No. 08700.008292/2013-76. Settlement agreement approved by the Tribunal on 5 February 2014

Praxair/Linde, Concentration Act No. 08700.007777/2017-76

Purchase of a subsidiary of Cisco Systems, Inc by Technicolor SA, Concentration Act No. 08700.011836/ 2015-49

UTC Óleo e Gás SA and Aurizônia Petróleo SA, Concentration Act No. 08700.008289/2013-52. Settlement agreement approved by the Tribunal on 5 February 2014

CANADA

R v Béton Régional Inc, Federal Court Trial Division No. T-58-95, 16 January 1995

CHINA

Beijing CNR/Hitachi, 21 April 2016 MOFCOM

Canon/Toshiba Medical Systems, 16 December 2016 MOFCOM

Dade Holdings/Jilin Sichang Pharmaceutical, 21 April 2016 MOFCOM

New United Group/Bombardier Transportation Sweden, 21 April 2016 MOFCOM

Gaoji Pharmaceuticals/Henan Baijia Haoyisheng Pharmaceuticals, 21 December 2018 SAMR

OCI/Tokuyama Malaysia, 21 April 2017 MOFCOM

Paper Excellence BV/Eldorado, 30 July 2018 SAMR

DENMARK

Circle K Denmark A/S and Shell, 26 June 2019 DCCA

KPMG Denmark & EY, 14/07180 SAM/MAN/JKK/CWA, 17 December 2016 DCCA

Norgesgruppen/Dagrofa, 13/05331/MNI/MST/STP, 23 October 2013 DCCA

Norgesgruppen/Dagrofa, MEDS-13/05331/STP/MNI/MST, 25 October 2013 DCCA

SEAS-NVE Holding A/S and Syd Energi Holding A/S, Case No 91250-00002-18, 21 and 22 June 2018 DCCA

EUROPEAN UNION

Altice/PT Portugal (Case M.7993) Commission decision of 24 April 2018 C(2018) 2418 final

AP Møller (Case No IV/M.969) Commission decision of 10 February 1999

Baywa/Clean Energy Trading (Case COMP/M.8758) Commission decision of 7 December 2017 C(2017) 8560 final

British-American Tobacco Company Ltd and RJ Reynolds Industries Inc v Commission (Cases 142 and 156/84) [1987] ECR 04487

Caterpillar/MWM (Case COMP/M.6106) Commission decision of 19 October 2011 C(2011)7434 final

Courage v Crehan (Case C-453/99) [2001] ECR I-6297

Delimitis v Henninger Bräu (Case C-234/89) [1991] ECR I-00935

Electrabel/Compagnie nationale du Rhône (Case COMP/M.4994) Commission decision of 10 June 2009 C (2009) 4416

Ernst & Young P/S v Konkurrencerådet (Case C-633/16) EU:C:2018:371

Europemballage Corp and Continental Can Co v Commission (Case C 6/72) [1973] ECR 215

Facebook/WhatsApp (Case M.8228) Commission decision of 17 May 2017 C(2017) 3192 final

Ineos/Kerling (Case COMP/M.4734) Commission decision of 30 January 2018 C(2008) 379 final

Lufthansa/Certain Air Berlin Assets (Case COMP/M.8633) Commission decision of 27 October 2017 C(2017) 7355 final

Manfredi v Lloyd Adriatico Assicurazioni SpA and others (Joined Cases C-295/04–298/04) [2006] ECR I-6619

Marine Harvest ASA v Commission (Case T-704-14) EU:T:2017:753

Marine Harvest/Morpol (Case COMP/M.7184) Commission decision of 23 July 2014 C(2014) 5089 final

Orica/Dyno (Case COMP/M.4151) Commission decision of 11 April 2006 Samsung/AST (Case No IV/M.980) Commission decision of 18 February 1998

SG-Greffe (2006) D/202009

SJ Johnson/Sara Lee (Case COMP/M.5969) Commission decision of 11 February 2011 C(2011) 1001 final

T-Mobile Netherlands BV and others v Raad van bestuur van der Nederlandse Mededingingsautoriteit (Case C-8/08) [2009] ECR I-04529

Yara/Kemira Growhow (Case COMP/M.4730) Commission decision of 21 September 2007 SG-Greffe(2007) D/205611

FINLAND

St1 Oy/Lämpöpuisto Oy, 1 March 2017 FCCA

VR-Yhtymä Oy/Avecra Oy, 3 July 2017 FCCA

FRANCE

Altice, Decision No 16-D-24 of 8 November 2016, FCA

British Steel/Ascoval, Decision No 19-DCC-96 of 16 May 2019, FCA

Cooperl/Financière Turenne Lafayette, Decision No 17-DCC-169 of 20 October 2017, FCA

Eurotunnel/SeaFrance, Decision No 12-DCC-154 of 7 November 2012, FCA

Finegee/Heineken France, Decision No 06-D-31 of 20 October 2006, Conseil de la concurrence

Gibert Joseph/Gibert Jeune, Decision No 17-DCC-186 of 10 November 2017, FCA

ICG/Courtepaille, Decision No 15-DCC-47 of 5 May 2015, FCA

Plukon/Duc, Decision No 17-DCC-10 of 27 January 2017, FCA

Practices implemented in the pay-TV sector, Decision No 10-D-32 of 16 November 2010, FCA

GERMANY

Bundeskartellamt order of 27 November 2003 – B 6-51/02, WuW/E DE-V 885 (not publicly available, reference in Bundeskartellamt, Activity Report 2003/2004 (German only))

Bundeskartellampt order of 5 October 2015 – B2-47/14 (not publicly available, reference in Bundeskartellamt press release of 5 October 2015 "Demerger of organic dairies Andechser and Söbbeke")

Druck- und Verlagshaus Frankfurt am Main GmbH, 13 February 2009, Bundeskartellamt

EDEKA/Kaiser's Tengelmann, (Case KVR 57/16) DE:BGH:2017:141117BKVR57.16.0, Decision of the German Federal Court of Justice of 14 November 2017

Homag/IMA, 22 June 2005, Bundeskartellamt

Interseroh, 10 May 2011, Bundeskartellamt

Kart (Case VI-W) Higher Regional Court of Düsseldorf, order of 3 April 2018, 2/18

Mars/Nutro, 15 December 2008, Bundeskartellamt

INDIA

Adani Transmission Limited/Reliance Electric Generation and Supply Limited, Order of the CCI under Section 43A of the Competition Act dated 30 July 2018 in Combination Registration C-2018/01/547

Baxalta Incorporated/Baxter International Inc, Order of the CCI under Section 43A of the Competition Act dated 8 March 2016 in Combination Registration C-2015/07/297

Bharti Airtel Limited/Tata Teleservices Limited, Order of the CCI under Section 43A of the Competition Act dated 27 August 2018 in Combination Registration C-2017/10/5311

Builders Association of India v Cement Manufacturers' Association [2016] SCC OnLine CCI 46

Builders Association of India v Cement Manufacturers' Association, Competition Appeal No. 22–26 of 2017 NCLAT

Chhatwal Group Trust/Dilip Builcon Limited, Order of the CCI under Section 43A of the Competition Act dated 8 August 2018 in Combination Registration C-2018/01/544

Competition Commission of India v Thomas Cook (India) Ltd & Anr [2018] 6 SCC 549

Eli Lilly & Company/Novartis AG, Order of the CCI under Section 43A of the Competition Act dated 14 July 2016 in Combination Registration C-2015/07/289

GE Energy Europe BV/GE/GEIF Alstom India Limited/Alstom T&D India Limited, Order of the CCI under Section 43A of the Competition Act dated 16 February 2016 in Combination Registration C-2015/01/241

Google LLC & Ors v Competition Commission of India & Ors, Competition Appeal No. 18 of 2018 NCLAT

Hindustan Colas Private Limited/Shell India Markets Private Limited, Order of the CCI under Section 43A of the Competition Act dated 14 September 2016 in Combination Registration No. C-2015/08/299

Intellect Design Arena Limited/Polaris Financial Technology Limited, Order of the CCI under Section 43A of the Competition Act dated 7 May 2018 in Combination Registration C-2015/12/348

LT Foods Limited/Hindustan Unilever Limited, Order of the CCI under Section 43A of the Competition Act dated 11 May 2018 in Combination Registration C-2016/04/387

Matrimony.com Limited v Google LLC [2018] SCC OnLine CCI 1

Piramal Enterprises Limited/Shriram Transport Finance Company/Shriram Capital Limited/Shriram City Union Finance Limited, Order of the CCI under Section 43A of the Competition Act dated 2 May 2016 in Combination Registration C-2015/02/249

Piyush Joshi v Competition Commission of India, Competition Appeal No. 32 of 2017 (Old Appeal No. 43 of 2016) (2 July 2019)

SCM Solifert Limited & Anr v Competition Commission of India [2018] 6 SCC 631

SCM Solifert Limited/Mangalore Chemicals and Fertilizers Limited, Order of the CCI under Section 43A of the Competition Act dated 10 February 2015 in Combination Registration C-2014/05/175

UltraTech Cement/Jaiprakash Associates Limited, Order of the CCI under Section 43A of the Competition Act dated 12 March 2018 in Combination Registration C-2015/02/246

ISRAEL

Akstel Ltd v Kalma V Industry, Aluminum Glass and Forging Marketing Ltd (Civil Appeal 6233/02) Supreme Court (4 February 2004)Antitrust Director v Baron-Fishman Communication Ltd and Yedioth Achronot Ltd (Antitrust Case) Competition Tribunal (13 January 2004)

Antitrust Director v Prinir (Hadas 1987) Ltd and Milos (1989) Ltd (Antitrust Case 704/07, No 5001400) Competition Tribunal (5 April 2009)

Antitrust Director v El-Har Engineering and Building Ltd and Taan Groundworks Ltd (Antitrust Case 37104-01-17, No 501224) Competition Tribunal (3 April 2017)

Determination 3001319 of the Antitrust Director regarding actual merger between Koor Industries Ltd. and Bank Hapoalim (12 November 1996)

Antitrust Director v SOS Energy Express Ltd, Agalim Investments Ltd and Adina Mesasa (Antitrust case 3333-10-18, No 501602) Competition Tribunal (4 October 2018)

Antitrust Director v Tal Hel Yasca Ltd and Fresh and Smooth Part 2 Ltd (Antitrust case 41804-03-18, No 501489) Competition Tribunal (10 April 2018)

The State of Israel v Ehud Friedlander (Criminal Case 1268/01) (5 September 2004)

The State of Israel v Electrochemical Industries (Protrom) Ltd et al. (Criminal Case 300/95) (9 June 1996)

Tivall (1993) Ltd v Chef Hayam (1994) Ltd [2001] (SCL) 4465/98 Judgment 56(1)56

JAPAN

Canon/Toshiba Medical Systems Corporation, 30 June 2016, Japan Fair Trade Commission

KOREA

DI Semicon, Case No 2007jeil2879 (business transfer), KFTC

GE Medical Holding AB, Case No 2007jei2562 (merger registration), KFTC

Kolon Corp, Case No 2005kigyul0765 (interlocking directorate), KFTC

Korail Tourism Development Co Ltd, Case No 2006gyulhap4610 (merger registration), KFTC

Mittal Steel Germany GmbH, Case No 2006gyulhap0154 (share acquisition), KFTC

Ramen Cartel Case, Case No 2013du25924 decided 24 December 2015, Korean Supreme Court

Shinhan Card Co Ltd, Case No 2008jijang2118 (formation of a new company), KFTC

SK Chemicals, Case No 2005kigyul 0774 (share acquisition), KFTC

Techno Semichem Co Ltd and Mitsubishi Chemical Co Ltd, Case No 2008jei0129 (formation of a new company), KFTC

MEXICO

Mexico Multifamily Fund VIII (Cayman) LP y otros, Case No VCN-001-2017, COFECE (18 May 2017)

Panasonic Corporation y otros, Case No VCN-002-2017, COFECE (4 May 2017)

Santander SA and Banco Popular Español SA, No VCN-003-2017, COFECE (7 December 2017)

SOUTH AFRICA

American Natural Soda Ash Corporation and Another v Competition Commission of South Africa (554/03) [2005] ZASCA 42; [2005] 3 All SA 1 (SCA)

Competition Commission of South Africa v Standard Bank of South Africa Ltd (FTN228Feb16) [2016] ZACT 56 (CT)

Competition Commission v Deican Investments (Pty) Ltd & New Seasons Investments Holding (Pty) Ltd (FTN151Aug15), Competition Commission v Dickerson Investments (Pty) Ltd & Nodus Equity (Pty) Ltd, (FTN127Aug15) (LM027May16) [2016] ZACT 49 (CT)

Competition Commission v Dunlop Industrial Products (Pty) Ltd & Another, Case No 018689, Competition Tribunal of South Africa (Order of 9 July 2014)

Competition Commission v Edgars Consolidated Stores Ltd and another, Case No 95/FN/Dec02, Competition Tribunal of South Africa (Order of 24 March 2003)

Competition Commission v Life Healthcare Group (Pty) Ltd & Joint Medical Holdings Ltd (FTN229Feb16) [2016] ZACT 26 (CT)

Competition Commission v Macsteel Services Centre SA (Pty) Ltd & Unique Ventilation and Support Systems (Pty) Ltd, Case No FTN154Nov16, Competition Tribunal of South Africa (Order of 21 February 2018)

Competition Commission v Pangbourne Properties Limited and others (16246) [2013] ZACT 15 (CT)

Competition Commission v Structa Technology (Pty) Ltd, Dorbyl Engineering Management Company (Pty) Ltd & Fastpulse Trading 26 (Pty) Ltd (83/LM/Nov02) [2003] ZACT 18 (CT)

Competition Commission v Trade Call Investments Apparel (Pty) Ltd and Seardel Group Trading (Pty) Ltd, Case No FTN114Jul18, Competition Tribunal of South Africa, (Order of 15 August 2018)

Competition Commission v WBHO Construction (Pty) Ltd & Another (69/AM/Oct10) [2010] ZACT 77 (CT)

Distillers Corporation (SA) Ltd and Stellenbosch Farmers Winery Group Ltd (08/LM/Feb02) [2003] ZACT 15 (CT)

Harmony Gold Mining Company Limited v Gold Fields Limited and others [2005] ZACAC 4

Murray & Roberts Holdings Ltd v Aton Holdings GMBH, Aton Austria Holdings GmbH and the Competition Commission, Case No IDT079Jun18, Competition Tribunal of South Africa (Order of 6 June 2018)

Netcare Hospital Group (Pty) Ltd and Community Hospital Group (Pty) Ltd (27/CR/Mar07) [2008] ZACT 19 (CT)

SOS Support Public Broadcasting Coalition and Others v South African Broadcasting Corporation (SOC) Limited and Others [2018] ZACC 37

SWEDEN

Carnegie Investment Bank AB, Dnr. 480/2010, 23 September 2010, SCA

SCA v Alfa Quality Moving AB (PMT 7498-16) 29 November 2017, Patent and Market Court

SCA v Scandorama AB & Ölvemarks Holiday AB (T 19974-10), 24 February 2012, Stockholm District Court

SCA v Swedbank Franchise AB /Svensk Fastighetsförmedling AB (T 3629-14) 16 December 2014, Stockholm District Court

SWITZERLAND

BKW-AEK/Comtop; RPW 1997/2, 237, ComCo

Curti & Co AG, RPW 1998/4, 613, ComCo

Ernst & Emmi Gruppe/Swiss Dairy Food, RPW 2003/3, 529, ComCo

Etablissements Ed Cherix and Filanosa SA/Edipresse SA, RPW 2003/2, 443, ComCo

NZZ-Espace-Der Bund: Vorläufiger Vollzug, RPW 2004/1, 152, ComCo

Phm Holding, der Simon et Membrez SA und der Termiboîtes SA, RPW 2014/1, 316, ComCo

ProVAG Versicherungen AG und der PROVITA Gesundheitsversicherung AG, RPW 2013/2, 222, ComCo

Rhône-Poulenc SA/Merck & Co, RPW 2001/2, 443, Bundesgericht

Schaeffler/Continental, RPW 2009/1, 85, ComCo

Schweizerische National-Versicherungs-Gesellschaft/Coop Leben, RPW 2002/3, 524, ComCo

Schweizerische Post/BEVO, RPW 1998/2, 355, ComCo

X/C-AG und D-AG, RPW 2000/2, 257, ComCo

TURKEY

Ajans Press (No E. 2011/961, K. 2017/4523) 29 December 2017, 13th Chamber of the Council of State

Ajans Press, No 10-66/1402-523, 21 October 2010, Turkish Competition Board

Anayurt, No 14-22/422-186, 25 June 2014, Turkish Competition Board

APMT BV/Grup Maritim TCB SL, No 16-16/267-118, 11 May 2016, Turkish Competition Board

Boyner/YKM, No 12-44/1359-M, 20 September 2012, Turkish Competition Board

Camargo Corrêa SA, No 12-24/665-187, 3 May 2012, Turkish Competition Board

Cegedim, 10-56/1089-411, 26 August 2010, Turkish Competition Board

CVR Inc/Inco Limited, No 07-11/71-23, 7 February 2007, Turkish Competition Board

Fairless-Simsmetal, No 09-42/1057-269, 16 September 2009, Turkish Competition Board

Longsheng, No 11-33/723-226, 2 June 2011, Turkish Competition Board

PETDER II, No 11-48/1215-428, 22 September 2011, Turkish Competition Board

Prysmian, No 11-15/259-87, 10 March 2011, Turkish Competition Board

Tekno Ray, No 12-08/224-55, 23 February 2012, Turkish Competition Board

Total SA, No 06-92/1186-355, 20 December 2006, Turkish Competition Board

UKRAINE

ACNielsen Ukraine LLC, Auchan Ukraine Hypermarket LLC, Metro Cash and Carry LLC, Fozzy-Food LLC, Novus Ukraine LLC, Enterprise with 100% foreign investment "BILLA-UKRAINE" and others, Case No 242-26.13/150-12, Decision of the Anti-Monopoly Committee of Ukraine of 29 April 2015

Blossom Investments OÜ (TAS Group)/PrJSC Dniprometyz, Case No 24-26.13/50-18, Decision of the Anti-Monopoly Committee of Ukraine of 25 April 2018

Cisco Systems Inc/One Mainstream Inc, Case No 24-26.13/20-16, Decision of the Anti-Monopoly Committee of Ukraine of 31 May 2016

Infox LLC, Brociti Investments Ltd/KUB-GAZ LLC, Case No 24-26.13/142-16, Decision of the Anti-Monopoly Committee of Ukraine of 27 December 2016

PJSC Kirovogradavtotrans/Dominion-Kirovograd LLC, Case No 24-26.13/97-14, Decision of the Anti-Monopoly Committee of Ukraine of 1 December 2015

UNITED KINGDOM

Ausurus/MWR (29 May 2019) Competition and Markets Authority

Electro Rent Corporation/Test Equipment Asset Management and Microlease (21 February 2019) Competition and Markets Authority

Electro Rent v Competition and Markets Authority [2019] CAT 4

UNITED STATES

FTC v Chicago Bridge & Iron Company and Pitt-Des Moines Inc, No. 05-60192 (5th Cir 2 July 2008)

In re Bosley and Aderans, File No. 121 0184 (2013)

In re Commonwealth Land Title Insurance Co, 126 FTC 680 (1998)

In re Insilco Corp, 125 FTC 293 (1998)

In re Torrington and Universal Bearings, 114 FTC 283 (1991)

Steves & Sons Inc v Jeld-Wen Inc, 3:16-cv-00545 345, F Supp 3d 614 (ED Va 2018)

United States v Computer Associates International, Inc, 01-02062 (DDC 2002)

United States v Duke Energy and Calpine Corporation, 1:17-cv-00116 (DDC 2017)

United States v Input/Output, Inc and Laitram, 99-0912 (DDC 1999)

United States v Qualcomm and Flarion, 1:06CV00672 (DDC 2006)

United States v Smithfield Foods and Premium Standard Farms, 1:10-cv-00120 (DDC 2010)

United States v Titan Wheel International, 96-1040 (DDC 1996)

US v Atlantic Richfield and UF Genetics, 91-3267 (DDC 1992)

US v Atlantic Richfield and Union Carbide, 91-0205 (DDC 1991)

US v Automatic Data Processing, 1:96CV00606 (DCC 1996)

US v Flakeboard Am Ltd and SierraPine, 3:14-cv-04949 (DDC 2014)

US v Gemstar-TV Guide International, Inc and TV Guide, Inc, 03-0198 (DDC 2003)

US v Hearst Trust, 1:01CV02119 (DCC 2001)

US v Mahle GmbH, 1:97CV01404 (DCC 1997)

US v Parker-Hannifin and CLARCOR, 1:17-cv-01354 (2018)

US v Sara Lee Corporation, 1:96CD00196 (DCC 1996)

US v ValueAct, 16-cv-01672, (2016)

PRESENTATION AND SYNTHESIS OF GLOBAL SURVEY RESULTS

Catriona Hatton and Yves Comtois
(Baker Botts LLP)
Andrea Hamilton
(McDermott Will & Emery LLP)

1. Why a Survey? Overview of Objectives and Methods

It is widely recognized that for M&A and capital markets to work effectively and efficiently, companies must be able to conduct effective due diligence, engage in integration planning, and put appropriate measures in place to protect the value of the target business between signing and closing. This necessarily requires a degree of pre-closing interaction between companies to an M&A transaction. In addition, many transactions require advance regulatory (competition or other) approvals in one or often more jurisdictions and in most of these cases, the parties must suspend closing pending review and clearance. During these waiting periods – which themselves can vary significantly – companies conduct integration planning work in preparation for "Day 1" post-closing. As pre-closing periods can be lengthy, acquirers may also be concerned about preserving the value of their investment.

These elements of M&A are not new. In recent years however, there has been a significant rise in the enforcement of rules to prevent so-called "gun-jumping" by competition authorities worldwide. At their core, gun-jumping rules require parties to transactions that require competition approval to preserve the pre-transaction status quo until the relevant authority completes its review and authorises the transaction. This is often referred to as the "standstill obligation".

Rules to prevent gun-jumping enforce the standstill obligation in two ways – namely, by penalising parties for failing to notify a reportable transaction altogether, or for prematurely completing their transaction in whole or in part during the standstill period. In this sense, these rules cover different scenarios, raise different issues and – unsurprisingly – are treated differently by competition authorities. In the first category "*failure-to-file*" parties do not notify a reportable transaction prior to closing and may not have even realised that they had an obligation to file. In the second category ("*premature implementation*"), parties recognize the notification requirement and notify, but nevertheless subsequently engage in conduct that is tantamount to the partial or full completion of the transaction prior to obtaining the required clearances.

The rise in gun-jumping enforcement has highlighted questions about permissible pre-closing conduct by parties to M&A transactions. The standstill requirement can create tension with the need of parties to a transaction to interact with one another to some extent in order to conduct due diligence, engage in integration planning and protect the value of the target business. The rise in enforcement has also led to questions about whether pre-closing conduct is governed by merger control rules, substantive antitrust rules, or both.

Taken together, the rise in gun-jumping enforcement, combined with apparent divergence in gun-jumping rules and practices across jurisdictions and a general lack of guidance from competition law enforcement agencies, presents practical challenges for businesses and their advisers. In addition, variations in the approach to sanctioning gun-jumping can result in inconsistent and arguably unfair treatment for companies across jurisdictions. This combination of uncertainty, divergence and rising enforcement risks chilling legitimate economic activity.

Against this background, the Mergers Working Group (MWG) of the Antitrust Committee of the International Bar Association (IBA) formulated the first multijurisdictional survey concerning gun-jumping (the Survey) to explore a number of these issues.[1] The MWG's guiding principle is that merger control/antitrust rules and enforcement should work towards best practices to support the effective and efficient operation of M&A markets and merger review processes, and that such rules should also create a transparent environment in which transactions can take place.

The MWG designed the survey by considering critical issues and questions that companies and their advisors can face in ensuring compliance during M&A processes in light of merger control rules and substantive antitrust laws. These issues were then transformed into concrete questions that were addressed to experts in each of the 21 jurisdictions covered by the Survey. The results of the Survey are reflected in each of the following chapters and are summarised here.

The MWG envisages that this Survey will contribute to such objectives by providing a comparative guide concerning the regulation of gun-jumping across 21 major jurisdictions, encompassing all global regions and including jurisdictions with both established and newer merger control systems. Specifically, the jurisdictions included in the Survey were: Australia, Brazil, Canada, China, Denmark, the EU, Finland, France, Germany, India, Israel, Japan, Korea, Mexico, South Africa, Sweden, Switzerland, Turkey, Ukraine, the United Kingdom and the United States.

In addition to this introduction and summary of findings, the Survey includes a country-specific chapter for each jurisdiction. Each chapter, in turn, is presented in two parts in order to provide a comprehensive overview of the state of the law concerning gun-jumping in that jurisdiction, along with a readily comparable summary chart :

- Part 1 relates to conduct that could infringe relevant merger control legislation and the standstill obligation in particular. It discusses the basic parameters of the applicable merger control system in that jurisdiction; whether the system imposes a standstill obligation on merging parties preventing them from implementing a notifiable transaction prior to approval and the scope of that obligation; and whether exceptions to the standstill obligation exist. It also covers the relevant authority's investigative powers and applicable penalties for violations of the standstill obligation, as well as actual enforcement activities, including the specific conduct that has been found to constitute gun-jumping, and current enforcement trends.
- Part 2 assesses the extent to which the pre-closing conduct of merging parties could also be subject to the jurisdiction's general substantive antitrust laws, such as rules prohibiting anticompetitive agreements and illegal restraints of trade between firms.
- Each chapter concludes with an annex that provides a summary of the type of conduct that has, or that could, infringe either merger control rules or substantive antitrust rules in the jurisdiction. This is intended to cover a range of conduct that is typical in M&A processes.

---

1 For more information about the International Bar Association, please refer to: <https://www.ibanet.org/>. For more information about the Antitrust Committee of the IBA and the Mergers Working Group, please refer to: <https://www.ibanet.org/LPD/Antitrust-Section/Antitrust/Default.aspx>, and for specific information about the work of the Mergers Working Group, please refer to: <https://www.ibanet.org/LPD/Antitrust-Section/Antitrust/WorkingGroupSubmissions.aspx#filter=.mergers>.

This introductory chapter provides a high-level overview of the Survey's key results and concludes by noting that clear, international best practices would provide helpful guidance in this complex area. By providing an overview of gun-jumping theory and practical enforcement in a number of jurisdictions worldwide, the MWG hopes to contribute to the debate and discussion in this dynamic area, while providing some insight to the international business community, their advisors as well as to competition authorities.

2. Overview of Key Results

Overall, the Survey showed that in virtually all jurisdictions, competition authorities have the ability to address "gun-jumping" rules because the applicable merger control laws include tools to enforce the standstill obligation. In addition, although not used frequently, substantive antitrust laws are also available as an enforcement tool to address pre-closing collaboration between competitors.

Although the power to enforce gun-jumping rules exists under the merger control laws of virtually all jurisdictions consulted, the Survey showed that enforcement varies significantly by jurisdiction. Variation was identified in terms of available sanctions, the nature of conduct that leads to enforcement and the level of practical enforcement.

2.1. Current Status of "Gun-Jumping" Enforcement

2.1.1. *Existence of a "Standstill Obligation"*

All jurisdictions surveyed have a mandatory merger control regime except for Australia and the UK.[2] Further, all jurisdictions with a mandatory notification regime impose a standstill obligation on merging parties.

As a general matter, the Survey confirmed that the standstill obligation is enforced by sanctioning two broad categories of conduct which cover a wide range of conduct. As noted above, the first category involves proceeding with a notifiable transaction without having notified the merger to the required authority – i.e., failure-to-file. The second category involves implementing – in whole or in part – a notifiable transaction prior to obtaining clearance from the authority and/or prior to the expiration of the applicable waiting period – i.e., "premature implementation".

By definition, no standstill obligation exists for merger control systems that are voluntary (i.e. Australia and the UK in this survey). However, parties in these jurisdictions may be requested or required to provide a commitment or undertaking not to close (or to not engage in any further integration) pending the review of a transaction by the competition authority and penalties may be imposed for non-compliance.

---

2 At the time of writing, the Chairman of the UK Competition and Markets Authority (CMA), has proposed sweeping changes to the enforcement of competition law in the UK, including with respect to the merger control regime which at present is voluntary. These changes have been proposed in light of the UK's expected exit from the EU. Among the proposals the transitioning of the UK system to a hybrid merger control system, in which larger, cross-border transactions would be subject to mandatory filings (including a standstill obligation) while smaller transactions would continue to fall within the voluntary filing system. See Letter from Andrew Tyrie, CMA Chair, to the Secretary of State for Business and Industrial Strategy, 21 February 2019, at 41–3. It is unclear whether such changes will proceed.

2.1.2. *Nature of the "Gun-jumping" Offence and Applicable Sanctions*

In virtually all jurisdictions surveyed, gun-jumping is considered to constitute an infringement of applicable merger control rules and is subject to penalties under these rules. Only Australia, where merger control is voluntary, and Sweden do not envisage specific penalties for gun-jumping.[3,4] In jurisdictions with mandatory merger control systems, the Survey confirmed that the merger control rules include enforcement tools to address gun-jumping. Indeed, voluntary merger control systems also have some ability to impose and enforce a standstill obligation in individual cases through "hold separate" orders.

The Survey revealed that in most jurisdictions (16 out of 21), gun-jumping is an administrative infringement of the relevant merger control rules, which is punishable by fines. Only a small number of jurisdictions (5 out of 21) consider gun-jumping to constitute criminal conduct. Of the jurisdictions that consider gun-jumping to constitute criminal conduct, only two (Denmark and Japan) consider it to be purely criminal conduct. The remaining three jurisdictions (Canada, Israel and Switzerland) consider gun-jumping to constitute both an administrative and a criminal offence. Of all of the jurisdictions that consider gun-jumping to constitute criminal conduct, only Israel includes the possibility of jail sentences – although none have been imposed to date.[5]

Administrative Penalties are the Dominant form of Penalty for Gun-Jumping

(limited to jurisdictions in which penalties are envisaged)

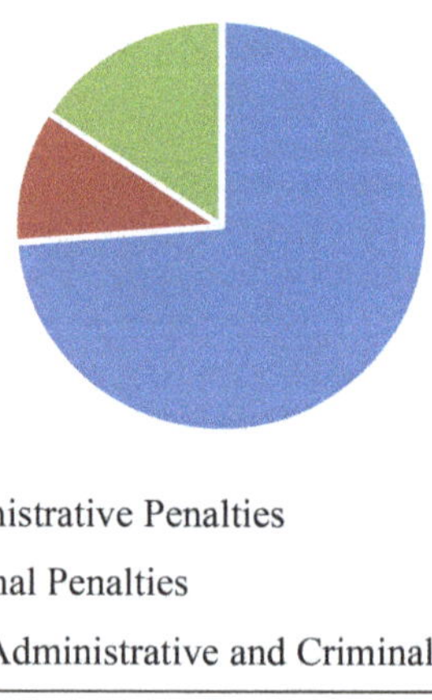

3 Although the UK's merger control system is voluntary, specific fines are set out for failure to comply with an initial enforcement order imposed by the CMA.

4 In Sweden, a hold separate order may be imposed, under penalty of fine – for which there is no maximum level. In Australia, parties may be requested or required not to close, and pre-closing conduct can also be enforced under substantive antitrust rules. If there is non-compliance with a formal undertaking not to complete given in the context of an application for merger authorisation, the authority can enforce the undertaking in the Federal Court, and seek orders including the giving up of any financial benefit gained from the breach, and compensation for any other loss or damage as a result of the breach.

5 In the case of Switzerland, criminal gun-jumping penalties apply only to individuals, while administrative penalties apply to the corporate group.

With the exception of Canada, no jurisdiction distinguishes between the type of conduct that comprises gun-jumping when imposing sanctions. In Canada, criminal fines are envisaged for gun-jumping cases that are based on a failure-to-file while administrative penalties (fines) are envisaged for gun-jumping cases that are based on "premature implementation." No other jurisdiction makes such a distinction in determining whether the rules prohibiting gun-jumping have been infringed and a penalty should be imposed.

Once an infringement of the gun-jumping rules is established, penalties are usually imposed on the corporate group, not on individuals. Of the 19 jurisdictions that envisage penalties for gun-jumping, only five (France, Germany, Israel, Korea and Switzerland) envisage the possibility of individual penalties in addition to penalties imposed on the corporate group. In all but one of these five jurisdictions, the penalty envisaged for individuals is in the form of fines – only in Israel is a custodial sentence contemplated.

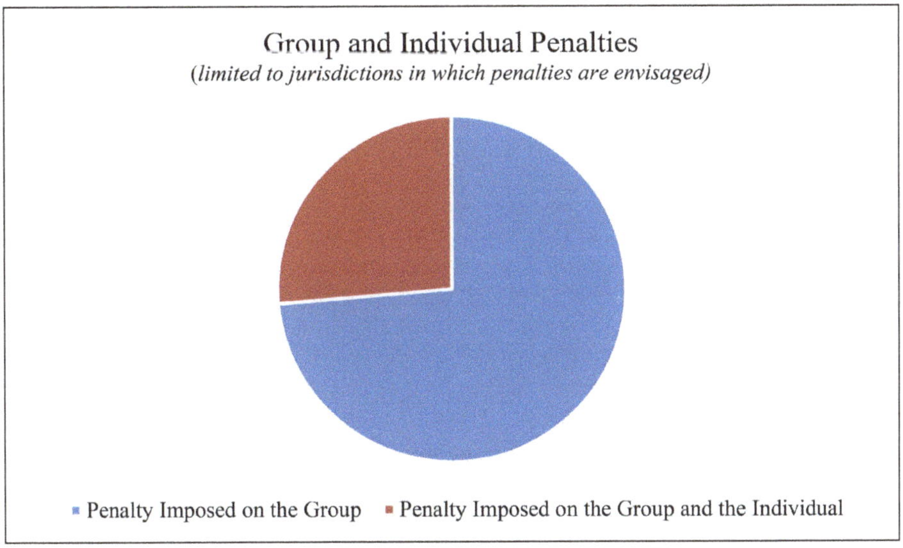

The Survey also revealed significant differences between jurisdictions regarding the basis for calculating fines as well as the maximum level of fines that can be imposed for gun-jumping offences. In turn, this can lead to questions of fairness.

Across the 19 jurisdictions in which fines may be imposed, several different models are employed. (summarised in *Annex 1*). The dominant model for calculating a fine, – reported in 11 jurisdictions and spearheaded by the EU – is to establish a fine in which the maximum penalty is based on a percentage of the infringing firm's turnover (revenue) on either a domestic or global basis.

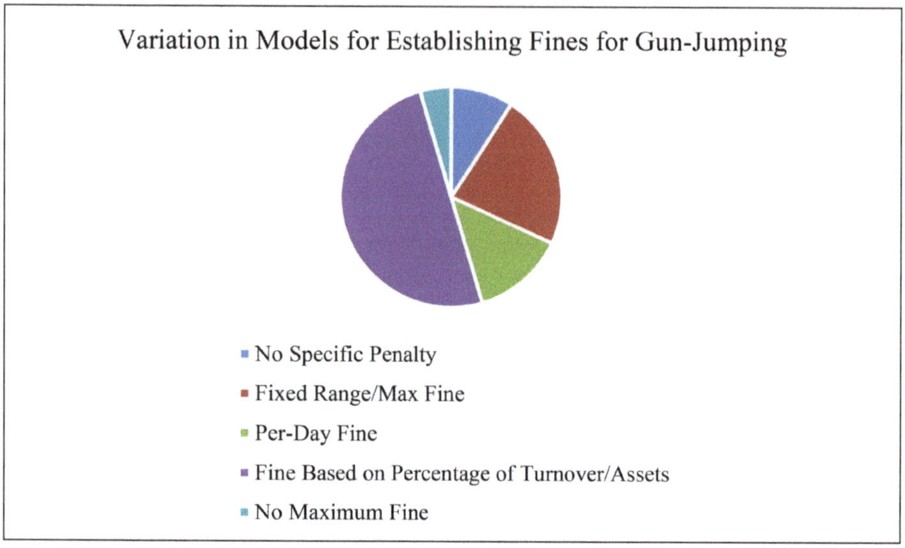

In five jurisdictions, either a maximum fixed fine (or range of fines) is prescribed (Brazil, China, Japan, Korea and Switzerland). In three jurisdictions, a maximum per-day fine (Canada, Israel and the United States) may be imposed. Of the 11 jurisdictions in which a fine based on the percentage of turnover is envisaged, the calculation is generally based on global turnover (8 of 11 jurisdictions: EU, Finland, Germany, India, Israel, Mexico, Ukraine and the UK), while in three jurisdictions the basis for the fine is local turnover (France, South Africa and Turkey). The percentage on which the fine is based also varies significantly, ranging from only 0.1% of local turnover in Turkey to a maximum of 10% of global turnover in the EU (and several other jurisdictions). Turkey is the only jurisdiction in which a minimum floor applies to the fine. There is no maximum penalty for fines imposed in one jurisdiction – Denmark.

The result is that the consequences for infringing gun-jumping rules vary significantly across jurisdictions, with the highest fines imposed in jurisdictions that determine a maximum fine on the basis of a percentage of global turnover – essentially, the EU model. Variation in the level of penalty for antitrust offences across jurisdictions is not a phenomenon unique to gun-jumping; however, it does suggest different levels of priority in terms of deterrence – particularly when considered together with actual enforcement. It can also lead to questions of transparency and fairness, especially as the specific conduct that can give rise to enforcement is not always clear (as discussed in section 2.2 below).

Finally, and as discussed in greater detail below, the Survey also showed that substantive antitrust laws are generally not used to enforce gun-jumping, although they could theoretically do so.[6]

6 Three exceptions were noted, with one case reported in each of Australia, Canada and the United States.

2.1.3. *Exemptions and Derogations from the "Standstill Obligation"*

Only a minority of jurisdictions surveyed recognize exemptions or derogations to the standstill obligation. A key distinction between "exemptions" and "derogations" is that an exemption is automatic if certain conditions are met, while a derogation requires a positive decision by the competition authority, making them much more difficult to achieve in practice. The Survey showed that exemptions and derogations typically come in three forms: (i) "public bid" exemptions; (ii) case-by-case derogations (typically granted only where the target is in financial distress); and (iii) carve-outs. Of the three, public bid exemptions are the most common type of exception from the standstill obligation, while derogations are rarely granted. Carve-outs are generally not permitted, with a couple of exceptions. Each of these is discussed in detail below.

Exemptions from the Standstill Obligation

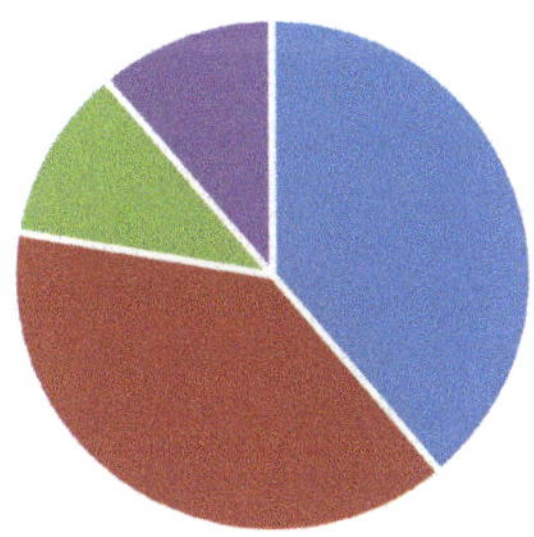

2.1.3.1. *Public Bid Exemptions*

The Survey indicated that, to some extent, a "public bid exemption" is available in seven jurisdictions – mainly in Europe and resembling the approach in the EU Merger Regulation ("EUMR").[7] Article 7(2) of the EUMR provides that public bids, or a series of transactions in securities on a stock exchange, by which control is acquired from various sellers, may be implemented without prior notification when certain conditions are met. In particular, parties relying on Article 7(2) EUMR are obliged to notify their transaction to the European Commission immediately. The acquirer is also obliged not to exercise the voting rights attached to the acquired shares until the transaction

7 Council Regulation (EC) No 139/2004 of 20 January 2004 on the control of concentrations between undertakings EU Merger Regulation [2004] OJ L 24/1.

is approved by the European Commission. Exceptionally, the acquirer may vote such shares to maintain the full value of the investment, based on an individually-granted derogation.

In addition to the EU, public bid exemptions are available in Brazil and in five European countries: Denmark, Finland, France, Germany and Sweden.

The remaining 14 jurisdictions surveyed do not have a public bid exemption. However, Israel has unique rules which provide that parties are not prohibited from transferring shares and consideration to an external trustee, provided that as a result of the transfer the acquirer does obtain additional rights with respect to the target. In the United States, the Hart-Scott-Rodino Act (HSR)[8] regime provides for a shorter standstill period – 15 calendar days instead of the standard 30 calendar days – in the case of a cash tender offer (or a transfer in a bankruptcy).

2.1.3.2. *Other Derogations to the Standstill Obligation*

In addition to the public bid exemption discussed above, the Survey showed that the laws of the EU. Denmark, Finland, France, Germany and Sweden as well as Switzerland and Brazil, allow for derogations to the standstill obligation in limited circumstances. With the exception of Switzerland, this list overlaps with the jurisdictions in which a public bid exemption is also available.

This essentially means that parties to notifiable transactions in these jurisdictions can, in principle, request an exemption to the standstill obligation on a case-by-case basis from the relevant authority. However, in practice derogations are granted only in exceptional circumstances (e.g., when complying with the standstill obligation would jeopardize the viability of the acquired business – for instance, due to the target's financial distress) and may be accompanied by conditions on the parties.

Apart from derogations, three jurisdictions (Canada, Japan and the United States) allow parties to notifiable transactions to request "early termination" of the standstill period. The effect of early termination is to release parties from the standstill obligation at an earlier stage than would normally be the case. For completeness, it should be mentioned that the relevant authorities in the other jurisdictions surveyed also generally have discretion to conclude their investigations before the end of the waiting period. The difference in Canada, Japan and the United States is that the rules of these jurisdictions include a formal mechanism to request that the standstill period be terminated early.

2.1.3.3. *Carve-outs*

Conceptually, a jurisdictional "carve-out" involves a scenario in which a transaction is closed on a global basis, but where a specific jurisdiction (or local activities) is excluded from the closing pending review and approval by the relevant competition authority. The Survey showed that carve-outs are generally not permitted and are considered to violate

---

8 Hart-Scott-Rodino Antitrust Improvements Act of 1976, 15 USC §18a.

the standstill obligation.[9] For example, Brazil's competition authority has announced that it would investigate IBM and Red Hat for gun-jumping by allegedly closing their transaction globally, subject to unilaterally carving out Brazil where the transaction remains pending.[10]

The Survey, however, also showed some nuance with respect to the availability of carve-outs in Israel, Mexico, Denmark and South Africa. Parties to a transaction executed outside of Israel may "carve out" Israel pending the receipt of competition approval in Israel, provided that the transaction will not affect competition in the domestic Israeli market. Mexico has a somewhat similar approach for "multijurisdictional" transactions. Although the law does not specifically recognize carve-outs, the parties may negotiate a carve-out of the Mexican part of the transaction, provided that competition will not be affected in Mexico until the parties receive competition approval in Mexico. The availability of a carve-out in Denmark and South Africa is not expressly envisaged, but cannot be ruled out. If available, parties wishing to carve out Denmark pending the receipt of competition approval would need to demonstrate that competition in Denmark would not be impacted. Similarly, in South Africa, parties seeking a carve-out would need to demonstrate – at a minimum – that they had not acquired control of the target business in South Africa, which may in turn depend on the nature of the target's business. It is unclear if such a request would be granted in practice.

2.1.4. *Enforcement in Practice Varies Considerably*

While virtually all of the jurisdictions surveyed have the ability to investigate and take enforcement action against gun-jumping to some extent, the Survey showed that actual enforcement varies considerably. This is evident in at least three ways: differences in the frequency of gun-jumping enforcement; differences in the types of cases brought; and differences in the types of sanctions imposed where gun-jumping infringements are found. Each of these is discussed in greater detail below.

2.1.4.1. *Differences in the Frequency of Enforcement*

Of the 19 jurisdictions with standstill obligations, the frequency with which gun-jumping cases are pursued varies fairly significantly. Six of these jurisdictions reported no, or very few, gun-jumping cases (Canada, Finland, Israel, Japan, Sweden and Switzerland). Four jurisdictions Denmark, France, Germany and Mexico, reported increasing levels of enforcement, typically in the wake of one or more high-profile cases. Nine jurisdictions (Brazil, China, EU, India, Korea, South Africa, Turkey, Ukraine and United States) reported a significant history of gun-jumping enforcement (which in some cases has

---

9 E.g. in Brazil, CA 08700.011836/2015-49 (*purchase of a subsidiary of Cisco Systems, Inc by Technicolor SA*); in India, *Baxalta Incorporated/Baxter International Inc* (Order of the CCI under Section 43A of the Competition Act dated 8 March 2016 in Combination Registration C-2015/07/297), and *Eli Lilly & Company/Novartis AG* (Order of the CCI under Section 43A of the Competition Act dated 14 July 2016 in Combination Registration C-2015/07/289).

10 See Mlex, "IBM, Red Hat face gun-jumping investigation in Brazil" (MLex 16 July 2019), reprinting a statement from CADE announcing the investigation.

varied over time). The United States has a particularly extensive history of gun-jumping enforcement. In Korea, enforcement has focused on relatively small cases.

The Survey also supported a fairly widespread perception that enforcement is on an upward trend. Reports from around 20% of jurisdictions surveyed (Denmark, France, Germany and Mexico) indicated an increase in recent enforcement – in many cases following a major case in the jurisdiction.

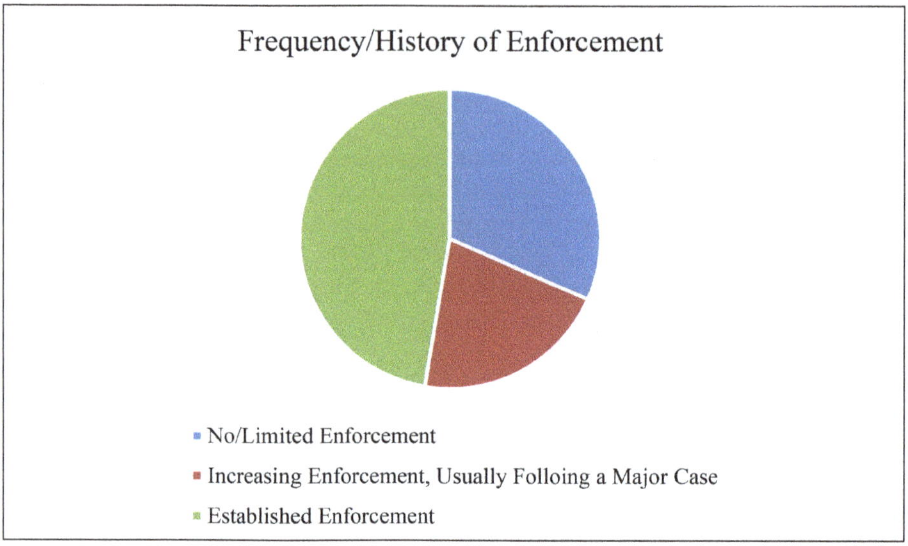

Notably, there do not appear to be obvious reasons underlying the differences in the frequency of enforcement across the jurisdictions surveyed. Multiple regions are represented in each of the categories identified above – i.e., no/limited enforcement, increasing enforcement and sustained enforcement track record. Likewise, each category includes jurisdictions with established and newer merger control systems, although there is a slight nuance as it appears that jurisdictions with established traditions of merger control tend to bring cases more frequently (e.g., the US, EU, Brazil). In addition, the Survey indicated that European jurisdictions are more likely to either have an established history, or an increasing practice, of gun-jumping enforcement (only Finland, Sweden and Switzerland reported limited enforcement in practice).

2.1.4.2. *Failure-to-File Cases Account for the Majority of Gun-Jumping Enforcement*

A second trend that emerged from the Survey is that the vast majority of reported cases on gun-jumping relate to the failure of companies to submit filings for notifiable transactions – i.e. failure-to-file cases. Gun-jumping cases based on premature implementation cases are less frequent.

In seven of the jurisdictions (China, Finland, Israel, Japan, Korea, Mexico and Switzerland), failure-to-file cases are the *only* type of conduct that appears to have been sanctioned as a violation of gun-jumping rules. Ukraine almost falls into this category as well, since most enforcement to date has involved failure-to-file cases. In most other jurisdictions, (Brazil, Denmark, EU, France, Germany, India, South Africa, Turkey and the US) a mix of failure-to-file and premature implementation cases were reported.[11] The cases identified by the Survey that involved theories of premature implementation also tended to involve a failure-to-file (or at least a late filing), with the notable exception of the French Competition Authority's (FCA) decision in *Altice*[12], which was brought only on the basis of premature implementation. Thus, it appears that in all jurisdictions that enforce gun-jumping rules, failure-to-file remains the primary basis of enforcement, although premature implementation enforcement appears to be increasing.

One probable reason for the focus on failure-to-file cases may be that such cases are somewhat easier to bring as the offense can be more objectively ascertained and typically does not require the type of nuanced assessment that may be needed for cases involving alleged full or partial premature implementation. Another possible reason for the apparent divergence is that jurisdictions with more recent traditions of merger control may prefer to prioritize failure-to-file cases to enforce the mandatory nature of their merger control regimes. In contrast, premature implementation cases are more difficult to identify and investigate – notably because parties do not publicise their pre-closing conduct.

2.1.4.3. *Significant Variation in Sanctions Imposed*

The third area of divergence in gun-jumping enforcement identified is the strikingly wide spectrum of sanctions that have been imposed in gun-jumping cases – in both failure-to-file cases and premature implementation cases.

Of the jurisdictions surveyed, fines (converted to euros for ease of comparison) imposed by competition authorities for failure-to-file in individual cases ranged from €1,800 in Ukraine to €28 million in the EU. The fines imposed by the European Commission are significantly higher when compared to other surveyed jurisdictions.

By way of example, the Antimonopoly Committee of Ukraine (AMC) imposed a wide range of fines in individual cases, ranging from the lowest fine (€1,800) to a relatively high fine of €1.8 million.[13] The Korea Fair Trade Commission (KFTC), imposed the next lowest fines in individual cases for failure-to-file among the jurisdictions surveyed, with the lowest fine reported at €5,800.[14] (It should, however, be noted that the KFTC has investigated a large volume of smaller transactions which, naturally, would attract a lower

---

11 Although not a breach of the standstill obligation, the UK CMA recently imposed fines in two cases on companies found to have infringed initial enforcement orders to hold their respective businesses separate. There were no reported cases of breach of the standstill obligation in Sweden or breach of an undertaking not to complete in Australia (the latter of which has a voluntary merger control system and no specific standstill obligation).

12 *Altice,* Decision No. 16-D-24 of 8 November 2016.

13 Case No 24-26.13/97-14 – *PJSC Kirovogradavtotrans/Dominion-Kirovograd LLC*, Decision of the Anti-Monopoly Committee of Ukraine of 1 December 2015.

14 See *Techno Semichem Co Ltd and Mitsubishi Chemical Co Ltd* (Case No 2008jei0129) – fine of approx. €5,800; *GE Medical Holding AB* (Case No 2007jei2562) – fine of approx. €11,500.

fine.) China's competition authority, the State Administration for Market Regulation of China (SAMR) (and its predecessor agency, MOFCOM) imposed slightly higher – but still relatively low – fines in individual cases, including – by way of example – fines of approximately €38,000 and €50,000.[15] The Competition Commission of Switzerland (ComCo) likewise has imposed comparatively low fines, including a fine of €61,000 in an individual case.[16]

Notably, Korea, China and Switzerland have maximum fixed fines which are capped at a relatively modest level. However, the existence of a fixed fine alone does not explain all relatively low fines, given that the Ukraine AMC imposes fines based on a percentage of turnover and has imposed both low and high fines.[17] Similarly, the Administrative Council for Economic Defence of Brazil (CADE) also has a fixed maximum fine level, and yet imposed fines five times higher than ComCo and 26 times higher than the KFTC, with fines in individual cases totalling hundreds of thousands of euros.[18] Likewise, in Denmark, where there is no fixed/maximum level of fine, reported sanctions appear to be somewhat higher, with a reported fine of approximately €500,000.[19] The model of determining the administrative fine therefore does not appear to be decisive as to whether a fine is relatively low, or high.

Fines imposed by the United States antitrust authorities – the US Department of Justice (DOJ) and the Federal Trade Commission (FTC), which are based on a fixed fine per day (maximum), generally reflect a higher level of penalty. Indeed, fines from reported cases range from hundreds of thousands to approximately €4.2 million.[20]

The highest fines arose in jurisdictions where fines are capped at a percentage of a corporate group's turnover, although there is also significant variation in failure-to-file enforcement cases in these jurisdictions as well. For example, while Mexico's Federal Economic Competition Commission (Cofece) has imposed relatively high fines – including fines of around €2.4 million in one case –,[21] the European Commission has imposed the highest fines – by far – for failure-to-file. The European Commission has imposed fines of €20 million in

---

15 See "MOFCOM fines Canon for failure to notify its acquisition of Toshiba Medical Systems Corporation" (MOFCOM decision, 16 December 2016) <http://fldj.mofcom.gov.cn/article/ztxx/201701/20170102495433.shtml>; "MOFCOM fines Bombardier Transportation Sweden and New United Group for failure to notify their establishment of a new joint venture" (MOFCOM decision, 21 April 2016) <http://fldj.mofcom.gov.cn/article/ztxx/201605/20160501311081.shtml>. MOFCOM imposed fines of €38,000 on Canon, and €50,000 on Bombardier, for their respective failures to file.

16 See *Curti & Co AG* RPW 1998/4, 613) (fine of approx. €61,000).

17 See e.g., *PJSC Kirovogradavtotrans/Dominion-Kirovograd LLC* n 13; Case No 24-26.13/50-18 – *Blossom Investments OÜ (TAS Group)/PrJSC Dniprometyz*, Decision of the Anti-Monopoly Committee of Ukraine of 25 April 2018.

18 See Concentration Act 08700.002655/2016-11 (*Blue Cycle/Shimano*) – fine of approx. €311,000.

19 See case on the unlawful implementation of the merger between SEAS-NVE and Syd Energi, case number 91250-00002-18, available in Danish at <https://www.kfst.dk/media/50750/20180704-boedeforelaeg-seas-nve.pdf> – fine of approx. €500,000.

20 The US antitrust agencies imposed fines encompassing a variety of fine levels, including approx. €205,000 on Leucadia National Corporation, approx. €555,500 in the case of Len Blavatnik, and just over €760,000 in *US v Smithfield Foods and Premium Standard Farms* 1:10-cv-00120.

21 See *Panasonic/Ficosa* (Case No VCN-002-2017), imposing a fine of approx. €2.4 million.

two separate cases, and most recently a fine of €28 million for a gun-jumping case based on a failure-to-file.[22]

Taken together, it is clear that gun-jumping cases based on a failure-to-file have resulted in significant variation in fines across the jurisdictions consulted. The *Canon/Toshiba* case provides an illustration of the variations in fine levels for essentially the same conduct. This case resulted in gun-jumping enforcement based on failures-to-file in multiple jurisdictions. In China, Canon was fined approximately €38,000, while both Canon and Toshiba were fined approximately €4.3 million in the United States.[23] The European Commission imposed a fine on Canon of €28 million.[24] However, in Japan, Canon and Toshiba were issued a "caution."[25] Clearly, the stakes of gun-jumping for failure-to-file vary significantly and present different levels of risk for companies.

Significant variations in fine levels were also observed for premature implementation cases. By way of illustration, fines of approximately €130,000 imposed by the Competition Commission of India (CCI) of India were the lowest reported fines for conduct that amounts to premature implementation.[26] Examples from the US include a fine of €4,200,000 ($5 million) imposed by a US federal court for pre-closing actions that violated both the HSR rules and the Sherman Act,[27] which is a provision of substantive antitrust law.[28] Finally, at the high end of the spectrum, examples include a fine of €80 million imposed by the FCA,[29] and a fine of €125 million recently imposed by the European Commission.[30]

The Survey thus clearly showed that cases involving gun-jumping based on premature implementation appear to be subject to comparatively higher fines than failures-to-file. This is unsurprising as, at least in principle, conduct giving rise to a premature implementation case may be more likely to involve a conscious decision to complete a notifiable transaction, in whole or in part, prior to receiving required approvals. In

---

22 See e.g. Case T-704/14, *Marine Harvest ASA v Commission* EU:T:2017:753 (upholding a fine of €20 million); Case No. COMP/M.4994 – *Electrabel Compagnie nationale du Rhône* C(2009) 4416 (decision of 10 June 2009). See also European Commission Press Release, "Mergers: Commission fines Canon €28 million for partially implementing its acquisition of Toshiba Medical Systems Corporation before notification and merger control approval" (27 June 2019).

23 See US Department of Justice Press Release, "Canon Inc., Toshiba Corporation Agree to Pay $5 Million for Violating Federal Antitrust Laws" (10 June 2019); "MOFCOM fines Canon for failure to notify its acquisition of Toshiba Medical Systems Corporation" n 15.

24 European Commission Press Release, "Mergers: Commission fines Canon €28 million for partially implementing its acquisition of Toshiba Medical Systems Corporation before notification and merger control approval" (27 June 2019) <http://europa.eu/rapid/press-release_IP-19-3429_en.htm>.

25 See <https://www.jftc.go.jp/en/pressreleases/yearly-2016/June/160630.html>.

26 See *Eli Lilly & Company/Novartis AG*n 9. See also e.g., *SCM Solifert /Mangalore Chemicals and Fertilizers Limited*, Order of the CCI under Section 43A of the Competition Act dated 10 February 2015 in Combination Registration C-2014/05/175 (fine of approx. €258,000).

27 See US Department of Justice Press Release, "Canon Inc., Toshiba Corporation Agree to Pay $5 Million for Violating Federal Antitrust Laws" (10 June 2019).

28 See *US v Flakeboard Am Ltd and SierraPine* (2014) 3:14-cv-04949.

29 FCA Press Release, "The Autorité de la concurrence fines the Altice group 80 million euros for the premature completion of two mergers notified in 2014" (8 November 2016): <http://www.autoritedelaconcurrence.fr/user/standard.php?id_rub=630&id_article=2900&lang=en>.

30 Case M.7993 – *Altice/PT Portugal* C(2018) 2418 final.

this respect, it bears mention that these cases may have been notified to the relevant authorities and were based on the parties' specific pre-closing conduct, which was found to constitute full or partial premature implementation. There is little guidance from competition authorities on the subject of premature implementation; yet, companies face clear risks given the possibility (and varying degrees) of fines that can be imposed for such conduct during the M&A process.

2.2. Conduct that Has Been Found to Constitute Gun-Jumping

2.2.1. *Categories of Conduct Covered*

The failure-to-file category captures most of the gun-jumping enforcement cases to date. Such violations are intrinsically linked to the application of each jurisdiction's specific rules and thresholds on merger notification. In most cases the application of these rules is not controversial, although there can be some debate on such requirements as shown by the recent EU case of *Marine Harvest*.[31] The exact breadth and scope of what constitutes a failure-to-file may not always be clear, especially in jurisdictions where merger control and gun-jumping enforcement is relatively new.

Premature implementation cases, however, raise significantly more questions and tend to account for most of the "grey zones" in enforcement. This is unsurprising, since it is precisely in this area that the requirements and rationale of the standstill obligation, on the one hand, and the parties' legitimate interests of appraising and preserving the value of the target business and of planning integration pending clearance, on the other, can sometimes clash. It is in this area where questions typically arise for companies seeking to comply with the standstill obligation.

2.2.2. *Little Formal Guidance Available*

There is little guidance to date that clarifies or elaborates on the scope of standstill obligations, and in particular the specific conduct that can constitute premature implementation. This is a significant concern given that there are legitimate questions about what conduct actually constitutes gun-jumping in practice, and serious risks for companies that fail to comply.

Only four of the 21 jurisdictions make available some form of guidance on gun-jumping (Brazil, France, South Africa and the United States). Brazil's and South Africa's respective competition authorities have promulgated formal guidelines, while informal guidance has been made available from competition authorities in France and the United States.[32]

---

31 Case T-704-14 *Marine Harvest ASA v Commission* EU:T:2017:753, paras 292–374.

32 See also comments of the IBA MWG: "Mergers Working Group submission to Brazil's Administrative Council for Economic Defense (CADE) on administrative procedure to investigate transactions"; "Working Group Response to consultation by the Brazilian Antitrust Authority (CADE) regarding procedures for late notifications of mergers, gun jumping and settlement"; "Working Group Response on the application of gun jumping provisions in Israeli national law" available at <https://www.ibanet.org/LPD/Antitrust-Section/Antitrust/WorkingGroupSubmissions.aspx#filter=.mergers>.

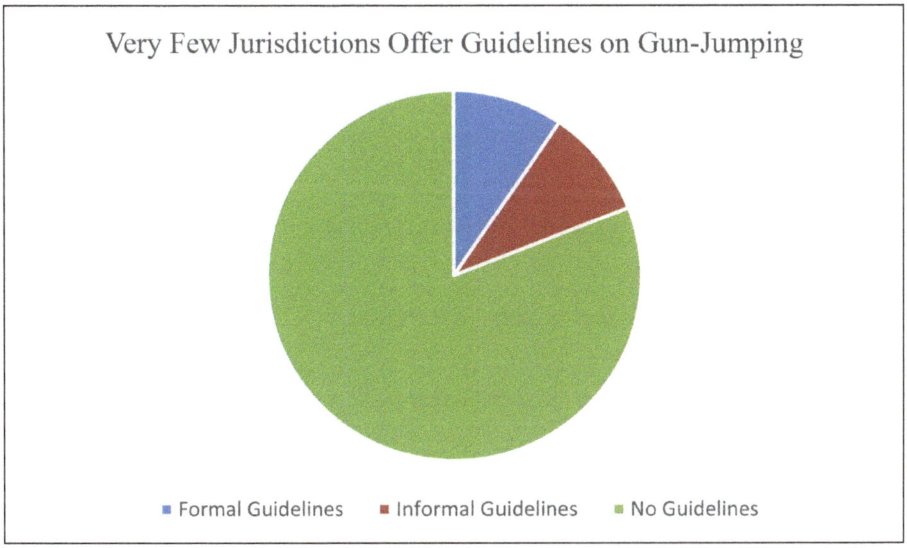

By way of example, the guidelines issued by CADE[33] briefly discuss the types of conduct that may constitute a breach of the standstill obligation, broken down in three broad categories:

- the exchange of competitively sensitive information;
- contract terms contained in the merger agreement itself that may lead to premature integration of the parties' activities (such as pre-closing non-compete obligations, or provisions allowing one of the parties the ability to directly interfere in the other party's business strategies that do not constitute a mere protection against deviation from the normal course of business); and
- problematic pre-clearance conduct (such as the integration of the parties' sales forces, or the appointment by one party of members to a decision-making body of the other party).

These guidelines issued by CADE also highlight in very general terms a few best practices for avoiding gun-jumping pitfalls (such as the use of clean teams and confidentiality agreements). While they are not comprehensive or detailed, they provide a welcome contribution to clarifying the scope of conduct that may constitute gun-jumping and best practices for companies to assist in their compliance efforts. These guidelines also raise important questions. For example, the guidelines include the exchange of information between parties as a type of conduct that can give rise to premature implementation and be sanctioned under merger control rules. However, it remains unclear the type of information exchange that would actually give rise to the full or partial completion of a transaction, as opposed to raising a straightforward substantive antitrust issue that is distinct from merger control.

---

33 CADE's guidelines were published in 2016, and are available at <http://www.cade.gov.br/acesso-a-informacao/publicacoes-institucionais/guias_do_Cade/guideline-gun-jumping-september.pdf>.

The FCA has not published formal guidelines, but its President has shared her personal views on the *Altice* decision and suggested some guiding principles going forward in a recently released publication.[34] *Altice* was a landmark case in France, representing by far the highest fine imposed for gun-jumping, and involving a wide range of conduct. The President emphasised that acquirers have legitimate interests in ensuring that the target's business continues to be managed in the ordinary course during the "standstill" period in order to preserve the value of their investment, and stated that the *Altice* decision does not question this principle. However, she also stressed that what constitutes the "ordinary course" will vary from business to business and that covenants limiting the target's business autonomy must be limited and proportional to decisions capable of having a negative impact on the value of the business.[35]

In the United States, the FTC has posted a brief blog in which it described the pitfalls companies should avoid during the pre-merger review process.[36] The document primarily deals with the issue of information exchange during the pre-merger phase and the importance of developing and sticking to a compliance strategy. As noted above, the focus on information exchange again raises the important question of the extent to which the exchange of information amounts to the premature completion of a transaction and subject to enforcement under merger control rules, as opposed to a straightforward antitrust issue best addressed under substantive antitrust rules.

Finally, in April 2019, the South African Competition Commission ("SACC") issued "Guidelines for the Determination of Administrative Penalties for Failure to Notify a Merger Contrary to the Competition Act".[37] The guidelines set out the South African Competition Commission's proposed approach to determining penalties and provide a few examples of conduct that has been regarded as prior implementation of a merger in violation of the standstill obligation. Among the (several) cited examples is the advance payment (in part or full) by the acquirer of the target business.[38]

Taken together, these materials demonstrate at least two common elements. First, they all stress the importance of putting in place a structured and documented process in order to avoid gun-jumping pitfalls (e.g., through the use of clean teams and confidentiality agreements). Second, they recognize the legitimacy of merging parties' interest in protecting the value of the business being sold and purchased, and preventing deviations from the ordinary course of business as a means of preserving that value.

While helpful, these principles are generally uncontroversial and are generally understood as standard practices for companies seeking to comply with the M&A process. What existing guidance lacks is a more detailed and practical approach to help merging parties

---

34 Isabelle de Silva, "Gun jumping: Quelles sont les pratiques à éviter?", Concurrences No 3-2018, 55-66.

35 ibid, 73-4.

36 See <https://www.ftc.gov/news-events/blogs/competition-matters/2018/03/avoiding-antitrust-pitfalls-during-pre-merger>.

37 See "Guidelines for the determination of administrative penalties for failure to notify mergers and implementation of mergers contrary to the Competition Act No 89 of 1998, as amended", available at <https://www.gov.za/sites/default/files/gcis_document/201903/42337gon473.pdf>.

38 Ibid, para 5.5.15.

to navigate the M&A process and comply with merger control rules, and to help competition authorities focus their enforcement efforts. This, of course, would require that principles be derived from typical M&A conduct and be adaptable for use across different types of business and industries. The clear goal of such principles would be to ensure that the parties not engage in conduct that would undermine the effectiveness of merger control-related enforcement decisions

2.2.3. *Recent European Law Provides Additional Guidance*

The significant cases recently decided by the courts of the European Union and the FCA have set out useful basic principles that have helped in delineating the legal scope of the standstill obligation. In general, these cases link the violation of the standstill obligation to a premature exercise of control or decisive influence over all or part of the target business.

The Court of Justice of the European Union, in a preliminary ruling, concluded that the standstill obligation applies only to actions which "*in whole or in part, in fact or in law, contribute [] to the change of control of the undertaking.*"[39] This led the court to conclude that the target's termination of a cooperation agreement with an international network of accountants prior to merger approval did not infringe the standstill obligation. Even though the termination was conditionally linked to the overall transaction, it did not appear to contribute to a change of control over the target's business. Notably, the European Commission's recent press release announcing its *Canon* decision noted that the conduct at issue contributed to the change of control over Toshiba Medical Systems Corporation using language with similarities to that used by the Court of Justice.[40]

The FCA also recently provided insight as to when the standstill obligation is violated in its *Altice* decision.[41] The decision equates gun-jumping to premature (i.e. pre-clearance) completion of a transaction. The decision goes on to state that the completion of a transaction is effective when the ownership of all or part of the target's assets and the rights attached thereto are effectively transferred to the buyer before the approval of the merger. It may *also* be considered to be effective when, regardless of the transfer of assets, the buyer nevertheless exercises a decisive influence over all or part of the target's activities. The question remains, however, as to what – factually – will generally constitute the exercise of a decisive influence in this context.

Both decisions also reinforce the proposition that buyers have a legitimate interest in wanting to preserve the value of the target business during the review period and may thus be justified in attempting to limit the target's ability to deviate from the ordinary course of business. The difficulty remains in defining what constitutes the "ordinary course" in a given case. Yet, this is essential in drawing the line between a legitimate attempt to protect the value of the target business and an undue exercise of influence over it.

---

39 Case C-633/16 – *Ernst & Young P/S v Konkurrencerådet* EU:C:2018:371, para 39.

40 European Commission Press Release n 24.

41 *Altice* n 12, para 193–4.

2.2.3.1. *Types of Conduct Challenged to Date*

Although the enforcement of gun-jumping is on the rise, the Survey reflects that most of these cases reflect failure-to-file cases. The number of cases, on a global basis, that have condemned the premature implementation of a transaction (and that go beyond a mere failure-to-file or closing while clearance is pending) remains limited.

The cases identified in this Survey can be classified according to the various types of conduct challenged. Basing such a summary on a modest number of cases does have inherent limitations in that the categories of conduct are difficult to delineate, are not mutually exclusive, may include a number of different types of conduct and may also not be exhaustive. The cases reported in the Survey also do not support the conclusion that the risk of gun-jumping is higher or lower at any given stage of an M&A transaction. To the contrary, much of the type of conduct identified in reported cases can occur pre- or post-signing.

Nevertheless, this attempt to categorize the types of conduct found to constitute or contribute to gun-jumping is provided to attempt to clarify what conduct is risky and has been – or may be – subject to challenge. For a fuller assessment of the specific conduct that has been, or could be, challenged in a given jurisdiction, please refer to the applicable country chapter.

2.2.3.2. *Conduct leading to de facto Change of Control*

The first discernible category of conduct that has given rise to findings of gun-jumping relates to actions that lead to a de facto change of control. The types of conduct that have led to this finding are summarized below (although the list is illustrative and non-exhaustive).

Restrictive provisions in a purchase agreement. The European Commission's recent decision in *Altice* focused on provisions in the purchase agreement that gave the purchaser (Altice) veto rights over decisions concerning the target's (PT Portugal's) ordinary course business decisions pre-closing.[42] According to the Commission, these rights gave the purchaser the ability to exercise decisive influence over the target, and thus led to a de facto change of control. The Commission stated that the relevant test was whether the purchaser had the *possibility* to exercise decisive influence, not whether it actually did so.

The specific types of veto rights obtained by the purchaser included:

- Requiring purchaser approval for "*appointment, dismissal and changes to the terms of any officer or director.*"
- Requiring purchaser approval relating to the target's pricing policies and commercial terms.

---

42 *Altice/PT Portugal* n 30.

- Requiring purchaser approval to enter into, terminate or modify contracts. This encompassed ordinary course of business activity because the monetary threshold for identifying impacted contracts was relatively low.

Approval of ordinary course procurement contracts. The case of *Smithfield Foods* in the United States also involved a purchaser (Smithfield Foods) which was found to have taken operational control of the target (Premium Standard) prior to closing (and before obtaining antitrust approval).[43] In this case, after signing the agreement but prior to closing, the target needed to continue procuring hogs in the ordinary course of business, consistent with its past practice. However, instead of engaging in ordinary course procurement, the target presented three procurement contracts to the purchaser and sought its consent, including to the contractual terms (including price, quantity and duration). The purchaser was found to have exercised operational control over the target pre-closing (and pre-approval) by approving the target's ordinary course procurement contracts.

Assuming day-to-day operational responsibilities. The *Duke Energy* case in the United States involved a purchaser (Duke Energy) which was alleged to have entered into a "tolling agreement" alongside the purchase agreement, which gave it operational control over the target (Osprey Energy Center), a competing supplier of wholesale electricity. Specifically, pursuant to the tolling agreement, the purchaser began exercising control over the target's output and retained the day-to-day profits (and losses) from the operation of the target's plant. The purchaser also bore all risk of changes in the market price for fuel and the market price for energy. The DOJ's complaint alleged that "[b]*ased on these potential risks and rewards* [the purchaser] *decided exactly how much energy would be generated by the plant on an hour-by-hour basis, and relayed those detailed instructions each day to plant personnel.*"[44] By assuming operational control over the target's day-to-day activities, the purchaser was accused of prematurely taking beneficial ownership over the target prior to receiving competition approval, and prior to closing. The case was resolved via settlement.[45]

Approval of ordinary course strategic decisions. In the *Altice* decision in France, the FCA found that purchaser acquired de facto control because it intervened in the target's day-to-day management by approving a number of strategic decisions – both within and outside the scope of the purchase agreement.[46] For example, these included:

- Purchaser approval of certain target investments, which were also outside the scope of the purchase agreement.
- Purchaser approval of target's participation in a call for tenders for a strategic project.
- Purchaser intervention in target's commercial policy regarding promotional campaigns for certain customers.

---

43 *United States v Smithfield Foods and Premium Standard Farms* 1:10-cv-00120.

44 *United States v Duke Energy and Calpine Corporation* 1:17-cv-00116.

45 See US Department of Justice Press Release, "Justice Department Reaches Settlement with Duke Energy Corporation for Violating Premerger Notification and Waiting Period Requirements" (18 January 2017), <https://www.justice.gov/opa/pr/justice-department-reaches-settlement-duke-energy-corporation-violating-premerger>.

46 *Altice* n 12.

- Purchaser approval of an amendment to a contract between target and a third party, as well as the renewal of another contract between target and a separate third party.
- Engaging in integration planning for the parties' respective networks in a way to limit services provided by third parties.

By intervening in management's day-to-day strategic activities, among other things – both within and outside the scope of the purchase agreement – purchaser was found to have obtained de facto control over target prior to receiving competition approval.[47]

Similarly, in the Indian case of *LT Foods*[48] the purchaser was found to have imposed restrictions on the target's promotional spending and the target's decisions to enter/exit any geographical territories. The target was also obliged to introduce its third party suppliers to the purchaser and to hand over certain inventories to the purchaser. By engaging in this conduct (among other things), the CCI found that the acquirer had failed to respect the standstill obligation and thus violated the applicable rules on gun-jumping.

Likewise, in the case of *Ajans Press*[49] in Turkey, gun-jumping was found where an acquirer interfered in the day-to-day management of the target, for example by:[50]

- Assigning telephone numbers for the target;
- Integrating the target company in the buyer's network, including physical integration of the target and the acquirer;
- Having purchaser management organize meetings attended by target staff; and
- Interfering in broadcast subscriptions of the target.

Finally, in the *Macsteel Services* case in South Africa, a purchaser was found to have involved itself in the operations and affairs of the target prior to obtaining competition approval, by appointing directors, recommending a name change, and providing administrative services to the target (including company secretarial duties among other things).[51]

2.2.3.3. *The Parties Cease to Act as Independent Companies*

This category of conduct is conceptually linked, and complementary, to the category of conduct described above – i.e., conduct found to lead to a de facto change of

---

47 The time of competition approval appears to be the critical date in terms of the standstill obligation. However, in principle, implementation prior to closing could still constitute an infringement of the substantive antitrust rules in most jurisdictions – although such cases are rare in practice.

48 *LT Foods Limited/Hindustan Unilever* Limited, Order of the CCI under Section 43A of the Competition Act dated 11 May 2018 in Combination Registration C-2016/04/387.

49 *Ajans Press* (10-66/1402-523) and dated 21 October 2010.

50 See also *Cegedim* (Turkey) 10-56/1089-411 and dated 26 August 2010, in which the purchaser was found to have engaged in gun-jumping because, among other things, it appointed the vice-chairman of the acquirer to the target's board of directors, interfered in the target's invoicing practices and interfered in the target's employment affairs. In *Tekno Ray* (Turkey) 12-08/224-55 and 23 February 2012, the purchaser obtained the right to influence day-to-day management and long-term strategic decisions of the target prior to obtaining competition approval.

51 *Competition Commission v Macsteel Services Centre SA (Pty) Ltd & Unique Ventiliation and Support Systems (Pty) Ltd* (Case No FTN154Nov16).

control. This is because when parties cease to act as independent companies, this provides a strong indication that the acquirer has the ability to exercise decisive influence or has prematurely assumed beneficial ownership of the target. Nevertheless, it is helpful to note that where parties cease to act as independent companies prior to obtaining competition approval and prior to closing, this creates significant risks of gun-jumping.

Approval of investments and contracts. Other examples of conduct from the European Commission's recent *Altice* decision (and in addition to the conduct discussed above), include a finding that the purchaser had direct involvement in a decision by the target regarding investments necessary to fulfil a non-material (i.e. ordinary course) customer contract .[52] The purchaser was also involved with the target's decisions vis-à-vis third party suppliers, including in the renewal of a third-party supply contract, as well as in the selection and subsequent negotiations with other third party suppliers. This provided further indication that the purchaser and target had ceased to act as independent companies prior to receiving competition approval, and prior to closing.

Coordinating commercial strategy. In the *Altice* case in France, the FCA's decision noted that that the parties had coordinated and implemented certain strategies. These included the joint development of new product offerings.[53] The FCA also found coordination with respect to the potential acquisition of a third party, which the target had originally envisaged. The parties' coordination of strategy was evidence that they had ceased to act as independent companies during the standstill period.

Supply chain changes. The German Federal Cartel Office (FCO) decision in *EDEKA/Kaiser's Tengelmann*[54] found that the parties had failed to act as independent companies during the standstill period by engaging in the following types of activity:

- The target began sourcing its purchases through the purchaser's existing supply network.
- The target was obliged to devalue or shut-down certain branches which were not cost efficient, as well as certain storage units or production sites.
- The target began reducing administrative staff.

The *Ajans Press* case in Turkey also involved the sharing of supply sources.[55]

Preparation of combined customer lists. In the Turkish *Ajans Press* case, the purchaser was found to have prepared shared customer lists during the standstill period, and to have also arranged for joint studies to be performed. This was viewed as an indication that the parties had ceased to act as independent companies during the standstill period.[56]

---

52 *Altice/PT Portugal* n 30.

53 *Altice* n 12.

54 See Case KVR 57/16, *EDEKA/Kaiser's Tengelmann,* Decision of the German Federal Court of Justice of 14 November 2018.

55 *Ajans Press*, n 49.

56 ibid.

Physical merging of office space. Also in the *Ajans Press* case, the parties were found to have physically merged their offices. This was regarded as a further indication that they had ceased to act as independent companies during the standstill period.[57]

2.2.3.4. *Exchange of Competitively Sensitive Information*

The exchange of competitively sensitive information is a delicate area, both in merger control and under substantive antitrust rules. In an M&A context, however, certain exchanges of commercially sensitive information must take place for M&A to occur – for example, to enable due diligence and integration planning.

Competition authorities generally recognize that, in an M&A context, certain information exchanges are lawful – even if undertaken between competitors. However, it is also generally recognized that such exchanges should be accompanied by certain safeguards, such as confidentiality or non-disclosure agreements and – where necessary – clean team arrangements. Indeed, in the European Commission's decision in *Altice*, the Commission stated that "*exchanges of business-related information between a potential acquirer and a vendor could be, if properly conducted, a normal part of the acquisition process, if the nature and purpose of such exchanges are directly related to the potential acquirer's need to assess the value of the business*".[58]

The type of conduct described in this section involves information exchanges that were carried out without the benefit of any safeguards to protect the sensitivity of the information shared. It follows that putting in place appropriate safeguards, such as non-disclosure agreements and clean team arrangements if appropriate, are an essential component of M&A compliance. As also noted in Section 2.2.2 above, however, these cases also raise important questions as to when information exchanges between parties amount to the premature implementation of a transaction. Presumably, unless the exchange of information between parties rises to that level, the exchange of commercially sensitive information is, in effect, a substantive antitrust infringement penalised under the merger control rules.

For example, in the European Commission's *Altice* decision, although the transaction involved competitors, the parties had not put in place a confidentiality agreement or a clean team arrangement.[59] In addition, the Commission noted that exchanges of commercially sensitive information had taken place long after the due diligence phase of the transaction and – according to the Commission – were not justified for the purposes of evaluating the target's business. The situation was exacerbated by the fact that the information exchanged was granular, non-aggregated and current – which made it all the more commercially sensitive.

In the FCA's *Altice* decision[60], the FCA noted that the purchaser's management team, as well as in-house lawyers, had systematic access to detailed and sensitive information

---

57 ibid.

58 *Altice/PT Portugal* n 30.

59 ibid.

60 *Altice* n 12.

regarding the target's business. Yet, there were no safeguards put in place, such as a confidentiality agreement or a clean team arrangement. The purchaser also implemented a weekly surveillance of the target's economic performance, which allowed the purchaser further access to current, commercially sensitive information prior to receiving competition approval.

2.2.3.5. *Partial Execution of the Contractual Arrangement*

This category covers a wide range of conduct or actions that are linked to more technical aspects of the parties' execution of the merger agreement. Some of the practices included here appear remote from the exercise of control or decisive influence. In that sense they appear to suggest an approach to gun-jumping which is broader and somewhat more formalistic than the approach laid out by the Court of Justice of the EU in the *Ernst & Young* case. As such, the Survey did not reveal a consensus that the type of conduct below *should* constitute gun-jumping. Nevertheless, this category of conduct is included here as it reflects conduct that has been the subject of actual enforcement in two jurisdictions.

Payment of Consideration Prior to Receiving Competition Approval. In two of the jurisdictions surveyed (Brazil and India), payment of the purchase price before competition approval was granted constituted a violation of the standstill obligation. This occurred in the *UTC Óleo e Gás* case in Brazil, although it should be noted that the payment of a 20% down-payment was considered acceptable.[61] It also occurred in the *LT Foods* case in India a number of cases in India such as the *LT Foods* case, the *Hindustan Colas* case, as well as the *Chhatwal Group Trust* case.[62]

Absence of Conditions Precedent Relating to Competition Approval. Among other factors, CADE identified the absence of a clause in the purchase agreement indicating that prior approval by CADE was a condition precedent for closing the transaction in prior cases.[63]

Depositing Shares in an Escrow Account. In the *Solifert* case in India, the CCI found that depositing shares in an escrow account prior to obtaining competition clearance would infringe the standstill obligation.[64]

2.2.4. *Summary of Conduct Challenged to Date*

Section 2.2.4 above sets out the types of conduct that have been challenged to date as premature implementation of a transaction, in violation of the applicable standstill provision. This should be read with caution as it is based on a limited number of cases which

---

61 *CA 08700.008292/2013-76 (acquisition by UTC Óleo e Gás of a 50% share from Potióleo).*

62 *LT Foods Limited/Hindustan Unilever* Limited, n 48; *Hindustan Colas Private Limited/Shell India Markets Private Limited,* Order of the CCI under Section 43A of the Competition Act dated 14 September 2016 in Combination Registration No. C-2015/08/299; *Chhatwal Group Trust/Dilip Builcon Limited*, Order of the CCI under Section 43A of the Competition Act dated 8 August 2018 in Combination Registration C-2018/01/544.

63 *CA 08700.005775/2013-19 (acquisition by OGX of a 40% share from Petrobras of a concession contract); CA 08700.000137/2015-73 (contract between Gasmig and GásLocal for gas supply).*

64 *SCM Solifert Limited/Mangalore Chemicals and Fertilizers Limited* n 26.

are themselves highly fact-specific and many involved multiple types of conduct that collectively led to a finding that gun-jumping had occurred. Subject to these caveats, the following summary is provided in an effort to distil six specific types of conduct that have contributed to a finding that the standstill obligation was infringed in the jurisdictions surveyed.

Restrictive provisions in purchase agreement, including, veto rights over the target's decisions regarding ordinary course matters prior to the receipt of competition approval, such as: – Pricing policies and commercial terms; – Certain personnel decisions; – Entering into, terminating or modifying non-material contracts (and it should be noted that determining the materiality threshold is important); – Non-material investments (and, again, determining the materiality threshold is important).	**Assuming responsibility over the Target's day-to-day operations (whether or not part of the purchase agreement), prior to the receipt of competition approval, for example:** – Control over target's output; – Assuming target's operational profits and losses from; – Communicating operational instructions to target's staff; and – Joint customer communications.
Intervening in target's ordinary course strategic decisions (whether or not part of the purchase agreement) prior to the receipt of competition approval and closing, such as decisions relating to: – Responding to calls for tenders, in particular for strategic projects; – Coordination of commercial strategies; – Promotional activities, including spending; – Customer outreach (including preparation of shared customer lists); – Decisions to enter/exit geographical territories; – Introduction of new products; – Third party suppliers, including changes to target's supply chain; – Closing down operations; – Reducing administrative staff; and – Invoicing practices.	**Physically merging the parties' activities, for example:** – Merging office space; – Physically integrating the parties' physical operations; – Assigning the target new telephone numbers, or printing new business cards for target personnel.

Exchange of commercially sensitive information in the absence of safeguards, such as :	**Certain acts, or failures to act, under the purchase agreement, for example:**
– Failing to enter into confidentiality or non-disclosure agreements (and clean team arrangements where warranted) . – Engaging in activity that results in the disclosure of competitively sensitive information – e.g., through personnel appointments, access to IT databases, etc.	– In certain jurisdictions (Brazil and India, in particular), the payment of the full purchase price prior to the receipt of competition approval. – Depositing shares to be acquired in escrow. – Failing to include conditions precedent in the purchase agreement relating to applicable competition approvals.

2.3. Gun-Jumping as a Violation of the Substantive Antitrust Laws

Conduct that can give rise to a finding that parties to a transaction failed to observe an applicable standstill obligation includes, among other things, information exchanges and coordination of strategic pricing or other competitive activity prior to obtaining required competition approval and closing the transaction. In principle, such pre-closing conduct can have similar impacts as an illegal restraint of trade or an unlawful horizontal agreement between competitors – which are prohibited under substantive antitrust laws, such as Section 1 of the Sherman Act (United States) or Article 101 of the Treaty on the Functioning of the European Union (TFEU). It follows that, at least theoretically, the substantive antitrust rules can also be used to address certain conduct that can constitute gun-jumping.

The Survey explored the extent to which this type of gun-jumping activity *had* or *could* be caught under each jurisdiction's substantive antitrust laws, in lieu of, or in addition to, being challenged as a procedural violation of merger control laws. This is an important area of inquiry, in particular as the substantive antitrust rules continue to apply after merger control clearance has been obtained until the closing of the transaction. In addition, the stakes at play can be high, in particular as many of the jurisdictions consulted can impose serious penalties for such conduct under the substantive antitrust rules (e.g., concerning cartels). For example:

- In Brazil, gun-jumping is punishable by fines ranging from approximately €12,500 to €12.5 million.[65] However, fines for infringing the substantive antitrust laws regarding illegal horizontal arrangements range from 0.1% to 20% of the infringing group's annual turnover, in addition to criminal sanctions.
- In China, the maximum fine for gun-jumping is around €63,000.[66] However, fines for infringing the substantive antitrust laws regarding illegal horizontal agreements can reach up to 10% of turnover.
- In India, the maximum fine for gun-jumping is amount equal to 1% of the total turnover or assets of the parties. However, fines for illegal horizontal behaviour can be up to an amount equal to 10% of a party's turnover.

---

65 These amounts have been converted to euros at currently prevailing rates to enable like-for-like comparisons. The fine range in local currency is BRL 60,000 to BRL 60 million.

66 The maximum fine in local currency is RMB 500,000.

- In Korea, the maximum fine for gun-jumping is around €77,000.[67] However, the total fine that can be imposed for infringing the substantive antitrust laws is up to 10% of the a party's relevant turnover.
- In Switzerland, the maximum fine for gun-jumping is around €880,000.[68] However, the total fine that can be imposed for infringing the substantive antitrust laws relating to "cartels" is up to 10% of an infringing party's Swiss turnover for the last three years in which the cartel was active.
- In Ukraine, fines for gun-jumping can be up to 5% of the global turnover. However, fines under the substantive antitrust laws can equal an amount of up to 10% of an infringing party's global turnover.

In various other jurisdictions, including the EU, Finland, Israel and South Africa, the upper limits of fines for gun-jumping and for breaching the substantive antitrust laws are the same. It should be noted that the potential maximum penalties in the EU are particularly high and that in Israel the potential term of imprisonment for infringing the substantive antitrust laws was recently extended to five years.

The results of the Survey on the application of the relevant substantive antitrust laws to conduct that can comprise gun-jumping under the relevant merger control rules were unequivocal. In all jurisdictions, illegal pre-clearance/closing conduct by competitors who are involved in a potential merger transaction (such as exchanging competitively sensitive information, or coordinating strategic conduct) can typically also be challenged under the applicable substantive antitrust rules.

Despite the availability of substantive antitrust laws as enforcement tools, the Survey found that these laws have rarely been used to address gun-jumping in practice. Indeed, conduct that constitutes a violation of the standstill obligation, either as a failure-to-file or as premature implementation, has normally been addressed as a violation of the merger control laws and parallel enforcement under substantive antitrust rules occurred only in very few cases. Arguably, this result is not surprising, as using the merger control rules to conclude that the standstill obligation was breached is, in practice, more straightforward than demonstrating how conduct between parties can have a negative impact on competition under substantive antitrust rules.

The European Commission's recent decision in *Altice/PT Portugal* provides a good illustration of this practice. The Commission's decision in that case was based in part on the unlawful exchange of competitively sensitive information between competitors, which might have been considered as a violation of Article 101 TFEU rather than a premature acquisition of control. However, the Commission considered the information exchange as a factor in deciding that Altice had undertaken a premature acquisition of control by exercising decisive control over the target, thus infringing the EUMR.[69]

Similarly, in a separate case involving Altice, the FCA found that the parties had engaged in the unlawful exchange of information. However, the FCA exclusively applied the

---

67 The maximum fine in local currency is KRW 100 million.

68 The maximum fine in local currency is CHF 1 million.

69 *Altice/PT Portugal* n 30.

merger control rules and considered that this conduct was a contributing element to the parties' premature implementation of the transaction.[70]

The Survey showed only a few exceptions to the general observation that competition authorities have not applied the substantive antitrust rules to conduct that can be subject to enforcement under the merger control rules.

For example, in a 2014 case in the United States (*Flakeboard America Limited/Sierra Pine*[71]), the target closed a mill that competed with the acquirer's mills, while the merger transaction was under review. It emerged that the parties had worked together concerning the content and the timing of the announcement of the mill's closure. It was also discovered that they worked together to transition the mill's customers to the acquirer's competing mill, including by sharing competitively sensitive information. The conduct was challenged as both a violation of the HSR (gun-jumping) and of Section 1 of the Sherman Act.

In addition, in an older case in Canada, the Competition Bureau challenged pre-closing pricing coordination of merging parties as a violation of the criminal conspiracy offence in Canada. The parties agreed to a prohibition order on a consent basis (no fines were imposed) and the merger did not proceed.[72]

Circumstances are different in jurisdictions that do not have a standstill obligation because their systems are voluntary. In these jurisdictions, enforcement can take place on the basis that parties have violated a hold separate order (such as an initial enforcement order in the UK). In addition, general challenges to illegal pre-closing conduct can take place under the substantive antitrust laws. The ongoing *Cryosite* case in Australia is a case in point. The Australia Competition and Consumer Commission (ACCC) has alleged that merging parties engaged in customer allocation after signing but before completing their transaction (an asset sale agreement). The parties' pre-closing conduct is currently being challenged by the ACCC under the civil cartel provisions of the Australia Competition and Consumer Act 2010.[73] At the time of writing, the case remains pending.

Overall, three conclusions emerge from the Survey regarding the use of the substantive antitrust laws as an enforcement tool for conduct that gives rise to gun-jumping:

- In general, substantive antitrust laws can be used to address certain types of conduct that comprises gun-jumping under merger control rules in premature implementation cases.
- While such enforcement is theoretically possible, in practice it has rarely occurred and most competition authorities have focused on the merger control standstill rules to address gun-jumping.
- Jurisdictions with voluntary merger control systems, which have no standstill obligation, may need to rely on the substantive antitrust rules to address coordination that takes place prior to closing. However, such enforcement has been infrequent in the two surveyed jurisdictions with voluntary regimes.

---

70 *Altice* n 12.

71 *US v Flakeboard Am Ltd and Sierra Pine*, n 28.

72 *R v Béton Régional Inc* No. T-58-95, 16 January 1995.

73 Competition and Consumer Act 2010.

3. A need for best practices?

Taken as a whole, the results of this Survey indicate that enforcement tools to address infringements of the standstill obligation – in effect, gun-jumping – are broadly available to jurisdictions in all regions and in both established and newer merger control systems. At the same time, it is also clear that competition authorities can also use substantive antitrust rules as an enforcement tool with respect to parties' pre-clearance/closing conduct – although they typically do not do so and rely instead on merger control rules.

The Survey also showed that there are significant differences in the extent of enforcement, judged by frequency of cases under the merger control rules, in terms of the type of cases brought (failure-to-file compared with premature implementation) and the penalties imposed. These differences do not appear to be fully explained by geography, or by how "established" or "new" the merger control system in question happens to be.

In addition, the specific types of conduct that have been considered to violate the standstill obligation through premature implementation are varied. However, there appears to be a broad consensus that:

- Conduct that enables a purchaser to exercise decisive influence or beneficial ownership over a target will violate the standstill obligation. However, given that there are still relatively few decided cases, all of which involve a variety of conduct, there is still uncertainty as to what conduct will be regarded as sufficient to meet the decisive influence or beneficial ownership criteria.
- Purchasers are able to impose certain restrictions on a target in order to protect the value of their proposed investment. However, such restrictions should not include intervening in, or directing, the target's ordinary course of business activity.
- Pre-closing disclosure of competitively sensitive information is recognized as a legitimate and necessary part of due diligence and integration planning, which enables M&A transactions to take place. In such cases, however, safeguards should be put in place to avoid breaches of standstill obligations and substantive antitrust rules.

However, identifying the precise type of conduct remains difficult as it must be derived from very limited guidance made available by competition authorities – which often rely on general principles – and existing case law. As gun-jumping is an emerging area in many of the jurisdictions consulted, this means that there is little practical guidance that can be applied to particular cases. Case law that exists is often very fact-specific and often involves a number of different types of contributing conduct, which can make it difficult for companies and their advisors to identify specific actions that are likely to lead to legal risk. Moreover, there are a number of activities, such as integration planning, which have become customary in global M&A practice, and which have so far received very little attention from the enforcers. For these areas, there is very little guidance available.

In addition to these difficulties, the existing cases also have revealed certain types of conduct that – in some jurisdictions – have been found to technically comprise gun-jumping, even though there is no consensus. For instance, this includes the timing of payment of consideration, failing to note competition approvals in the purchase agreement as a condition precedent, or depositing shares in escrow. While the latter type of conduct is limited to only two jurisdictions, it points to unhelpful variation that can lead to uncertainty for companies in M&A processes – particularly multijurisdictional processes.

Against this background, it appears that clear principles to help guide companies through the M&A process would be useful, especially as the stakes relating to possible gun-jumping violations increase. One suggested guiding principle is that conduct undertaken to protect the value of a business generally should be allowed, provided that the purchaser does not intervene in the target's ordinary course activity prior to receiving required competition approvals. As such, any guidance should include at least the following:

- Best practices should reflect that companies are permitted to take legitimate steps necessary to protect the value of the business to be acquired during the pendency of an antitrust review.
- Further, best practices should expressly acknowledge the need for proper due diligence and integration planning, which necessarily involves the exchange of certain competitively sensitive information, and provide guidance the general limits of such exchanges as well as on appropriate safeguards such as clean teams and confidentiality agreements.
- Best practices should reflect the fact that the merger control-specific standstill obligations have the purpose of and are limited to ensuring the effectiveness of eventual decisions by the competition authority and do not serve the general regulation of potentially anti-competitive behaviour that takes place in the context of an M&A transaction.
- In addition to these core principles, best practices should also provide examples of permitted and prohibited conduct to help businesses understand the limits of permissible conduct. Such examples can be drawn from existing cases and guidance. In addition, companies and their advisors can usefully contribute to the process by identifying the types of conduct that are essential for effective and efficient M&A processes but do not impede the target's ability to operate in the ordinary course.

In addition to providing assistance to companies navigating the M&A process and seeking to comply with applicable merger control rules, such best practices covering these basic issues could also assist competition authorities considering enforcement of gun-jumping cases and help lead to greater convergence.

Annex 1

Jurisdictions	Criminal sanctions	Administrative Fines (failure-to-file/breach of standstill)[74]
Australia	No	N/A
Brazil	No	~€12,500-€12.5 million
Canada	Failure-to-file ≤€33K	≤€6,500 per day
China	No	≤€63,000
Denmark	No maximum fine specified	No
EU	No	≤10% global turnover
Finland	No	≤10% global turnover
France	No	≤5% domestic turnover (individuals ≤€1.5million)
Germany	No	≤ 10% global turnover (individuals ≤€1million)
India	No	≤1% global turnover or assets
Israel	Jail: maximum of 3-5 years Fines: ≤€1million and ≤€7,000 per day (half of these maximum amounts for individuals)	≤8% global turnover (up to a maximum of €6million) (individuals ≤€250,000)
Japan	≤€16,000	No
Korea	No	≤€77,000 (individuals ≤€7,700)
Mexico	No	≤5% annual accruable income
South Africa	No	≤10% domestic turnover South African turnover (≤25% for repeat offences)
Sweden	No	None
Switzerland	Individuals: ≤€18,000	≤€880,000 (individuals ≤€18,000)
Turkey	No	≤0.1% domestic turnover (minimum of €2,800)

►

74 For illustrative purposes only, fine levels have been estimated in euros (at rates prevailing in July 2019) to enable a like-for-like comparison on the relative level of fines. For specific levels of fine in local currency, please refer to the jurisdiction-specific chapters.

Jurisdictions	Criminal sanctions	Administrative Fines (failure-to-file/breach of standstill)[74]
Ukraine	No	≤5% global turnover
UK	No	≤5% global turnover (breach of hold separate order)
US	No	≤€35,000 per day

AUSTRALIA

Paul Schoff and Miranda Noble
(MinterEllison)

Part 1:
Merger Control and the "Standstill Obligation"

1. Please identify the relevant merger control legislation in your jurisdiction. Please provide a link to the relevant legislation (if possible, in English) and also indicate:

- **whether the merger control system is mandatory or voluntary,**
- **the relevant authority, and**
- **the duration of the review period.**

Australia's merger control regime is governed by the Competition and Consumer Act 2010 (Cth) (CCA)[1] and is administered and enforced by the Australian Competition and Consumer Commission (ACCC), with a limited role undertaken by the Australian Competition Tribunal (Tribunal).

Voluntary notification

There is no mandatory merger notification or filing requirement under the CCA (or any other legislation) in Australia.

Merger notification is therefore voluntary under the CCA and the voluntary regime is non-suspensory – it contains no standstill obligation. There is no penalty for failing to notify the ACCC. Rather, the risk associated with not notifying the ACCC arises from the ACCC's ability to bring proceedings and seek a range of orders from the Federal Court where it considers there has been, or may have been, a breach of section 50 of the CCA (which prohibits a corporation or person from directly or indirectly acquiring shares or assets if it would have the effect, or be likely to have the effect, of substantially lessening competition in a market in Australia).

The ACCC recommends that proposed acquisitions should be notified to it where certain voluntary notification thresholds are met. These thresholds, however, are indicative only and mergers that do not meet them may still raise competition concerns (including vertical mergers), and as such may be investigated by the ACCC, even if notification is not made. Equally, mergers above the thresholds in certain circumstances may not warrant notification or investigation.

Overview of clearance processes

Following reforms to the CCA in November 2017, there are now two avenues by which parties may seek to have the ACCC approve an acquisition:

---

1 Available at <https://www.legislation.gov.au/Details/C2017C00375>.

- informal merger clearance; and
- merger authorization.

Informal Merger Clearance

The ACCC routinely investigates proposed acquisitions at the request of a purchaser or vendor, and in most cases will provide a letter indicating whether it has any objections to the acquisition. This amounts to an "informal clearance" that is widely relied upon by Australian businesses. Informal clearance remains the most flexible and least costly option (particularly for non-controversial transactions).

For each merger notified to the ACCC, the ACCC makes an initial confidential pre-assessment to determine whether further review is required. If the ACCC forms the view that the risk of a substantial lessening of competition is low, it may decide that no further inquiry or public review is required. In other cases, the ACCC may decide there is a low risk of a substantial lessening of competition after conducting targeted market inquiries and decide no public review is necessary. In either case, these mergers are considered to be "pre-assessed".

For mergers that cannot be pre-assessed, the ACCC will then proceed to conduct a public review.

There is no statutory basis for this informal process, which therefore means that the informal clearance provided by the ACCC is not protected from legal action under section 50 of the CCA. Accordingly, impacted third parties and the ACCC may still take action against merging parties (although this would be highly unusual in practice).

The length of time it will take the ACCC to respond to a request for informal clearance varies according to the particular circumstances of the matter and whether or not it proceeds to a public review. Typically, a confidential pre-assessment can be provided within 4–6 weeks of a request by the merger parties, but can take longer in complex matters or if the ACCC wishes to conduct targeted market inquiries once the transaction is public. Once in a public review, it will typically take 8–12 weeks from the commencement of the ACCC's public review for the ACCC to reach a decision to either clear a proposed transaction or move into "Phase II" by releasing a "statement of issues" (**SOI**). While the indicative timeline for the second stage of the process will depend on the nature and complexity of the merger and the responses received to the statement of issues, the ACCC generally expects to form a final view within 8–12 weeks of publishing the SOI.

Merger Authorization

Prior to 6 November 2017, applications for merger authorization were made to the Tribunal. Following the reforms to the CCA, an application for merger authorization is now made directly to the ACCC, with a right to apply to the Tribunal for review of the ACCC's decision. The Tribunal's review is limited to the merits of the application, with the Tribunal being limited to the information, documents and evidence submitted to the ACCC.

Under this new authorization process, the ACCC assesses proposed mergers pursuant to section 90(7) of the CCA, whereby the ACCC may grant merger authorization if it is satisfied that:

- the proposed acquisition would not be likely to substantially lessen competition; or
- the likely public benefit from the proposed acquisition outweighs the likely public detriment.

The duration of the merger authorization process is a statutory 90 days from the application being validly lodged, unless extended. Unlike the informal merger review process, merger authorization provides statutory protection from legal action under section 50 of the CCA. The previous authorization process that was undertaken by making an application to the Tribunal was rarely (but successfully) used. Since the introduction of the new process, there has been one merger authorization application, filed in April 2019, which was authorized on a conditional basis (with divestments) in July 2019.

2. **Does the merger control system in your jurisdiction impose a "*standstill obligation*" – meaning, that the transaction cannot be implemented prior to completing the merger control process? (Please cite the relevant legislation.) Please also indicate the *legal scope* of the standstill obligation according to the relevant legislation (e.g. the parties to the transaction cannot effect a change of control, cannot take steps towards implementation, etc.).**

There is no specific standstill obligation under the CCA. However, there are certain circumstances where a commitment or undertaking not to complete a transaction is required or requested.

Informal merger clearance

In the informal clearance context, the ACCC may request that merger parties provide a voluntary commitment or undertaking not to complete before it has completed its review. This is typically in situations where the ACCC is investigating a controversial or complex merger that has not been notified and/or where completion is planned before the ACCC has had an opportunity to carry out its review. There are no specific guidelines on the circumstances in which these voluntary commitments or undertakings will be required or the form that they must take. These sometimes take the form of a letter, however, the ACCC generally prefers the undertaking to be in the form of a court-enforceable undertaking under s 87B of the CCA, as this enables the ACCC to enforce the undertaking in the Federal Court if there is non-compliance. In terms of content, these typically involve a simple undertaking to not complete while the transaction is being considered (rather than specific and detailed commitments to not engage in certain conduct that could constitute premature implementation).

In practice, parties who are requested to provide such a commitment or undertaking usually do so. In theory, if the parties refused to do so, the ACCC could make an application in the Federal Court for interim or interlocutory injunction to prevent completion. Such interim or interlocutory relief requires the court to be satisfied that:

- there is a serious issue to be tried; and
- the balance of convenience favors the granting of the interim injunction.

Additionally, the ACCC may also seek such an injunction to prevent completion in circumstances where it is bringing proceedings for a breach or potential breach of section 50 and/or another substantive antitrust law in respect of a transaction. For example, in proceedings against Pacific National and Aurizon in the Federal Court, the ACCC alleged, among other things, that the parties reached an understanding in relation to Aurizon's intermodal business that had or would likely have the effect of substantially lessening competition.[2] The ACCC sought (among other orders) an injunction to prevent Aurizon from completing the transaction and obtained an interim injunction to prevent Aurizon from closing its Queensland intermodal business while the case was being determined.[3] Aurizon subsequently announced the sale of its Queensland intermodal business to Linfox (which the ACCC did not oppose).[4] The proceeding against Pacific National and Aurizon was recently dismissed by the Federal Court on the basis of a long term behavioral undertaking offered by Pacific National.

Merger authorization

Authorization cannot be granted for transactions that have completed.

The CCA requires that, if making an application to the ACCC for merger authorization, the applicant must provide a court-enforceable undertaking under s 87B of the CCA to not complete the acquisition to which the authorization relates while the ACCC is considering the application. This operates to preclude completion until the merger authorization process is finished.

The specific form of this undertaking is prescribed in Annexure A of the merger authorization form. This involves a simple undertaking to not complete while the transaction is being considered (rather than specific and detailed commitments to not engage in certain conduct that could constitute premature implementation). The ACCC may publish such an undertaking.

The ACCC can apply to enforce such an undertaking in the Federal Court if there is non-compliance.

3. Have the relevant authorities in your jurisdiction issued internal or external guidelines concerning the scope of the standstill obligation, and/or their authority to enforce it? Please provide a copy/link of such guidance, if possible in English.

Not applicable. There is no specific standstill obligation under the CCA.

The ACCC has not published any formal or informal guidance with respect to the content or approach to requesting, in the context of the informal clearance process, an undertaking to not complete. In the context of merger authorization, other than references to the requirement to provide a s 87B undertaking to not complete as part of the application, there is no specific guidance around such undertakings.

---

2 Australian Competition and Consumer Commission v Pacific National Pty Limited (No 2) [2019] FCA 669.

3 Australian Competition and Consumer Commission v Pacific National Pty Ltd [2018] FCA 1221.

4 <https://www.accc.gov.au/media-release/accc-will-not-oppose-proposed-sale-of-aurizon%E2%80%99s-queensland-intermodal-business>.

4. **Are there any exceptions to the standstill obligation – for example, through derogation or "carve out"? Please describe the circumstances in which this is possible. Please also describe the relevant process, e.g. do parties need to apply to the authority for a derogation from the standstill obligation? If so, how long is the approval process? If there are specific cases addressing these issues, please identify them.**

   Not applicable. There is no specific standstill obligation under the CCA.

5. **Does a public bid exception exist in your jurisdiction? (For example, under the EU Merger Regulation it is possible to acquire shares as part of a public bid, provided that the shares are not exercised until the acquisition is cleared by the Commission.) If such an exception exists in your jurisdiction, please describe how it is applied.**

   Not applicable. There is no specific standstill obligation under the CCA.

6. **What powers does the relevant authority have to investigate and enforce violations of the standstill obligation? Are dawn raids possible? What timing applies to investigation/enforcement proceedings?**

   Not applicable. There is no standstill obligation under the CCA.

   With respect to voluntary commitments or undertakings to not complete (including in the context of a merger authorization application), the ACCC will actively monitor compliance with that undertaking, for example, by seeking updates from the parties confirming that completion has not occurred and requesting advance notice if the parties propose to proceed to completion despite the undertaking.

   Where that commitment is in the form of a s 87B undertaking, the ACCC's compulsory information-gathering powers extend to monitoring a contravention or potential contravention of any term of a s 87B undertaking.

   If there is non-compliance with a s 87B undertaking to not complete, the ACCC can seek to enforce the undertaking in the Federal Court. The ACCC may seek orders from the court directing compliance with the undertaking, the giving up of any financial benefit gained from the breach, compensation for any other loss or damage as a result of the breach, or any other appropriate orders. Additionally, in the merger authorization context, where the CCA requires a s 87B undertaking to not complete while the authorization application is considered, completing the transaction in breach of that undertaking will prevent authorization being granted – as authorization cannot be given for transactions that have completed.

   If a voluntary undertaking to not complete is not given in the form of a s 87B undertaking (but less formally, for example, by way of letter), there is no formal ability for the ACCC to enforce the commitment.

   Relevantly, if parties fail to comply with a commitment or undertaking to not complete and proceed to complete the transaction, the ACCC will then treat the matter as a *completed* merger. Reviews of completed mergers will generally undergo a different (and longer) process from reviews of proposed acquisitions, and will not be reviewed in accordance with the ordinary processes outlined in the ACCC's merger guidelines. Rather, they are treated as investigations of potential breaches of the CCA that have occurred, and the ACCC may proceed to seek orders as may be appropriate for a substantive breach of section 50, including divestment.

7. What are the possible penalties for violating the standstill obligation? Are there criminal sanctions, including on individuals? Have these been applied in practice? Is there a difference in enforcement between transactions involving domestic companies and "foreign-to-foreign" transactions? Does the authority have the power to unwind transactions implemented in breach of the standstill obligation? If so, has the authority made use of that power in practice? If yes, please provide examples.

Given there is no specific standstill obligation in Australia, there are no corresponding penalties that apply.

If there is non-compliance with a s 87B undertaking to not complete, the ACCC can seek to enforce the undertaking in the Federal Court. The ACCC may seek orders from the court directing compliance with the undertaking, the giving up of any financial benefit gained from the breach, compensation for any other loss or damage as a result of the breach, or any other appropriate orders.

If a voluntary undertaking is not given in a s 87B undertaking, there is no formal ability for the ACCC to enforce the commitment or seek pecuniary penalties for non-compliance.

For completeness, we note that an action alleging a contravention of section 50 (the substantive prohibition on anticompetitive acquisitions and mergers) may be brought by either the ACCC or a private party. Action may be brought even after a merger has been completed.

An example of the ACCC taking action *after completion* of an acquisition that had not been notified related to Primary Health Care Limited's acquisition of certain pathology assets from Healthscope Limited. The parties completed the transaction without notifying the ACCC, despite the ACCC stating that the parties were on notice that the ACCC would have serious concerns with the transaction.[5] The ACCC commenced a public review of the transaction soon after completion. Around 16 months later, the ACCC closed its investigation after the parties provided onerous divestment undertakings to essentially unwind and reverse the transaction.[6]

While the Australian clearance regime is voluntary, this matter highlights the risks of completing a contentious acquisition without seeking and obtaining ACCC clearance.

8. How does the relevant authority typically learn of potential violations of the standstill obligation? Does the authority actively monitor the trade press?

There is no specific standstill obligation under the CCA.

With respect to voluntary commitments or undertakings to not complete (or undertaking to not complete in the merger authorization context), see Question 6.

---

5 <https://www.accc.gov.au/media-release/accc-acts-to-restore-competition-for-pathology-services-in-queensland>.

6 <https://www.accc.gov.au/public-registers/mergers-registers/public-informal-merger-reviews/primary-health-care-limited-acquisition-of-pathology-assets-previously-operated-by-healthscope-in-queensland>.

For completeness, it is not uncommon for the ACCC to learn of transactions that have not been voluntarily notified and open a review of its own accord. This applies both to transactions which have completed and which have not yet closed. The ACCC can become aware of such transactions through media attention, complaints from affected stakeholders such as customers or competitors, consultation or referrals from other government bodies such as the Foreign Investment Review Board (**FIRB**) or through the ACCC's own monitoring activities.

9. **Please describe the relevant authority's enforcement of the standstill obligation. If there have been cases, please describe the specific conduct that was found to violate the standstill provision and the criteria applied by the relevant authority or court. Has the relevant authority considered the market impact of the conduct? (Please refer to the Annex.)**

Not applicable. There is no specific standstill obligation under the CCA.

With respect to voluntary commitments or undertakings to not complete (or undertakings to not complete required to be provided in the merger authorization context), we are not aware of any cases where action was taken against parties for failing to comply with those undertakings.

10. **In cases involving alleged violations of the standstill obligation under the relevant merger control laws, has the relevant authority (or court) *also* considered the substantive antitrust laws? (Please refer to the Annex.)**

Not applicable. There is no specific standstill obligation under the CCA.

11. **Is private enforcement of the standstill obligation possible?**

Not applicable. There is no specific standstill obligation under the CCA.

For completeness, the CCA does permit private enforcement of section 50, although injunctive relief is not available to private parties. Section 50 is primarily enforced by the ACCC, with private enforcement being limited.

12. **Please describe the private law risks/consequences (i.e. contractual/validity consequences) for transactions that are subject to notification, but which are completed without notification/approval. Please identify any relevant cases and describe them.**

Not applicable. The merger notification regime under the CCA is voluntary.

However, as noted in Question 7 above, in *Primary Health Care Limited/ Healthscope Limited*, the parties completed the transaction without notifying the ACCC, and the parties ultimately provided onerous divestment undertakings to essentially unwind and reverse the transaction.

For completeness, there may be contractual consequences for transactions where the ACCC declines to grant informal clearance or authorization, or where the ACCC takes enforcement action by reason that a transaction contravenes section 50.

13. **Please describe policy and enforcement trends in your jurisdiction.**

The ACCC is a sophisticated regulator and takes a tough stance in respect of merger enforcement.

The ACCC has ramped up investigations of complex mergers through the imposition of a more document-heavy approach to evidence-gathering, particularly for transactions progressing into a Phase II review. This is done with the stated intention of ensuring that it is better prepared to litigate to prevent anticompetitive mergers from proceeding. This includes the use of tools such as notices issued under section 155 of the CCA requiring merger parties to furnish information and produce documents.

In this context, the ACCC recently confirmed its increased use of section 155 notices, stating that in the last financial year (2017/18) they issued significantly more notices (89) compared with the previous financial year (44), and with the vast majority of notices concentrated in a relatively small number of matters. They confirmed that these have involved both notices for information and documents and, importantly, oral examinations which enable the ACCC to "test lines of inquiry with key stakeholders, including the executives of the merger parties, under oath".

The ACCC is also increasingly examining the circumstances in which a transaction is entered into, ancillary arrangements and potential "gun-jumping" behavior. The ACCC has recently warned that it is not just taking a narrow merger assessment during its reviews and "will consider any other related agreements to determine whether they would, combined with the acquisition, be likely to substantially lessen competition or whether separately they potentially breach other provisions in the CCA". In this context, the ACCC instituted proceedings for substantive breaches of the CCA against parties involved in two separate transactions relating to pre-signing and pre-completion – namely, the proceedings against Cryosite for alleged gun-jumping (discussed below) and the proceedings against Pacific National and Aurizon relation to dealings related to the sale of Aurizon's assets (discussed above).

Part 2: Substantive Antitrust Law in an M&A Context

1. **Please identify the relevant *substantive antitrust laws* in your jurisdiction that can potentially apply in an M&A context (e.g. for the EU, this would include Article 101 of the Treaty on the Functioning of the European Union). Please provide a link to the relevant legislation (if possible, in English).**

All of Australia's substantive antitrust laws are set out in the Competition and Consumer Act 2010 (Cth) (**CCA**).[7]

Australia's merger control regime consists of two prohibitions.

- Section 50 of the CCA prohibits a corporation or person from directly or indirectly acquiring shares or assets if it would have the effect, or would be likely to have the effect, of substantially lessening competition in a market in Australia.
- Section 50A prohibits acquisitions of shares occurring outside Australia, where that acquisition would result in a change of control in an Australian corporation, which results, or would be likely to result, in a substantial lessening of competition and would not give rise to a net benefit offsetting the lessening of competition.

Anti-overlap provisions in the CCA apply so that where an acquisition is subject to both the section 50 and section 50A prohibitions, the section 50 provision will apply.

Anticompetitive conduct and concerted practices

Until a merger completes, firms are considered to be competitors or potential competitors. As such, the provisions of the CCA relating to cartel conduct will apply until and unless the transaction completes and the parties become part of the same corporate group.

The CCA prohibits parties (that are or are likely to be in competition) from entering into or giving effect to, contracts, arrangements or understandings containing a provision:

- with the purpose or effect of fixing, controlling or maintaining prices;
- with the purpose of:
  - restricting or limiting production, capacity, supply or acquisition of goods or services;

7 Available at: <https://www.legislation.gov.au/Details/C2017C00375>.

- allocating customers, suppliers or territories; and/or
- rigging bids or tender processes.

Cartel conduct is a civil prohibition and a criminal offense in Australia, and (among other consequences) exposes individuals to potential terms of imprisonment of up to 10 years.

In the merger context, material risks can arise where parties seek to prematurely integrate or align business activities (or jointly undertake activities) prior to closing, as at that point they are still, for the purposes of the CCA, in competition with each other.

Merger parties also need to be conscious of the other prohibitions on anticompetitive conduct (which apply regardless of whether the parties are competitors) including the prohibition on contracts, arrangements, understandings or concerted practices that have the purpose, effect or likely effect of substantially lessening competition. The "concerted practice" prohibition operates to capture coordinated or cooperative conduct that falls short of the requisite commitment in respect of contracts, arrangements or understandings.

2. Do any guidelines exist in your jurisdiction concerning the application of the substantive antitrust laws in an M&A context – whether internal to the relevant authority, or external, formal or informal (e.g. speeches)? If so, please provide a copy/link to such guidance.

The ACCC has published numerous guidelines to assist parties in the merger clearance processes. These include:

- *Merger Guidelines 2008*: these guidelines provide an overview of the ACCC's approach to mergers and section 50;
- *Informal Merger Review Process Guidelines 2013*: these guidelines assist parties with the procedures involved in the informal clearance process, in the absence of statutory guidance; and
- *Merger Authorisation Guidelines 2018*: these guidelines provide information on the statutory and procedural elements that need to be satisfied in order to seek merger authorization from the ACCC. These guidelines were updated following amendments to the CCA relevant to the merger authorization process came into force on 6 November 2017.

The ACCC recently published (brief) guidance on gun-jumping risks in the merger context. The ACCC explained that the term is used, in Australia, "when merger parties start coordinating their activities or behaving as one entity instead of as competitors during the period before a merger or acquisition is completed (including where the ACCC is still conducting a merger review)", and that gun-jumping conduct, particularly if it involves market-sharing or price-fixing, will risk breaching Australian competition laws prohibiting cartel and other anticompetitive conduct.

The ACCC further explained that the gun-jumping conduct that (from the ACCC's perspective) may be at risk under the CCA includes:

- sharing current and competitively sensitive information beyond what is required for integration-planning and to conduct due diligence;

- placing unreasonable restrictions on the target's business activities or impeding its ability to compete, for example by restricting its ability to make new business investments; and
- taking steps to integrate the acquirer's and target's businesses or to coordinate their pricing or dealings with customers, such as joint marketing or referring the target's customers to the acquirer.

Relevantly, the ACCC further highlighted that, in Australia:

- pre-merger gun-jumping may breach Australian competition law regardless of whether or not the merger parties notify the ACCC of a proposed transaction; and
- completing a transaction does not remove the risk of the ACCC taking legal action in respect of any gun-jumping conduct that occurred before the transaction was completed.

The ACCC has not published guidelines dedicated solely to the exchange of competitively sensitive information. However, the ACCC's gun-jumping guidance refers to risks arising in the context of information exchange, and (in that context) notes that "usually parties implement information-sharing confidentiality restrictions, such as ensuring a select group of employees responsible for viewing competitively sensitive information necessary for merger planning are not also involved in commercial decisions". The ACCC's *Guidelines on Concerted Practices* (2018) may also be of relevance to the extent they cover potential competition issues that may arise through the exchange of competitively sensitive information between competitors.

3. **As a general matter (not limited to M&A), how are the substantive antitrust laws enforced with respect to the exchange of competitively sensitive information between competing firms? Please also indicate the relevance of anti-competitive effects or intent in such enforcement.**

The exchange of competitively sensitive information between firms is an example of conduct that may be caught within the ambit of cartel conduct (if the exchange involved or led to a cartel arrangement) and/or a concerted practice, as explained above. The prohibition against concerted practices prohibits such conduct where there is a purpose, effect or likely effect of substantially lessening competition. The conduct of merger parties may raise concerns under the prohibition against concerted practices if they exchange competitively sensitive information (such as future pricing, output or capacity) in circumstances where that exchange is intended to or would have the likely effect of substantially lessening competition.

The remedies for engaging in cartel conduct and concerted practices are outlined below.

4. **Have there been any cases in your jurisdiction in which the substantive antitrust laws were enforced in an M&A context? Please describe/explain and cite any such cases. (See also Annex.)**

Norcast S.ár.L v Bradken Limited (No 2) [2013] FCA 235

This private litigation involved the application of the cartel provisions under the CCA in the context of bids in an M&A sale process, whereby Norcast (Vendor) sold NWS to a subsidiary of Castle Harlan. The Vendor alleged that Bradken Limited (Bradken) had entered into a contract, arrangement or understanding with Castle Harlan that contained a bid-rigging provision, whereby it was agreed that Castle Harlan would bid and that Bradken would not bid for the acquisition of NWS. Castle Harlan then on-sold NWS to Bradken, an Australian mining company, on the same day, generating a significant profit. The Vendor alleged that a higher price would have been paid had the parties not engaged in bid-rigging. The court held that the "flip" constituted both misleading and deceptive conduct and bid-rigging, given the coordination between Bradken and Castle Harlan, who were inferred to be competitors. The Court held that this amounted to coordination that was concealed from the Vendor, resulting in a finding of cartel conduct.

ACCC v Cryosite [2019] FCA 116

The ACCC instituted proceedings in the Federal Court against Cryosite Limited (Cryosite) in the first "gun-jumping" case instituted in Australia in July 2018.[8]

The ACCC alleged Cryosite engaged in cartel conduct in respect of its entry into an asset sale agreement (Agreement) with Cell Care Australia Pty Ltd (Cell Care) in June 2017. Cryosite and Cell Care are the only private suppliers of cord blood and tissue banking services in Australia.

The ACCC alleged that the Agreement involved a provision which required Cryosite to refer all customer enquiries to Cell Care after signing but prior to completion. The ACCC alleged this constituted cartel conduct, in that it allocated potential customers from Cryosite to Cell Care and effectively restricted the supply of Cryosite's services to new customers.

The ACCC also challenged another provision of the Agreement which restrained Cell Care from dealing with any Cryosite customers who had used Cryosite's services in the five years preceding completion of the transaction, and alleged that there was an ancillary arrangement in which Cell Care agreed it would not market to Cryosite's existing customers prior to completion.

In a decision in February 2019, the Court found (by consent) that Cryosite engaged in cartel conduct with respect to the relevant provision in the Agreement, and in subsequently giving effect to that provision. Cryosite admitted that the provision was designed to restrict the supply of Cryosite's services to new customers and to allocate potential customers to Cell Care. Cryosite was ultimately fined A$1.05 million.

ACCC v Pacific National Pty Ltd (No 2) [2019] FCA 669

In July 2018, the ACCC instituted proceedings in the Federal Court against Pacific National (PN) and Aurizon (Aurizon) for alleged anticompetitive conduct regarding an understanding the parties had reached whereby Aurizon would close part of its intermodal freight business and sell other parts to PN with the purpose or likely effect of substantially lessening competition. The ACCC alleged that the effect of the understanding was that Aurizon would stop competing with

---

8 <https://www.accc.gov.au/media-release/accc-institutes-proceedings-against-cryosite-for-alleged-cartel-conduct>.

PN in respect of the supply of intermodal freight and bulk steel rail linehaul services in Australia.

In May 2019, the Federal Court dismissed the ACCC's proceedings against PN and Aurizon. The Court stated that it would have found the proposed acquisition to have the likely effect of substantially lessening competition in breach of the CCA, had it not been for the undertaking offered by PN which would prevent it from providing discriminatory access.

5. Are the substantive antitrust laws more likely to apply at specific stages of the transaction – i.e. at an early stage, or prior to closing (or does it not make a difference)? Do companies face ongoing risk following the consummation (or failure) of their transaction for conduct that allegedly occurred pre-closing (pre-failure)?

The substantive antitrust provisions under the CCA apply regardless of the stage of the transaction. As noted above, the ACCC has explicitly stated that completing a transaction does not remove the risk of the ACCC taking legal action in respect of any gun-jumping conduct that occurred before the transaction was completed.

The standard limitation period for civil prohibitions is six years. There is no limitation period for criminal offenses (such as a cartel offense).

6. Please explain how the relevant authority enforces (or could enforce) the substantive antitrust laws in an M&A context. How would the investigation occur, and what timing constraints would apply?

The ACCC is likely to investigate potential contraventions of the substantive antitrust provisions of the CCA in parallel with any merger clearance or authorization process. The ACCC has explained that where the ACCC is concerned that merger parties may have "jumped the gun", it will investigate whether the conduct in question contravenes the prohibitions on cartel conduct, involves an anticompetitive arrangement or constitutes an anticompetitive acquisition in breach of section 50 of the CCA.

The ACCC is unlikely to be constrained by any clearance or authorization process timelines in conducting its investigation or reaching its decision in respect of potential breaches of the substantive antitrust provisions of the CCA. Any such investigation or action is likely to continue following its clearance/authorization and completion of a transaction. Indeed, the ACCC has stated that gun-jumping may *delay* the ACCC's consideration of the proposed merger, if the ACCC suspends its assessment of a merger while it investigates the conduct.

7. Is private enforcement of the substantive antitrust laws possible in an M&A context, and has it occurred?

The CCA permits private enforcement of the substantive antitrust provisions, although the remedies available to a private party may differ from those available to the ACCC. The provisions, however, are primarily enforced by the ACCC.

Norcast S.ár.L v Bradken Limited (No 2) [2013] FCA 235 is an example of private litigation being initiated in respect of the (then new) cartel prohibitions/offenses in an M&A context.

8. Could behavior subject to the substantive antitrust laws also be caught under the merger control rules/standstill obligation? (Please also refer to the Annex.)

Not applicable. There is no specific standstill obligation under the CCA.

9. Please describe the penalties for infringing the substantive antitrust laws. Please indicate whether these include criminal penalties, including individual criminal penalties. As a practical matter, how have these been applied in the context of an M&A transaction?

The potential penalties that may be applied in respect of a transaction that breaches the substantive antitrust laws (i.e. not section 50) are set out below.

Contravention of the prohibitions/offenses on cartel conduct will expose:

- a corporation to criminal fines or civil penalties for each breach of up to the greater of:
  - A$10 million;
  - three times the value of the benefit to the cartel (when that benefit can be determined); or
  - 10% of the group's annual turnover in the preceding 12 months; and
- an individual to:
  - criminal liability of up to 10 years' imprisonment and fines of up to A$420,000 per breach; or
  - civil liability for pecuniary penalties of A$500,000 per breach.

Breach of the other substantive antitrust provisions will expose:

- a corporation to civil penalties for each breach of up to the greater of:
  - A$10 million;
  - three times the value of the benefit to the conduct (when that benefit can be determined); or
  - 10% of the group's annual turnover in the preceding 12 months; and
- an individual to civil liability for pecuniary penalties of A$500,000 per breach.

For all substantive antitrust provisions, the ACCC may also seek a range of other orders such as injunctions, declarations, divestitures, damages, adverse publicity, disqualification and other broad remedial orders.

In *Norcast S.ár.L v Bradken Limited (No 2)* (see Questions 4 and 7) the plaintiffs were awarded damages which were calculated as the difference between the purchase price paid for NWS by Castle Harlan to the Vendor and the purchase price paid for NWS by Bradken to Castle Harlan. The Court held that this was a reasonable estimate of the amount Bradken might have paid for NWS, absent the bid-rigging agreement.

In *ACCC v Cryosite* (see Question 4), the parties jointly sought (and were granted) declarations of contravention and orders for the payment of A$1.05 million. The Court determined that the maximum penalty would be A$10 million because the value of the benefit of the conduct cannot be quantified and 10% of Cryosite's annual revenue would be in the order of A$1 million. While the penalties were at the lower end of the maximum available, the Court noted that "in light of Cryosite's size and financial position, the proposed penalties could not reasonably be regarded as an acceptable cost of doing business, and could be expected to render any risk/benefit analysis materially less palatable to other potential wrongdoers". In determining the appropriate penalty, the Court also noted:

- that market-sharing, including when it is undertaken in the context of a proposed or anticipated sale of business, is cartel conduct which causes serious harm to consumers, other businesses and the economy;
- the potential for permanent structural market change to be caused by both pre-completion cartel conduct and acquisitions that contravene the merger control provisions; and
- the fact that Cryosite had received legal advice and that it did not engage in conduct with the intention to contravene the CCA.

10. Please describe policy and enforcement trends in your jurisdiction.

The ACCC has used its loss in the case of *ACCC v Pacific National Pty Ltd (No 2)* [2019] FCA 669 to highlight the challenges it faces in opposing mergers in Court, and to continue advocating for a potential change to the legal standard and/or how that standard is approached in Australia. It has raised concerns that "the bar for establishing a likely substantial lessening of competition is being raised to a height that is failing to protect competition and ultimately consumers".

The ACCC is aggressively seeking higher penalties for breaches of the substantive antitrust provisions, and it is common for it to appeal penalty decisions to seek larger penalties. It has recently flagged a change in its approach to penalties and settlement, following an OECD report that Australia is lagging behind other jurisdictions in the level of penalties imposed, especially in the context of large companies and conduct that has lasted for long periods of time.[9] It has flagged that it will push for penalties in the "hundreds" of millions of dollars.

The ACCC is also pursuing criminal action for cartel conduct with more vigor, and is referring more cartel matters to the Commonwealth Department of Public Prosecutions (CDPP) (which is the prosecutorial body at the Federal level) for criminal prosecution. The first criminal conviction was handed down in August 2017, whereby a Japanese corporation pleaded guilty and was fined A$25 million for one rolled-up charge. Since these first proceedings, criminal cartel charges have been laid – against companies and individuals – in five other matters.

The ACCC's stated policy is to take criminal action and seek higher penalties to ensure senior management and company boards, as well as shareholders, prioritize competition law compliance.

---

9 Rod Sims, "Release of the OECD's Pecuniary Penalties for Competition Law Infringements in Australia Report" (Speech at Workshop on Australian Pecuniary Penalties for Competition Law Infringements, 26 March 2018) <https://www.accc.gov.au/speech/release-of-the-oecd%E2%80%99s-pecuniary-penalties-for-competition-law-infringements-in-australia-report>.

Brent Fisse, "The Federal Court of Australia issues its first decision on cartel liability under the Competition and Consumer Act 2010: a wake-up call to those doing private equity deals (Norcast v Bradken)" 19 March 2013, e-Competitions Bulletin March 2013, Art. N° 51500

Julie Clarke, "The Federal Court of Australia hands down its first decision involving a bid rigging case after the entry into force of new cartel laws (Norcast/ Bradken)" 19 March 2013, e-Competitions Bulletin March 2013, Art. N° 52518

Annex

Table 1: Actual Enforcement of Specific Conduct under the Relevant Merger Control Rules and Substantive Antitrust Laws

Please identify whether the following type of conduct has been subject to investigation/enforcement in your jurisdiction, under the merger control laws or substantive antitrust laws. Please cite any such case(s) and provide a brief description in the table below.

Specific Conduct	Actual Enforcement under Merger Control Laws	Actual Enforcement under Substantive Antitrust Laws
Pre-signing due diligence	N/A (there is no specific standstill obligation under the CCA)	No
Post-signing/pre-approval due diligence		*ACCC v Cryosite* [2019] FCA 116 – This involved alleged cartel conduct post-signing but prior to completion (see Part 2 Question 4 for a brief description)
Post-approval/pre-closing due diligence		No
Use of "clean teams"		No
Restrictions on the target in an M&A agreement, e.g. buyer approval required for: – Investments above a certain level; – New business above a certain level; – Other obligations to consult/obtain approval from the buyer before closing.		*ACCC v Cryosite* [2019] FCA 116 – This involved alleged cartel conduct regarding referral of prospective customers prior to completion (see Part 2 Question 4 for a brief description)
Joint marketing		No
Joint presentations (e.g. industry fairs)		No
Joint communications		No

Specific Conduct	Actual Enforcement under Merger Control Laws	Actual Enforcement under Substantive Antitrust Laws
Strategy/planning regarding customers	N/A (there is no specific standstill obligation under the CCA)	*ACCC v Cryosite* [2019] FCA 116 – This involved alleged cartel conduct regarding referral of prospective customers prior to completion (see Part 2 Question 4 for a brief description)
Strategy/planning regarding suppliers		No
Third party contract novation		No
Personnel Issues: – Secondments – Retention Strategies		No
IT Planning/Database Migration		No
Other		*ACCC v Pacific National Pty Ltd (No 2)* [2019] FCA 669 – These proceedings involved alleged breaches of substantive provisions of the CCA regarding circumstances around entry into a proposed transaction including the proposed closure of part of the vendor's business (see Part 1 Question 2 and Part 2 Question 4 for a brief description). *Norcast S.ár.L v Bradken Limited (No 2)* [2013] FCA 235 – This involved
		bid-rigging in the context of the M&A sale process (see Part 2 Question 4 for a brief description)

Table 2: Hypothetical Enforcement of Specific Conduct under the Relevant Merger Control Rules and Substantive Antitrust Laws

For any conduct that is *not* the subject of actual enforcement (Table 1), please indicate in the Table below whether the conduct identified *could potentially* be enforced under the merger control laws and/or substantive antitrust laws.

Specific Conduct	Hypothetical Enforcement under Merger Control Laws	Hypothetical Enforcement under Substantive Antitrust Laws
Pre-signing due diligence	N/A (there is no specific standstill obligation under the CCA)	Depending on the circumstances, information exchange during due diligence could raise risks under the concerted practices prohibition.
Post-signing/pre-approval due diligence		Depending on the circumstances, information exchange during due diligence could raise risks under the concerted practices prohibition.
Post-approval/pre-closing due diligence		Depending on the circumstances, information exchange during due diligence could raise risks under the concerted practices prohibition.
Use of "clean teams"		Depending on the circumstances, information exchange during due diligence, including through "clean teams", could raise risks under the concerted practices prohibition.
Restrictions on the target in an M&A agreement, e.g. buyer approval required for: – Investments above a certain level; – New business above a certain level; – Other obligations to consult/obtain approval from the buyer before closing.		Depending on the circumstances, restrictions on the target could raise risks under cartel prohibitions/ offenses, or the prohibition on arrangements or concerted practices with the purpose or likely effect of a substantial lessening of competition.

Specific Conduct	Hypothetical Enforcement under Merger Control Laws	Hypothetical Enforcement under Substantive Antitrust Laws
Joint marketing	N/A (there is no specific standstill obligation under the CCA)	Depending on the circumstances, joint activities prior to closing could raise risks under cartel prohibitions/offenses, or the prohibition on arrangements or concerted practices with the purpose or likely effect of a substantial lessening of competition.
Joint presentations (e.g. industry fairs)		Depending on the circumstances, joint activities prior to closing could raise risks under cartel prohibitions/offenses, or the prohibition on arrangements or concerted practices with the purpose or likely effect of a substantial lessening of competition.
Joint communications		Depending on the circumstances, joint activities prior to closing could raise risks under cartel prohibitions/offenses, or the prohibition on arrangements or concerted practices with the purpose or likely effect of a substantial lessening of competition.
Strategy/planning regarding customers		Depending on the circumstances, joint planning or arrangements regarding customers prior to closing could raise risks under cartel prohibitions/offenses, or the prohibition on arrangements or concerted practices with the purpose or likely effect of a substantial lessening of competition.
Strategy/planning regarding suppliers		Depending on the circumstances, joint planning or arrangements regarding suppliers prior to closing could raise risks under cartel prohibitions/offenses, or the prohibition on arrangements or concerted practices with the purpose or likely effect of a substantial lessening of competition.

Specific Conduct	Hypothetical Enforcement under Merger Control Laws	Hypothetical Enforcement under Substantive Antitrust Laws
Third party contract novation	N/A (there is no specific standstill obligation under the CCA)	Depending on the circumstances, arrangements around third-party contract novation prior to closing could raise risks under cartel prohibitions/offenses, or the prohibition on arrangements or concerted practices with the purpose or likely effect of a substantial lessening of competition.
Personnel Issues: Secondments Retention Strategies		Depending on the circumstances, arrangements around employees (e.g. secondments pre-closing) prior to closing could raise risks under cartel prohibitions/offenses, or the prohibition on arrangements or concerted practices with the purpose or likely effect of a substantial lessening of competition.
IT Planning/Database Migration		Depending on the circumstances, IT/data migration (involving the exchange of information) prior to closing could raise risks under the concerted practices prohibition, cartel prohibitions/offenses, or the prohibition on arrangements or concerted practices with the purpose or likely effect of a substantial lessening of competition.
Other		Depending on the circumstances, any other premature alignment or coordination of activities prior to closing could raise risks under the concerted practices prohibition, cartel prohibitions/offenses, or the prohibition on arrangements or concerted practices with the purpose or likely effect of a substantial lessening of competition.

BRAZIL

Cristianne Zarzur and Marcos Garrido
(Pinheiro Neto Advogados)

Part 1: Merger Control and the "Standstill Obligation"

1. **Please identify the relevant merger control legislation in your jurisdiction. Please provide a link to the relevant legislation (if possible, in English) and also indicate:**
   - **whether the merger control system is mandatory or voluntary,**
   - **the relevant authority, and**
   - **the duration of the review period.**

   The principal merger control legislation in Brazil is Law No 12.529/11[1] (**Brazilian Competition Law**), which sets out the Brazilian System for Protection of Competition, setting forth general rules for the mandatory merger control system (Articles 88 to 90), preventive measures and sanctions for violations against the economic order.

   The relevant antitrust authority in Brazil is the Administrative Council for Economic Defense (**CADE**). The merger control system is mandatory and therefore all concentration acts that meet the turnover thresholds should be notified.

   CADE's Resolution 2/2012 regulates the merger control system and provides for overall filing procedures and exceptions. CADE's Internal Regulations (**RICADE**) also provide certain rules related to merger control (Articles 106 *et seq.*), including gun-jumping.

   The statutory timeframe for review of notified mergers is 240 days, starting on the day of filing, and can be extended for: (i) 60 days, upon the parties' request, or (ii) 90 days, further to a reasoned decision issued by CADE. On average, simple transactions eligible for the fast-track procedure are decided in 20 to 30 calendar days.

2. **Does the merger control system in your jurisdiction impose a "*standstill obligation*" – meaning, that the transaction cannot be implemented prior to completing the merger control process? (Please cite the relevant legislation.) Please also indicate the *legal scope* of the standstill obligation according to the relevant legislation (e.g. the parties to the transaction cannot effect a change of control, cannot take steps towards implementation, etc.).**

   Yes, concentration acts whose filing is mandatory in Brazil may not be consummated until cleared by CADE (Article 88, s 3 of the Brazilian Competition Law).

---

1 <http://www.cade.gov.br/assuntos/internacional/legislacao/law-no-12529-2011-english-version-from-18-05-2012.pdf/view>.

Generally speaking, RICADE establishes that the parties to a reportable transaction must keep physical structures and competitive conditions unchanged until CADE's final decision. CADE's *Internal Regulations and the Gun-Jumping Guidelines* also prohibit transfers of assets or the exercise of any influence of one of the deal parties over the other, as well as any exchange of competitively sensitive information not strictly necessary for execution of the formal binding instrument between the parties.

3. **Have the relevant authorities in your jurisdiction issued internal or external guidelines concerning the scope of the standstill obligation, and/or their authority to enforce it? Please provide a copy/link of such guidance, if possible in English.**

Yes, CADE issued the *Gun-Jumping Guidelines*[2] with a view to providing a mechanism of administrative transparency and orientation with no binding effects. In addition, CADE issued Resolution 24 in July 2019, which establishes specific procedures for investigating possible breaches to the standstill obligation. Most importantly, this Resolution also sets out objective criteria for the application of fines in the event a violation is confirmed by CADE. Further details are provided below.

4. **Are there any exceptions to the standstill obligation – for example, through derogation or "carve out"? Please describe the circumstances in which this is possible. Please also describe the relevant process, e.g. do parties need to apply to the authority for a derogation from the standstill obligation? If so, how long is the approval process? If there are specific cases addressing these issues, please identify them.**

According to RICADE (Article 114), the parties notifying a merger may, on an exceptional basis, request a preliminary authorization for the consummation of the merger, in cases where (i) there is no danger of irreparable damage to the competition conditions in the market; (ii) the measures whose authorization is requested are fully reversible; *and* (iii) the notifying party is able to prove the imminent occurrence of substantial and irreversible financial damage to the purchased company if the exceptional authorization for the consummation of the merger is not granted.

CADE's General Superintendence shall issue an opinion on the request within 30 days of filing. Such opinion is then sent to the Tribunal, which in turn must decide within 30 days of its receipt.

In addition, past rulings issued by CADE have established that (i) a carve-out agreement, pursuant to which parties decide to isolate Brazil and proceed with the closing, or partial implementation, of a multijurisdictional transaction in other countries, constitutes gun-jumping in Brazil; and that (ii) down payments and break-up fees are acceptable, as long as they are typical of business transactions and proportional in the circumstances of the particular case.

5. **Does a public bid exception exist in your jurisdiction? (For example, under the EU Merger Regulation it is possible to acquire shares as part of a public**

---

2 <http://www.cade.gov.br/acesso-a-informacao/publicacoes-institucionais/guias_do_Cade/guideline-gun-jumping-september.pdf>.

bid, provided that the shares are not exercised until the acquisition is cleared by the Commission.) If such an exception exists in your jurisdiction, please describe how it is applied.

Article 107 of RICADE establishes that public offers for securities may be notified as from the time of their publication and are not subject to CADE's prior approval. However, the exercise of political rights attached to the purchased interest by means of the public offer shall be forbidden until final clearance. In principle, nothing would prevent the acquirer from requesting a derogation from CADE, to exercise voting rights of the shares acquired prior to clearance, if this is necessary to protect the value of the investment (Article 107, s 2). Transactions executed on the stock markets are subject to this same rule (Article 108).

6. **What powers does the relevant authority have to investigate and enforce violations of the standstill obligation? Are dawn raids possible? What timing applies to investigation/enforcement proceedings?**

In June 2015, in order to bring more legal certainty to investigations relating to gun-jumping, CADE issued Resolution 13, which has now been replaced by Resolution 24. Issued by CADE in July 2019, Resolution 24 outlines specific administrative proceedings to scrutinize (i) reportable transactions that have been filed and were consummated before CADE's clearance; (ii) reportable transactions that have not been filed and were consummated before CADE's clearance; and (iii) transactions that do not meet the filing thresholds (so not subject to mandatory review), but whose notification may be requested by CADE.

It should be noted that, among the possible sanctions for violating the standstill obligation, the authorities may commence an administrative proceeding to investigate alleged violations to the economic order. Accordingly, the Brazilian Competition Law allows for dawn raids in these circumstances. In addition, as part of its investigative powers, CADE is allowed, among other actions, to (i) request information, documents and/or oral clarification from any individual or legal entity, as well as from public or private bodies; (ii) make inspections at the principal place of business, establishment, office, branch or subsidiary of a company under investigation, of inventories, effects, papers of any kind, commercial records, computers and electronic files, and is entitled to take or request copies of any documents or electronic data.

The authority's investigation is not subject to any specific term which in practice will vary depending on the need to collect evidence and overall instruction. The statute of limitations for CADE to impose penalties on parties for breaching the standstill obligation is five years, counted as from the material event related to the breach.

7. **What are the possible penalties for violating the standstill obligation? Are there criminal sanctions, including on individuals? Have these been applied in practice? Is there a difference in enforcement between transactions involving domestic companies and "foreign-to-foreign" transactions? Does the authority have the power to unwind transactions implemented in breach of the standstill obligation? If so, has the authority made use of that power in practice? If yes, please provide examples.**

Penalties for gun-jumping practices in Brazil comprise fines, ranging from BRL 60,000 to BRL 60 million, in addition to the possible annulment of the acts (e.g. total or partial implementation of the transaction) performed by the parties before obtaining CADE's approval and the commencement of an administrative investigation into potential anticompetitive conduct. Such penalties were initially imposed by CADE at its own discretion, taking into consideration such aspects as the parties' good faith, the extent of competitive harm and the parties' economic capacity, among others. In July 2019, however, CADE issued Resolution 24, which sets out objective criteria for the application of fines due to the breach of the standstill obligation.

Accordingly, Article 21 of Resolution 24 states that the penalty to be applied for breaching the standstill obligation should be adopted pursuant to the following methodology:

- Base penalty in the amount of BRL 60,000.
- Aggravating circumstances:
  - By the duration of the breach, in the amount equivalent to 0.01% of the value of the transaction per day of delay, counted from the date of consummation until notification of the concentration act or amendment, if any;
  - by the severity of the conduct, up to 4% of the value of the transaction, depending on the ultimate decision to be taken by CADE on the concentration act;
  - by intentionality, up to 0.4% of the average turnover of the economic group or conglomerate in the year prior to consummation of the transaction, depending on the good faith of the parties.
- Reduction for the time of notification, which will be applied to the value of the base penalty and the increases for aggravating circumstances, and will be equivalent to:
  - 50% in cases of spontaneous notification of the concentration act, prior to receipt of the complaint or representation of the *ex officio* investigation by the General Superintendence or by any members of CADE's Tribunal;
  - 30% in cases of notification after receipt of the complaint or representation but prior to the initiation of the formal proceedings;
  - 20% in cases of notification after the initiation of formal proceedings and before the final decision is rendered by CADE's Tribunal.

The final value of the fine will be subject to monetary correction and, in cases of recidivism, the base penalty and any increase for the breach duration may be doubled, depending on specific circumstances.

Since the Brazilian Competition Law came into effect, CADE has had the opportunity to examine some cases in which gun-jumping issues emerged. Some of those cases definitely served as grounds for certain statements made by CADE in its *Gun-Jumping Guidelines*. Within this context, CADE has held that the following acts constitute gun-jumping if performed prior to antitrust clearance:

- Payment of the price, since this would alter the competitive dynamics between the parties in terms of profits and obligations (note that in the merger 08700.003462/201679 *Hypermarcas SA/Reckitt Benckiser Ltda*, a down payment of 20% was accepted by the authorities);

- Effective participation of one party in the decisions to be taken by the other party, such as consolidation of management or interference in operational activities;
- Joint presentation of the companies to the public as if they were already merged;
- Press releases to the media and investors publicizing the deal closing/ consummation;
- Participation by the acquirer in the target company's costs and results;
- Sharing of information and decision-making power with regard to commercially and competitively sensitive matters;
- Absence of a clause in the agreement indicating that CADE clearance is a condition precedent for closing of the deal. Even though this has not been considered as a breach per se in past rulings, CADE has made reference to such absence in conjunction with other material breaches;
- Carve-out agreements (pursuant to which parties decide to isolate Brazil and proceed with the closing, or partial implementation, of a multijurisdictional transaction in other countries).

There are no criminal sanctions for the mere violation of the standstill obligation (assuming that it does not concern any type of collusion between the companies) and no difference between transactions involving domestic companies and foreign-to-foreign transactions.

8. How does the relevant authority typically learn of potential violations of the standstill obligation? Does the authority actively monitor the trade press?

CADE can learn of a potential violation through internal investigations (e.g. monitoring the trade press), but more often through complaints made by third parties or information provided by the Public Prosecutor's Office, etc.

9. Please describe the relevant authority's enforcement of the standstill obligation. If there have been cases, please describe the specific conduct that was found to violate the standstill provision and the criteria applied by the relevant authority or court. Has the relevant authority considered the market impact of the conduct? (Please refer to the Annex.)

Please refer to Question 7 above and Annex – Table 1.

The first section of the *Gun-Jumping Guidelines* divides the activities related to concentration acts that may raise certain concerns into three main groups: (i) exchange of sensitive information between market players; (ii) definition of contract clauses that govern the relationship between market players, and (iii) activities carried out by the parties before and during implementation of the concentration acts.

As for the first group, the *Gun-Jumping Guidelines* seek to prevent commercially sensitive information being exchanged between the parties before final clearance. This includes, for instance, information referring to specific data about costs; capacity level and expansion plans; marketing strategies; product pricing (prices and discounts); main customers and secured discounts; payroll; main suppliers and contractual terms and conditions of supply; non-public information about trademarks, patents and research & development; future acquisition plans; and competitive strategies.

Contractual provisions that may lead to gun-jumping issues include: full or partial advance payment (except for typical down payments, deposits in escrow accounts or break-up fees); clauses establishing that the contract-effective date precedes its closing (implying interactions between the parties); non-compete obligations prior to closing; clauses providing for the influence of one party on the strategic and sensitive business aspects of the other; as well as any clauses establishing activities that cannot be reversed at a later time or whose reversal would require significant expenditure.

Finally, the third category mentioned in the *Gun-Jumping Guidelines* includes activities related to the receipt of profits/earn-outs; transfer and/or usufruct of assets; exercise of voting rights or relevant influence; development of joint sale or marketing strategies for products; joint management; integration of sales force; exclusive licensing of intellectual property to the other party; joint development of products; nomination of members for decision-making bodies; and interruption of investments.[3]

10. In cases involving alleged violations of the standstill obligation under the relevant merger control laws, has the relevant authority (or court) *also* considered the substantive antitrust laws? (Please refer to the Annex.)

We have not identified any relevant case in this regard. Even though the commencement of administrative proceedings to investigate possible anticompetitive practices arising from the violation of the standstill obligation is allowed by the Brazilian Competition Law, precedents on gun-jumping mostly refer to cases in which parties entered into a settlement with the authorities under which they acknowledge they had taken measures that were not allowed before obtaining CADE's approval for their deals and agreeing to pay a financial contribution to end the proceedings.

11. Is private enforcement of the standstill obligation possible?

CADE is allowed to enforce its jurisdiction through the judiciary in the event parties to a reportable concentration act have committed a breach. Third parties, whose interests may be affected by a violation of the economic order, may also

---

3 CADE's precedents that served as a basis for the Gun-Jumping Guidelines include: Concentration Act No. 08700.008289/2013-52. Notifying Parties: UTC Óleo e Gás SA and Aurizônia Petróleo SA. Settlement agreement approved by the Tribunal on 5 February 2014; Concentration Act No. 08700.008292/2013-76. Notifying Parties: Potióleo SA and UTC Óleo e Gás SA. Settlement agreement approved by the Tribunal on 5 February 2014; Concentration Act No. 08700.002285/2014-41. Notifying Parties: FIAT SpA and Chrysler Group LLC. Settlement agreement approved by the Tribunal on 14 May 2014; Procedure to Investigate Concentration Act No. 08700.007160/2013-27 – Parties: JBS SA, Tinto Holding Ltda, Unilav Industrial Ltda, Flora Produtos de Higiene e Limpeza Ltda and Tramonto Alimentos SA, judged by the Tribunal on 17 August 2016; Concentration Act No. 08700.010394/2014-32. Notifying Parties: Goiás Verde Alimentos Ltda, Brasfrigo Alimentos Ltda and Brasfrigo S/A. Settlement agreement approved by the Tribunal on 22 April 2015; Concentration Act. No. 08700.000137/2015-73. Notifying Parties: GNL Gemini Comercialização e Logística Ltda and Companhia de Gás de Minas Gerais. Settlement agreement approved by the Tribunal on 24 June 2015.

seek redress before the courts by requesting the end of the parties' practice, including indemnification for possible losses.

12. Please describe the private law risks/consequences (i.e. contractual/validity consequences) for transactions that are subject to notification, but which are completed without notification/approval. Please identify any relevant cases and describe them.

As discussed in Question 7, penalties for gun-jumping practices in Brazil include fines, the commencement of an administrative proceeding, and the annulment of the acts performed by the parties before obtaining CADE's approval. Depending on the impact of the transaction on the market, therefore, CADE may determine that the agreement(s) entered into by the parties are void and that any acts performed in that regard should be reversed.

In the procedure to investigate *Concentration Act 08700.002655/2016-11 (Blue Cycle/Shimano)*, which relates to the formation of a joint venture for the exclusive distribution of Shimano's cycling products in Brazil, for the first time CADE ordered the annulment of the transaction (at least provisionally, until completion of the final review). Specifically, the object of the JV was to create a new company focused on the exclusive distribution of Shimano's bike parts to the over-the-counter segment in Brazil. CADE became aware of the transaction through a complaint received early in 2016 (after its closing). CADE then initiated an investigation and requested further information from the defendants, and the reason why they had not filed for review. In response, the companies mentioned that the transaction was not submitted to CADE because they were not aware of such an obligation prior to closing. CADE's Tribunal concluded that the parties had committed gun-jumping, imposed a fine of BRL 1.5 million and ordered the annulment of the distribution agreement until the final review of the transaction by the authorities. After analyzing the merits of the transaction, the concentration act was fully approved by CADE and the distribution agreement was re-established.

13. Please describe policy and enforcement trends in your jurisdiction.

After almost seven years since the Brazilian Competition Law came into effect, CADE has gone a long way in its efforts to enhance transparency and bring more legal certainty to investigations on gun-jumping issues. This has been made clear through the publication of the *Gun-Jumping Guidelines* and precedents on the subject. It is expected that this trend will continue, with the authorities continually enforcing its rules.

Part 2: Substantive Antitrust Law in an M&A Context

1. **Please identify the relevant *substantive antitrust laws* in your jurisdiction that can potentially apply in an M&A context (e.g. for the EU, this would include Article 101 of the Treaty on the Functioning of the European Union). Please provide a link to the relevant legislation (if possible, in English).**

Article 36 of the Brazilian Competition Law defines anticompetitive practices as the acts intended or otherwise able to produce the following effects, even if any such effects are not achieved, regardless of the agent's fault: (i) to limit, restrain or in any way harm open competition or free enterprise; (ii) to control a relevant market of a certain product or service; (iii) to increase profits arbitrarily; and (iv) abuse of a dominant position.

Paragraph 3 of Article 36 lists the types of conduct that may be considered as anticompetitive practices. These conducts are punishable if they can actually or even potentially produce harmful effects on competition and could potentially be applied in an M&A context.

2. **Do any guidelines exist in your jurisdiction concerning the application of the substantive antitrust laws in an M&A context – whether internal to the relevant authority, or external, formal or informal (e.g. speeches)? If so, please provide a copy/link to such guidance.**

As mentioned in Part 1, in July 2019, CADE issued Resolution 24, which sets forth specific administrative proceedings to scrutinize (i) reportable transactions that have been filed and were consummated before CADE's clearance; (ii) reportable transactions that have not been filed and were consummated before CADE's clearance; and (iii) transactions that do not meet the filing thresholds (thus not subject to mandatory review), but whose notification may be requested by CADE. In July 2016, CADE issued guidelines to orient stakeholders and propose best practices related to horizontal mergers (*Guia para análise de atos de concentração horizontal*).

In addition, the *Gun-Jumping Guidelines* list, as activities that might constitute gun-jumping, (i) the exchange of information between economic agents involved in a merger; (ii) definition of contractual clauses governing the relationship between economic agents; and (iii) the activities of the parties before and during the implementation of a merger. As far as the exchange of information is concerned, the *Guidelines* identify the following as being sensitive and requiring increased attention: (a) costs of the companies involved; (b) capacity level and plans for expansion; (c) marketing strategies; (d) product pricing (prices and deductions); (e) main customers and deductions ensured; (f) employees' wages; (g) main suppliers and the terms of contracts signed with them; (h) non-public information on marks and patents and research & development; (i) plans for future acquisitions; (j) competition strategies, etc.

In this context, procedures to reduce the risk of gun-jumping may be generally described as follows:

- General rule: competitors are not allowed to exchange information about prices, costs, clients, suppliers and any data that can be considered competitively sensitive;
- What is permitted: the exchange of information in a due diligence context, as long as the following measures are observed:
  - information requested by the acquiring party's clean team has to be restricted to what is strictly necessary for the transaction;
  - information must be aggregated, anonymous and historical;
  - information must be transmitted through a clean team (an independent committee which is the only communication channel between the companies);
  - written records are kept of every information request.

3. As a general matter (not limited to M&A), how are the substantive antitrust laws enforced with respect to the exchange of competitively sensitive information between competing firms? Please also indicate the relevance of anticompetitive effects or intent in such enforcement.

The Brazilian regime has adopted a mechanism based on subjective criteria, in which the determination on whether a given practice constitutes an economic violation must be made on a case-by-case basis. The new Brazilian Competition Law envisions no specific substantive test for verification of an antitrust violation, but rather sets out broad and generic principles to aid the analysis of each case (application of the rule of reason). In addition, CADE adopts the effects doctrine, meaning that the authority can investigate practices fully or partially performed within Brazilian territory or even fully performed abroad provided that they produce or are capable of producing effects in Brazil.

Finally, and differently from other anticompetitive conduct, cartels are considered a per se violation of the law in Brazil, meaning that the anticompetitive effects of the practice do not need to be proved, and are rather presumed.

As regards the exchange of competitively sensitive information in particular, the *Gun-Jumping Guidelines* expressly recognize that "it is known that any merger implies the sharing of information between the parties to some extent, especially during the due diligence that generally precedes mergers and acquisitions". For further details on the procedures recommended by the guidelines, please refer to Question 2.

4. Have there been any cases in your jurisdiction in which the substantive antitrust laws were enforced in an M&A context? Please describe/explain and cite any such cases. (See also Annex.)

In Brazil, violation of the standstill obligation may give rise to penalties under Article 36 and 88 of the Competition Law. The latter relates to the mere fact that the parties should wait for clearance before implementing the transaction. It is therefore a more straightforward analysis to determine whether the parties have performed any conduct related to the implementation of the deal and/or exchanged sensitive information before they were allowed to. The analysis to be performed under Article 36 examines the extent to which such conduct affected the market and therefore could be qualified as an anticompetitive practice.

So far, most cases involving an assessment of the standstill obligation have been settled between CADE and the involved parties with the recognition of a breach of Article 88. We are not aware of investigations involving Article 36 in the context of an M&A.

Further, in certain merger cases analyzed by CADE, the authorities questioned the use of restrictive clauses and decided to analyze further a given practice:

- *Concentration Act 08700.007777/2017-76 (Praxair/Linde)*: as part of the merger review, CADE asked how frequently exclusive supply and most-favored nation clauses were used by the companies and why. The transaction was ultimately approved by CADE subject to the divestment of certain assets and the investigation closed after the parties provided justification for the use of such clauses.
- *Concentration Act 08700.009988/2014-09 (Condor/Tigre)*: during the final ruling of the merger case, CADE rejected the transaction and decided to open proceedings to investigate possible anticompetitive practices related to the use of clauses restricting competition, which could increase the probability of exercising coordinated power. The investigation is still ongoing.
- *Concentration Act 08012.011323/2010-81 (Allpark/Bagattini/CGB)*: during the analysis of the merger filing, CADE found evidence of collusion in the parking market and decided to open a cartel investigation. The case was settled by certain defendants and in August 2018 a final ruling was issued with the conviction of one company and its director under Article 36 of the Competition Law.

5. Are the substantive antitrust laws more likely to apply at specific stages of the transaction – i.e. at an early stage, or prior to closing (or does it not make a difference)? Do companies face ongoing risk following the consummation (or failure) of their transaction for conduct that allegedly occurred pre-closing (pre-failure)?

In Brazil, the application of substantive antitrust laws occurs before clearance by CADE, and therefore before closing. This may be the case, for instance, when there is an exchange of sensitive information without proper safeguards during the course of negotiations of the contracts or even after signing. The parties would be still considered as independent players and any type of coordination or exchange of sensitive information could give rise to the application of antitrust laws.

It may also be the case that the authorities come to the conclusion that certain peculiarities of the market warrant an in-depth analysis and therefore determine the need to open proceedings in this respect.

The statute of limitations for CADE to impose penalties on parties for breaching the standstill obligation is five years, counted from the material event related to the breach. As discussed above, CADE may also consider that the actions taken by the parties before clearance constitute collusion between competitors contrary to Article 36. In such a case, there is a major ongoing debate on the length of the statute of limitations for an investigation. Since participation in a cartel is considered a crime in Brazil, CADE usually considers the limitation period of 12 years for commencing an investigation (which is the term provided by the criminal law).

6. Please explain how the relevant authority enforces (or could enforce) the substantive antitrust laws in an M&A context. How would the investigation occur, and what timing constraints would apply?

Considering that Brazil enforces a standstill obligation, under which parties to a transaction whose filing is mandatory are prohibited from implementing or consummating the merger before clearance, it is expected that no breach is committed before that. It may be the case, however, that the authorities identify certain issues during their analysis, usually related to the relevant market under scrutiny, and determine that the opening of a broader inquiry into the market's practices is warranted.

Such an investigation would need to follow its own specific rules, detailing the particular object of the analysis, and all affected parties (not necessarily only those involved in the merger case) would be granted the opportunity to a full defense. Please refer to Question 4 for a few examples in this respect.

7. Is private enforcement of the substantive antitrust laws possible in an M&A context, and has it occurred?

CADE is allowed to enforce its jurisdiction through the judiciary in the event parties fail to comply with the substantive antitrust laws. As is the case for the private enforcement of the standstill obligation (see discussion above), third parties whose interests may be affected by a violation of the economic order may also seek redress before the courts by requesting that the parties end their practice, including indemnification for possible losses.

8. Could behavior subject to the substantive antitrust laws also be caught under the merger control rules/standstill obligation? (Please also refer to the Annex.)

Yes, for instance, the exchange of sensitive information by the parties to a transaction whose filing is mandatory would be subject to the substantive antitrust laws and would also likely to be caught under the merger control rules.

9. Please describe the penalties for infringing the substantive antitrust laws. Please indicate whether these include criminal penalties, including individual criminal penalties. As a practical matter, how have these been applied in the context of an M&A transaction?

With regard to possible penalties, defendants in administrative proceedings for anticompetitive practices may be liable to payment of a fine ranging from 0.1% to 20% of the turnover (gross revenue) of the company, group or conglomerate, which was achieved during the financial year immediately before the initiation of the proceedings in the field of business affected by the anticompetitive practice.

Other sanctions can be imposed on the defendants, such as: (i) at the offender's expense, half-page publication of the summary sentence in a court-appointed newspaper for two consecutive days, within one to three consecutive weeks;

(ii) ineligibility for obtaining finance from official financial institutions or for participating in bidding processes involving purchases, sales, works, services or utility concessions with the federal, state, municipal and Federal District authorities and related entities, as well as with indirect administration entities, for a period of at least five years; (iii) inscription of the offender on the Brazilian Consumer Protection Register; (iv) recommendation that the relevant government entities: (a) grant compulsory licenses for intellectual property rights held by the offender, when the offense is related to use of such rights; and (b) deny the offender a right to installment payment of federal overdue debts, or order full or partial cancellation of tax incentives or public subsidies; (v) the company's spin-off, transfer of corporate control, sale of assets, or partial discontinuance of activities; (vi) prohibition from doing business under its own name or as representative of a legal entity, for up to five years; and (vii) any other act or measure necessary to eliminate the harmful effects to competition.

Participation in a cartel is contrary to Article 36 and can lead to criminal sanctions.

10. Please describe policy and enforcement trends in your jurisdiction.

The material law and guidelines issued by CADE significantly increased predictability and legal certainty. Even though most of the cases decided so far in Brazil involving gun-jumping practices were settled with the authorities, parties must be aware that the antitrust laws may be applied in this context and therefore it is important to be careful in negotiations preceding the deal, drafting of contracts and measures that could be taken after signing and before closing.

Barbara Rosenberg, Pierre Honoré, "Brazil: Merger control regime further to the 2012 reform" September 2014, Concurrences Review N° 3-2014, Art. N° 67805

Mariana Tavares de Araujo, "International Cooperation & Convergence to International Best Practices: The Brazilian Experience" in Eleanor Fox, Harry First, Nicolas Charbit, Elisa Ramundo (eds) "Antitrust in Emerging and Developing Countries: Featuring Africa, Brazil, China, India, Mexico – Conference Papers 2nd Edition" (Concurrences 2015) 179

Annex

Table 1: Actual Enforcement of Specific Conduct under the Relevant Merger Control Rules and Substantive Antitrust Laws

Please identify whether the following type of conduct has been subject to investigation/enforcement in your jurisdiction, under the merger control laws or substantive antitrust laws. Please cite any such case(s) and provide a brief description in the table below.

Specific Conduct	Actual Enforcement under Merger Control Laws	Actual Enforcement under Substantive Antitrust Laws
Pre-signing due diligence	No	No
Post-signing/ pre-approval due diligence	No	No
Post-approval/pre-closing due diligence	No	No
Use of "clean teams"	No	No
Restrictions on the target in an M&A agreement, e.g. buyer approval required for: Investments above a certain level; New business above a certain level; Other obligations to consult/obtain approval from the buyer before closing.	No	No

Specific Conduct	Actual Enforcement under Merger Control Laws	Actual Enforcement under Substantive Antitrust Laws
Joint marketing	*CA 08700.010394/2014-32 (acquisition of certain assets belonging to Brasfrigo Ltda and Brasfrigo S/A by Goiás Verde Ltda)* – The parties understood that filing was not mandatory because only the seller's group would exceed the higher turnover threshold. CADE opened an investigation, ultimately concluding that filing was mandatory and that sales had been made by the target which included specific references to the buyer. CADE and the parties entered into an agreement for a pecuniary contribution of BRL 3 million.	No
Joint presentations (e.g. industry fairs)	No	No
Joint communications	*CA 08700.011836/2015-49 (purchase of a subsidiary of Cisco Systems, Inc by Technicolor SA)* – During the analysis of the transaction (and before the Brazilian antitrust clearance) CADE became aware of a potential violation, due to the public announcement of the global closing on Technicolor's website. Three days later, the applicants informed CADE of the global closing and after a month presented a carve-out agreement as a justification, alleging that it would preserve competitive conditions in the Brazilian market until CADE's approval. Nonetheless, CADE determined that there had been a violation since the transaction was implemented before clearance,	No

Specific Conduct	Actual Enforcement under Merger Control Laws	Actual Enforcement under Substantive Antitrust Laws
Joint communications	and that neither the urgency nor the absence of anticompetitive impact could justify the prior consummation of the merger. Specifically, regarding the carve-out agreement, CADE stressed that it should not be accepted as a measure to exclude or mitigate gun-jumping penalties, following international best practices. CADE and the parties entered into an agreement setting forth a pecuniary contribution of BRL 30 million. *CA 8700.002285/2014-41 (consolidation of Chrysler's control by Fiat.)*: CADE concluded that the transaction was notified after closing. Among other factors, CADE mentioned that the public announcement of the transaction's closing before approval constituted a violation of the standstill obligation. CADE and the parties entered into an agreement for a pecuniary contribution of BRL 600,000.	No
Strategy/planning regarding customers	No	No
Strategy/planning regarding suppliers	No	No
Third party contract novation	No	No
Personnel Issues: – Secondments – Retention Strategies	No	No
IT Planning/Database Migration	No	No

Specific Conduct	Actual Enforcement under Merger Control Laws	Actual Enforcement under Substantive Antitrust Laws
Other: *Failure to notify a reportable transaction*	*CA 08700.002655/2016-11 (formation of Blue Cycle to act as the exclusive distributor of Shimano's products in Brazil)* – CADE became aware of the transaction after closing. Penalty of BRL 1.5 million and the provisional nullity of the contract were imposed by CADE. *CA 08700.007160/2013-27 (rental contract between Tramonto and JBS)* – CADE determined that the applicants knew that the transaction was reportable and intentionally did not notify. Penalty of BRL 388,718.45 was imposed by CADE. *CA 08700.007612/2016-13 (acquisition of Fratelli Dorazio Investments Ltd, Mataboi Foods Ltd, subsidiary by JBJ Agropecuária Ltda)* – The parties e admitted that closing took place before approval. CADE and the parties entered into an agreement for a pecuniary contribution of BRL 664,983. *08700.010071/2015-20 (acquisition of assets by the Enzo Group from the Group Smaff, including inventory and trademark representation)* – The Enzo Group maintained that there was no notification because the transaction involved the acquisition of assets. CADE became aware of the transaction after a complaint made by a third party and entered into an agreement with the parties for a	No

Specific Conduct	Actual Enforcement under Merger Control Laws	Actual Enforcement under Substantive Antitrust Laws
Other: Failure to notify a reportable transaction	pecuniary contribution of BRL 700,000. The case was decided on in October 2018 and brings certain objective parameters for calculating penalties for gun-jumping violations including (i) the value of the transaction; (ii) days of delay; (iii) financial situation of the parties; and (iv) recurrence. *08700.004924/2015-94 (acquisition of assets in at least 6 different transactions from 2012 to 2015 by the SAGA Group, mostly related to car dealers)* – The case was commenced after a complaint was sent to the authorities. CADE and the parties entered into an agreement for a pecuniary contribution of BRL 2 million.	No
Other: The absence of a clause in the agreement indicating that CADE clearance is a condition precedent for closing the deal	*CA 08700.005775/2013-19 (acquisition by OGX of a 40% share from Petrobras of a concession contract)* – Among other factors, CADE determined that the absence of a clause in the agreement indicating that the authority's clearance is a condition precedent for closing violated the standstill obligation. CADE and the parties entered into an agreement for a pecuniary contribution of BRL 3 million. *CA 08700.008292/2013-76 (acquisition by UTC Óleo e Gás of a 50% share from Potióleo)* – Among other factors, CADE determined that the absence	*No*

Specific Conduct	Actual Enforcement under Merger Control Laws	Actual Enforcement under Substantive Antitrust Laws
Other: *The absence of a clause in the agreement indicating that CADE clearance is a condition precedent for closing the deal*	of a clause in the agreement indicating that the authority's clearance is a condition precedent for closing violated the standstill obligation. CADE and the parties entered into an agreement for a pecuniary contribution of BRL 60,000. *CA 08700.000137/2015-73 (contract between Gasmig and GásLocal for gas supply)* – Among other factors, CADE determined that the absence of a clause in the agreement indicating that the authority's clearance is a condition precedent for closing violated the standstill obligation. CADE and the parties entered into an agreement for a pecuniary contribution of BRL 90,000.	*No*
Other Payment of the price	*CA 08700.008292/2013-76 (acquisition by UTC Óleo e Gás of a 50% share from Potióleo)* – Among other factors, CADE determined that the payment of the first installment of the total price prior to clearance violated the standstill obligation. CADE and the parties entered into an agreement for a pecuniary contribution of BRL 60,000. *CA 08700.008289/2013-52 (acquisition by UTC Óleo e Gás of a 37% equity owned by Aurizônia Petróleo in a contract related to the exploitation of hydrocarbon)* – Among other factors, CADE determined that the immediate obligation to pay the value of the transaction prior	No

Specific Conduct	Actual Enforcement under Merger Control Laws	Actual Enforcement under Substantive Antitrust Laws
Other Payment of the price	to clearance violated the standstill obligation. CADE and the parties entered into an agreement for a pecuniary contribution of BRL 60,000. *CA 8700.002285/2014-41 (consolidation of Chrysler's control by Fiat)* – CADE concluded that the transaction was notified after closing. Among other factors, CADE mentioned that payment of the price prior to clearance constituted a breach of the standstill obligation. CADE and the parties entered into an agreement for a pecuniary contribution of BRL 600,000. *CA 08700.000137/2015-73 (contract between Gasmig and GásLocal concerning gas supply)* – Among other factors, CADE determined that payments made in the context of the contract, and prior to clearance, to (i) redeem investments and (ii) acquire a supply tank violated the standstill obligation. CADE and the parties entered into an agreement for a pecuniary contribution of BRL 90,000.	No
Other Decision-making power with regard to commercially and competitively sensitive matters of the target	*CA 08700.005775/2013-19 (acquisition by OGX of 40% share from Petrobras of a concession contract)* – Among other factors, CADE determined that the contractual provisions ensured OGX's effective participation as a partner in the asset before final approval. CADE and the parties entered	*No*

Specific Conduct	Actual Enforcement under Merger Control Laws	Actual Enforcement under Substantive Antitrust Laws
	into an agreement for a pecuniary contribution of BRL 3 million	
Other Decision-making power with regard to commercially and competitively sensitive matters of the target	*CA 08700.008292/2013-76 (acquisition by UTC Óleo e Gás of a 50% share from Potióleo)* – Among other factors, CADE determined that the contract contained clauses providing UTC rights and obligations, such as participating in the costs and results of the target company and receiving the payment of a reward immediately after signing (i.e. premature implementation). CADE and the parties entered into an agreement for a pecuniary contribution of BRL 60,000. *CA 08700.008289/2013-52 (acquisition by UTC Óleo e Gás of a 37% equity owned by Aurizônia Petróleo in a contract related to the exploitation of hydrocarbon)* – Among other factors, CADE determined that the contract contained clauses providing UTC rights and obligations, such as participating in the costs and results of the target company and receiving the payment of a reward immediately after signing (i.e. premature implementation). CADE and the parties entered into an agreement for a pecuniary contribution of BRL 60,000.	*No*

Specific Conduct	Actual Enforcement under Merger Control Laws	Actual Enforcement under Substantive Antitrust Laws
Other Steps towards closing prior to CADE's approval	*CA 08700.010394/2014-32 (acquisitions of certain assets belonging to Brasfrigo Ltda and Brasfrigo S/A by Goiás Verde Ltda)* – The parties understood that filing was not mandatory because only the seller's group would exceed the higher turnover threshold. CADE opened an investigation, ultimately concluding that filing was mandatory and determined that there had been an immediate transfer of property of the assets, including product barcodes. CADE and the parties entered into an agreement for a pecuniary contribution of BRL 3 million. *CA 08700.000137/2015-73 (contract between Gasmig and GásLocal concerning gas supply)* – CADE concluded that there was strong evidence to suggest that the applicants had taken steps towards closing the transaction after signing the contract and before the authority's approval (e.g. payments made in connection with contemplated investments, supply of gas to third parties). In addition, the agreement entered by the parties had no specific provisions about the submission of the transaction to CADE. CADE and the parties entered into an agreement for a pecuniary contribution of BRL 90,000.	No

Table 2: Hypothetical Enforcement of Specific Conduct under the Relevant Merger Control Rules and Substantive Antitrust Laws

For any conduct that is *not* the subject of actual enforcement (Table 1), please indicate in the Table below whether the conduct identified *could potentially* be enforced under the merger control laws and/or substantive antitrust laws.

Specific Conduct	Hypothetical Enforcement under Merger Control Laws	Hypothetical Enforcement under Substantive Antitrust Laws
Pre-signing due diligence	N/A (if restricted to information which is strictly necessary for the signature of the formal instrument binding the parties)	N/A (if restricted to information which is strictly necessary for the signature of the formal instrument binding the parties)
Post-signing/pre-approval due diligence	Information exchange has to be limited to what is strictly necessary to complete the transaction (see Question 2 of Part 2)	Information exchange has to be limited to what is strictly necessary to complete the transaction (see Question 2 of Part 2)
Post-approval/pre-closing due diligence	There is no specific guidance in this respect, but one could assume that the exchange of information is allowed in connection with the closing activities	There is no specific guidance in this respect, but one could assume that the exchange of information is allowed in connection with the closing activities
Use of "clean teams"	Clean teams are allowed and encouraged by the *Gun-Jumping Guidelines*	Clean teams are allowed and encouraged by the *Gun-Jumping Guidelines*
Restrictions on the target in an M&A agreement, e.g. buyer approval required for: Investments above a certain level; New business above a certain level; Other obligations to consult/obtain approval from the buyer before closing.	Restrictions are allowed if they are generally related to the maintenance of ordinary course of business activities.	Restrictions are allowed if they are generally related to the maintenance of ordinary course of business activities.

Specific Conduct	Hypothetical Enforcement under Merger Control Laws	Hypothetical Enforcement under Substantive Antitrust Laws
Joint marketing	Subject of actual enforcement (Table 1)	May be subject to investigation.
Joint presentations (e.g. industry fairs)	Subject of actual enforcement (Table 1)	May be subject to investigation.
Joint communications	May be subject to investigation depending on the content of the communication	May be subject to investigation depending on the content of the communication
Strategy/planning regarding customers	Subject of actual enforcement (Table 1)	May be subject to investigation.
Strategy/planning regarding suppliers	Subject of actual enforcement (Table 1)	May be subject to investigation.
Third party contract novation	Subject of actual enforcement (Table 1)	May be subject to investigation.
Personnel Issues: Secondments Retention Strategies	Subject of actual enforcement (Table 1)	May be subject to investigation.
IT Planning/Database Migration	Subject of actual enforcement (Table 1)	May be subject to investigation.
Other	N/A	N/A

As mentioned above, apart from cartels, the Brazilian regime has adopted a mechanism based on subjective criteria, in which the determination of whether a given practice constitutes a violation must be made on a case-by-case basis. Law 12.529/11 envisions no specific substantive test for verification of an antitrust violation, but rather sets forth broad and generic principles to aid the analysis of each case (application of the rule of reason). This rationale is also applied to standstill obligation investigations in Brazil.

CANADA

Neil Campbell
(McMillan LLP)

Part 1: Merger Control and the "Standstill Obligation"

1. **Please identify the relevant merger control legislation in your jurisdiction. Please provide a link to the relevant legislation (if possible, in English) and also indicate:**
   - **whether the merger control system is mandatory or voluntary,**
   - **the relevant authority, and**
   - **the duration of the review period.**

Legislation: Competition Act (RSC 1985, c. C-34) Part VIII (mergers) and Part IX (pre-notifiable transactions)[1]

– whether the merger control system is mandatory or voluntary:

There is mandatory pre-merger notification for certain types of merger and acquisition transactions that exceed specified financial thresholds (Part IX). There is also a possibility for mergers that fall below the thresholds to be reviewed before or up to one year after closing (Part VIII).

– the relevant authority:

The Commissioner of Competition (**Commissioner**), supported by the Competition Bureau (**CCB**), is responsible for enforcement of the Act including the review of mergers.[2]

If a transaction is challenged, the proceedings are adjudicated by the Competition Tribunal.[3]

– Duration of the review period:

Pre-notifiable transactions are subject to an initial suspensory ("no-close") period of 30 days. If a Supplementary Information Request is issued, the no-close period is extended until 30 days after the Request is responded to. The review process may also extend beyond the no-close period.

2. **Does the merger control system in your jurisdiction impose a "*standstill obligation*" – meaning, that the transaction cannot be implemented prior to completing the merger control process? (Please cite the relevant legislation.) Please also indicate the *legal scope* of the standstill obligation according to the relevant legislation (e.g. the parties to the transaction cannot effect a change of control, cannot take steps towards implementation, etc.).**

---

1 <http://laws.justice.gc.ca/eng/acts/C-34/index.html>.

2 <http://www.competitionbureau.gc.ca/eic/site/cb-bc.nsf/eng/home>.

3 <http://www.ct-tc.gc.ca/Home.asp>.

The suspensory period referenced above is found in section 123 of the Competition Act. The scope of the no-close obligation is that the proposed transaction "shall not be completed". This provides the merging parties with substantial flexibility to engage in due diligence, transition planning and other steps moving towards completion (subject to compliance with the substantive laws relating to collaboration between competitors – see Part 2 below).

3. **Have the relevant authorities in your jurisdiction issued internal or external guidelines concerning the scope of the standstill obligation, and/or their authority to enforce it? Please provide a copy/link of such guidance, if possible in English.**

The CCB has not issued guidelines regarding the standstill/no-close obligation.

4. **Are there any exceptions to the standstill obligation – for example, through derogation or "carve out"? Please describe the circumstances in which this is possible. Please also describe the relevant process, e.g. do parties need to apply to the authority for a derogation from the standstill obligation? If so, how long is the approval process? If there are specific cases addressing these issues, please identify them.**

The Commissioner has the power to terminate the suspensory period earlier than its scheduled expiry date. This power is usually invoked at the request of the merging parties when the CCB has concluded that a transaction is not anticompetitive.

Otherwise, there are no exceptions or derogations to the standstill/no-close obligation regarding transactions that meet the mandatory notification thresholds, including by way of carve-out.

5. **Does a public bid exception exist in your jurisdiction? (For example, under the EU Merger Regulation it is possible to acquire shares as part of a public bid, provided that the shares are not exercised until the acquisition is cleared by the Commission.) If such an exception exists in your jurisdiction, please describe how it is applied.**

No.

6. **What powers does the relevant authority have to investigate and enforce violations of the standstill obligation? Are dawn raids possible? What timing applies to investigation/enforcement proceedings?**

Non-compliance with the pre-notification requirements in Part IX of the Act is an offense under section 65(2) of the Act. In addition, the Commissioner may seek administrative monetary penalties and other remedies under section 123.1 when there has been a failure to comply with the no-close obligation.

The CCB has the same powers of investigation in respect of breaches the suspensory obligations as it does for other matters. These powers include the ability to obtain and execute search warrants as well as powers to subpoena the production of documents and responses to written interrogatories and to examine individuals under oath (see Part II of the Act).

There are no fixed timing rules for such investigations or any resulting enforcement proceedings.

7. **What are the possible penalties for violating the standstill obligation? Are there criminal sanctions, including on individuals? Have these been applied in practice? Is there a difference in enforcement between transactions involving domestic companies and "foreign-to-foreign" transactions? Does the authority have the power to unwind transactions implemented in breach of the standstill obligation? If so, has the authority made use of that power in practice? If yes, please provide examples.**

Possible Penalties: The penalty for the section 65(2) offense of failing to provide a complete pre-notification filing is a fine of up to C$50,000. Directors and officers who participated in the contravention are subject to the same potential penalty. In addition, the administrative monetary penalties that may be imposed for non-compliance with the no-close obligation may be up to C$10,000 per day (section 123.1(d)).

Domestic v Foreign-to-Foreign Transactions: Both types of transaction are subject to the same framework, as summarized above.

Power to Unwind: The Commissioner may apply to the Tribunal or a court for a divestiture or dissolution order (section 123.1(c)).

Other Remedies: The Commissioner may seek court orders to require the production of information that is required to be supplied under Part IX, an interim order prohibiting any steps directed towards completion of a transaction until Part IX has been complied with, and/or any other relief the court considers appropriate (section 123.1(a) and (b)).

8. **How does the relevant authority typically learn of potential violations of the standstill obligation? Does the authority actively monitor the trade press?**

The CCB may learn about violations of the filing and no-close requirements in the course of the review of a transaction or through complaints from other market participants. The CCB's Merger Intelligence and Notification Unit also actively monitors business and trade media, and periodically contacts parties to check whether an announced transaction exceeds the notification thresholds.

9. **Please describe the relevant authority's enforcement of the standstill obligation. If there have been cases, please describe the specific conduct that was found to violate the standstill provision and the criteria applied by the relevant authority or court. Has the relevant authority considered the market impact of the conduct? (Please refer to the Annex.)**

There are no reported cases on conduct found to be in breach of either section 65(2) of the Act (failure to file) or of section 123.1 (failure to comply with the no-close obligation).

10. **In cases involving alleged violations of the standstill obligation under the relevant merger control laws, has the relevant authority (or court) *also* considered the substantive antitrust laws? (Please refer to the Annex.)**

See discussion under Question 4 of Part 2.

11. **Is private enforcement of the standstill obligation possible?**

No. The Act does not provide any private rights of action to enforce the pre-notification filing or no-close obligations.

12. Please describe the private law risks/consequences (i.e. contractual/validity consequences) for transactions that are subject to notification, but which are completed without notification/approval. Please identify any relevant cases and describe them.

Aside from the representations/warranties, covenants or other provisions negotiated as part of the transaction agreements, there are no private law risks or consequences of completing a transaction without notification.

13. Please describe policy and enforcement trends in your jurisdiction.

The CCB has a well-established track record for active enforcement of the merger, criminal and other provisions of the Act. The CCB has recently expanded its focus on identifying mergers that may have required pre-notification filings or that warrant review even though the filing thresholds are not met. No other specific trends have been identified in respect of gun-jumping issues.

Part 2: Substantive Antitrust Law in an M&A Context

1. **Please identify the relevant *substantive antitrust laws* in your jurisdiction that can potentially apply in an M&A context (e.g. for the EU, this would include Article 101 of the Treaty on the Functioning of the European Union). Please provide a link to the relevant legislation (if possible, in English).**

   Conspiracy in Restraint of Trade: Section 45 of the Act establishes the criminal offense of conspiracy in restraint of trade. Agreements between competitors to fix, raise or increase prices, allocate customers or markets, or restrict output, are per se illegal. In an M&A context, an agreement to go out of business or shut down a business could constitute an output restriction agreement. Similarly, back-to-back buy – sell agreements involving two markets in which the parties are competitors could constitute agreement to allocate markets.

   Foreign-Directed Conspiracy: Section 46 of the Act establishes a related offense in respect of foreign-directed conspiracies. It is a criminal offense for a Canadian corporation to implement price increases or other illegal conspiracies in restraint of trade (i.e. conduct that would contravene Section 45 of the Act) entered into by companies or individuals outside Canada. This provision is designed to allow enforcement action to be taken against Canadian subsidiaries whose foreign parent corporations may be difficult to prosecute in Canada.

   Bid-rigging: Section 47 of the Act establishes a criminal offense in respect of bid-rigging. Agreements to coordinate bids, to not bid or to withdraw a bid previously submitted, in response to a call or request for bids or tenders, are per se illegal criminal offenses.

   Other Types of Competitor Collaboration: Other coordination between competitors is subject to a non-criminal "reviewable practice" in section 90.1 of the Act. The competitive effects test ("substantial lessening or prevention of competition") and the factors to be considered in making such a determination are the same as for merger transactions.

   Exemption for Affiliates: The foregoing conduct is not an offense if all the parties to a transaction are affiliates. However, the parties to a merger transaction do not become affiliates until the transaction is consummated.

   Legislation: See link in footnote for the relevant legislative provisions.[4]

2. **Do any guidelines exist in your jurisdiction concerning the application of the substantive antitrust laws in an M&A context – whether internal to the**

---

4 <http://laws.justice.gc.ca/eng/acts/C-34/index.html>.

relevant authority, or external, formal or informal (e.g. speeches)? If so, please provide a copy/link to such guidance.

The CCB has not provided comprehensive guidance regarding the potential application of the various substantive provisions dealing with competitor agreements to M&A situations. However, it has stated that "an agreement to abstain from making material changes to a business pending consummation of a merger" would be regarded as an ancillary restraint which normally would be assessed under the competitor agreements practice (section 90.1), not the conspiracy offense (section 45). See Competition Bureau Canada, *Competitor Collaboration Guidelines* (2009) p12.[5]

3. **As a general matter (not limited to M&A), how are the substantive antitrust laws enforced with respect to the exchange of competitively sensitive information between competing firms? Please also indicate the relevance of anti-competitive effects or intent in such enforcement.**

In general, exchanges of competitively sensitive information may be enforced criminally if they facilitate a price-fixing, market allocation or output restriction agreement between competitors, or bid-rigging, contrary to sections 45–47 of the Act (see discussion under Question 1).

Otherwise, exchanges of competitively sensitive information would be assessed pursuant to the competitor agreements reviewable practice, which has a "substantial lessening or prevention of competition" test (see discussion under Question 1).

4. **Have there been any cases in your jurisdiction in which the substantive antitrust laws were enforced in an M&A context? Please describe/explain and cite any such cases. (See also Annex.)**

In *R v Béton Régional Inc*, the acquirer ordered a subsidiary of the target company to raise its prices for cement after the parties had reached an agreement in principle related to the sale of the business, but before the merger was completed. After a CCB investigation, the parties agreed to a prohibition order on a consent basis (no fine imposed) and the merger did not proceed.

We are aware of one other investigation of pre-merger coordination related to potential price increases that the CCB investigated as a possible violation of the conspiracy offense. However, the file was closed and there is no public explanation of the CCB's reasoning or conclusions.

5. **Are the substantive antitrust laws more likely to apply at specific stages of the transaction – i.e. at an early stage, or prior to closing (or does it not make a difference)? Do companies face ongoing risk following the consummation (or failure) of their transaction for conduct that allegedly occurred pre-closing (pre-failure)?**

The substantive laws relating to competitor collaboration are potentially applicable at any stage prior to closing of a transaction. However, in practice, it may be less likely for the CCB to pursue enforcement action under the conspiracy offense for conduct occurring during the period after a transaction has been cleared by the Commissioner and prior to closing. Similarly, the competitive effects test for competitor collaborations is the same as for mergers, so it is unlikely that the

---

5 Available at <http://www.competitionbureau.gc.ca/eic/site/cb-bc.nsf/eng/03177.html>.

competitor agreements reviewable practice would be invoked in respect of conduct after a merger had cleared and prior to closing.

As indicated in Question 4, there has been at least one case where, post-closing, the CCB conducted an in-depth criminal investigation relating to alleged coordinated pre-closing price increases by the two parties to the merger.

6. Please explain how the relevant authority enforces (or could enforce) the substantive antitrust laws in an M&A context. How would the investigation occur, and what timing constraints would apply?

If the CCB becomes aware that conduct constituting a criminal conspiracy may have occurred (e.g. pre-closing price coordination by the merging parties), it may conduct an in-depth investigation including through the use of formal search or subpoena powers (see Question 7 in Part 1). Such an investigation may be undertaken at any time pre-closing or post-closing. There is no limitation period in respect of enforcement of criminal offenses in the Act.

If the CCB concludes that there is evidence that a criminal offense has been committed, it refers the evidence to the Public Prosecution Service of Canada (**PPSC**). The PPSC may lay charges against the merging companies, as well as company personnel or others who participated in, aided or counseled the illegal conduct.

As a practical matter, section 90.1 may be of limited utility to the CCB in respect of gun-jumping activity. The competitive effects test, the limited scope of the remedy available (a prohibition order), and the requirement to seek such a remedy through litigation before the Tribunal, make it unlikely that the CCB would have enough time and would choose to deploy resources to seek a remedial order in respect of conduct that may have been anticompetitive but did not appear to constitute a criminal conspiracy.

7. Is private enforcement of the substantive antitrust laws possible in an M&A context, and has it occurred?

Private parties (e.g. affected customers) have a private right of action under section 36 of the Act to recover damages (plus their costs of investigation) from parties whose conduct has contravened sections 45–47. The cause of action can be pursued regardless of whether the CCB has initiated proceedings in respect of any alleged criminal offense. The claims can also be pursued using class action procedures if there are multiple affected parties.

There are no reported cases where the potentially unlawful pre-closing conduct of merging parties has been the object of a private right of action under section 36 of the Act.

8. Could behavior subject to the substantive antitrust laws also be caught under the merger control rules/standstill obligation? (Please also refer to the Annex.)

Since the standstill obligation focuses on completion of the transaction (see Question 2 in Part 1), this normally does not overlap with the substantive antitrust provisions.

9. Please describe the penalties for infringing the substantive antitrust laws. Please indicate whether these include criminal penalties, including individual criminal penalties. As a practical matter, how have these been applied in the context of an M&A transaction?

The conspiracy offense is subject to criminal penalties of up to C$25 million per count (infraction). The foreign-directed conspiracy and bid-rigging provisions are subject to a fine at the discretion of the court (no stated maximum).

Individuals who participated in the commission of an offense, or who assisted or counselled the commission of an offense (which are general Criminal Code provisions applicable to all criminal offenses) are also subject to similar fines and/ or to imprisonment for up to 14 years.

Other than the two cases mentioned in Question 4, we are not aware of any cases where the substantive antitrust laws have been applied in the context of an M&A transaction.

10. Please describe policy and enforcement trends in your jurisdiction.

The CCB has a well-established track record for active enforcement of the merger, criminal and other provisions of the Act. However, no specific trends have been identified in respect of gun-jumping issues.

Annex

Table 1: Actual Enforcement of Specific Conduct under the Relevant Merger Control Rules and Substantive Antitrust Laws

Please identify whether the following type of conduct has been subject to investigation/enforcement in your jurisdiction, under the merger control laws or substantive antitrust laws. Please cite any such case(s) and provide a brief description in the table below.

Specific Conduct	Actual Enforcement under Merger Control Laws	Actual Enforcement under Substantive Antitrust Laws
Pre-signing due diligence	No	No
Post-signing/pre-approval due diligence	No	No
Post-approval/pre-closing due diligence	No	No
Use of "clean teams"	No	No
Restrictions on the target in an M&A agreement, e.g. buyer approval required for: – Investments above a certain level; – New business above a certain level; – Other obligations to consult/obtain approval from the buyer before closing.	No	No
Joint marketing	No	No
Joint presentations (e.g. industry fairs)	No	No
Joint communications	No	No
Strategy/planning regarding customers	No	No

Specific Conduct	Actual Enforcement under Merger Control Laws	Actual Enforcement under Substantive Antitrust Laws
Strategy/planning regarding suppliers	No	No
Third party contract novation	No	No
Personnel Issues: – Secondments – Retention Strategies	No	No
IT Planning/Database Migration	No	No
Other	No	*R v Béton Régional Inc* (pre-closing pricing coordination – see Question 4 of Part 2).

Table 2: Hypothetical Enforcement of Specific Conduct under the Relevant Merger Control Rules and Substantive Antitrust Laws

For any conduct that is *not* the subject of actual enforcement (Table 1), please indicate in the Table below whether the conduct identified *could potentially* be enforced under the merger control laws and/or substantive antitrust laws.

Specific Conduct	Hypothetical Enforcement under Merger Control Laws	Hypothetical Enforcement under Substantive Antitrust Laws
Pre-signing due diligence		Depending on circumstances, all types of conduct could raise issues under the substantive laws relating to collaboration with competitors
Post-signing/pre-approval due diligence		
Post-approval/pre-closing due diligence		
Use of "clean teams"		

Specific Conduct	Hypothetical Enforcement under Merger Control Laws	Hypothetical Enforcement under Substantive Antitrust Laws
Restrictions on the target in an M&A agreement, e.g. buyer approval required for: – Investments above a certain level; – New business above a certain level; – Other obligations to consult/obtain approval from the buyer before closing.	Depending on circumstances, could raise issues under the standstill/ no-close obligation.	
Joint marketing		
Joint presentations (e.g. industry fairs)		
Joint communications		
Strategy/planning regarding customers		
Strategy/planning regarding suppliers		
Third party contract novation		
Personnel Issues: Secondments Retention Strategies		
IT Planning/Database Migration		
Other		

CHINA

Alastair Mordaunt
(Freshfields Bruckhaus Deringer LLP)
Michael Han
(Fangda Partners)

Part 1: Merger Control and the "Standstill Obligation"

1. **Please identify the relevant merger control legislation in your jurisdiction. Please provide a link to the relevant legislation (if possible, in English) and also indicate:**
   - **whether the merger control system is mandatory or voluntary,**
   - **the relevant authority, and**
   - **the duration of the review period.**

The Anti-Monopoly Law of People's Republic of China (**AML**)[6] (which entered into force on 1 August 2008) contains a chapter entitled "Concentration of undertakings". This chapter deals with the merger control regime in China.

The AML is supplemented by a large number of implementing regulations, guidelines and measures dealing with various areas including notification thresholds and procedural, documentary and substantive matters.

The merger control system established by the AML is mandatory. If the notification thresholds are met, the parties to the transaction are obliged to file with the authority and cannot close before clearance is obtained (see Question 2 below). For non-reportable transactions, the parties can file their cases with the authority on a voluntary basis while the authority has the discretion to decide whether to review the transactions or not. The Anti-Monopoly Bureau of State Administration for Market Regulation (**SAMR**) has jurisdiction for merger control enforcement.[7]

The maximum statutory review period is 180 calendar days, which is divided into three phases: Phase I (30 days), Phase II (90 calendar days), and Extended Phase II (60 calendar days).

2. **Does the merger control system in your jurisdiction impose a "*standstill obligation*" – meaning, that the transaction cannot be implemented prior to completing the merger control process? (Please cite the relevant legislation.) Please also indicate the *legal scope* of the standstill obligation according to the**

---

6 An English translation of the AML can be found here: <http://english.mofcom.gov.cn/article/policyrelease/Businessregulations/201303/20130300045909.shtml>.

7 From the introduction of the merger control regime in China in 2008 until early 2018, the Ministry of Commerce of the People's Republic of China (MOFCOM) was the authority in charge of merger control enforcement in China. As part of an institutional reform plan published by the State Council of the People's Republic of China in March 2018, MOFCOM's merger control function was merged with the other two agencies previously overseeing antitrust enforcement in China, i.e. the Price Supervision and Anti-Monopoly Bureau at the National Development and Reform Commission and the Anti-Monopoly and Anti-Unfair Competition Bureau of the State Administration for Industry and Commerce, into a consolidated Anti-Monopoly Bureau under the newly established SAMR.

relevant legislation (e.g. the parties to the transaction cannot effect a change of control, cannot take steps towards implementation, etc.).

Yes. The standstill obligation is clearly established by the AML.

Art. 21 of the AML: "Where a concentration of undertakings meets the relevant thresholds for notification as stipulated by the State Council, the undertakings shall file a notification with the Anti-Monopoly Enforcement Authority under the State Council; without notification with the Anti-Monopoly Enforcement Authority under the State Council, the undertakings shall be prohibited from implementing the concentration."

Art. 25 of the AML: "Within 30 days from the date of receipt of the documents and materials that are consistent with provisions of Article 23 of this Law as submitted by the undertakings, the Anti-Monopoly Enforcement Authority under the State Council shall initiate the preliminary review, make a decision whether or not to initiate further review, and notify the undertakings in writing. **Before obtaining the decision of the Anti-Monopoly Enforcement Authority under the State Council, undertakings shall not implement the concentration.**

"Where the Anti-Monopoly Enforcement Authority under the State Council decides not to initiate further review or makes no decision within the time limit, the undertakings may implement the concentration."

Art. 26 of the AML: "Where the Anti-Monopoly Enforcement Authority under the State Council decides to initiate further review, it shall complete the review within 90 days from the date of the decision, make a decision whether or not to prohibit the concentration of undertakings and notify the undertakings in writing; in case of a decision to prohibit the concentration of undertakings, the Anti-Monopoly Enforcement Authority under the State Council shall state its reasons thereof. **During the period of the further review, undertakings shall not implement the concentration**..."

The Chinese merger control legislation does not specify the legal scope of the standstill obligation but merely generally prohibits the parties to the transaction from implementation prior to clearance of the merger filing by the authority.

3. **Have the relevant authorities in your jurisdiction issued internal or external guidelines concerning the scope of the standstill obligation, and/or their authority to enforce it? Please provide a copy/link of such guidance, if possible in English.**

No. No guidelines concerning the scope of the standstill obligation have been issued. For completeness, the Chinese merger control authority issued the Interim Measures on the Investigation and Handling of Failure to File Concentrations of Undertakings Pursuant to Applicable Laws (**Interim Measures**)[8] in 2011, which came into force in 2012. The Interim Measures mainly provide the procedural rules governing the authority's investigation and handling of failure-to-file cases.

4. **Are there any exceptions to the standstill obligation – for example, through derogation or "carve out"? Please describe the circumstances in which this**

---

8 Available in Chinese at: <http://fldj.mofcom.gov.cn/article/c/201201/20120107921682.shtml>.

is possible. Please also describe the relevant process, e.g. do parties need to apply to the authority for a derogation from the standstill obligation? If so, how long is the approval process? If there are specific cases addressing these issues, please identify them.

No. There are no exceptions to the standstill obligation under Chinese merger control rules. Derogation or "carve out" is not a feasible option for parties to get around the standstill obligation.

5. **Does a public bid exception exist in your jurisdiction? (For example, under the EU Merger Regulation it is possible to acquire shares as part of a public bid, provided that the shares are not exercised until the acquisition is cleared by the Commission.) If such an exception exists in your jurisdiction, please describe how it is applied.**

There is no exception for public bids under Chinese merger control rules and so it is not possible to acquire shares as part of a public bid before receiving clearance from the SAMR. The party is obliged to notify the reportable transaction with the SAMR after the announcement of a public bid is published. No further details or guidance is provided on this. However, in practice, the SAMR may expedite the review process when a transaction is subject to public takeover rules.

6. **What powers does the relevant authority have to investigate and enforce violations of the standstill obligation? Are dawn raids possible? What timing applies to investigation/enforcement proceedings?**

Pursuant to the AML, the SAMR is empowered to:

- Inspect the business premises or other places of the investigated undertaking;
- Interview relevant parties;
- Examine and copy relevant documents and materials;
- Seal or seize relevant evidence; and
- Examine bank accounts.

The timing for investigation and enforcement proceedings relating to possible violations of the standstill obligations are as follows:

- Preliminary investigation: 60 calendar days. During the preliminary investigation period, the SAMR will decide whether or not the transaction under investigation is a concentration that the parties failed to notify pursuant to applicable laws.
- Further investigation: 180 calendar days. During the further investigation period, the SAMR will review the notification materials submitted by the parties to assess the competition effects of the transaction.

7. **What are the possible penalties for violating the standstill obligation? Are there criminal sanctions, including on individuals? Have these been applied in practice? Is there a difference in enforcement between transactions involving domestic companies and "foreign-to-foreign" transactions? Does the authority have the power to unwind transactions implemented in breach of the standstill obligation? If so, has the authority made use of that power in practice? If yes, please provide examples.**

Under Chinese merger control rules, there are no criminal sanctions either on undertakings or individuals. The possible penalties for undertakings violating the standstill obligation include:

- A fine of up to RMB 500,000; and
- An order to unwind the deal by requiring the parties to take any measure necessary to restore the pre-merger market structure including ceasing implementation of the concentration, disposal of shares or assets, and transfer of business.

According to the Interim Measures, the authority shall take certain factors into consideration when making the penalty decision, which include the nature, gravity and duration of the failure to file behavior as well as the assessment of anticompetitive effects of the transaction. However, it is unclear whether the authority can order a deal to be unwound for failure to notify in the absence of anticompetitive effects. Based on the literal interpretation of the rules, the finding that a failure to file transaction has anticompetitive effects is not a precondition for the penalty of unwinding the deal although it is likely to be a very important factor.

In practice, the authority (formerly MOFCOM and currently the SAMR) has fined many undertakings for violation of the standstill obligation while it has not ordered any transaction to be unwound. The highest fine imposed for this offense so far on a single undertaking has been a fine of RMB 400,000 imposed in two cases: on Bombardier Transportation Sweden[9] in 2016, due to the intentional nature of the failure to notify, and the fact that the undertaking had been penalized for a similar offense before; and on a domestic pharmaceutical company[10] in 2018 for failure to notify, although the authority did not specify the factors affecting the level of fine in its decision. To date, the authority has not found any failure to notify case where the transaction had anticompetitive effects.

Enforcement is carried out on a non-discriminatory basis and has caught transactions involving domestic companies and foreign-to-foreign transactions. To date, the vast majority of transactions caught by the authority involved at least one domestic company. However, the authority also has imposed fines in foreign-to-foreign transactions, for example, Canon Inc's acquisition of Toshiba Medical Systems Corporation[11] in 2016, OCI Corporation's acquisition of Tokuyama (Malaysia) Corporation[12] in 2017, and Paper Excellence BV's acquisition of Eldorado[13] in 2018.

---

9 "MOFCOM fines Bombardier Transportation Sweden and New United Group for failure to notify their establishment of a new joint venture" (MOFCOM decision, 21 April 2016) <http://fldj.mofcom.gov.cn/article/ztxx/201605/20160501311081.shtml>.

10 "SAMR fines Gaoji Pharmaceuticals for failure to notify its acquisition of Henan Baijia Haoyisheng Pharmaceuticals" (SAMR decision, 21 December 2018) <http://gkml.samr.gov.cn/nsjg/bgt/201902/t20190216_288684.html>.

11 "MOFCOM fines Canon for failure to notify its acquisition of Toshiba Medical Systems Corporation" (MOFCOM decision, 16 December 2016) <http://fldj.mofcom.gov.cn/article/ztxx/201701/20170102495433.shtml>.

12 "MOFCOM fines OCI Corporation for failure to notify its acquisition of Tokuyama (Malaysia) Corporation" (MOFCOM decision, 21 April 2017) <http://fldj.mofcom.gov.cn/article/ztxx/201705/20170502568693.shtml>.

13 "SAMR fines Paper Excellence BV for failure to notify its acquisition of Eldorado" (SAMR decision, 30 July 2018) <http://www.competitionlaw.cn/info/1025/26320.htm>.

8. How does the relevant authority typically learn of potential violations of the standstill obligation? Does the authority actively monitor the trade press?

In most cases, the authority learns of potential violations by third-party complaints or as a result of the undertakings concerned self-reporting to the authority.

It is unknown whether the authority actively monitors the trade press.

9. Please describe the relevant authority's enforcement of the standstill obligation. If there have been cases, please describe the specific conduct that was found to violate the standstill provision and the criteria applied by the relevant authority or court. Has the relevant authority considered the market impact of the conduct? (Please refer to the Annex.)

The authority has imposed monetary penalties in a large number of cases where the parties completed a transaction or partly completed a multi-step transaction prior to notification to the authority. The authority considered the impact of the transaction on competition in each case. All reported cases so far concern a failure to file, i.e. there are **no** cases where parties were found to have prematurely closed or implemented, prior to clearance, a transaction that they had notified to the authority.

In practice, the authority focuses more on the closing of a transaction, e.g. the transfer of shares/assets or the establishment of a joint venture. It has not enforced any specific conduct listed in the Annex (Table 1).

As regards consideration of the market impact of the transaction, please see Question 7 above.

10. In cases involving alleged violations of the standstill obligation under the relevant merger control laws, has the relevant authority (or court) *also* considered the substantive antitrust laws? (Please refer to the Annex.)

No. We are not aware of any reported gun-jumping cases where the authority has considered the potential violation of any substantive antitrust laws.

11. Is private enforcement of the standstill obligation possible?

No. Private parties can make complaints to the authority but they cannot bring a lawsuit to court for a violation of the standstill obligation.

12. Please describe the private law risks/consequences (i.e. contractual/validity consequences) for transactions that are subject to notification, but which are completed without notification/approval. Please identify any relevant cases and describe them.

No private law risks/consequences in China. There may be contractual consequences if parties complete a transaction prior to notification/approval.

13. Please describe policy and enforcement trends in your jurisdiction.

From a merger control perspective, gun-jumping is and will continue to be an enforcement priority of the SAMR. There has been a significant increase in the number of gun-jumping cases. Although the AML has been in effect since 2008, the first major gun-jumping case was MOFCOM's 2016 fine of Canon Inc for failure to notify its acquisition of Toshiba Medical Systems Corporation before implementing the first step in the transaction.[14] This case was also notable because the transaction in question did not involve a China-headquartered entity.

In addition, the authority is studying the possibility of imposing heavier penalties on undertakings that fail to notify their transactions, aiming to increase the financial impact of violation and strengthen deterrence.

From a policy perspective, towards the end of 2017, MOFCOM solicited comments on a draft of its new *Measures for Review of Concentrations of Undertakings*. In July 2018, the SAMR solicited comments on a draft of its new *Measures for Notification of Concentrations of Undertakings*. These new measures are intended to clarify the definition of "concentrations of undertakings", how to calculate turnover, particular procedural points in the notification and review process, as well as the authority's power to investigate transactions. Although a final version of these drafts has not yet been promulgated, these measures are likely to give welcome clarification to the merger filing and review process.

As noted above, another significant development has been the announced merger of the antitrust functions of three antitrust enforcement agencies – the National Development and Reform Commission (**NDRC**), the State Administration for Industry and Commerce (**SAIC**), and MOFCOM. Following the merger, the former Director General of the Anti-Monopoly Bureau at MOFCOM, Mr Zhenguo Wu, was appointed Director General of the Anti-Monopoly Bureau at SAMR. Given that the three former merger review divisions within the Anti-Monopoly Bureau at MOFCOM have been kept and many of the officials involved in mergers have remained in office, including the former leadership of the Anti-Monopoly Bureau at MOFCOM, the changes that will be brought to China's merger control enforcement, including in relation to gun-jumping violations, if any, are expected to be gradual and incremental.

---

14 See n 6.

Part 2: Substantive Antitrust Law in an M&A Context

1. **Please identify the relevant *substantive antitrust laws* in your jurisdiction that can potentially apply in an M&A context (e.g. for the EU, this would include Article 101 of the Treaty on the Functioning of the European Union). Please provide a link to the relevant legislation (if possible, in English).**

   The primary substantive legal provisions that may apply are contained in Arts. 13, 14, and 17 of the AML.[15]

   There are particular substantive risks where parties to an M&A transaction are competitors, as they will remain competitors until the merger transaction is cleared. There is a risk, therefore, that an exchange of commercially sensitive information before the transaction is cleared (particularly if the transaction is later aborted) could lead to coordination between these competitors. This would include information about future plans and intentions that are shared during the course of merger negotiations. The SAMR may therefore have concerns that the pre-clearance exchange of information could lead to concerted conduct designed to eliminate or restrict competition which would be treated as a monopoly agreement between these competing undertakings. This could therefore be considered a violation of Art. 13 of the AML, and could potentially result in fines of up to 10% of the sales revenue achieved by the company in the previous year (Art. 46 of the AML).

2. **Do any guidelines exist in your jurisdiction concerning the application of the substantive antitrust laws in an M&A context – whether internal to the relevant authority, or external, formal or informal (e.g. speeches)? If so, please provide a copy/link to such guidance.**

   Although guidance specific to the application of substantive antitrust laws in an M&A context is not available, there is more general guidance on the application of the AML to M&A in the context of merger review, including:

   - The 2008 *Provisions of the State Council on the Thresholds for Declaring Concentrations of Business Operators* (which contains the turnover thresholds for merger notifications)[16]
   - The 2009 *Measures on Review of Concentrations of Undertakings*[17]

---

15 An English translation of the AML can be found here: <http://english.mofcom.gov.cn/article/policyrelease/Businessregulations/201303/20130300045909.shtml>.

16 Available in Chinese at: <http://www.gov.cn/zwgk/2008-08/04/content_1063769.htm>.

17 An unofficial English translation of these measures can be found at: <http://sg2.mofcom.gov.cn/article/Nocategory/200912/20091206715333.shtml>; an English version of the new draft measures together with the IBA's comments can be found here: <https://www.ibanet.org/Document/Default.aspx?DocumentUid=761DBCB8-

- The 2014 *Guidance Opinion on Notification of Concentrations of Undertakings*[18]
- The 2014 *Rules regarding the notification and review of simple transactions.*[19]

3. As a general matter (not limited to M&A), how are the substantive antitrust laws enforced with respect to the exchange of competitively sensitive information between competing firms? Please also indicate the relevance of anticompetitive effects or intent in such enforcement.

Unlike in the EU, for example, there is no clear definition of what might be considered "competitively sensitive information" in the PRC. Information exchange is also not considered a standalone violation of the AML, but may otherwise facilitate parallel conduct between competing undertakings.

Some guidance has been provided by the NDRC in relation to industry associations and the possible risks of hub-and-spoke information exchanges. The 2017 *Industry Association Price Behavior Guidance*[20] contains some insight into the type of information the NDRC may consider problematic to exchange, including pricing information, and non-public information about competitors. However, it is important to note that enforcement authorities will still have to show that an information exchange is part of a larger concerted practice or anticompetitive agreement. Enforcement authorities must show that there is an intent to share competitively sensitive information as part of a concerted practice or anticompetitive agreement, which has anticompetitive effects.

4. Have there been any cases in your jurisdiction in which the substantive antitrust laws were enforced in an M&A context? Please describe/explain and cite any such cases. (See also Annex.)

We are not aware of any reported cases where this has occurred.

There have not been any public referrals between the previous three agencies (MOFCOM, the SAIC and the NDRC), although this may change with the merger of the three agencies into the new SAMR.

5. Are the substantive antitrust laws more likely to apply at specific stages of the transaction – i.e. at an early stage, or prior to closing (or does it not make a difference)? Do companies face ongoing risk following the consummation (or failure) of their transaction for conduct that allegedly occurred pre-closing (pre-failure)?

As there have been no cases so far, it is not possible to determine this at the moment.

6. Please explain how the relevant authority enforces (or could enforce) the substantive antitrust laws in an M&A context. How would the investigation occur, and what timing constraints would apply?

D30B-4C6E-B68C-A91F491BE0D0>.

18 Available in Chinese at: <http://fldj.mofcom.gov.cn/article/i/201406/20140600614679.shtml>.

19 Available in Chinese at: <http://fldj.mofcom.gov.cn/article/i/201404/20140400555353.shtml>.

20 Available in Chinese at: <http://www.ndrc.gov.cn/gzdt/201707/t20170725_855402.html>.

As there have been no cases so far, it is not possible to determine this at the moment.

7. **Is private enforcement of the substantive antitrust laws possible in an M&A context, and has it occurred?**

Art. 50 of the AML imposes civil liability on undertakings whose monopolistic conduct has caused losses to another person. The courts are also obliged to accept civil actions for alleged anti-monopoly violations regardless of whether there is a prior decision from an anti-monopoly enforcement authority (under Art. 2, Provisions of the Supreme People's Court on Several Issues Concerning the Application of Law in the Trial of Civil Dispute Cases Arising from Monopolistic Conduct (Supreme People's Court Provisions on Monopolistic Conduct)*)*. Parties can bring either standalone or follow-on actions via a civil case as long as they are able to satisfy the four conditions contained in Art. 119 of the *Civil Procedure Law*, namely that:

i. The claimant is an interested party to the action;

ii. There is a specified defendant;

iii. There are specific claims, facts, and reasons; and

iv. The court has jurisdiction to hear the case.

To date, however, there have been no published decisions of private enforcement actions specific to the application of substantive antitrust laws to an M&A transaction.

8. **Could behavior subject to the substantive antitrust laws also be caught under the merger control rules/standstill obligation? (Please also refer to the Annex.)**

As there have been no cases so far, it is not possible to determine this at the moment.

9. **Please describe the penalties for infringing the substantive antitrust laws. Please indicate whether these include criminal penalties, including individual criminal penalties. As a practical matter, how have these been applied in the context of an M&A transaction?**

Penalties for infringement of the substantive antitrust laws in China under Arts. 46 & 47 of the AML may be up to 10% of the undertaking's total sales in the previous year. There are no criminal penalties for substantive antitrust law breaches.

For the penalties for failure to notify under the AML, please refer to Question 8 in Part 1.

10. **Please describe policy and enforcement trends in your jurisdiction.**

Please refer to Question 14 in Part 1.

Allan Fels, Xiaoye Wang, Wendy Ng, Adrian Emch, "The Chinese MOFCOM releases three decisions sanctioning companies for failure to notify their transactions for antitrust review (Dade Holdings/Jilin Sichang Pharmaceutical; New United Group/Bombardier Transportation Sweden; Beijing CNR/Hitachi)" 4 May 2016, e-Competitions Bulletin May 2016, Art. N° 88614

Zhan Hao, Xiang Li, "The Chinese MOFCOM fines several undertakings for breaches of merger notification rules (FJEI/FPID; Nanjing Puzhen/Bombardier Sweden; BestTv/Microsoft)" 29 September 2015, e-Competitions Bulletin September 2015, Art. N° 76702

Wendy Ng, Allan Fels, Adrian Emch, Xiaoye Wang, "The Chinese MOFCOM fines a merger in medical imaging market for gun jumping (Canon/Toshiba Medical Systems)" 16 December 2016, e-Competitions Bulletin December 2016, Art. N° 88642

Adrian Emch, "The Chinese MOFCOM rules that a foreign-to-foreign deal 'jumped the gun' in breach of antitrust rules (Canon/Toshiba Medical Systems)" 16 December 2016, e-Competitions Bulletin December 2016, Art. N° 82646

Annex

Table 1: Actual Enforcement of Specific Conduct under the Relevant Merger Control Rules and Substantive Antitrust Laws

Please identify whether the following type of conduct has been subject to investigation/enforcement in your jurisdiction, under the merger control laws or substantive antitrust laws. Please cite any such case(s) and provide a brief description in the table below.

Specific Conduct	Actual Enforcement under Merger Control Laws	Actual Enforcement under Substantive Antitrust Laws
Pre-signing due diligence	No	No
Post-signing/pre-approval due diligence	No	No
Post-approval/pre-closing due diligence	No	No
Use of "clean teams"	No	No
Restrictions on the target in an M&A agreement, e.g. buyer approval required for: Investments above a certain level; New business above a certain level; Other obligations to consult/ obtain approval from the buyer before closing.	No	No
Joint marketing	No	No
Joint presentations (e.g. industry fairs)	No	No
Joint communications	No	No
Strategy/planning regarding customers	No	No
Strategy/planning regarding suppliers	No	No

▶

Specific Conduct	Actual Enforcement under Merger Control Laws	Actual Enforcement under Substantive Antitrust Laws
Third party contract novation	No	No
Personnel Issues: Secondments Retention Strategies	No	No
IT Planning/Database Migration	No	No
Other	See comment below	No

In China, to date, the authority has only investigated and imposed fines in transactions which have been completed or partly completed (i.e. in a scenario of establishment of a joint venture, the new joint venture obtains the business license in China;[21] in a scenario of share/assets acquisition, the transfer of shares/assets is completed; in a multi-step transaction, some steps are completed) prior to notification to the authority. The authority has not enforced any specific conduct listed above or similar conduct in any case.

Table 2: Hypothetical Enforcement of Specific Conduct under the Relevant Merger Control Rules and Substantive Antitrust Laws

For any conduct that is *not* the subject of actual enforcement (Table 1), please indicate in the Table below whether the conduct identified *could potentially* be enforced under the merger control laws and/or substantive antitrust laws.

Specific Conduct	Hypothetical Enforcement under Merger Control Laws	Hypothetical Enforcement under Substantive Antitrust Laws
Pre-signing due diligence	Yes. [Risk arises where, e.g., competitively sensitive information is exchanged.]	Yes. [An exchange of commercially sensitive information at this stage could potentially lead to concerns that the transaction is intended to facilitate a concerted practice, which would constitute a prohibited monopoly agreement under Art. 13 of the AML.]

[21] The business license of an entity is that entity's certificate of incorporation in China. In the authority's view, obtaining a business license of a new JV prior to clearance means the transaction has been implemented.

Specific Conduct	Hypothetical Enforcement under Merger Control Laws	Hypothetical Enforcement under Substantive Antitrust Laws
Post-signing/pre-approval due diligence	Yes. [Risk arises where, e.g., competitively sensitive information is exchanged.]	Yes. [An exchange of commercially sensitive information at this stage could potentially lead to concerns that the transaction is intended to facilitate a concerted practice, which would constitute a prohibited monopoly agreement under Art. 13 of the AML.]
Post-approval/pre-closing due diligence	–	Yes. [An exchange of commercially sensitive information at this stage could potentially lead to concerns that the transaction is intended to facilitate a concerted practice, which would constitute a prohibited monopoly agreement under Art. 13 of the AML.]
Use of "clean teams"	Yes. [Risk arises where the clean team is not set up correctly.]	Yes. [Risk arises where the clean team is not set up correctly.]
Restrictions on the target in an M&A agreement, e.g. buyer approval required for: Investments above a certain level; New business above a certain level; Other obligations to consult/obtain approval from the buyer before closing.	Yes. [Risk arises where, e.g., the matters subject to the buyer's approval are regarded as strategic matters of the target, such that it would be considered as exercising control over the target prior to clearance.]	Yes. [Risks arise especially where such restrictions are imposed on the target before case clearance when the buyer and target are considered as two independent entities. In that case, if the buyer and the target are competitors, such pre-clearance restrictions (particularly in relation to pricing, sales volumes, and future business plans of the target) could lead

Specific Conduct	Hypothetical Enforcement under Merger Control Laws	Hypothetical Enforcement under Substantive Antitrust Laws
		to concerns that the arrangement is intended to facilitate a concerted practice, which would constitute a prohibited monopoly agreement under Art. 13 of the AML. If the target is a downstream distributor of the buyer, then such pre-clearance restrictions (particularly in relation to pricing) could potentially constitute resale price maintenance, which is prohibited under Art. 14 of the AML. The risk would be much lower if such restrictions are imposed on the target after clearance and before closing.]
Joint marketing	Yes. [Risk arises where, e.g., parties act in front of customers and other third parties as though they are already one entity.]	Yes. [An exchange of commercially sensitive information at this stage (particularly in relation to pricing, volumes, and future plans) could potentially lead to concerns that the transaction is intended to facilitate a concerted practice, which would constitute a prohibited monopoly agreement under Art. 13 of the AML.]

Specific Conduct	Hypothetical Enforcement under Merger Control Laws	Hypothetical Enforcement under Substantive Antitrust Laws
Joint presentations (e.g. industry fairs)	Yes. [Risk arises where, e.g., parties act in front of customers and other third parties as though they are already one entity.]	Yes. [An exchange of commercially sensitive information at this stage (particularly in relation to pricing, volumes, and future plans) could potentially lead to concerns that the transaction is intended to facilitate a concerted practice, which would constitute a prohibited monopoly agreement under Art. 13 of the AML.]
Joint communications	Yes. [Risk arises where, e.g., parties act in front of customers and other third parties as though they are already one entity.]	Yes. [An exchange of commercially sensitive information at this stage (particularly in relation to pricing, volumes, and future plans) could potentially lead to concerns that the transaction is intended to facilitate a concerted practice, which would constitute a prohibited monopoly agreement under Art. 13 of the AML.]
Strategy/planning regarding customers	Yes. [Risk arises where, e.g., competitively sensitive information is exchanged.]	Yes. [An exchange of commercially sensitive information at this stage (future plans) could potentially lead to concerns that the transaction is intended to facilitate a concerted practice, which would constitute a prohibited monopoly agreement under Art. 13 of the AML.]

Specific Conduct	Hypothetical Enforcement under Merger Control Laws	Hypothetical Enforcement under Substantive Antitrust Laws
Strategy/planning regarding suppliers	Yes. [Risk arises where, e.g., competitively sensitive information is exchanged.]	Yes. [An exchange of commercially sensitive information at this stage (future plans) could potentially lead to concerns that the transaction is intended to facilitate a concerted practice, which would constitute a prohibited monopoly agreement under Art. 13 of the AML.]
Third party contract novation	Yes.	–
Personnel Issues: Secondments Retention Strategies	Yes.	Yes. [An exchange of commercially sensitive information at this stage (e.g. from employees seconded to the other party, or seconded employees returning to their original employer) could potentially lead to concerns that the transaction is intended to facilitate a concerted practice, which would constitute a prohibited monopoly agreement under Art. 13 of the AML.]
IT Planning/Database Migration	Yes.	Yes. [An exchange of commercially sensitive information at this stage could potentially lead to concerns that the transaction is intended to facilitate a concerted practice, which would constitute a prohibited monopoly agreement under Art. 13 of the AML.]
Other	–	–

For certain conduct identified above, there is a risk that they would be enforced under the merger control laws. However, given lack of guidance from specific legislation and precedents concerning the scope of standstill obligation, it is hard to predict the enforcement practice of the SAMR. Generally speaking, acting as one entity in joint actions in front of customers and other third parties, and exchanging competitively sensitive information (without appropriate safeguards) prior to receiving clearance from the SAMR would incur antitrust risk.

DENMARK

Jens Munk Plum
(Kromann Reumert)

Part 1: Merger Control and the "Standstill Obligation"

1. **Please identify the relevant merger control legislation in your jurisdiction. Please provide a link to the relevant legislation (if possible, in English) and also indicate:**
   - **whether the merger control system is mandatory or voluntary,**
   - **the relevant authority, and**
   - **the duration of the review period.**

Merger control in Denmark is governed on a national level in Part 4 of the Danish Competition Act (Consolidation Act No. 155 of 1 March 2018).

Under section 12b of the Competition Act, a merger covered by the Act shall be notified to the Danish Competition and Consumer Authority (**DCCA**). A merger is covered by the Act if it satisfies certain turnover thresholds laid out in section 12(1).

Once a transaction is notified, the DCCA decides no later than 25 working days after the notification whether the merger will be approved pursuant to section 12d(1). This period may be extended up to 35 working days if one or more of the undertakings propose commitments.

The DCCA may also decide to initiate a further investigation of a merger, after which the DCCA has 90 working days to decide on the approval of the merger. This period may be extended by up to 20 working days if one or more of the undertakings propose commitments. The period may further be extended by up to 20 working days if one or more of the undertakings request or consent to the extension.

The DCCA receives notification and prepares decisions that are generally taken by the Danish Competition Council (**DCC**), which is the main responsible body for enforcing the Danish Competition Act. The DCC takes decisions in both Phase 1 and Phase 2 cases. In practice, however, the DCAA, which is under the DCC, is in charge of the day-to-day administration of the Competition Act and prepares the decisions of the DCC. Thus, the DCCA acts as secretariat for the DCC and has been delegated competence to make decisions in certain specified types of matters which include simplified and ordinary merger procedures and other matters that do not pose new issues or issues of more general interest.

2. **Does the merger control system in your jurisdiction impose a "*standstill obligation*" – meaning, that the transaction cannot be implemented prior to completing the merger control process? (Please cite the relevant legislation.) Please also indicate the *legal scope* of the standstill obligation according to the relevant legislation (e.g. the parties to the transaction cannot effect a change of control, cannot take steps towards implementation, etc.).**

As stated under Question 1, a merger covered by the Act must be notified to the DCCA. Under section 12c(5) a merger that is subject to the Competition Act shall not be completed until it has been notified to, and approved by, the DCCA.

Consequently, a merger covered by the Act must be notified to the DCCA, and until it has been approved by the DCCA (or the DCC, as applicable) the merger must not be completed.

The standstill obligation entails a ban on the partial or full implementation of the merger before the approval by the DCCA. Recent case law on the standstill obligation has clarified the scope of the standstill obligation to the effect that only measures that are part of establishing a change of control are covered by the prohibition (see Question 9 and the reference to the merger between EY and KPMG Denmark).

3. Have the relevant authorities in your jurisdiction issued internal or external guidelines concerning the scope of the standstill obligation, and/or their authority to enforce it? Please provide a copy/link of such guidance, if possible in English.

The DCCA has not issued guidelines concerning the standstill obligation. It has however issued a set of general guidelines on merger control (in Danish) including a short section on the ban on early implementation.[1]

4. Are there any exceptions to the standstill obligation – for example, through derogation or "carve out"? Please describe the circumstances in which this is possible. Please also describe the relevant process, e.g. do parties need to apply to the authority for a derogation from the standstill obligation? If so, how long is the approval process? If there are specific cases addressing these issues, please identify them.

There are two exceptions to the standstill obligation in the Competition Act.

- Under section 12c(5), second sentence, the standstill obligation does not prevent the implementation of a public takeover bid provided that the merger is notified immediately to the DCCA and the acquirer does not exercise the voting rights until it has been approved by the DCCA.
- Under section 12c(6), the DCCA may grant an exemption from the standstill obligation. This must be based on a reasoned request by the parties and may have conditions attached.

While no exemption needs to be granted under section 12c(5), under section 12c(6) parties will need to formally request an exemption. There is no formal process established for this. Parties will need to prepare a reasoned request with sufficient documentation showing the necessity of getting an exemption. The main criteria for deciding whether an exemption can be granted is the potential impact on effective competition that the merger may have. If a merger does not pose any threat to competition, an exemption will most likely be granted. If such a request is submitted during the merger review period, it will normally have the

---

1 <https://www.kfst.dk/vejledninger/kfst/dansk/2018/20180628-vejledning-om-fusionskontrol/>.

effect of postponing the merger review as the case-handlers will have to focus their resources on the requested exemption. The DCCA has, in a number of instances, granted such exemptions, e.g. for parties to enter into supply agreements for a full-function joint venture not yet being cleared.

There is no case law showing that the DCCA has been confronted with and accepted a situation where merging parties have carved out Denmark pending clearance, while closing the remaining transaction. While theoretically a carve-out solution should not be excluded, the DCCA would most likely require very solid evidence to the effect that the carve-out arrangement would not affect effective competition in Denmark, should the DCCA/DCC decide to prohibit the merger. The scope of a carve-out model in Denmark would most likely be very limited, if it exists at all.

5. Does a public bid exception exist in your jurisdiction? (For example, under the EU Merger Regulation it is possible to acquire shares as part of a public bid, provided that the shares are not exercised until the acquisition is cleared by the Commission.) If such an exception exists in your jurisdiction, please describe how it is applied.

As indicated in Question 4, the standstill obligation does not prevent the implementation of a public takeover bid provided that the merger is notified immediately to the DCCA and the acquirer does not exercise the voting rights until it has been approved.

This exception is a duplicate of the similar exception in Art. 7(2) EUMR and is applied similarly to the way the European Commission applies this article.

6. What powers does the relevant authority have to investigate and enforce violations of the standstill obligation? Are dawn raids possible? What timing applies to investigation/enforcement proceedings?

Under section 17 of the Competition Act, the DCCA may request any information necessary to carry out the tasks under the Act.

The DCCA has the same powers to investigate and enforce violations of the standstill obligation as they have in any other case concerning violations of competition rules. This also means that they can conduct dawn raids.

7. What are the possible penalties for violating the standstill obligation? Are there criminal sanctions, including on individuals? Have these been applied in practice? Is there a difference in enforcement between transactions involving domestic companies and "foreign-to-foreign" transactions? Does the authority have the power to unwind transactions implemented in breach of the standstill obligation? If so, has the authority made use of that power in practice? If yes, please provide examples.

First of all, the DCCA or the DCC, depending on the nature of the case, may find that there has been an infringement of the standstill obligation and may issue an order to that effect. Further, under section 23(1)(vii), failure to notify the DCCA of a merger that is subject to the Act or the violation of the standstill obligation may be punished with a fine, which is a criminal sanction. The DCCA has recently referred two undertakings to the public prosecutor which fined each of them

DKK 4 million for failure to notify and for violating the standstill obligation by implementing the merger without having obtained clearance.[2]

More recently, in June 2019, Circle K accepted an out-of-court settlement to pay a fine of DKK 6 million for failure to notify a transaction.[3] Circle K had notified the primary transaction to the European Commission and received a clearance decision; however, a separate part of the transaction was not covered by the Commission's clearance and should therefore have been notified separately to the DCCA. Since Circle K had not notified the latter part of the transaction, it accepted to pay the fine to settle the matter.[4]

There is no reason to believe that the DCCA would treat foreign-to-foreign mergers more leniently than local mergers when looking at potential violations of the standstill obligation.

Under section 12g, the DCCA also has the power to prohibit a merger that has been implemented in violation of the standstill obligation, provided it gives rise to a substantial impediment of effective competition. It remains unclear, and there is no case law determining if the DCCA can prohibit a merger even if the merger itself does not raise any concerns. Alternatively, the DCCA may issue orders requiring a separation of the merged entity as well as any other measure necessary to reinstall effective competition. These powers have not yet been used in practice.

8. How does the relevant authority typically learn of potential violations of the standstill obligation? Does the authority actively monitor the trade press?

Typically, the cases on violation of the standstill obligation are brought to the attention of the DCCA following the notification of a merger and in the subsequent investigation; or when an undertaking notifies the DCCA of a different merger following a failure to notify the DCCA of a previous merger.

9. Please describe the relevant authority's enforcement of the standstill obligation. If there have been cases, please describe the specific conduct that was found to violate the standstill provision and the criteria applied by the relevant authority or court. Has the relevant authority considered the market impact of the conduct? (Please refer to the Annex.)

Recent years have seen an increase in the amount of enforcement of the standstill obligation, most notably in the case of the merger between EY and KPMG Denmark. In its decision, the Competition Council found that the parties had violated the standstill obligation by terminating a cooperation agreement with KPMG International.[5]

---

2 See case on the unlawful implementation of the merger between SEAS-NVE and Syd Energi, case number 91250-00002-18, available in Danish at: <https://www.kfst.dk/media/50750/20180704-boedeforelaeg-seas-nve.pdf>.

3 *Circle K Denmark A/S and Shell*, 26 June 2019 DCCA

4 A case summary is available in English at the DCCA's website at <https://www.en.kfst.dk/nyheder/kfst/english/judgements/20190626-company-accepts-fine-for-not-notifying-a-merger/>.

5 See *Ernst & Young* decision by the Danish Competition Council in case 14/07180.

On appeal to the Danish Maritime and Commercial High Court, a preliminary reference was brought before the CJEU on the interpretation of Art 7(1) EUMR.[6] In its judgment, the Court found that the termination of the cooperation agreement did not constitute an unlawful implementation of the merger. The Court held that a concentration is implemented "only by a transaction which, in whole or in part, in fact or in law, contributes to the change in control of the target undertaking". The DCC subsequently accepted the claims submitted to the court by EY to the effect that the DCC had been wrong, and the case has now been closed.

In a different case, two energy service providers, SEAS-NVE and Syd Energi were found to have violated section 12b of the Competition Act by failing to notify the DCCA, and were subsequently fined DKK 4 million.[7] SEAS-NVE and Syd Energi had acquired joint control over Clever A/S – a company that provides charging stations for electric cars. The acquisition was found to be covered by the merger control rules, and as such the merger should have been notified to the DCCA.

10. In cases involving alleged violations of the standstill obligation under the relevant merger control laws, has the relevant authority (or court) *also* considered the substantive antitrust laws? (Please refer to the Annex.)

Where a transaction is subject to the rules on merger control, the general antitrust rules do not apply to the transaction as such. This also means that within the ambit of the transaction giving rise to the merger, both the parties' conduct preceding the signing of the agreement, and their conduct between signing and closing, may be assessed under the merger rules but also under the general antitrust rules. To the extent that such conduct clearly exceeds what can be considered the ambit of the transaction, the general rules could apply. A case on the violation of the standstill obligation would therefore most likely only involve the antitrust rules, if it was found to fall outside the scope of the merger control rules by its nature.

In the recent case of EY and KPMG Denmark, the Competition Council did not consider whether there had been a breach of antitrust rules.

11. Is private enforcement of the standstill obligation possible?

This issue is not addressed in the Competition Act, or in the preparatory works of the Competition Act. In our view it seems doubtful that private parties could initiate enforcement of the standstill obligation in the courts without prior involvement of the DCCA.

12. Please describe the private law risks/consequences (i.e. contractual/validity consequences) for transactions that are subject to notification, but which are completed without notification/approval. Please identify any relevant cases and describe them.

To our knowledge there are no cases that have involved these issues. From a private law perspective, the risk of violating the standstill obligation would be that the merger agreement could likely be considered null and void, and that parties therefore would stand in a situation with no instrument to govern the relationship.

---

6 See case C-633/16 Ernst & Young, EU:C:2018:371.

7 See n 2.

Provided the conditions under Danish tort law are met, a seller is likely to be able to claim damages for any loss suffered in circumstances where the seller has given up control and is confronted with a buyer that has violated the standstill obligation and the DCCA or DCC (as applicable) has ordered the merger to be dissolved.

13. Please describe policy and enforcement trends in your jurisdiction.

As indicated under Question 9, recent years have seen an increase in the cases on breach of the standstill obligation.

Part 2: Substantive Antitrust Law in an M&A Context

1. **Please identify the relevant *substantive antitrust laws* in your jurisdiction that can potentially apply in an M&A context (e.g. for the EU, this would include Article 101 of the Treaty on the Functioning of the European Union). Please provide a link to the relevant legislation (if possible, in English).**

The general provisions concerning anticompetitive agreements and abuse of a dominant position are found in section 6(1) and section 11(1) of the Danish Competition Act.

The merger rules apply to transactions that bring about a change in control, and this is what is covered by the merger clearance. Merger clearance does not include explicit approval of any agreements that are made which constitute important elements of the transactions for the parties. Such agreements will be subject to the general competition rules – namely, section 6(1) and section 11(1) of the Competition Act. In the case concerning the acquisition of joint control by Norgesgruppen/Dagrofa[8], the DCCA conducted the merger review and gave clearance, while at the same time investigating and preparing a decision under section 6(1) that approved the franchise concept to be applied by Dagrofa following the merger clearance. Thus, the DCCA made two separate decisions: i) the merger clearance (substantively assessed under the merger control rules), and ii) an assessment of the franchise concept (under section 6(1)), finding it also unproblematic.

Similarly, a merger clearance does not imply an explicit clearance of ancillary agreements. If agreements fall within the scope of the European Commission guidelines on ancillary restraints, the DCCA is unlikely to challenge such agreements. However, if agreements have a scope going beyond the Commission guidelines, the DCCA may investigate whether such agreements are acceptable.[9]

2. **Do any guidelines exist in your jurisdiction concerning the application of the substantive antitrust laws in an M&A context – whether internal to the relevant authority, or external, formal or informal (e.g. speeches)? If so, please provide a copy/link to such guidance.**

---

8 DCC decision of 23 October 2013 in case: 13/05331 (section 6(1)) and DCCA decision of 25 October 2013 in case MEDS-13/05331 (merger clearance). Link to the decision under section 6(1): <https://www.kfst.dk/media/13350/20131023-dagrofa-aftaler-om-omstrukturering.pdf>. Link to the merger clearance decision: <https://www.kfst.dk/media/13350/20131025-norgesgruppen-danmark-aps-erhvervelse-af-faelles-kontrol-sammen-med-kfi-erhvervsdrivende-f.pdf>.

9 <https://www.retsinformation.dk/Forms/R0710.aspx?id=199825>.

To date, the DCCA has not issued guidelines concerning antitrust laws in an M&A context.

3. As a general matter (not limited to M&A), how are the substantive antitrust laws enforced with respect to the exchange of competitively sensitive information between competing firms? Please also indicate the relevance of anti-competitive effects or intent in such enforcement.

In order for the parties to be able to make an informed decision as to whether or not the transaction should proceed, the exchange of sensitive information is a necessary step in assessing the potential merger. Such exchanges are likely to be considered ancillary and unproblematic, subject to the parties putting in place the appropriate measures. These include safeguards such as non-disclosure agreements, limiting of the number of persons involved and implementing protective measures to ensure that persons with a direct market-related responsibility do not participate in due diligence concerning their area of activity. Provided the situation concerns a genuine transaction, the exchange of information is not likely to give rise to issues under section 6(1) of the Competition Act.

Following the signing of the merger agreement, the exchange of information must be limited to that which is necessary to preserve the value of the target undertaking up until the closing of the merger. In this regard, the DCCA is likely to follow the principles laid out by the European Commission in the *Altice* case.[10]

The DCCA has yet to bring a case applying section 6(1) of the Competition Act to the exchange of sensitive information during a merger review. In our view, this is not likely to happen as the DCCA would most likely treat the exchange of information as conduct to be assessed primarily under the standstill obligation, unless it goes beyond what is necessary for the purpose of the transaction.[11]

Section 6(1) of the Competition Act theoretically still applies following clearance but before closing, as a new economic entity has not yet been created. Enforcement, however, has never actually been attempted and it is unlikely to happen.

4. Have there been any cases in your jurisdiction in which the substantive antitrust laws were enforced in an M&A context? Please describe/explain and cite any such cases. (See also Annex.)

Please see Question 1 in relation to the acquisition of joint control by Norgesgruppen of Dagrofa.[12] To our knowledge, this is the only case where Danish Competition Authorities have made parallel (and separate) assessments under the merger control rules and the substantive antitrust laws, but there is nothing to indicate that it could not happen again in a similar situation.

With regard to merging parties' pre-merger conduct, there are no cases where such conduct has been examined under the substantive antitrust rules/section 6(1), as opposed to the standstill obligation/merger control rules.

---

10 Case M.7993 *Altice/PT Portugal* (Art. 14(2)), 24 April 2018.

11 Section 12c(5) of the Competition Act.

12 n 8.

5. Are the substantive antitrust laws more likely to apply at specific stages of the transaction – i.e. at an early stage, or prior to closing (or does it not make a difference)? Do companies face ongoing risk following the consummation (or failure) of their transaction for conduct that allegedly occurred pre-closing (pre-failure)?

In our view, the answer to this question is no.

One could consider whether the substantive rules could become applicable to the exchange of sensitive information in the period following clearance but before closing. Theoretically, the undertakings are still competitors in this period. However, it would seem unlikely that the DCCA would initiate enforcement procedures against such conduct, provided closing takes place shortly after clearance.

6. Please explain how the relevant authority enforces (or could enforce) the substantive antitrust laws in an M&A context. How would the investigation occur, and what timing constraints would apply?

There is very little guidance on this issue. In the *Norgesgruppen/Dagrofa*[13] case referred to above, the substantive rules were applied in parallel with the ongoing merger review, and issues relating to the franchise concept and hence subject to the substantive rules were also discussed in the merger pre-notification phase. It is likely that the DCCA would aim to follow a similar procedure in similar cases.

7. Is private enforcement of the substantive antitrust laws possible in an M&A context, and has it occurred?

Yes, in principle it is possible for private parties to initiate enforcement in the courts of the substantive rules against a pending merger. It has to our knowledge never happened and we would assume that Danish courts would be reluctant to interfere in the M&A process if it is subject to a pending mandatory merger control review.

8. Could behavior subject to the substantive antitrust laws also be caught under the merger control rules/standstill obligation? (Please also refer to the Annex.)

As mentioned in Question 1, there is a distinction between what a merger clearance will cover and what is subject to the substantive antitrust rules. A merger clearance will cover the transaction that brings about a change of control. It will not cover any behavior that is not a necessary element in establishing a change of control. Agreements made in the course of the transaction but falling outside this criterion may be ancillary and thereby not considered a restriction of competition, or they may go further than that and thus be subject to the substantive antitrust rules.

9. Please describe the penalties for infringing the substantive antitrust laws. Please indicate whether these include criminal penalties, including individual criminal penalties. As a practical matter, how have these been applied in the context of an M&A transaction?

Under section 23(1) of the Competition Act, a party that infringes the antitrust laws shall be punished with fines (which are criminal in nature). The fines depend on the gravity of the infringement.

---

13 ibid.

Less serious infringements may be fined with a base amount of between DKK 400,000 and DKK 4 million. Serious infringements have a range for fines of DKK 4 million to DKK 20 million. Very serious infringements have a base amount at DKK 20 million and upwards. The base amount is adjusted, based on gravity and duration. Fines may not exceed 10% of the group's turnover.

Individuals may be punished with fines of at least DKK 50,000 and under particularly aggravating circumstances at least DKK 200,000. Individuals participating in a cartel in breach of section 6(1) may be subject to imprisonment for up to 18 months. Under particularly aggravating circumstances the punishment may increase to imprisonment for up to six years.

Prison sentences for individuals have yet to be applied by the courts.

10. Please describe policy and enforcement trends in your jurisdiction.

Generally speaking, the DCCA is very active, implying that they will investigate most cases where infringements could be discussed, be it smaller or larger cases. The DCCA is known to be quite thorough in its reviews. In merger cases, the DCCA to a large extent relies on econometric and quantitative analyses and it is fair to say that the threshold for intervention has been going down during the recent years.

Michael Klöcker, "The Danish Competition and Consumer Authority refers its first gun-jumping case to the public prosecutor (KPMG/EY)" 11 June 2015, e-Competitions Bulletin June 2015, Art. N° 73857

Michael Klöcker, "The Danish Competition and Consumer Authority holds that companies have pre-implemented a merger under scrutiny, leading to the first case of gun jumping (KPMG/EY)" 17 December 2014, e-Competitions Bulletin December 2014, Art. N° 70935

Eric David, Marco Plankensteiner, "The EU Court of Justice puts an end to the extensive interpretation by some competition authorities of the concept of gun jumping (Ernst & Young)" 31 May 2018, e-Competitions Bulletin May 2018, Art. N° 87374

Sara Moya Izquierdo, Miguel Troncoso Ferrer, Clara García Fernández, "Advocate General Wahl excludes gun-jumping in a case involving a takeover in the auditing sector (Ernst & Young)" 18 January 2018, e-Competitions Bulletin January 2018, Art. N° 86160

Caroline Ruiz Palmer, Andrea L Hamilton, David Henry, "The EU Court of Justice provides guidance on the merger notification obligation in the EU regulation (Ernst & Young)" 31 May 2018, e-Competitions Bulletin May 2018, Art. N° 88783

Jean-François Bellis, Valérie Lefever, "Standstill obligation: The Court of Justice of the European Union recalls that a merger is only subject to notification when there is a change of control of the targeted undertaking, with the result that a cooperation agreement may be denounced before the notification of the operation and before its clearance by competition authorities (Ernst & Young)" 31 May 2018, Concurrences Review N° 3-2018, Art. N° 87784

Annex

Table 1: Actual Enforcement of Specific Conduct under the Relevant Merger Control Rules and Substantive Antitrust Laws

Please identify whether the following type of conduct has been subject to investigation/enforcement in your jurisdiction, under the merger control laws or substantive antitrust laws. Please cite any such case(s) and provide a brief description in the table below.

Specific Conduct	Actual Enforcement under Merger Control Laws	Actual Enforcement under Substantive Antitrust Laws
Pre-signing due diligence	No	No
Post-signing/pre-approval due diligence	No	No
Post-approval/pre-closing due diligence	No	No
Use of "clean teams"	No	No
Restrictions on the target in an M&A agreement, e.g. buyer approval required for: Investments above a certain level; New business above a certain level; Other obligations to consult/obtain approval from the buyer before closing.	No	No
Joint marketing	In the *EY/KPMG* case, complainants suggested that the parties were undertaking joint marketing. The DCCA did not find any infringement.	No
Joint presentations (e.g. industry fairs)	No	No

Specific Conduct	Actual Enforcement under Merger Control Laws	Actual Enforcement under Substantive Antitrust Laws
Joint communications	No	No
Strategy/planning regarding customers	No	No
Strategy/planning regarding suppliers	No	No
Third party contract novation	No	No
Personnel Issues: Secondments Retention Strategies	No	No
IT Planning/Database Migration	No	No
Other	No	No

Table 2: Hypothetical Enforcement of Specific Conduct under the Relevant Merger Control Rules and Substantive Antitrust Laws

For any conduct that is *not* the subject of actual enforcement (Table 1), please indicate in the Table below whether the conduct identified *could potentially* be enforced under the merger control laws and/or substantive antitrust laws.

Specific Conduct	Hypothetical Enforcement under Merger Control Laws	Hypothetical Enforcement under Substantive Antitrust Laws
Pre-signing due diligence	Could be challenged under the standstill obligation.	Only if the transaction and process are considered a scam to hide cartel behavior.
Post-signing/pre-approval due diligence	Could be challenged under the standstill obligation.	No
Post-approval/pre-closing due diligence	Could be challenged under the standstill obligation.	No
Use of "clean teams"	Could be challenged under the standstill obligation.	No

Specific Conduct	Hypothetical Enforcement under Merger Control Laws	Hypothetical Enforcement under Substantive Antitrust Laws
Restrictions on the target in an M&A agreement, e.g. buyer approval required for: Investments above a certain level; New business above a certain level; Other obligations to consult/ obtain approval from the buyer before closing.	This would likely be an issue that the DCCA would investigate, particularly following the *Altice* decision.	No
Joint marketing	This would likely be an issue that the DCCA would investigate, particularly following the *Altice* decision.	No
Joint presentations (e.g. industry fairs)	This would likely be an issue that the DCCA would investigate, particularly following the *Altice* decision.	No
Joint communications	This would likely be an issue that the DCCA would investigate, particularly following the *Altice* decision.	No
Strategy/planning regarding customers	Provided such planning is made subject to sufficient clean team restrictions, it would not seem likely that this would be investigated.	No
Strategy/planning regarding suppliers	Provided such planning is made subject to sufficient clean team restrictions, it would not seem likely that this would be investigated.	No

Specific Conduct	Hypothetical Enforcement under Merger Control Laws	Hypothetical Enforcement under Substantive Antitrust Laws
Third party contract novation	Following the *EY/ KPMG* case, a novation of contracts subject to merger clearance would not seem likely to be considered a violation of the standstill obligation.	No
Personnel Issues: Secondments Retention Strategies	Subject to ensuring protection of confidential information, it would not seem likely that this would be investigated.	No
IT Planning/Database Migration	Provided such planning is made subject to sufficient clean team restrictions, it would not seem likely that this would be investigated.	No
Other		

EUROPEAN UNION

Andrea Hamilton
(McDermott Will & Emery LLP)

Part 1: Merger Control and the "Standstill Obligation"

1. **Please identify the relevant merger control legislation in your jurisdiction. Please provide a link to the relevant legislation (if possible, in English) and also indicate:**
   - **whether the merger control system is mandatory or voluntary,**
   - **the relevant authority, and**
   - **the duration of the review period.**

The EU Merger Regulation (EC) 139/2004[1] (**EUMR**), which is enforced by the European Commission, provides that "concentrations" with a "Community Dimension" must be notified and approved before they can be completed. The merger control system is mandatory, and there are no exceptions.

The EUMR defines a "concentration" as a merger or two or more previously independent undertakings or parts of undertakings, or the acquisition of direct or indirect control of the whole or parts of another undertaking, resulting in a lasting change of control. The definition of "concentration" extends to the creation and change of control over "full-function" joint ventures. Concentrations are only subject to prior notification and approval from the Commission when they have a "Community dimension" – meaning that they meet certain revenue thresholds.

Once a concentration is formally filed with (notified to) the European Commission following customary pre-notification, the 25-working-day Phase 1 review period begins, which can be extended to 35 working days when the parties offer commitments. At the conclusion of Phase 1, the Commission can approve the transaction unconditionally or subject to commitments, or can open an in-depth Phase 2 investigation. A Phase 2 investigation has a basic duration of 90 working days, and can be extended to 125 working days.

2. **Does the merger control system in your jurisdiction impose a "*standstill obligation*" – meaning, that the transaction cannot be implemented prior to completing the merger control process? (Please cite the relevant legislation.) Please also indicate the *legal scope* of the standstill obligation according to the relevant legislation (e.g. the parties to the transaction cannot effect a change of control, cannot take steps towards implementation, etc.).**

Yes. Article 4(1) EUMR requires that "[c]oncentrations with a Community dimension ... be notified to the Commission prior to their implementation". Article 7(1) EUMR further provides that a concentration with a Community dimension "shall not

[1] <http://eur-lex.europa.eu/legal-content/EN/ALL/?uri=CELEX:32004R0139>.

be implemented either before its notification or until it has been declared compatible with the common market". The EUMR thus requires the advance notification of a notifiable transaction, and prohibits the completion of that transaction before it is approved by the Commission. Further, the General Court has confirmed that a failure to notify under Article 4(1) will also automatically violate the "standstill" obligation of Article 7(1). In effect, the failure to notify a concentration to the Commission can thus infringe two separate provisions of the EUMR.[2]

Article 7(1) EUMR does not, by its terms, clarify the scope of the standstill obligation, and in particular the specific conduct that can constitute premature implementation.[3] In a recent case, however, the Court of Justice concluded that the standstill obligation only applies to actions which "in whole or in part, in fact or in law, [contribute] to the change of control of the target undertaking".[4] While a welcome clarification, this standard leaves room for interpretation.

3. **Have the relevant authorities in your jurisdiction issued internal or external guidelines concerning the scope of the standstill obligation, and/or their authority to enforce it? Please provide a copy/link of such guidance, if possible in English.**

The Commission has not issued guidelines on the scope of the standstill provision. It, however, investigated violations of the standstill obligation and issued decisions, some of which have been challenged before the General Court or the Court of Justice of the European Union. To some extent, guidance may be derived through these cases.[5]

4. **Are there any exceptions to the standstill obligation – for example, through derogation or "carve out"? Please describe the circumstances in which this is possible. Please also describe the relevant process, e.g. do parties need to apply to the authority for a derogation from the standstill obligation? If so, how long is the approval process? If there are specific cases addressing these issues, please identify them.**

There two limited exceptions to the standstill obligation and in limited circumstances parties may apply for a derogation from the standstill obligation.

4.1 Exceptions

Article 7(2) EUMR provides that public bids or a series of transactions in securities on a stock exchange by which control is acquired from various sellers may be implemented without prior notification to the Commission. This exception requires that transaction is notified to the Commission without delay. It also requires that

---

2 Case T-704-14 *Marine Harvest ASA v Commission* EU:T:2017:753, paras 292–374.

3 Case C-633/16 *Ernst & Young P/S v Konkurrencerådet* EU:C:2018:371, para 39.

4 ibid, para 62.

5 See OECD, *Suspensory Effects of Merger Notifications and Gun Jumping – Note by the European Union*, 27 November 2018, Section 6 (recommending that guidance be derived from leading gun-jumping cases). Indeed, the Director of Competition and State Aid for the EFTA Surveillance Authority reportedly said that the lack of legal clarity over which specific activities can be considered "gun-jumping" and the need for a case-by-case assessment means that the prospect of publishing guidance will likely take years. See Michael Acton, "EU gun-jumping guidelines could take years, EFTA official says" (*MLex Market Insight* 30 January 2019).

the acquirer not exercise the voting rights of the shares acquired, or does so only to maintain the full value of its investment based on a derogation from the Commission pursuant to Article 7(3) EUMR (see section 4.2, below). Notably, Article 7(2) was the subject of a recent case decided by the General Court, *Marine Harvest v Commission*.[6] In that case, the Court upheld the Commission's imposition of a fine of €20 million for acquiring de facto control over a target without prior notification or approval. Marine Harvest's defense rested on Article 7(2), but the Court upheld the Commission's reasoning that this did not apply since Marine Harvest acquired de facto control through a minority acquisition from a single seller.

In addition, Article 7(4) EUMR preserves the validity of transactions in securities traded on a market (unless the buyer and seller knew, or ought to have known, that advance notification was required).

4.2 Derogation

Parties to a notifiable transaction may request a derogation from the standstill obligation to allow implementation, or partial implementation, prior to the completion of the Commission's review and approval of the transaction. An application for derogation may be made at any time, before or after the transaction is notified to the Commission.

In practice, derogations are only granted in exceptional circumstances, where the Commission determines that the harm to the parties, or to a third party, resulting from the standstill obligation is greater than the threat to competition posed by the transaction. The applicant must show that the threats to business resulting from the standstill obligation are real, not hypothetical – for instance, that a target is in financial distress and the derogation is needed to preserve its viability.[7]

The Commission may also subject a grant of derogation to commitments and obligations to ensure conditions of effective competition. The breach of these conditions invalidates the derogation, and may subject a party to fines and/or periodic penalty payments.[8]

5. Does a public bid exception exist in your jurisdiction? (For example, under the EU Merger Regulation it is possible to acquire shares as part of a public bid, provided that the shares are not exercised until the acquisition is cleared by the Commission.) If such an exception exists in your jurisdiction, please describe how it is applied.

Yes. Article 7(2) EUMR provides for a public bid exception, as indicated in Question 4, above. The Commission applies Article 7(2) strictly, as evidenced by its enforcement record.

---

6 n 2.

7 To illustrate the Commission's approach, see e.g. Case COMP/M.8758 *Baywa/Clean Energy Trading* (decision of 7 December 2017); Case COMP/M.8633 *Lufthansa/Certain Air Berlin Assets* (decision of 27 October 2017); Case COMP/M.5969 *SJ Johnson/Sara Lee* (decision of 11 February 2011); Case COMP/M.4151 *Orica/Dyno* (decision of 11 April 2006).

8 Article 14(2)(d) EUMR (providing for a fine of up to 10% of group turnover); Article 15(2) (to enforce compliance with an obligation (attached to a derogation) imposed by decision under Article 7(3).

Most recently, in 2017 the General Court upheld a fine of €20 million that the Commission imposed on Marine Harvest in a case involving Article 7(2).[9] Marine Harvest argued that Article 7(2) applied because its 2012 acquisition of 48.5% of the shares of Morpol, the target, was part of a larger transaction that included a 2013 public bid and constituted a series of transactions in securities.

The Commission, upheld by the General Court, rejected these arguments, concluding that the 2012 share purchase was not conditional on the 2013 public bid and was not part of the same transaction. In addition, because the sellers in the 2012 acquisition were ultimately controlled by the same person, the sale did not involve "various sellers" as required by Article 7(2). The Commission's analysis in this case is in line with its prior practice in *Yara/Kemira Growhow* (2007), which also involved Article 7(2).[10] Marine Harvest has appealed the General Court's ruling to the Court of Justice of the European Union.

6. What powers does the relevant authority have to investigate and enforce violations of the standstill obligation? Are dawn raids possible? What timing applies to investigation/enforcement proceedings?

The Commission has the power to request information[11] under Article 11 EUMR and to conduct on-site inspections (dawn raids) at the premises of the parties to the transaction under Article 13 EUMR. The Commission has, in the past, exercised its authority to conduct dawn raids, notably to determine whether exchanges of competitively sensitive information had occurred, leading to premature implementation in violation of the standstill obligation.[12] In terms of timing, gun-jumping investigations are not subject to the same time frame as merger review and can be lengthy.

7. What are the possible penalties for violating the standstill obligation? Are there criminal sanctions, including on individuals? Have these been applied in practice? Is there a difference in enforcement between transactions involving domestic companies and "foreign-to-foreign" transactions? Does the authority have the power to unwind transactions implemented in breach of the standstill obligation? If so, has the authority made use of that power in practice? If yes, please provide examples.

Under Article 14(2)(b) EUMR, the Commission can impose fines of up to 10% of the aggregate turnover of the undertakings concerned in the preceding financial year, as well as interim measures for the violation of the standstill obligation. These penalties apply irrespective of whether the infringement was committed negligently or intentionally and despite the fact that clearance might be ultimately obtained and the transaction raises no competition concerns. Fines can be separately imposed for infringements of both Article 4(1) EUMR, pursuant to Article 14.2(a), and Article 7(1) EUMR, pursuant to Article 14.2(b).

---

9 n 2. (currently on appeal to the Court of Justice of the European Union).

10 Case COMP/M.4730 *Yara/Kemira Growhow* (decision of 21 September 2007), paras 6–7.

11 See generally Case M.7993 *Altice/PT Portugal* (decision of 24 April 2018) (numerous references to requests for information, and the Commission's extensive reliance on information derived through these requests).

12 See e.g. European Commission Memo 07/573, "Mergers: Commission has carried out inspections in the S PVC sector" (13 December 2007), available at <http://europa.eu/rapid/press-release_MEMO-07-573_en.htm>.

Notably, the upper limit on fines for infringing the EUMR is identical to the upper limit of fines for infringing the substantive antitrust rules. However, while guidelines exist on the setting of fines under the substantive antitrust rules,[13] no such guidelines exist on the setting of fines under the EUMR. This can lead to differences in practice as to the level of fines that could theoretically be imposed.

8. How does the relevant authority typically learn of potential violations of the standstill obligation? Does the authority actively monitor the trade press?

One important way in which the Commission can become aware of a potential violation of the standstill obligation is through the review of company documents. Such access can provide the Commission with the opportunity to observe the extent of information exchange between the parties and pre-merger coordination.

The Commission also monitors the press. For instance, in *Altice/PT Portugal*, the Commission identified reports in the Portuguese press "regarding visits by Altice executives to PT Portugal prior to the adoption by the Commission of the Clearance Decision".[14] This prompted the Commission to request further information and ultimately open an investigation. The Commission can learn of possible infringements of the standstill obligation through other means, including information received from third parties – or through other sources.

9. Please describe the relevant authority's enforcement of the standstill obligation. If there have been cases, please describe the specific conduct that was found to violate the standstill provision and the criteria applied by the relevant authority or court. Has the relevant authority considered the market impact of the conduct? (Please refer to the Annex.)

The European Commission's enforcement of procedural violations of the EUMR has significantly increased in recent years. Recent enforcement has encompassed violations of the standstill obligation, as well as other procedural violations, including the provision of incorrect or misleading information – and cases remain pending at the time of writing.[15]

Until recently, the Commission's prior decisions have mainly focused on cases involving a failure to file a notifiable transaction. The Commission's current enforcement activity, in contrast, addresses more complex situations involving questions over what type of conduct will give rise to partial or full implementation of a concentration prior to receiving approval, thus violating the standstill provision in the EUMR. Over time, the Commission has significantly increased the level of penalties imposed.

Historically, there was very little enforcement of failure-to-file cases. Indeed, in 1998, the Commission fined Samsung the equivalent of €32,000 for a negligent

---

13 See European Commission, Guidelines on the method of setting fines imposed pursuant to Article 23(2)(a) of Regulation No 1/2003 (OJ C 210) (9 January 2006).

14 *Altice/PT Portugal* (n 11), para 12.

15 See European Commission, Press Release, "Mergers: Commission alleges Merck and Sigma-Aldrich, General Electric, and Canon breached EU merger procedural rules" (6 July 2017), available at <http://europa.eu/rapid/press-release_IP-17-1924_en.htm>.

failure to file, which Samsung self-reported.[16] The next year, the Commission fined AP Møller the equivalent of €219,000 for a failure to file a reportable transaction.[17] Although the Commission found "gross negligence" in that case, this was mitigated by a lack of enforcement history.

Ten years later, the Commission significantly increased its enforcement of failure to file, namely in the *Electrabel*[18] and *Marine Harvest* cases. Even though both cases were ultimately notified, each resulted in a fine of €20 million being imposed on the notifying party. Both cases were upheld when challenged before the General Court and CJEU, and show a hardening approach by the Commission toward procedural infringements. Notably, the Commission ultimately cleared the transactions (unconditionally in *Electrabel* and conditionally in *Marine Harvest*).

The Commission's current enforcement has focused on more complex situations involving conduct that leads to partial or full implementation of a concentration in violation of the standstill obligation. Historically, the Commission investigated possible conduct leading to premature implementation of a transaction in a few earlier cases, but these cases did not result in a decision.[19] Thus, until recently there has been relatively little guidance or decisional practice on the specific conduct that will be found to constitute partial or full implementation of a concentration in violation of the standstill obligation in the EUMR.

On 31 May 2018, however, the CJEU issued a ruling on the scope of Article 7(1), in *Ernst & Young P/S v Konkurrencerådet.*[20] That case addressed an alleged violation of the standstill obligation in Ernst & Young's (**EY**) acquisition of KPMG's Danish unit (**KPMG Denmark**). Following EY's agreement to acquire KPMG Denmark, which was subject to antitrust approval in Denmark, KPMG Denmark terminated its cooperation agreement with KPMG International. The key question in the case was whether that termination violated the standstill obligation.

The CJEU acknowledged that Article 7(1), by its terms, "does not, in itself, clarify the scope of the prohibition…"[21] but concluded that the standstill obligation only applies to actions which "in whole or in part, in fact or in law, [contribute] to the change of control of the target undertaking".[22] The Court went on to conclude that the termination of the cooperation agreement was conditionally linked to the overall transaction, but did not appear to contribute to a change of control of KPMG Denmark. As such, it did not appear to violate the standstill obligation.

---

16 Case No IV/M.980 *Samsung/AST* (decision of 18 February 1998).

17 Case No IV/M.969 *AP Møller* (decision of 10 February 1999).

18 Case COMP/M.4994 *Electrabel/Compagnie nationale du Rhône* C(2009) 4416 (decision of 10 June 2009).

19 See e.g. European Commission Memo 07/573 (n 12); and Case COMP/M.4734 *Ineos/Kerling* (decision of 30 January 2018); *Yara/Kemira Growhow* (n 10); European Commission Press Release, "Commission warns BERTELSMANN and KIRCH against infringement of European merger control" (1 December 1997), <http://europa.eu/rapid/press-release_IP-97-1062_en.htm?locale=en>; Case COMP/M.6106 Caterpillar/MWM (decision of 19 October 2011), para 14.

20 Case C-633/16 *Ernst & Young P/S v Konkurrencerådet* EU:C:2018:371.

21 ibid, para 39.

22 ibid, para 62.

This case followed a decision by the Commission on 24 April 2018 to impose a fine of €124.5 million on Altice for violating Articles 4(1) and 7(1) in connection with its acquisition of PT Portugal, a direct competitor in certain markets. In that case, the Commission focused on how the parties' substantive conduct led to a de facto change of control "before obtaining the Commission's clearance, and in some cases, even before its notification of the merger".[23] At a high level, the specific conduct at issue included provisions of the purchase agreement through which Altice "acquir[ed] the legal right to exercise decisive influence over PT Portugal, for example by granting Altice veto rights over decisions concerning PT Portugal's ordinary business".[24] In addition, the Commission found that:

> Altice actually exercised decisive influence over aspects of PT Portugal's business, for example by giving PT Portugal instructions on how to carry out a marketing campaign and by seeking and receiving detailed commercially sensitive information about PT Portugal outside the framework of any confidentiality agreement.[25]

In addition, the Commission also cited extensive bilateral exchanges of competitively sensitive information after the conclusion of the diligence process, and without appropriate safeguards, such as clean teams.[26]

More recently, on 27 June 2019 the Commission imposed a fine of €28 million on Canon in connection with the premature implementation of its acquisition of Toshiba Medical Systems Corporation (**TMSC**). This case involved a two-step or "warehousing" transaction. The first step involved the acquisition of 95% of the share capital of TMSC for 800 million by an interim purchaser, established indirectly by Toshiba and Canon. At the same time, Canon acquired the remaining 5% of TMSC shares for €5.28 billion, with an option to acquire the 95% stake. In the second step, Canon exercised the option, acquiring 100% of the shares of TMSC. Only the second step was notified to the Commission for approval.

In its press release, the Commission noted that the first and second steps of the transaction together formed "a single, notifiable merger".[27] The Commission found that the first step "contributed to the acquisition of final control over TMSC, which occurred with the second step … [and was] necessary for Canon to gain control over TMSC." By completing the first step, the Commission concluded that Canon had partially implemented its acquisition of TMSC without prior notification to the Commission. For this reason, the Commission fined Canon €28 million. Canon has indicated its intention to appeal.[28]

---

23 European Commission Press release: "Commission fines Altice €125 million for breaching EU rules and controlling PT Portugal before obtaining merger approval" (24 April 2018) <http://europa.eu/rapid/press-release_IP-18-3522_en.htm>.

24 ibid.

25 ibid.

26 Please refer to the Annex for a more granular review of the types of conduct at issue in *Altice/PT Portugal.*

27 European Commission Press Release, "Mergers: Commission fines Canon €28 million for partially implementing its acquisition of Toshiba Medical Systems Corporation before notification and merger control approval" (27 June 2019) <http://europa.eu/rapid/press-release_IP-19-3429_en.htm>.

28 See MLex, "Canon to appeal EU's EUR 28 million 'gun-jumping' fine" (*MLex Market Insight* 27 June 2019).

Taken together, the current enforcement approach and climate should cause parties to take care to ensure that their pre-closing conduct does not effectively confer control on the purchaser. This requires consideration of the transaction structure and purchase agreement itself, as well as conduct at key stages of the M&A transaction, including the diligence process and planning for the integrated company.

10. In cases involving alleged violations of the standstill obligation under the relevant merger control laws, has the relevant authority (or court) *also* considered the substantive antitrust laws? (Please refer to the Annex.)

To date, the Commission's enforcement of the standstill obligation has been in the context of the EUMR. The Commission has, however, noted the possibility that the substantive antitrust laws, in particular Article 101 TFEU, could also apply.[29]

11. Is private enforcement of the standstill obligation possible?

The European Commission's ultimate decision to approve or prohibit concentrations notified under the EUMR can, under some circumstances, be challenged by private parties. We are not aware of a case in which a private plaintiff has successfully brought an action for a violation of the standstill obligation.

12. Please describe the private law risks/consequences (i.e. contractual/validity consequences) for transactions that are subject to notification, but which are completed without notification/approval. Please identify any relevant cases and describe them.

Violation of the standstill obligation set out in Article 7(1) EUMR can in principle present private law risks/consequences, to the extent that it raises doubts about the legitimacy of a transaction. This risk is largely theoretical, however, given the safeguards contained in Article 7(4), which recognize that the validity of the transaction depends on the ultimate decision of the Commission to approve, conditionally approve or prohibit the transaction.[30] Thus, until the Commission issues such a decision, agreements effecting the transaction are unenforceable, but not void. It follows that violation of the standstill provision itself is unlikely to lead to significant exposure, as courts would be unlikely to rule on any private enforcement claim until the Commission issued its final decision on the transaction's validity.[31] To date we are aware of no significant enforcement directly resulting from a violation of the standstill obligation.

13. Please describe policy and enforcement trends in your jurisdiction.

Please refer to Question 10 above.

---

[29] See e.g. European Commission Memo 07/573 (n 12).

[30] Recital 34 of the EUMR states that "in the interests of legal certainty the validity of transactions must … be protected as much as possible".

[31] See e.g. Case C-234/89 *Delimitis v Henninger Bräu* [1991] ECR I-00935. This case provides some guidance by analogy. It arose in a different context, namely during the then-existing regime by which certain agreements required advance notification to the European Commission. The case involved a challenge to a beer distribution agreement. The Court of Justice ruled that if a national court considered that the Commission could conclude that the agreement did not infringe the antitrust laws, then "the national court may decide to stay the proceedings or to adopt interim measures pursuant to its national rules of procedure. A stay of proceedings or the adoption of interim measures should also be envisaged where there is a risk of conflicting decisions." See also CJ Cook & CS Kerse, *EC Merger Control* (5th edn, Sweet & Maxwell 2009), 149–50.

In addition, it should be noted that the Commission has generally increased its enforcement of procedural infringements of the EUMR, not limited to violations of the standstill obligation. Notably, the Commission has also increased enforcement relating to parties to a notifiable concentration providing the Commission with incorrect or misleading information in violation of the EUMR. The Commission recently imposed a fine on Facebook of €110 million for providing the Commission with incorrect or misleading information in connection with its acquisition of WhatsApp.[32]

The Commission has investigated at least two other cases involving the alleged provision of incorrect of misleading information.[33] This includes General Electric's acquisition of LM Wind, which was notified to and approved by the European Commission in 2017. On 8 April 2019, the European Commission imposed a fine of €52 million on General Electric for providing the Commission with incorrect information in connection with the 2017 review.[34] The Commission is also investigating Merck and Sigma-Aldrich for the provision of incorrect or misleading information in connection with their 2015 concentration which was notified to the Commission in 2015. The Commission's investigation of Merck and Sigma-Aldrich remains pending. The provision of incorrect or misleading information is punishable with a fine of up to 1% of an undertaking's worldwide turnover.[35]

---

32 Case M.8228 *Facebook/WhatsApp* (decision of 17 May 2017).

33 European Commission Press Release (n 15).

34 European Commission, Press Release, "Mergers: European Commission fines General Electric €52 million for providing incorrect information in LM Wind Takeover" (8 April 2019) <http://europa.eu/rapid/press-release_IP-19-2049_en.htm>.

35 EUMR, Article 14.1.

Part 2: Substantive Antitrust Law in an M&A Context

1. **Please identify the relevant *substantive antitrust laws* in your jurisdiction that can potentially apply in an M&A context (e.g. for the EU, this would include Article 101 of the Treaty on the Functioning of the European Union). Please provide a link to the relevant legislation (if possible, in English).**

The primary substantive antitrust laws that can in principle apply in an M&A context are Articles 101 and 102 of the Treaty on the Functioning of the European Union (**TFEU**). Article 101 TFEU prohibits certain restrictive agreements, while Article 102 TFEU prohibits the abuse of a dominant position. As a practical matter, however, the substantive antitrust rules have only rarely been used to control mergers, in particular following the entry into force of the first merger regulation in 1989 (**Merger Regulation**).[36]

Historically, and prior to the introduction of the Merger Regulation, the European Commission concluded in a 1966 Memorandum that Article 85 (now Article 101 TFEU) did not apply to concentrations, but that Article 86 (now Article 102 TFEU) did.[37] The application – at least in principle – of Article 86 by the Commission to prohibit a transaction was confirmed in the landmark 1972 case of *Europemballage Corp and Continental Can Co v Commission*,[38] where the Court ruled that Article 86 prohibits mergers that strengthen a dominant position.[39] Notwithstanding the 1966 Memorandum, in 1987 the Court of Justice revived the possibility that Article 85 EC could be applied to concentrations in *BAT and RJ Reynolds Industries v Commission*.[40] In that case, the Court concluded that the acquisition of equity interests is not prima facie evidence of anticompetitive behavior, but could nevertheless facilitate such behavior.[41]

---

36 See OECD, *Investigations of Consummated and Non-Notifiable Mergers* (2014), para 19.

37 European Commission, "Memorandum on the Problem of Concentrations in the Common Market" (1966) Competition Series, No. 3, para 58, cited in Ethan Schwartz, "Politics as Usual: The History of European Community Merger Control" (1993) 18 Yale J Int'l L, 614, footnote 40.

38 Case C 6/72 *Europemballage Corp and Continental Can Co v Commission* [1973] ECR 215

39 European Commission, "First Report on Competition Policy" (April 1972), paras 81, 87–94 <http://ec.europa.eu/competition/publications/annual_report/ar_1971_en.pdf>.

40 Cases 142 and 156/84 *British-American Tobacco Company Ltd and RJ Reynolds Industries Inc v Commission* [1987] ECR 04487.

41 ibid; See OECD, *Investigations of Consummated and Non-Notifiable Mergers* (2014), para 19.

The Merger Regulation did not supplant the substantive antitrust laws.[42] As a practical matter, however, even if the substantive antitrust laws are theoretically applicable to the parties' conduct in an M&A transaction, enforcement has taken place under the EUMR.[43]

In contrast, transactions that are not subject to the EUMR (e.g. acquisitions of non-controlling minority stakes, the formation/acquisition of non-full-function joint ventures or transactions that lack a Community dimension), are subject to the substantive antitrust rules. In addition, such transactions may also be subject to national merger control laws or substantive antitrust laws of EU Member States.

2. **Do any guidelines exist in your jurisdiction concerning the application of the substantive antitrust laws in an M&A context – whether internal to the relevant authority, or external, formal or informal (e.g. speeches)? If so, please provide a copy/link to such guidance.**

The European Commission has issued guidance concerning the antitrust treatment of horizontal[44] and non-horizontal[45] transactions (in the context of the EUMR), as well as the application of Article 101 TFEU to horizontal cooperation agreements,[46] vertical agreements[47] and technology transfer agreements.[48] These guidelines provide insight into the antitrust treatment of certain concentrations and agreements. However, they do not address the antitrust treatment of certain conduct between parties to a transaction during the life of an M&A transaction, for instance concerning diligence activities and integration planning.

3. **As a general matter (not limited to M&A), how are the substantive antitrust laws enforced with respect to the exchange of competitively sensitive information between competing firms? Please also indicate the relevance of anti-competitive effects or intent in such enforcement.**

As a general matter, the Court of Justice of the European Union has upheld a decision finding that the exchange of competitively sensitive information between competitors infringed Article 101(1) TFEU "by object".[49] It is not necessary to show that an infringement by object led to anticompetitive effects.

The Commission's enforcement of information exchange during an M&A transaction appears largely to have taken place under the EUMR (although the

---

42 Indeed, the first Merger Regulation and the subsequent EUMR recognize the ongoing applicability of Articles 85 and 86 EC (now Articles 101 and 102 TFEU), but note that these provisions are not "sufficient to cover all operations which may prove incompatible with the system of undistorted competition envisaged in the Treaty."

43 European Commission Press release (n 23).

44 European Commission, Guidelines on the assessment of horizontal mergers under the Council Regulation on the control of concentrations between undertakings [2004] OJ C 31.

45 European Commission, Guidelines on the assessment of non-horizontal mergers under the Council Regulation on the control of concentrations between undertakings [2008] OJ C 265.

46 European Commission, Guidelines on the applicability of Article 101 of the Treaty on the Functioning of the European Union to horizontal cooperation agreements [2011] OJ C 11.

47 European Commission, Guidelines on Vertical Restraints [2010] OJ C 130.

48 European Commission, Guidelines on the application of Article 101 of the Treaty on the Functioning of the European Union to technology transfer agreements [2014] OJ C 89.

49 Case C-8/08 *T-Mobile Netherlands BV and others v Raad van bestuur van der Nederlandse Mededingingsautoriteit* [2009] ECR I-04529.

Commission notes the relevance of Article 101 TFEU).[50] Despite limited decisional practice to date, the Commission's guidance concerning the application of Article 101 TFEU to horizontal cooperation agreements[51] provides some insight into its likely approach in an M&A context. In its guidance, the Commission has stated that the legal and economic context of the exchange, and intent, are relevant in determining whether an exchange of information between competitors infringes Article 101 TFEU:

> [a]ny information exchange with the objective of restricting competition on the market will be considered as a restriction of competition by object. In assessing whether an information exchange constitutes a restriction of competition by object, the Commission will pay particular attention to the legal and economic context in which the information exchange takes place.[52]

The legal and economic context of an M&A transaction is unique, as it will necessarily involve exchanges of competitively sensitive information between parties – who may be competitors – that would not otherwise occur. Indeed, the need for such exchanges appears to be at least implicitly recognized by the Commission, which states in its guidelines concerning remedies that:

> [c]ommitments should foresee that potential purchasers can carry out a due diligence exercise and obtain, dependent on the stage of the procedure, sufficient information concerning the divested business to allow the purchaser to fully assess the value, scope and commercial potential of the business, and have direct access to its personnel.[53]

This statement broadly reflects the need for exchange of competitively sensitive information that occurs in every M&A transaction, as acquiring parties need to conduct diligence to assess the full value of a business and adequately plan for its integration. Taken together, it appears that the Commission is likely to consider the specific circumstances of an M&A transaction in any assessment of whether an exchange of competitively sensitive information infringed Article 101 TFEU. The Commission has not issued guidance confirming this approach.

4. **Have there been any cases in your jurisdiction in which the substantive antitrust laws were enforced in an M&A context? Please describe/explain and cite any such cases. (See also Annex.)**

   Please refer to the responses to Questions 1 and 3.

5. **Are the substantive antitrust laws more likely to apply at specific stages of the transaction – i.e. at an early stage, or prior to closing (or does it not make a**

---

50 See e.g. Cases cited in Part 1 of this Questionnaire. See also European Commission Press Release, "Mergers: Commission has carried out inspections in the S-PVC sector" (n 12), noting applicability of Article 81 (now Article 101 TFEU).

51 See n 44.

52 ibid, para 72.

53 European Commission, Commission notice on remedies acceptable under Council Regulation (EC) No 139/2004 and under Commission Regulation (EC) No 802/2004 [2008] OJ C 267, para 116.

difference)? Do companies face ongoing risk following the consummation (or failure) of their transaction for conduct that allegedly occurred pre-closing (pre-failure)?

At this point, the Commission and court decisions do not provide a picture of the relative risk during the life of an M&A transaction. Indeed, the announcement of the recent Altice decision (albeit under the EUMR) is suggestive of conduct that could occur either pre- or post-signing. Thus, the specific state of a transaction may not make a significant difference in the relative risk that parties to an M&A transaction face.

In terms of ongoing risk for anticompetitive conduct, the Commission has three years to begin proceedings for alleged infringements of the EUMR.[54] The limitation period applicable to Article 101 TFEU can be found in Regulation 1/2003, which provides for a five-year limitation period.

6. **Please explain how the relevant authority enforces (or could enforce) the substantive antitrust laws in an M&A context. How would the investigation occur, and what timing constraints would apply?**

The substantive antitrust rules can be applied to M&A transactions that do not meet the EUMR thresholds for notification. A notable example is the abandoned plan for a production joint venture between Rio Tinto and BHP Billiton.[55] This transaction was not subject to the EUMR because it was not a "full-function" joint venture. Nevertheless, the Commission investigated the transaction under Article 101 TFEU. It is important to note that the time constraints that apply to transactions reviewed under the EUMR do not apply to investigations involving Article 101 TFEU, which are not time-limited and are subject to the procedural rules set out in Regulation 1/2003.

7. **Is private enforcement of the substantive antitrust laws possible in an M&A context, and has it occurred?**

Under settled case law and legislation, it is well established that private claimants may seek damages resulting from a violation of the substantive antitrust laws.[56] We are not, however, aware of successful private enforcement of M&A transactions using either Article 101 or 102 TFEU.

8. **Could behavior subject to the substantive antitrust laws also be caught under the merger control rules/standstill obligation? (Please also refer to the Annex.)**

Yes, at least in principle. Concentrations subject to the EUMR are in principle subject to both the EUMR and the substantive antitrust rules. To date, cases involving conduct that could be reviewed under the EUMR and substantive antitrust rules

---

54 Council Regulation (EEC) No. 2988/74, Art. 1 (discussed in para 95 of Case M.8228 *Facebook/Whatsapp* (decision of 17 May 2017)).

55 See European Commission, DG Competition's Management Plan 2011,18 <http://ec.europa.eu/competition/publications/annual_management_plan/amp_2011_en.pdf>.

56 See Directive 2014/104/EU of the European Parliament and of the Council of 26 November 2014 on certain rules governing actions for damages under national law for infringements of the competition law provisions of the Member States and of the European Union [2014] OJ L 349; see also Case C-453/99 *Courage v Crehan* [2001] ECR I-6297 and Joined Cases C-295/04–298/04, *Manfredi v Lloyd Adriatico Assicurazioni SpA and others* [2006] ECR I-6619.

(such as information exchange or pre-closing coordination) have been enforced under the EUMR.[57]

M&A transactions not subject to the EUMR are subject only to the substantive antitrust rules, and/or the merger control rules and substantive antitrust rules of EU Member States. Such M&A transactions include, for example, non-full-function joint ventures, acquisition of minority stakes that do not confer control and transactions that lack a Community dimension.

9. Please describe the penalties for infringing the substantive antitrust laws. Please indicate whether these include criminal penalties, including individual criminal penalties. As a practical matter, how have these been applied in the context of an M&A transaction?

As a general matter, companies found to have infringed Articles 101 and 102 TFEU are subject to a fine of up to 10% of group worldwide turnover, as well as injunctive relief. Articles 101 and 102 TFEU do not include criminal penalties. As discussed in Part 1, enforcement of antitrust violations in the context of M&A transactions have been based on the EUMR, including resulting penalties.

10. Please describe policy and enforcement trends in your jurisdiction.

The primary developments in the enforcement of the parties' conduct in M&A transactions relates to enforcement under the EUMR, not the substantive antitrust rules. We note, however, that the substantive antitrust rules form an important part of the Commission's enforcement tools with regard to M&A transactions, in particular for transactions that are not subject to the EUMR.[58]

Jean-Christophe Mauger, Massimiliano Kadar, "The EU Commission fines a leading company in salmon farming €20 million for breaching the standstill obligation and failing to meet notification requirements (Marine Harvest/Morpol)" 23 July 2014, e-Competitions Bulletin July 2014, Art. N° 69953

David Tayar, "Failure to notify: The European Commission fines the purchaser €20 million for taking control without prior EU merger clearance (Marine Harvest/Morpol)" 23 July 2014, Concurrences Review N° 4-2014, Art. N° 69965,

Caroline Ruiz Palmer, Andrea L Hamilton, David Henry, "The EU Court of Justice provides guidance on the merger notification obligation in the EU regulation (Ernst & Young)" 31 May 2018, e-Competitions Bulletin May 2018, Art. N° 88783

Eric David, Marco Plankensteiner, "The EU Court of Justice puts an end to the extensive interpretation by some competition authorities of the concept of gun jumping (Ernst & Young)" 31 May 2018, e-Competitions Bulletin May 2018, Art. N° 87374

---

57 See cases discussed in Part 1 of this Questionnaire.

58 See e.g. IBA Antitrust Committee, "Submission to the European Commission's Directorate General for Competition regarding the consultation on evaluation of procedural and jurisdictional aspects of EU merger control" 13 January 2017 <https://www.ibanet.org/LPD/Antitrust-Section/Antitrust/WorkingGroupSubmissions.aspx>.

Paul Culliford, Robert Bell, "The EU Court of Justice clarifies the scope of gun jumping prohibition by excluding cooperation agreements which don't contribute to the change in control of the target business (Ernst & Young)" 31 May 2018, e-Competitions Bulletin May 2018, Art. N° 88520

Porter Elliott, "The EU Commission publishes decision refusing derogation from standstill obligation in merger case in the consumer goods industry (SC Johnson/Sara Lee)" 11 February 2011, e-Competitions Bulletin February 2011, Art. N° 58281

John Gatti, Mary Loughran, "The European Commission conditionally approves an acquisition in the explosives and detonators industry (Orica/Dyno Nobel)" 23 May 2006, e-Competitions Bulletin May 2006, Art. N° 38260

John Gatti, Mary Loughran, "The European Commission conditionally clears a merger in the fertilizers industry (Yara/Kemira GrowHow)" 21 September 2007, e-Competitions Bulletin September 2007, Art. N° 37721

Guillaume Fabre, Olivier Billard, "Gun-jumping: The European Commission fines an undertaking for the early implementation of a concentration stemming from the clauses of the share purchase agreement and from the intervention of the acquirer into the commercial strategy of the target (Altice/PT Portugal)" 24 April 2018, Concurrences Review N° 4-2018, Art. N° 88262

Jean-François Bellis, Valérie Lefever, "Gun jumping: The European Commission imposes a fine of EUR 125.5 million to a multinational cable and telecommunications company based in the Netherlands for implementing its acquisition of the Portuguese telecommunications operator before notification or approval by the European Commission (Altice/PT Portugal)" 24 April 2018, Concurrences Review N° 3-2018, Art. N° 87789

Charles Bankes, Satyen Dhana, Peter Broadhurst, Ombline Ancelin, Koen Platteau, Peter Meyer, "The EU Commission publishes its decision in a gun-jumping case (Altice/PT Portugal)" 24 April 2018, e-Competitions Bulletin April 2018, Art. N° 87903

Porter Elliott, "The EU Commission imposes record €125 million fine to a multinational cable and telecommunications company for gun jumping (Altice/PT Portugal)" 24 April 2018, e-Competitions Bulletin April 2018, Art. N° 86838

Geraldine Emberger, John Kemp, "The European Commission fines a Korean electronic equipment manufacturer for failing to notify a merger (Samsung/AST)" 18 February 1998, e-Competitions Bulletin February 1998, Art. N° 39433

John Gatti, Mary Loughran, "The European Commission clears an acquisition in the production of PVC (Ineos/Kerling)" 30 January 2008, e-Competitions Bulletin January 2008, Art. N° 37716

Sergio Sorinas, Estelle Jegou, "The EU Commission unconditionally clears an acquisition in the genset sector (Caterpillar/MWM)" 19 October 2011, e-Competitions Bulletin October 2011, Art. N° 51790

Alain Ronzano, "Gun jumping: The European Commission sanctions a gun jumping for the fourth time (Canon/Toshiba Medical Systems)" 27 June 2019, Concurrences Review N° 2-2019, Art. N° 90938

Sara Ashall, James Webber, Matthew Readings, "The EU Commission imposes a fine of €28 million for "gun-jumping" on a Japanese manufacturer of imaging and optical products (Canon)" 27 June 2019, Bulletin e-Competitions June 2019, Art. N° 91012

Nicholas Levy, Maurits Dolmans, Christopher Cook, Francisco Enrique González-Díaz, Thomas Graf, François-Charles Laprévote, "The EU Commission fines a company for providing incorrect or misleading information during its investigations on a merger (Facebook/WhatsApp)" 18 May 2017, e-Competitions Bulletin May 2017, Art. N° 84276

Porter Elliott, "The EU Commission fines a company €52 million for providing incorrect information during merger review (General Electric", 8 April 2019, e-Competitions Bulletin April 2019, Art. N° 90354

José Rivas, "The European Court of Justice clarifies the notion of concerted practice and holds that a single meeting amongst competitors where they exchanged sensitive information can be caught by EU Antitrust rules (T-Mobile Netherlands)" 4 June 2009, e-Competitions Bulletin June 2009, Art. N° 35319

Eddy de Smijter, Denis O'Sullivan, "The European Court of Justice renders a preliminary ruling under article 234 EC considering issues raised in the European Commission's Green Paper on antitrust damages actions (Manfredi)" 13 July 2006, e-Competitions Bulletin July 2006, Art. N° 36562

Fabien Zivy," Action for damages: The ECJ holds that one must wait a little in order to know more (Manfredi)" 13 July 2006, Concurrences Review N° 4-2006, Art. N° 12495

Annex

Table 1: Actual Enforcement of Specific Conduct under the Relevant Merger Control Rules and Substantive Antitrust Laws

Please identify whether the following type of conduct has been subject to investigation/enforcement in your jurisdiction, under the merger control laws or substantive antitrust laws. Please cite any such case(s) and provide a brief description in the table below.

Specific Conduct	Actual Enforcement under Merger Control Laws	Actual Enforcement under Substantive Antitrust Laws
Pre-signing due diligence	In *Altice/PT Portugal* (Art 14(2) Procedure) The Commission recognized that "exchanges of business-related information between a potential acquirer and a vendor could be, if properly conducted, a normal part of the acquisition process, if the nature and purpose of such exchanges are directly related to the acquirer's need to assess the value of the business. Such situations normally arise as part of a due diligence process."[1]	Article 101 TFEU is in principle available to enforce the type of conduct referenced in this table. However, we are not aware of decisions to date that rely on Article 101 TFEU in relation to this conduct in an M&A context.

59 Case M.7993 *Altice/PT Portugal* (decision of 24 April 2018), para 437.

Specific Conduct	Actual Enforcement under Merger Control Laws	Actual Enforcement under Substantive Antitrust Laws
Pre-signing due diligence	However, and as a general matter, bilateral exchanges of information can be problematic where they take place "in the absence of any type of confidentiality arrangement, be it a clean-team-type of structure or any other measure aimed at limiting the number of individuals who would have access to the information and/or circulation".[2] Indeed, the exchange of information between companies before receiving the Commission's decision, without appropriate safeguards, was cited by the Commission as one of the factors contributing to its decision that Altice exercised decisive control over the target, thus infringing the EUMR.[3]	Article 101 TFEU is in principle available to enforce the type of conduct referenced in this table. However, we are not aware of decisions to date that rely on Article 101 TFEU in relation to this conduct in an M&A context.
Post-signing/pre-approval due diligence	See above	See above
Post-approval/pre-closing due diligence	See above	See above

60 *Altice/PT Portugal*, 438. It should be noted that the *Altice/PT Portugal* decision is in the context of bilateral exchanges between direct competitors (in certain markets) that extended beyond the diligence process.

61 *Altice/PT Portugal*, para 448. The Commission stated that the exchange of "strategic detailed information on the Target's commercial policy" and other information, together with other elements, show that "Altice exercised decisive influence over certain conducts pertaining to the Target".

Specific Conduct	Actual Enforcement under Merger Control Laws	Actual Enforcement under Substantive Antitrust Laws
Use of "clean teams"	See above. As a general matter, the Commission in *Alitice/PT Portugal* implied that the use of clean teams, alongside confidentiality agreements, can be a safeguard associated with legitimate and necessary exchanges of information between competitors in an M&A context.[4]	See above
Restrictions on the target in an M&A agreement, e.g. buyer approval required for: Investments above a certain level; New business above a certain level; Other obligations to consult/obtain approval from the buyer before closing.	Restrictions on the target in the M&A agreement were among the key conduct cited by the Commission in *Altice/PT Portugal*, which found that Altice infringed the EUMR by exercising decisive influence over the target before the Commission issued its clearance decision. This includes what the Commission characterized as: – Requiring acquirer approval for "the appointment, dismissal and changes to the terms of any officer or director".[5]	See above

62 *Altice/PT Portugal*, paras 53, 438. See also footnotes 60 and 221 for the Commission's definition of "clean team".

63 *Altice/PT Portugal*, paras 74–77. The Commission noted that "having a degree of oversight regarding the personnel of a target may be justified in order to preserve the value of the business between signing and closing… However, having a veto right over the appointment, dismissal and changes to the terms of employment of any officer or director goes beyond what is necessary for the purposes of value preservation and enables the acquirer to influence the commercial policy of the target."

Specific Conduct	Actual Enforcement under Merger Control Laws	Actual Enforcement under Substantive Antitrust Laws
Restrictions on the target in an M&A agreement, e.g. buyer approval required for: – Investments above a certain level; – New business above a certain level; – Other obligations to consult/obtain approval from the buyer before closing.	– Requiring acquirer approval relating to target's pricing policies and commercial terms.[6] – Requiring approval from the purchaser entering into, terminating or modifying contracts – with a low monetary threshold,[7] thus encompassing ordinary course activity.[8]	See above
Joint marketing	In *Altice/PT Portugal*, the Commission cited the involvement of the acquirer in the target's marketing campaign, and the related exchange of competitively sensitive information on a bilateral basis without appropriate safeguards, as indications that the acquirer exercised decisive influence over aspects of the target's business before receiving the Commission's clearance decision, thus infringing the EUMR.[9]	See above

64 *Altice/PT Portugal*, paras 78–84. The Commission clearly states that "the Commission does not consider that having the power to determine a target's pricing policies is either a valid or justifiable manner in which to preserve the value of a target business between signing and closing, regardless of whether the clause purportedly excludes pricing matters that fall within the ordinary course of business." (para 149).

65 The Commission further stated that monetary thresholds reflect what is strictly needed to preserve the value of the target business. See *Altice/PT Portugal*, paras 167, 583–4.

66 *Altice/PT Portugal*, paras 85–108.

67 *Altice/PT Portugal*. The campaign at issue related to a "post-paid mobile campaign targeted at the consumer segment in Portugal." (para 181).

Specific Conduct	Actual Enforcement under Merger Control Laws	Actual Enforcement under Substantive Antitrust Laws
Joint presentations (e.g. industry fairs)	We are not aware of enforcement to date covering joint presentations. However, given the extent of conduct encompassed in *Altice/PT Portugal*, it follows that joint presentations can – at least in principle – raise antitrust risks under merger control laws, especially if combined with other conduct.	See above
Joint communications	We are not aware of enforcement to date covering joint communications. However, given the extent of conduct encompassed in *Altice/PT Portugal*, it follows that joint communications can – at least in principle – raise antitrust risks under merger control laws, especially if combined with other conduct.	See above
Strategy/planning regarding customers	The *Altice/PT Portugal* decision suggests that joint strategy/planning relating to customers prior to receiving the Commission's clearance decision can raise antitrust risks.[10]	See above

▶

68 *Altice/PT Portugal*, paras 353–71. The Commission cited Altice's direct involvement in a decision regarding investments necessary to fulfill a customer contract. The contract itself was, in the Commission's view, too small to be "material" and the conduct also involved the bilateral exchange of competitively sensitive information.

Specific Conduct	Actual Enforcement under Merger Control Laws	Actual Enforcement under Substantive Antitrust Laws
Strategy/planning regarding suppliers	The *Altice/PT Portugal* decision identified both the acquirer's involvement in the renewal of a third-party supply contract, and in the separate selection and negotiation with other suppliers, as contributing to its conclusion that the acquirer exercised decisive influence over aspects of the target's business, thus infringing the EUMR.[11]	See above
Third party contract novation	In *KPMG*, the CJEU found that contract termination (by analogy, relevant to contract novation) infringes only if the conduct "in whole or in part, in fact or in law, contributes to the change of control of the target…"	See above
Personnel Issues: – Secondments – Retention Strategies	In *Altice/PT Portugal*, the Commission identified provisions in the M&A agreement that required acquirer approval for "the appointment, dismissal and changes to the terms of any officer or director"[12] as contributing to its conclusion that the acquirer exercised decisive influence over aspects of the target's business, thus infringing the EUMR.[13]	See above

69 *Altice/PT Portugal*, paras 220–304.

70 *Altice/PT Portugal*, paras 74–7. The Commission noted that "having a degree of oversight regarding the personnel of a target may be justified in order to preserve the value of the business between signing and closing […] However, having a veto right over the appointment, dismissal and changes to the terms of employment of any officer or director goes beyond what is necessary for the purposes of value preservation and enables the acquirer to influence the commercial policy of the target."

71 *Altice/PT Portugal*, paras 74–6. It should be noted, however, that the Commission considered that oversight regarding personnel may be appropriate "in respect of, for example, the retention of key employees who are integral to the value of the business, or in order to prevent material changes to the cost basis of the business" (para 75).

Specific Conduct	Actual Enforcement under Merger Control Laws	Actual Enforcement under Substantive Antitrust Laws
IT Planning/Database Migration	We are not aware of enforcement to date involving IT planning/ database migration	See above
Other	In *Canon/Toshiba*, the Commission concluded that a "two-step" warehousing structure can lead to premature implementation.[14]	

Table 2: Hypothetical Enforcement of Specific Conduct under the Relevant Merger Control Rules and Substantive Antitrust Laws

For any conduct that is *not* the subject of actual enforcement (Table 1), please indicate in the Table below whether the conduct identified *could potentially* be enforced under the merger control laws and/or substantive antitrust laws.

Please refer to the table above. As there have been relatively few investigations and decisions to date, the responses would not likely materially differ.

---

72 See Response to Question 9. See also European Commission Press Release, "Mergers: Commission fines Canon €28 million for partially implementing its acquisition of Toshiba Medical Systems Corporation before notification and merger control approval" (27 June 2019).

FINLAND

Niko Hukkinen
(Frontia)

Part 1: Merger Control and the "Standstill Obligation"

1. **Please identify the relevant merger control legislation in your jurisdiction. Please provide a link to the relevant legislation (if possible, in English) and also indicate:**
   - **whether the merger control system is mandatory or voluntary,**
   - **the relevant authority, and**
   - **the duration of the review period.**

   Merger control is governed on a national level by the Finnish Competition Act (no. 948/2011, as amended) (**Competition Act**).[1]

   According to section 21 of the Competition Act, it is **mandatory** to notify a concentration to the Finnish Competition and Consumer Authority (**FCCA**) if certain prescribed turnover thresholds are exceeded.

   The FCCA has no right to investigate transactions that fall below the turnover thresholds, although the FCCA has recently opined that an amendment changing this is needed to the Competition Act.

   In the first phase, within 23 working days from submission of a complete notification, the FCCA shall conclude that the transaction will not be caught by the Competition Act, decide to clear the concentration as such or with conditions, or decide to initiate a second-phase investigation. The concentration will be deemed approved if the FCCA fails to take any measures within the deadline.

   If the FCCA decides to initiate a second-phase investigation it must, within 69 working days (with a possible further extension of 46 working days by application to the Market Court) of such decision, either clear the concentration as such or with conditions, or request the Market Court to block it. Having received the FCCA's request to block a concentration, the Market Court has to clear the concentration as it is, clear it with conditions or prohibit the concentration within three months.

2. **Does the merger control system in your jurisdiction impose a "*standstill obligation*" – meaning, that the transaction cannot be implemented prior to completing the merger control process? (Please cite the relevant legislation.) Please also indicate the *legal scope* of the standstill obligation according to the relevant legislation (e.g. the parties to the transaction cannot effect a change of control, cannot take steps towards implementation, etc.).**

---

1 Official Act: <https://www.finlex.fi/fi/laki/ajantasa/2011/20110948>; FCCA's unofficial non-binding translation: <https://www.kkv.fi/en/facts-and-advice/competition-affairs/legislation-and-guidelines/competition-act/>.

Pursuant to section 27 of the Competition Act, **no measures** may be taken to put the concentration into effect prior to its clearance. However, when the Market Court is investigating a concentration upon the FCCA's request to block it, the prohibition to implement the concentration ceases after one month from such request, unless the Market Court orders the suspension to continue.

3. Have the relevant authorities in your jurisdiction issued internal or external guidelines concerning the scope of the standstill obligation, and/or their authority to enforce it? Please provide a copy/link of such guidance, if possible in English.

The FCCA has not issued guidelines concerning the standstill obligation specifically. However, the FCCA has issued general merger control guidelines.[2]

4. Are there any exceptions to the standstill obligation – for example, through derogation or "carve out"? Please describe the circumstances in which this is possible. Please also describe the relevant process, e.g. do parties need to apply to the authority for a derogation from the standstill obligation? If so, how long is the approval process? If there are specific cases addressing these issues, please identify them.

The FCCA may grant full or partial exemption from the standstill obligation upon request during the investigation period. If an exemption is granted, it is only briefly mentioned in the main final FCCA decision concerning the transaction in question, and there is no public information available on the FCCA's reasoning or length of the review process. In general, the FCCA can be expected to grant an exemption rather swiftly (approximately one week) in straightforward cases where no competition concerns are foreseen. On the other hand, if the deal is substantively problematic, an exemption can be expected to require rather strong justifications going beyond insignificant costs or administrative inconvenience caused by a delayed implementation, and also that the exempted implementation measures are reversible.

Partial closings and carve-out arrangements (i.e. to close the transaction in other jurisdictions but not in Finland, pending receipt of the FCCA's clearance) are not acceptable without a formal exemption from the FCCA.

5. Does a public bid exception exist in your jurisdiction? (For example, under the EU Merger Regulation it is possible to acquire shares as part of a public bid, provided that the shares are not exercised until the acquisition is cleared by the Commission.) If such an exception exists in your jurisdiction, please describe how it is applied.

Yes. A party that has launched a public bid can purchase the shares offered prior to clearance, but it may not use its voting rights until the FCCA has cleared the concentration. This also applies in certain cases where shares are redeemed.

6. What powers does the relevant authority have to investigate and enforce violations of the standstill obligation? Are dawn raids possible? What timing applies to investigation/enforcement proceedings?

---

2 English translation: <https://www.kkv.fi/globalassets/kkv-suomi/julkaisut/suuntaviivat/en/guidelines-1-2011-mergers.pdf>.

There are no specific rules on the FCCA's powers to investigate and enforce violations of the standstill obligation. However, pursuant to section 35 of the Competition Act, the FCCA may conduct dawn raids to supervise compliance with the Competition Act and any subsequent rules issued under it, and to assess concentrations. In practice, the FCCA has also carried out dawn raids in merger control investigations, although apparently not yet to investigate violations of standstill obligation. The FCCA may also oblige undertakings to provide all the information and documents needed to assess a concentration.

There are no binding time limits for the FCAA to reach a decision in a gun-jumping investigation. In general, depending on the complexity of the substance of the case, it can be expected that the decision by the FCCA is issued within two years.

7. What are the possible penalties for violating the standstill obligation? Are there criminal sanctions, including on individuals? Have these been applied in practice? Is there a difference in enforcement between transactions involving domestic companies and "foreign-to-foreign" transactions? Does the authority have the power to unwind transactions implemented in breach of the standstill obligation? If so, has the authority made use of that power in practice? If yes, please provide examples.

If a concentration is implemented before clearance, a fine of up to 10% of the total worldwide turnover of the relevant undertaking (group of companies) may be imposed. The fine is imposed by the Market Court upon proposal by the FCCA. The amount of the fine shall be based on an overall assessment, and in determining the amount, attention shall be paid to the nature and extent, the degree of gravity, and the duration of the infringement. A fine shall be imposed, unless the infringement is considered minor or the imposition of a fine is otherwise unnecessary for purposes of safeguarding competition.

Furthermore, the Market Court may – upon the proposal of the FCCA – prohibit a concentration or order it to be dissolved, for example, by requiring the undertakings concerned or assets brought together to be separated or by requiring the cessation of the joint control. Instead of prohibiting the concentration, the Market Court may also attach conditions on its clearance. The proposal to the Market Court by the FCCA must be notified to the parties within one year from the closing of the transaction.

These sanctions apply irrespective of whether the transaction involves foreign or purely domestic companies.

There are no decisions so far where sanctions were proposed by the FCCA for violations of the standstill obligation.

A violation of the standstill obligation does not give rise to criminal sanctions in Finland.

8. How does the relevant authority typically learn of potential violations of the standstill obligation? Does the authority actively monitor the trade press?

The FCCA actively monitors trade press and local newspapers. In addition, both companies and private individuals are able to submit anonymous tips to the FCCA.

9. Please describe the relevant authority's enforcement of the standstill obligation. If there have been cases, please describe the specific conduct that was

found to violate the standstill provision and the criteria applied by the relevant authority or court. Has the relevant authority considered the market impact of the conduct? (Please refer to the Annex.)

The Finnish case law is rather scarce with regard to the standstill obligation. There are no cases where the FCCA has proposed the imposition of fines to the Market Court. However, two recent cases can be mentioned where the FCCA has carried out a more detailed analysis of the situation.

In *St1 Oy/Lämpöpuisto Oy*, the transaction agreement had been signed on 17 June 2016 and the transaction implemented on 1 August 2016, but the notification submitted to the FCCA only on 2 February 2017. St1 Oy claimed that the failure to file resulted from an erroneous assessment by the parties and that the concentration was notified to the FCCA immediately after the mistake was discovered.

In *VR-Yhtymä Oy/Avecra Oy*, the transaction agreement had been signed on 23 May 2017, after which the purchase price had been paid and VR-Yhtymä had also appointed member to the board of Avecra. The concentration was notified to the FCCA on 16 June 2017. According to VR-Yhtymä, it had for several different reasons been difficult to assess whether the concentration was notifiable or not, which resulted in the failure to file. Upon discovery of the mistake, all other implementing measures had immediately been suspended and a notification submitted.

In both cases the FCCA noted that failure to file and gun-jumping are serious infringements but that there was no need to impose a fine in the particular cases. The FCCA's assessment was based on the fact that the failure to file was due to a genuine mistake, which was immediately rectified when discovered, and that the concentrations in questions did not have negative effects on market competition.

10. In cases involving alleged violations of the standstill obligation under the relevant merger control laws, has the relevant authority (or court) *also* considered the substantive antitrust laws? (Please refer to the Annex.)

Based on publicly available information there are no such cases.

11. Is private enforcement of the standstill obligation possible?

It is only the Market Court that can, following a proposal from the FCCA, impose sanctions for violations of the standstill obligation. Violation of the standstill obligation does not affect the validity of the transaction as such, and thus it is not possible for a Civil Court to nullify the transaction agreements. Therefore, it seems that potentially the main private enforcement possibility would be a claim for damages caused by a standstill violation.

12. Please describe the private law risks/consequences (i.e. contractual/validity consequences) for transactions that are subject to notification, but which are completed without notification/approval. Please identify any relevant cases and describe them.

See Question 12 above. There are no relevant cases in Finland.

13. Please describe policy and enforcement trends in your jurisdiction.

There are no particular policy or enforcement trends related to the standstill obligation in Finland. The FCCA has publicly stated that it closely follows possible gun-jumping violations and that it is prepared to take action when needed.

Part 2:
Substantive Antitrust Law in an M&A Context

1. **Please identify the relevant *substantive antitrust laws* in your jurisdiction that can potentially apply in an M&A context (e.g. for the EU, this would include Article 101 of the Treaty on the Functioning of the European Union). Please provide a link to the relevant legislation (if possible, in English).**

The relevant legislation is the Competition Act, which entered into force on 1 November 2011.[3]

Section 5 of the Competition Act, concerning agreements restrictive of competition, is in essence equivalent to Article 101 of the Treaty on the Functioning of the European Union (**TFEU**), and it also applies in an M&A context.

2. **Do any guidelines exist in your jurisdiction concerning the application of the substantive antitrust laws in an M&A context – whether internal to the relevant authority, or external, formal or informal (e.g. speeches)? If so, please provide a copy/link to such guidance.**

There are no specific guidelines concerning substantive antitrust laws in an M&A context. However, the FCCA's general merger control guidelines[4] mention (p25) that non-full-function joint ventures and agreements that regulate the commercial behavior of undertakings (with the exception of ancillary restraints) are reviewed under sections 5–7 of the Competition Act (equivalent to Articles 101 and 102 TFEU).

3. **As a general matter (not limited to M&A), how are the substantive antitrust laws enforced with respect to the exchange of competitively sensitive information between competing firms? Please also indicate the relevance of anticompetitive effects or intent in such enforcement.**

The rules in Finland are broadly similar to those in the EU. If the exchange of competitively sensitive information is part of an anticompetitive agreement between competing undertakings, e.g. a cartel agreement, the information exchange is considered part of the same violation of section 5 of the Competition Act. However, exchange of sensitive information may also in itself violate the prohibition against anticompetitive cooperation. The effects analysis is normally an instrumental part of an information exchange investigation, but information exchange can also constitute an infringement by object.

---

3 Official Act: <https://www.finlex.fi/fi/laki/ajantasa/2011/20110948>; FCCA's unofficial non-binding English translation: <https://www.kkv.fi/en/facts-and-advice/competition-affairs/legislation-and-guidelines/competition-act/>.

4 English version: <https://www.kkv.fi/globalassets/kkv-suomi/julkaisut/suuntaviivat/en/guidelines-1-2011-mergers.pdf>.

It should be noted that the FCCA requires (and issues frequent reminders) that the parties to a transaction may not exchange sensitive information before the implementation of the transaction. This may require the creation of separate clean teams or similar precautionary arrangements.

If the FCCA suspects illegal information exchange in the context of M&A (or otherwise), it will open a formal investigation under section 5 of the Competition Act. The FCCA may conduct dawn raids, order parties to supply inform and require persons who are likely to be in a position to provide relevant information to appear at a hearing to investigate potentially illegal information exchange. The FCCA can propose the imposition of fines to the Market Court, the maximum amount being 10% of the annual global turnover of the undertakings concerned.

4. **Have there been any cases in your jurisdiction in which the substantive antitrust laws were enforced in an M&A context? Please describe/explain and cite any such cases. (See also Annex.)**

Apart from the cases mentioned in Part 1 regarding early implementation of transactions, there are no cases related to enforcement of substantive antitrust laws in an M&A context.

5. **Are the substantive antitrust laws more likely to apply at specific stages of the transaction – i.e. at an early stage, or prior to closing (or does it not make a difference)? Do companies face ongoing risk following the consummation (or failure) of their transaction for conduct that allegedly occurred pre-closing (pre-failure)?**

Substantive antitrust laws apply during all stages of the transaction. However, the risk of exchange of sensitive information (or other anticompetitive cooperation) could in practice peak during the due diligence phase and possible in-depth investigation phase as the time between signing and closing is prolonged.

The merger control clearance and closing of the transaction do not remove the risk of investigations for conduct that occurred pre-closing or pre-clearance.

For the purposes of the administrative fine, the limitation period with regard to violations of substantive antitrust laws in an M&A context, as well for the breach of the standstill obligation, is five years from the infringement or, in the case of a continuous infringement, within five years of the date on which the violation ended (it can be questioned whether the closing of a transaction is a one-off infringement or a continuous one). On the other hand, the Market Court can order the dissolution of a transaction or impose conditions on a transaction only if the FCCA has submitted a proposal to that effect to the Market Court within one year from the closing of the transaction.

6. **Please explain how the relevant authority enforces (or could enforce) the substantive antitrust laws in an M&A context. How would the investigation occur, and what timing constraints would apply?**

Enforcement and investigation in an M&A context would be similar to a normal investigation of anticompetitive conduct on the market, i.e. the FCCA opens a separate investigation under section 5 of the Competition Act.

The FCCA can open an investigation on its own initiative or based on a complaint or hint, carry out dawn raids, order parties to supply information and require persons who are likely to be in a position to provide relevant information to appear at a hearing. Fines cannot be imposed unless a proposal has been made to the Market Court within five years of the date of the violation, or in the case of a continuous infringement, within five years of the date on which the violation ended. FCCA measures to investigate the infringement reset the limitation period.

7. Is private enforcement of the substantive antitrust laws possible in an M&A context, and has it occurred?

Yes, private enforcement based on violations of substantive antitrust laws in an M&A context is possible. Mainly this could mean private actions for damages or claims based on the nullity of illegal agreements. No relevant case law exists so far.

8. Could behavior subject to the substantive antitrust laws also be caught under the merger control rules/standstill obligation? (Please also refer to the Annex.)

Behavior such as coordination between the merging parties or exchanges of information before closing of the transaction can violate both the merger control standstill obligation and section 5 of the Competition Act.

9. Please describe the penalties for infringing the substantive antitrust laws. Please indicate whether these include criminal penalties, including individual criminal penalties. As a practical matter, how have these been applied in the context of an M&A transaction?

The main penalty for infringing substantive antitrust law in Finland is administrative fines, which may not exceed 10% of the annual global turnover of an undertaking concerned. The FCCA does not have the authority to impose fines on its own, but only to make a proposal of fines to the Market Court.

Criminal penalties cannot be imposed under Finnish law, neither on the companies nor on individuals.

10. Please describe policy and enforcement trends in your jurisdiction.

There are no particular policy or enforcement trends related to substantive antitrust laws in an M&A context in Finland.

Annex

Table 1: Actual Enforcement of Specific Conduct under the Relevant Merger Control Rules and Substantive Antitrust Laws

Please identify whether the following type of conduct has been subject to investigation/enforcement in your jurisdiction, under the merger control laws or substantive antitrust laws. Please cite any such case(s) and provide a brief description in the table below.

Specific Conduct	Actual Enforcement under Merger Control Laws	Actual Enforcement under Substantive Antitrust Laws
Pre-signing due diligence	No	No
Post-signing/pre-approval due diligence	No	No
Post-approval/pre-closing due diligence	No	No
Use of "clean teams"	No	No
Restrictions on the target in an M&A agreement, e.g. buyer approval required for: – Investments above a certain level; – New business above a certain level; – Other obligations to consult/obtain approval from the buyer before closing.	No	No
Joint marketing	No	No
Joint presentations (e.g. industry fairs)	No	No
Joint communications	No	No
Strategy/planning regarding customers	No	No
Strategy/planning regarding suppliers	No	No

Specific Conduct	Actual Enforcement under Merger Control Laws	Actual Enforcement under Substantive Antitrust Laws
Third party contract novation	No	No
Personnel Issues: Secondments Retention Strategies	No	No
IT Planning/Database Migration	No	No
Other	No	No

There exists no public information suggesting that any of the conduct in the table has been investigated by the FCCA.

Table 2: Hypothetical Enforcement of Specific Conduct under the Relevant Merger Control Rules and Substantive Antitrust Laws

For any conduct that is *not* the subject of actual enforcement (Table 1), please indicate in the Table below whether the conduct identified *could potentially* be enforced under the merger control laws and/or substantive antitrust laws.

Specific Conduct	Hypothetical Enforcement under Merger Control Laws	Hypothetical Enforcement under Substantive Antitrust Laws
Pre-signing due diligence	Yes	Yes (Information exchange)
Post-signing/pre-approval due diligence	Yes	Yes (Information exchange)
Post-approval/pre-closing due diligence	Yes	Yes (Information exchange)
Use of "clean teams"	Yes	Yes (Information exchange)
Restrictions on the target in an M&A agreement, e.g. buyer approval required for: – Investments above a certain level; – New business above a certain level; – Other obligations to consult/ obtain approval from the buyer before closing.	Yes	Yes (Information exchange; horizontal cooperation)

Specific Conduct	**Hypothetical Enforcement under Merger Control Laws**	**Hypothetical Enforcement under Substantive Antitrust Laws**
Joint marketing	Yes	Yes (Information exchange; horizontal cooperation)
Joint presentations (e.g. industry fairs)	Yes	Yes (Information exchange; horizontal cooperation)
Joint communications	Yes	Yes (Information exchange; horizontal cooperation)
Strategy/planning regarding customers	Yes	Yes (Information exchange; horizontal cooperation)
Strategy/planning regarding suppliers	Yes	Yes (Information exchange; horizontal cooperation)
Third party contract novation	Yes	Yes (Information exchange; horizontal cooperation)
Personnel Issues: – Secondments – Retention Strategies	Yes	Yes (Information exchange)
IT Planning/Database Migration	Yes	Yes (Information exchange)
Other		

FRANCE

Didier Théophile
(Darrois Villey Maillot Brochier)

Part 1:
Merger Control
and the "Standstill Obligation"

1. **Please identify the relevant merger control legislation in your jurisdiction. Please provide a link to the relevant legislation (if possible, in English) and also indicate:**
   - **whether the merger control system is mandatory or voluntary,**
   - **the relevant authority, and**
   - **the duration of the review period.**

Merger control is governed by Articles L430-1 to L430-10 of the French Commercial Code.[1]

The merger control system is mandatory. Prior to the formal notification the parties may submit a pre-notification – either a presentation of the transaction or a draft notification. Such pre-notification, while voluntary, is strongly recommended.

The relevant authority is the French Competition Authority (*Autorité de la concurrence*) (**FCA**). The French Minister of Economy has ancillary powers allowing them to intervene at two stages in the merger control process: (i) they may request an opening of a Phase II review within five working days of the FCA's decision following a Phase I review (the FCA may veto this request), and (ii) within 25 working days of the FCA's decision in a Phase II review, they may veto such decision and authorize or prohibit the merger for reasons related to public interest, other than the protection of competition (industrial development, competitiveness of the parties in the context of global competition, development or protection of employment).

The Phase I review period is 25 working days running from the date on which the notification has been deemed "complete" by the FCA. This period may be (i) extended by 15 working days if the parties offer commitments, (ii) suspended by the FCA (i.e. if the parties failed to inform the authority of a material fact or did not respond to a request for information within the prescribed time), or (iii) extended at the request of the parties for a maximum of 15 working days. The Phase II review period lasts 65 working days from the opening of Phase II and may be (i) extended by 20 working days if the parties offer commitments less than 20 working days before the expiry of Phase II, (ii) suspended by the FCA or (iii) suspended a maximum of 20 working days at the request of the parties.

2. **Does the merger control system in your jurisdiction impose a "standstill obligation" – meaning, that the transaction cannot be implemented prior to completing the merger control process? (Please cite the relevant legislation.)**

---

[1] Articles L430-1 to L430-10 of the French Commercial Code (French only): <https://www.legifrance.gouv.fr/affichCode.do;jsessionid=AB474472382AB3CD7905B9DE09422018.tplgfr23s_2?idSectionTA=LEGISCTA000006133185&cidTexte=LEGITEXT000005634379&dateTexte=20180326>.

Please also indicate the legal scope of the standstill obligation according to the relevant legislation (e.g. the parties to the transaction cannot effect a change of control, cannot take steps towards implementation, etc.).

Article L430-4 of the French Commercial Code provides for a standstill obligation. The actual completion of the transaction can only occur upon approval from the FCA. A transaction is deemed to be implemented when the change of control has taken place. The FCA considers that completion of a transaction is effective when the ownership of all or part of the target's assets and the rights attached thereto are effectively transferred to the buyer. It may also be considered to be effective when, regardless of the transfer of assets, the buyer nevertheless exercises a decisive influence over all or part of the target's activities.

3. **Have the relevant authorities in your jurisdiction issued internal or external guidelines concerning the scope of the standstill obligation, and/or their authority to enforce it? Please provide a copy/link of such guidance, if possible in English.**

The FCA has not issued any specific guidelines at this point. However, in July 2018, the President of the FCA published an article in the Revue Concurrence providing certain guidance.[2]

4. **Are there any exceptions to the standstill obligation – for example, through derogation or "carve out"? Please describe the circumstances in which this is possible. Please also describe the relevant process, e.g. do parties need to apply to the authority for a derogation from the standstill obligation? If so, how long is the approval process? If there are specific cases addressing these issues, please identify them.**

A derogation may be granted in exceptional circumstances. Pursuant to Article L430-4 of the French Commercial Code, the notifying parties may apply for derogation in case of a duly justified special need. Derogations are generally granted for acquisitions of undertakings subject to insolvency proceedings (undertakings in judicial reorganization or liquidation). Other exceptional circumstances may be the risk of imminent exit of the target firm, the opening of insolvency proceedings, or the purchaser's need to provide collateral or access financing in order to ensure the survival of the target firm.

2 See Isabelle de Silva, "Gun jumping: Quelles sont les pratiques à éviter?" Concurrences No 3-2018, 55–66 (French only).

In Cases No 12-DCC-154,[3] 17-DCC-169,[4] 17-DCC-186[5] and 19-DCC-96[6] for instance, the FCA granted derogations given that the target undertakings were subject to judicial reorganization and liquidation respectively. In Case No 15-DCC-47,[7] the derogation was justified by the purchaser's need to obtain financing as quickly as possible. In the press release regarding Case No 17-DCC-10,[8] the FCA referred to the financial difficulties of the target and the exceptional context (bird flu epidemic and the exceptionally low poultry prices).

The parties may request a derogation after the submission of the notification form. In the context of insolvency proceedings, the FCA's merger control guidelines provide that parties should apply for a derogation at least five business days before the decision of the Commercial Court assigning control of the target undertaking, and add this request to a notification filing which is as complete as possible (mentioning at least a presentation of the parties and the planned operation, a justification of the derogation request and a preliminary competition assessment). The FCA generally takes a few days to examine derogation requests (six days in Cases No 17-DCC-10 and 17-DCC-186).

The possibility of "carve out" is not provided for by the French legislation.

5. Does a public bid exception exist in your jurisdiction? (For example, under the EU Merger Regulation it is possible to acquire shares as part of a public bid, provided that the shares are not exercised until the acquisition is cleared by the Commission.) If such an exception exists in your jurisdiction, please describe how it is applied.

Article R.430-5 of the French Commercial Code provides for a public bid exception. It is an automatic derogation. The mechanism applies to public takeover bids, public exchange offers or acquisition of control through simple purchase of shares on a regulated market without the launch of a takeover bid.

Transfer of securities can take place before the FCA approves the decision. However, voting rights attached to the securities may not be exercised and the exercise of such rights before the FCA's approval would be subject to sanctions (unless

---

3 *Eurotunnel/SeaFrance* Decision No.12-DCC-154 of 7 November 2012, para 3 (French only) and FCA Press Release, "The Autorité de la concurrence clears, subject to conditions, the acquisition of certain SeaFrance assets by the Eurotunnel group" (8 November 2012): <http://www.autoritedelaconcurrence.fr/user/standard.php?id_rub=418&id_article=1996>.

4 *Cooperl/Financière Turenne Lafayette* Decision No. 17-DCC-169 of 20 October 2017, para 3 (French only) and FCA Press Release, "The Autorité de la concurrence clears the acquisition of full control of the cured meats' division of Financière Turenne Lafayette (Paul Prédault, Madrange…) by Coorperl Arc Atlantique (Brocéliande)" (23 October 2017) <http://www.autoritedelaconcurrence.fr/user/standard.php?id_rub=663&id_article=3051&lang=en>.

5 *Gibert Joseph/Gibert Jeune* Decision No. 17-DCC-186 of 10 November 2017, para 3 (French only) and FCA Press Release, "The Autorité de la concurrence clears the acquisition of Gibert Jeune's activity by Gibert Joseph" (15 November 2017): <http://www.autoritedelaconcurrence.fr/user/standard.php?id_rub=663&id_article=3065&lang=en>.

6 *British Steel/Ascoval* Decision No. 19-DCC-96 of 16 May 2019 (French only) and FCA Press Release, "The Autorité de la concurrence clears the takeover of the Ascoval company by the British Steel group" (17 May 2019): <http://www.autoritedelaconcurrence.fr/user/standard.php?id_rub=697&id_article=3412&lang=en>.

7 *ICG/Courtepaille* Decision No. 15-DCC-47 of 5 May 2015, para 6 (French only).

8 *Plukon/Duc* Decision No. 17-DCC-10 of 27 January 2017 (French only) and FCA Press Release, "The Autorité de la concurrence approves the acquisition of the Duc group by the Dutch Plukon group" (27 January 2017): <http://www.autoritedelaconcurrence.fr/user/standard.php?id_rub=663&id_article=2935&lang=en>.

the parties have applied for, and been granted, a derogation pursuant to Article L430-4 of the French Commercial Code).

6. What powers does the relevant authority have to investigate and enforce violations of the standstill obligation? Are dawn raids possible? What timing applies to investigation/enforcement proceedings?

The FCA may use all its regular powers of investigation. Dawn raids are possible. Proceedings are not subject to any specific timeline.

7. What are the possible penalties for violating the standstill obligation? Are there criminal sanctions, including on individuals? Have these been applied in practice? Is there a difference in enforcement between transactions involving domestic companies and "foreign-to-foreign" transactions? Does the authority have the power to unwind transactions implemented in breach of the standstill obligation? If so, has the authority made use of that power in practice? If yes, please provide examples.

The FCA may fine the concerned party as follows (maximum fines):

- corporate entities: 5% of pre-tax turnover in France from the previous financial year (plus, where applicable, the turnover in France of the acquired party over the same period); and
- individuals: €1.5 million.

Criminal sanctions are not provided. According to Article L430-8-II of the French Commercial Code, the FCA may impose financial penalties. It does not have the power to unwind the transaction in case of implementation of the transaction prior to approval (contrary to the failure to notify the transaction).

The financial penalties may be substantial, as illustrated in the *Altice* case, where the FCA fined Altice €80 million under Article L430-8-II. The FCA noted that it may take into account the anticompetitive effects of the infringement of Article L430-8 when determining the amount of the fine. Other factors which influence the level of the fine are, for instance, the duration of the infringement or the intentional behavior of the parties.[9]

8. How does the relevant authority typically learn of potential violations of the standstill obligation? Does the authority actively monitor the trade press?

The FCA may learn of potential violations by asking questions during the merger investigation for instance, or through a third-party complaint. The FCA also monitors the press.

9. Please describe the relevant authority's enforcement of the standstill obligation. If there have been cases, please describe the specific conduct that was found to violate the standstill provision and the criteria applied by the relevant authority or court. Has the relevant authority considered the market impact of the conduct? (Please refer to the Annex.)

---

9 *Altice* Decision No. 16-D-24 of 8 November 2016, para 334–53 (French only) and FCA Press Release, "The Autorité de la concurrence fines the Altice group 80 million euros for the premature completion of two mergers notified in 2014" (8 November 2016): <http://www.autoritedelaconcurrence.fr/user/standard.php?id_rub=630&id_article=2900&lang=en>.

In *Altice*, which is the first case imposing fines for violation of the standstill obligation, the FCA considered the control over the decisions of the target, the nature of the economic relations between the parties and the information that was exchanged between the parties during the period prior to approval. The FCA noted that Altice intervened in SFR's day-to-day management by approving a number of strategic decisions. The parties also coordinated regarding the potential acquisition of a third-party operator, OTL group. They also implemented in advance various coordinated strategies, notably during the negotiation and preparation of an important commercial project. Furthermore, the parties exchanged sensitive information. Regarding the acquisition of OTL, Altice also took a number of strategic decisions pursuant to the terms of the share purchase agreement. Moreover, Altice implemented a weekly surveillance of OTL's economic performance, which allowed Altice to gain access to commercially sensitive information. Finally, OTL's manager was instated as a member of SFR-Numericable's executive committee before the approval.[10]

10. In cases involving alleged violations of the standstill obligation under the relevant merger control laws, has the relevant authority (or court) also considered the substantive antitrust laws? (Please refer to the Annex.)

In *Altice*, the FCA exclusively applied merger control rules and considered the conduct to amount to an infringement of Article L430-8-II of the French Commercial Code (even as regards the exchange of information).[11]

11. Is private enforcement of the standstill obligation possible?

Private enforcement of the standstill obligation is possible. However, the author is not aware of such cases yet in France.

12. Please describe the private law risks/consequences (i.e. contractual/validity consequences) for transactions that are subject to notification, but which are completed without notification/approval. Please identify any relevant cases and describe them.

See response to Question 11.

13. Please describe policy and enforcement trends in your jurisdiction.

Gun-jumping is being strictly controlled; the FCA's future guidelines will provide clarification on how the FCA is planning to enforce the rules on gun-jumping.

---

10 *Altice*, para 196–291 (French only).

11 ibid, para 103–35 (French only)

Part 2: Substantive Antitrust Law in an M&A Context

1. **Please identify the relevant substantive antitrust laws in your jurisdiction that can potentially apply in an M&A context (e.g. for the EU, this would include Article 101 of the Treaty on the Functioning of the European Union). Please provide a link to the relevant legislation (if possible, in English).**

   The FCA may apply Article L420-1 of the French Commercial Code,[12] which is the equivalent of Article 101 TFEU. Situations in which this Article may be applied are, for instance, the creation of joint ventures that do not qualify as full-function (e.g. Case No 02-D-44[13]), the exchange of information during the suspensive period or ancillary restraints which are not strictly necessary to the merger (e.g. Cases No 06-D-31[14] and 10-D-32[15]).

2. **Do any guidelines exist in your jurisdiction concerning the application of the substantive antitrust laws in an M&A context – whether internal to the relevant authority, or external, formal or informal (e.g. speeches)? If so, please provide a copy/link to such guidance.**

   Other than a reference in the general merger control guidelines to joint ventures which are not full-function, there are no special guidelines on this topic at this stage.

3. **As a general matter (not limited to M&A), how are the substantive antitrust laws enforced with respect to the exchange of competitively sensitive information between competing firms? Please also indicate the relevance of anticompetitive effects or intent in such enforcement.**

   In general, exchanges of information between competitors may constitute an anticompetitive practice according to Article L420-1 of the French Commercial

---

12 Article L420-1 of the French Commercial code (French only): <https://www.legifrance.gouv.fr/affichCodeArticle.do;jsessionid=37C3622AB3A31F1F676ABB887E7F069C.tplgfr23s_3?idArticle=LEGIARTI000006231970&cidTexte=LEGITEXT000005634379&dateTexte=20180410&categorieLien=id&oldAction>.

13 Decision No. 02-D-44 of 11 July 2002 (French only) and FCA Press Release, "Water market: the Conseil de la concurrence asks the Minister to raise questions over the joint subsidiaries of CGE and SLDE" (17 July 2002): <http://www.autoritedelaconcurrence.fr/user/standard.php?id_rub=128&id_article=258>.

14 *Finegee/Heineken France* Decision No. 06-D-31 of 20 October 2006, Conseil de la concurrence (former FCA) (French only).

15 Decision No. 10-D-32 of 16 November 2010 on practices implemented in the pay-TV sector, para 158–78 (French only) and FCA Press Release, "Pay TV: The Autorité de la concurrence will investigate further into the exclusivities implemented by Groupe Canal Plus on the pay TV market – It issues today a decision in principle, so as to define the framework and limits of its assessment: it won't challenge the "Ceres" draft agreement signed with TF1 and M6 in January 2006 and the "Lagardère" one concluded in March 2006 with Groupe Lagardère, which are part of the Canal Plus/TPS merger cleared by the Economy Minister in August 2006" (16 November 2010): <http://www.autoritedelaconcurrence.fr/user/standard.php?id_rub=368&id_article=1499>.

Code. They may be part of a larger cartel, or be caught autonomously as a concerted practice. Exchanges of information may restrict competition by object or by effect. Exchanges of information would be restrictive by object if they relate to future pricing behavior, for instance. In order to determine the anticompetitive effects of an exchange of information, the FCA takes into consideration the structure of the market (transparency, concentration) and the characteristics of the information that is being exchanged (aggregate or individualized information, recurrent nature of the exchange; current or historical information). In certain cases, exchange of information may also constitute an abuse of dominant position.

4. Have there been any cases in your jurisdiction in which the substantive antitrust laws were enforced in an M&A context? Please describe/explain and cite any such cases. (See also Annex.)

In *Altice*, the FCA only enforced the merger control rules pursuant to Article L430-II-8 of the French Commercial Code, even as regards the exchange of commercially sensitive information. However, the FCA indicated in the decision that exchanges of information during the suspensive period may also be subject to Article L420-1.[16]

5. Are the substantive antitrust laws more likely to apply at specific stages of the transaction – i.e. at an early stage, or prior to closing (or does it not make a difference)? Do companies face ongoing risk following the consummation (or failure) of their transaction for conduct that allegedly occurred pre-closing (pre-failure)?

The parties to a transaction can be investigated post-closing for conduct that occurred pre-closing.

In our opinion, the following stages would be most at risk:

- *due diligence stage*: the exchange of information should be limited to what is strictly necessary. The involvement of operational personnel should be limited as much as possible. This is particularly important, as in the event of failure of the transaction the parties would continue to be competitors;
- *advanced integration planning stage between approval and closing*: during this time the parties remain competitors. Therefore, this is a sensitive period during which substantive antitrust laws may be enforced.

6. Please explain how the relevant authority enforces (or could enforce) the substantive antitrust laws in an M&A context. How would the investigation occur, and what timing constraints would apply?

Investigations may occur at any point in time, subject to information that would justify dawn raids. No particular timing constraints apply.

7. Is private enforcement of the substantive antitrust laws possible in an M&A context, and has it occurred?

Private enforcement of substantive antitrust laws would be possible in an M&A context. To the best of our knowledge, there is currently one case pending.

---

16 n 9, para 263.

8. Could behavior subject to the substantive antitrust laws also be caught under the merger control rules/standstill obligation? (Please also refer to the Annex.)

Behavior such as coordination between the merging parties or exchanges of information before closing of the transaction would also be considered to be in breach of the standstill obligation (subject to such action not being time-barred). Please note that the current decisional practice shows that the FCA might be more inclined to prohibit such behavior under merger control laws (see the *Altice* case[17]).

9. Please describe the penalties for infringing the substantive antitrust laws. Please indicate whether these include criminal penalties, including individual criminal penalties. As a practical matter, how have these been applied in the context of an M&A transaction?

If the offender is not a company, the maximum amount of the penalty is €3 million. The maximum amount of the penalty for a company is 10% of the highest worldwide turnover, net of tax, achieved in one of the financial years ended after the financial year preceding that in which the practices were implemented.

If any natural person takes a personal and decisive part in the design, organization or implementation of the practices referred to in Articles L420-1 and L420-2 of the French Commercial Code, criminal sanctions may be imposed (prison sentence of four years and a fine of €75,000).

10. Please describe policy and enforcement trends in your jurisdiction.

The FCA plans to revisit its merger guidelines and to simplify the notification process for simplified cases. A consultation was launched in October 2017 and some of the proposed measures have been implemented, or will be shortly, whereas others are still under examination.

Measures aimed at simplifying companies' administrative workload when notifying a concentration were adopted by Decree No. 2019-339, which entered into force on 21 April 2019.[18] The FCA is currently testing a new online notification procedure for concentrations which benefit from the simplified procedure which is expected to be operational before end of June 2019.[19]

The FCA also decided to pursue its reflection regarding the implementation of an *ex post* control system for transactions which do not fall within the FCA's jurisdiction and which raise "substantial competition concerns" in France.[20] A final position from the FCA is awaited in the course of 2019.

---

17 n 9.

18 Decree No. 2019-339 of 18 April 2019 regarding the simplification of the notification file of a merger control to the Autorité de la concurrence (French only): <https://www.legifrance.gouv.fr/affichTexte.do;jsessionid=40A2162D30C0C65A8E4F8B5BF3CB2142.tplgfr21s_2?cidTexte=JORFTEXT000038395295&dateTexte=&oldAction=rechJO&categorieLien=id&idJO=JORFCONT0000383952099>.

19 See FCA Press Release, "Modernization of merger control" (25 April 2019): <http://www.autoritedelaconcurrence.fr/user/standard.php?id_rub=697&id_article=3401&lang=en>.

20 See FCA summary, "Reform of merger law and *ex post* control": <http://www.autoritedelaconcurrence.fr/doc/note_controle_expost_en_final.pdf>.

Finally, the FCA announced that it would initiate a wider revision of its merger control guidelines to take into account developments in its decision practice in recent years.[21]

French Competition Authority, "The French Competition Authority clears, subject to conditions, a merger in the maritime transport sector (Eurotunnel/SeaFrance/MyFerryLink)" 7 November 2012, e-Competitions Bulletin November 2012, Art. N° 58521

Olivier Billard, Guillaume Fabre, "Jurisdiction: The French Competition Authority approves the acquisition of exclusive control over the assets of a firm in liquidation subject to commitments (SeaFrance)" May 2013, Concurrences Review N° 2-2013, Art. N° 52354

Porter Elliott, "The French Competition Authority clears a merger in the cured meat sector (Cooperl Arc Atlantique/Financière Turenne Lafayette)" 23 October 2017, e-Competitions Bulletin October 2017, Art. N° 85298

Alexis Baudelin, Sergio Sorinas, Marie Louvet, "Suspensive effect: The French Competition Authority grants a derogation to the suspensive effect of merger control for the acquisitions of a salted sausage business on the one hand and of certain assets in the ready-cooked meals sector on the other hand, in the context of an insolvency procedure, the former having been authorised and the latter having been subject to the opening of an in-depth investigation (Financière Turenne Lafayette – Cooperl Arc Atlantique; William Saurin)" 20 October 2017, Concurrences Review N° 1-2018, Art. N° 86227

Marie Louvet, Alexis Baudelin, Sergio Sorinas, "Insolvency procedure: The French Competition Authority clears the acquisition of sole control of a market player by one of its competitors in the books and stationery products retail sale sector and grants an exemption from the suspensive effect of merger control (Gibert Jeune – Gibert Joseph)" 10 November 2017, Concurrences Review N° 1-2018, Art. N° 86228

Alain Ronzano, "Sole control: The French Competition Authority publishes the decision authorizing the takeover of a French steel mill by a British group (Ascoval, British Steel)" 16 May 2019, Concurrences Review N° 2-2019, Art. N° 90803

Alain Ronzano, "Clearance: The French Competition Authority clears the acquisition of sole control of a major food services company by an investment group (Courtepaille/ICG)" 5 May 2015, Concurrences Review N° 3-2015, Art. N° 75352

Jean-Mathieu Cot, "Gun Jumping: The French Competition Authority imposes a €80 million fine for gun jumping (Altice)" 8 November 2016, Concurrences Review N° 2-2017, Art. N° 83946

---

21 See FCA Press Release, "Modernization and simplification of merger control" (7 June 2018): <http://www.autoritedelaconcurrence.fr/user/standard.php?lang=en&id_rub=684&id_article=3182>.

Christophe Lemaire, "Judicial review of merger commitments: The French Competition Council rules on its competence to assess practices in the course of the execution of commitments (Finegee C/Heineken)" 20 October 2006, Concurrences Review N° 1-2007, Art. N° 13113

Frédéric Marty, "Exclusivity clauses: The French Competition Authority conducts an additional inquiry into risks of anticompetitive preemption on the market for pay TV (Pay TV)" 16 November 2010, Concurrences Review N° 1-2011, Art. N° 34135

Annex

Table 1: Actual Enforcement of Specific Conduct under the Relevant Merger Control Rules and Substantive Antitrust Laws

Please identify whether the following type of conduct has been subject to investigation/enforcement in your jurisdiction, under the merger control laws or substantive antitrust laws. Please cite any such case(s) and provide a brief description in the table below.

Note that all examples regarding actual enforcement concern the Altice case[22]

Specific Conduct	Actual Enforcement under Merger Control Laws	Actual Enforcement under Substantive Antitrust Laws
Pre-signing due diligence	Exchange of information	No
Post-signing/pre-approval due diligence	Exchange of information	No
Post-approval/pre-closing due diligence	Exchange of information	No
Use of "clean teams"	The FCA recommends the implementation of clean teams with no operational personnel (clarified in a recent article of the president of the FCA).[15]	No

[22] *Altice* Decision No. 16-D-24 of 8 November 2016.

[23] n° 2.

Specific Conduct	Actual Enforcement under Merger Control Laws	Actual Enforcement under Substantive Antitrust Laws
Restrictions on the target in an M&A agreement, e.g. buyer approval required for: – Investments above a certain level; – New business above a certain level; – Other obligations to consult/obtain approval from the buyer before closing.	– Approval by Altice of a certain number of SFR's investments, beyond the scope of the M&A agreement. – The agreement between OTL and Numericable provides a number of restrictions on OTL's commercial freedom re: the level of authorized investments, prohibition to enter into or amend important contracts, prohibition to open new stores. OTL solicited Numericable's approval for the conclusion of certain contracts and the use of overdrafts.	No
Joint marketing	No	No
Joint presentations (e.g. industry fairs)	No	No
Joint communications	No	No
Strategy/planning regarding customers	– Altice approved SFR's participation in a call for tenders for a strategic project. – Altice intervened in SFR's commercial policy as regards promotional campaigns for SFR's internet customers.	No
Strategy/planning regarding suppliers	Planning the integration of the parties' networks in order to limit services provided by third parties.	No
Third party contract novation	Altice's approval was solicited for an amendment to a contract between SFR and Bouygues Telecom, as well as the renewal of a contract between SFR and Canal+.	No

Specific Conduct	Actual Enforcement under Merger Control Laws	Actual Enforcement under Substantive Antitrust Laws
Personnel Issues: – Secondments – Retention Strategies	Appointment of OTL's general manager as member of SFR-Numericable's executive committee.	No
IT Planning/Database Migration	No	No
Other	– Coordination between Altice and SFR for the acquisition of OTL group. – Contract between SFR and Numericable regarding the launch of the commercial project "marque blanche", which is a major change in SFR's commercial strategy.	No

Table 2: Hypothetical Enforcement of Specific Conduct under the Relevant Merger Control Rules and Substantive Antitrust Laws

For any conduct that is *not* the subject of actual enforcement (Table 1), please indicate in the Table below whether the conduct identified *could potentially* be enforced under the merger control laws and/or substantive antitrust laws.

Specific Conduct	Hypothetical Enforcement under Merger Control Laws	Hypothetical Enforcement under Substantive Antitrust Laws
Pre-signing due diligence	No	Yes
Post-signing/pre-approval due diligence	Yes	Yes
Post-approval/pre-closing due diligence		Yes
Use of "clean teams"	Yes	Yes
Restrictions on the target in an M&A agreement, e.g. buyer approval required for: Investments above a certain level; New business above a certain level; Other obligations to consult/ obtain approval from the buyer before closing.	Yes	No

Specific Conduct	Hypothetical Enforcement under Merger Control Laws	Hypothetical Enforcement under Substantive Antitrust Laws
Joint marketing	Yes	No
Joint presentations (e.g. industry fairs)	Yes	No
Joint communications	Yes	No
Strategy/planning regarding customers	Yes	No
Strategy/planning regarding suppliers	Yes	No
Third party contract novation	Yes	No
Personnel Issues: Secondments Retention Strategies	Yes	No
IT Planning/Database Migration	Yes	No
Other		

GERMANY

Christian Steinle
(Gleiss Lutz)

Part 1: Merger Control and the "Standstill Obligation"

1. **Please identify the relevant merger control legislation in your jurisdiction. Please provide a link to the relevant legislation (if possible, in English) and also indicate:**
   - **whether the merger control system is mandatory or voluntary,**
   - **the relevant authority, and**
   - **the duration of the review period.**

The relevant merger control legislation can be found in Chapter VII of the Act against Restraints of Competition (**GWB/ARC**).[1]

The examination of concentrations in Germany is the exclusive responsibility of the Bundeskartellamt (**Federal Cartel Office/BKartA**). In cases that are subject to merger control, the BKartA has, in principle, four months from receipt of the complete notification to examine the concentration, i.e. it may prohibit the merger within this period. It must, however, inform the notifying undertakings within one month of receipt of the notification (so-called "one-month letter") that it has initiated an examination of the concentration (main examination proceedings). Otherwise, the concentration is deemed to be cleared one month after receipt of the complete notification.[2] The main examination proceedings should be initiated if a further examination of the concentration is necessary (section 40(1) sentence 2 ARC).

2. **Does the merger control system in your jurisdiction impose a "standstill obligation" – meaning, that the transaction cannot be implemented prior to completing the merger control process? (Please cite the relevant legislation.) Please also indicate the legal scope of the standstill obligation according to the relevant legislation (e.g. the parties to the transaction cannot effect a change of control, cannot take steps towards implementation, etc.).**

Concentrations or mergers that are subject to control according to section 35(1) ARC must not be put into effect until the BKartA has cleared the transaction or the relevant waiting periods of one month or four months respectively are over.

---

1 An English Translation of the GWB is available at <https://www.gesetze-im-internet.de/englisch_gwb/englisch_gwb.html>.

2 This follows *mutatis mutandis* from s 40(2) sentence 2 ARC (cf. Bechtold/Bosch, *GWB: Commentary* (9th ed CH Beck 2018) §40, para 7). In practice, the BKartA informs the notifying undertakings of the clearance by stating that the preconditions to prohibit the concentration are not fulfilled.

Any legal transaction violating this prohibition is void (section 41(1) sentence 2 ARC). A violation of the prohibition of putting a concentration into effect constitutes an administrative offense (section 81(2) sentence 1 ARC).

There are different types of measures prohibited under the aforementioned provision:

- Premature influence on the management of the target company;
- De facto execution of the transaction by, for example, merging administrative functions of the two companies, taking on business as one entity, following the instructions of the future management or making joint sales of products;
- Formal closing of the transaction.

3. **Have the relevant authorities in your jurisdiction issued internal or external guidelines concerning the scope of the standstill obligation, and/or their authority to enforce it? Please provide a copy/link of such guidance, if possible in English.**

The BKartA publishes no such specific guidelines. Indications of the approach taken by the BKartA can be found in its "activity reports" (Tätigkeitsberichte) that are published every two years.

4. **Are there any exceptions to the standstill obligation – for example, through derogation or "carve out"? Please describe the circumstances in which this is possible. Please also describe the relevant process, e.g. do parties need to apply to the authority for a derogation from the standstill obligation? If so, how long is the approval process? If there are specific cases addressing these issues, please identify them.**

The BKartA may, on application, grant an exemption from the prohibition of putting a concentration into effect if the participating undertakings put forward important reasons for this, in particular to prevent serious damage to a participating undertaking or to a third party (section 41(2) ARC). This may be the case if the merger can only be executed in a certain time frame that the merger control would exceed or if requirements of foreign jurisdictions dictate the immediate execution of the merger. The exemption may be granted at any time, even prior to notification, and may be made subject to conditions and obligations.

It is possible for merging parties to apply for a "carve out" of Germany, i.e. to close the transaction in other jurisdictions but not in Germany, pending receipt of the BKartA's clearance. This would constitute an application for partial exemption from the prohibition of putting a concentration into effect, i.e. only insofar as Germany is concerned. The preconditions would be the same as described above.

However, in practice, an application for full or partial exemption under section 41(2) ARC is not usually a realistic option. The BKartA takes a very restrictive view in order to avoid being confronted with accomplished facts should it decide later to block the concentration. The review of such application usually takes just as long as the merger control proceeding. Therefore, such applications are largely unknown in practice.

5. **Does a public bid exception exist in your jurisdiction? (For example, under the EU Merger Regulation it is possible to acquire shares as part of a public bid, provided that the shares are not exercised until the acquisition is cleared**

by the Commission.) If such an exception exists in your jurisdiction, please describe how it is applied.

There is a public bid exception in section 41(1a) ARC – which is aligned with Article 7 (2) EUMR – allowing the acquisition of shares as part of a public takeover bid or by way of a number of legal transactions in securities at a stock exchange prior to clearance by the BKartA if the concentration is notified to the BKartA without undue delay and the acquirer does not exercise the voting rights attached to the shares or only exercises them to preserve the full value of its investment based on an exemption granted by the BKartA.

6. **What powers does the relevant authority have to investigate and enforce violations of the standstill obligation? Are dawn raids possible? What timing applies to investigation/enforcement proceedings?**

The BKartA generally has the power to perform any investigation that is deemed necessary (section 57(1) ARC).

In particular, it can request the disclosure of information regarding the economic situation as well as the surrender of documents from an undertaking. It may also inspect and examine business documents of undertakings on their premises during normal business hours (section 59(1) ARC). Searches outside normal business hours may be conducted only by order of a court. Searches are permissible if it is assumed that documents are located in the relevant premises which may be inspected and/or examined, and the surrender of which may be requested (section 59(4) ARC). The BKartA also has the power to seize objects which may be of importance as evidence in the investigation (section 58(1) ARC).

The BKartA is free to determine the timing of investigation/enforcement proceedings in gun-jumping cases. Once the BKartA has sufficient indication of such administrative offense, it usually starts to investigate rather quickly, within a few days or weeks.

7. **What are the possible penalties for violating the standstill obligation? Are there criminal sanctions, including on individuals? Have these been applied in practice? Is there a difference in enforcement between transactions involving domestic companies and "foreign-to-foreign" transactions? Does the authority have the power to unwind transactions implemented in breach of the standstill obligation? If so, has the authority made use of that power in practice? If yes, please provide examples.**

An administrative offense is committed by any person who intentionally or negligently violates the prohibition of putting a proposed merger into effect or participates in its implementation (section 81(2) sentence 1 ARC). The offense may be punished by a fine of up to €1 million (section 81(4) sentence 1 ARC). If a fine is imposed on an undertaking or an association of undertakings, the fine for each undertaking or association of undertakings participating in the infringement may not, beyond the abovementioned amount, exceed 10% of its total turnover in the preceding business year (section 81(4) sentence 2 ARC).

Any person who intentionally or negligently fails to notify a planned concentration correctly or completely or in time, or intentionally or negligently fails to make a notification that a concentration has been put into effect correctly or completely or in time, commits an administrative offense which may be punished by a regulatory fine of up to €100,000.

Gun-jumping does not give rise to criminal sanctions.

The BKartA has the power to unwind transactions in breach of the standstill obligation if the concentration fulfills the conditions for prohibition, i.e. if it would significantly impede effective competition (section 36(1) sentence 1 ARC). However, the Federal Minister of Economics and Technology has the power to authorize the concentration in spite of the BKartA's decision (section 41(3) ARC).

Due to practical difficulties in unwinding already-implemented concentrations, there have been very few cases where the BKartA enforced such an order, and even fewer of them have been successful. Examples of cases where unwinding measures were ordered by the BKartA include:

- BKartA, order of 27 November 2003 – B 6-51/02, WuW/E DE-V 885 (not publicly available; reference in BKartA, Activity Report 2003/2004, p24 *et seq.* [in German only])
- BKartA, order of 5 October 2015 – B2-47/14 (not publicly available; reference in BKartA, press release of 5 October 2015 "Demerger of organic dairies Andechser and Söbbeke").

In the first case, one of the largest German newspaper publishers, Westdeutsche Allgemeine Zeitungsverlag (**WAZ**), had held 60% of the shares in a regional German newspaper publisher, Ostthüringer Zeitung Verlag. WAZ failed to notify the acquisition of the remaining 40% in 1995 which, according to the BKartA, constituted a notifiable concentration. The BKartA prohibited the 40% acquisition in 2000. Three years later the BKartA ordered the divestiture of the 40% to a publisher not affiliated with WAZ. The decision became necessary because WAZ intended to sell these shares to a law professor not active as a newspaper publisher.

In the *Andechser/Söbbeke* case, the two then-largest organic dairies in Germany – Andechser Molkerei Scheitz GmbH and Molkerei Söbbeke GmbH – were integrated under the large French dairy Savencia SA (now known as Bongrain). In 1999 the company acquired shares in Andechser and between 2011 and 2013 also acquired Söbbeke. Savencia only succeeded in having the merger cleared in merger control proceedings in 2011 by submitting incorrect information.[3] Once it realized that the company had given false information, the BKartA initiated divestiture proceedings and carried out extensive investigations at the companies concerned and at all the organic dairies in Germany. In order to avoid the dissolution of the merger between Savencia and Söbbeke, which in the authority's view was necessary, Savencia offered to give up its participation in Andechser and to sell its shares. After this measure was implemented, the BKartA decided to end the divestiture proceedings against Savencia and Söbbeke.

In principle, there is no difference in the treatment of transactions whether they include domestic companies or not. However, the BKartA's legal means to enforce

3 Savencia's notification in 2011 did not correctly reflect the market situation and contained incomplete information on the further possibilities of the group exerting influence on Andechser Molkerei Scheitz GmbH. In reply to further queries during the first phase proceedings, it also submitted incorrect sales figures.

its order abroad are limited (of course) and subject to applicable conventions and treaties of public international law.

8. How does the relevant authority typically learn of potential violations of the standstill obligation? Does the authority actively monitor the trade press?

Typically, the BKartA will learn of potential violations by chance, especially while investigating another merger or via press reports.

9. Please describe the relevant authority's enforcement of the standstill obligation. If there have been cases, please describe the specific conduct that was found to violate the standstill provision and the criteria applied by the relevant authority or court. Has the relevant authority considered the market impact of the conduct? (Please refer to the Annex.)

In the most recent case from 2017 (KVR 57/16 – *EDEKA/Kaiser's Tengelmann*, Decision of the German Federal Court of Justice of 14 November 2018), the Federal Court of Justice (**Bundesgerichtshof/BGH**) ruled that certain conduct that does not yet constitute a concentration can nonetheless be considered a violation of the standstill obligation, if said conduct at least partially anticipates the effects of the planned concentration.

The two merging firms – two of the biggest food retailers in the German market – had already taken isolated measures in pursuing the planned concentration ahead of even filing the merger. These measures were subsequently prohibited by the BKartA with regard to the standstill obligation, even though the merger was not yet implemented in its entirety. The decision by the BKartA was then confirmed by the BGH.

The conduct in question was:

- The centralization of the purchase and payment of goods which were then to be distributed by the acquiring undertaking; and
- Closing down or economically devaluating certain venues of the acquired company ("carving out").

Other gun-jumping cases exist, some of which are publicly known (including the *Mars* case[4], the *Interseroh* case[5] and the *Homag* case[6]) However, in most of these cases the parties did not notify the transaction at all. In *Mars*, the company did notify the acquisition of US pet food manufacturer Nutro Products to the competition authorities in Germany, Austria and the USA. However, after clearance of the transaction in the USA and during the period of ongoing examination by the BKartA, Mars acquired the majority of the shares in Nutro Products. The BKartA

---

4 See German Federal Cartel Office Press Release, "Fine imposed against Mars for violating the prohibition to put a merger into effect" (15 December 2008) <https://www.bundeskartellamt.de/SharedDocs/Meldung/EN/Pressemitteilungen/2008/15_12_2008_Mars_Vollzugsverbot.html;jsessionid=0D3421E2474E12C10AF-D1ABE8543F370.1_cid362?nn=3591568>.

5 See German Federal Cartel Office Press Release, "Fine imposed on Interseroh for violating the prohibition to put a merger into effect before examination under merger control" (10 May 2011) <https://www.bundeskartellamt.de/SharedDocs/Meldung/EN/Pressemitteilungen/2011/10_05_2011_Intersehroh.html?nn=3591568>.

6 See German Federal Cartel Office Report, "Bericht des Bundeskartellamtes über seine Tätigkeit in den Jahren 2003/2004 sowie über die Lage und Entwicklung auf seinem Aufgabengebiet" (German only) (22 June 2005) p25 <https://www.bundeskartellamt.de/SharedDocs/Publikation/DE/Taetigkeitsberichte/Bundeskartellamt%20-%20Tätigkeitsbericht%202004.pdf?__blob=publicationFile&v=3>.

imposed a regulatory fine of €4.5 million which was the highest fine for violating the standstill obligation at the time. In *Interseroh*, the company's legal predecessor made use of its option to increase its share ownership in another company from 40% to 49%. At the same time the partnership agreement of this company was altered in order to provide that important decisions could only be made with the approval of Interseroh's legal predecessor. This acquisition of control was not notified before it was put into effect, although the BKartA had informed the companies of the obligation to do so in a previous merger control proceeding. In *Homag,* the parties did not notify the merger between Homag and IMA to the BKartA with the overall aim of trying to prevent a possible prohibition of the concentration.

The fines imposed by the BKartA vary from case to case. In *Mars*, the BKartA imposed a fine of €4.5 million due to the premature implementation of the transaction. In *Interseroh*, the BKartA imposed fines of €206,000 on Interseroh due to its failure to file. The fines in *Homag/IMA* are not publicly known. In another case involving the publishing house *Druck- und Verlagshaus Frankfurt,* the BKartA imposed a fine of €4.13 million due to the failure of the companies to file.[7]

10. In cases involving alleged violations of the standstill obligation under the relevant merger control laws, has the relevant authority (or court) also considered the substantive antitrust laws? (Please refer to the Annex.)

As yet, there are no known cases involving alleged violations of the standstill obligation where the BKartA or a court has also considered substantive antitrust laws. However, the antitrust laws are applicable while the standstill obligation is in effect, enabling the BKartA to prohibit any behavior that is deemed a violation of antitrust law.

11. Is private enforcement of the standstill obligation possible?

Whoever violates the standstill obligation is obliged to the person affected by the violation, to rectify the infringement and, where there is a risk of recurrence, to desist from further infringements. A claim for injunction also exists if an infringement is likely. Affected persons are competitors or other market participants impaired by the infringement (section 33 (1) and (2) ARC).

Such claims may also be asserted by certain associations with the legal capacity for the promotion of commercial or independent professional interests or other entities named in section 33(4) ARC.

12. Please describe the private law risks/consequences (i.e. contractual/validity consequences) for transactions that are subject to notification, but which are completed without notification/approval. Please identify any relevant cases and describe them.

All legal transactions violating the prohibition to implement a concentration that is subject to notification are void until the concentration is cleared by the BKartA. After clearance, the transactions become valid retroactively.

---

7 See German Federal Cartel Office Press Release, "Publishing House Druck- und Verlagshaus Frankfurt am Main GmbH fined for violating the prohibition of putting a concentration into effect" (13 February 2009) <https://www.bundeskartellamt.de/SharedDocs/Meldung/EN/Pressemitteilungen/2009/13_02_2009_DuV-Bußgeld.html>.

This leads to considerable insecurity for the participating undertakings until a final decision by the BKartA is made, since all transactions depend on the (uncertain) approval by the BKartA. For example, any payment that may have been made in advance could be subject to reclaim, should the BKartA later prohibit the concentration.

13. Please describe policy and enforcement trends in your jurisdiction.

The ninth amendment of the ARC in 2017 has brought along a new threshold (section 35(1a) ARC) that is supposed to enable the BKartA to enact control over mergers, notably in digital markets, where the target undertaking has considerable market potential, but as yet no – or no significant – turnover. The concentration is now subject to notification if the value of the transaction exceeds €400 million. In 2017 and 2018, the new threshold triggered more than 30 new cases (including informal consultations), none of which resulted in prohibitions. These include 18 formal "deal-value" notifications, with seven of those being withdrawn and 11 cleared. None of the cases led to a second-phase investigation, and the BKartA has not yet caught a so-called "killer acquisition".[8] The BKartA and the Austrian Bundeswettbewerbsbehörde (Federal Competition Authority) issued a joint guidance paper in 2018 that has helped reduce the legal uncertainty surrounding the new deal value threshold.[9]

---

8 MLex, "Merger-value thresholds catch few deals and no unicorns in Austria, officials say", (MLex 23 May 2019).

9 See German Federal Cartel Office and Austrian Federal Competition Authority, "Guidance on Transaction Value Thresholds for Mandatory Pre-merger Notification (section 35(1a) GWB and section 9(4) KartG)" (July 2018) <https://www.bundeskartellamt.de/SharedDocs/Publikation/EN/Leitfaden/Leitfaden_Transaktionsschwelle.pdf?__blob=publicationFile&v=2>.

Part 2: Substantive Antitrust Law in an M&A Context

1. **Please identify the relevant substantive antitrust laws in your jurisdiction that can potentially apply in an M&A context (e.g. for the EU, this would include Article 101 of the Treaty on the Functioning of the European Union). Please provide a link to the relevant legislation (if possible, in English).**

   The relevant antitrust laws can be found in Chapter 1 of the ARC.[10]

2. **Do any guidelines exist in your jurisdiction concerning the application of the substantive antitrust laws in an M&A context – whether internal to the relevant authority, or external, formal or informal (e.g. speeches)? If so, please provide a copy/link to such guidance.**

   There are no specific guidelines on the application of substantive antitrust laws in an M&A context.

3. **As a general matter (not limited to M&A), how are the substantive antitrust laws enforced with respect to the exchange of competitively sensitive information between competing firms? Please also indicate the relevance of anti-competitive effects or intent in such enforcement.**

   In recent years the BKartA has become more active in enforcing antitrust laws on competing firms that exchange competitively sensitive information, mainly by fining them for such conduct. This concerns cases where participating undertakings exchanged information on future business plans and strategies, future pricing, current negotiations with opposing market participants, planned introduction of new products or other information which allowed them to ascertain the future endeavors of the other firm.

   Mostly, the BKartA considered such conduct to constitute an intended restriction of competition. It was therefore not necessary to determine if the conduct also had anticompetitive effects.

4. **Have there been any cases in your jurisdiction in which the substantive antitrust laws were enforced in an M&A context? Please describe/explain and cite any such cases. (See also Annex.)**

   Merger control and antitrust law can be applied side by side and independently from one another (so called "double control"). Thus, the establishment of a joint venture can be subject to merger control and to antitrust law if the concentration leads to a restriction of competition according to section 1 ARC beyond the mere concentration itself. Additionally, the clearance of a transaction by the BKartA in merger

---

10 An English version is available at <https://www.gesetze-im-internet.de/englisch_gwb/englisch_gwb.html>.

control does not prevent it from later starting an investigation regarding a possible antitrust violation, unless explicitly provided otherwise in the clearance decision.

Most cases where antitrust law was enforced in an M&A context involve a joint venture between two competitors. In these cases, the joint venture was considered likely to bring about coordinated behavior between the two competitors. Depending on the circumstances of the case at hand, a violation of antitrust laws could be found to exist where the common undertaking does not fulfill all the necessary functions that an independent firm would normally have and is instead only used for a specific set of tasks provided by the parent companies (e.g. common production, common acquisition of goods).

The BKartA has stated that in cases in which the two founding companies and their joint venture remain competitors in the same market, a violation of antitrust law is regularly to be expected. The same is said to be true in cases where the founding companies and the joint venture are competitors, but the parents on the one hand and the joint venture on the other are active in different geographical markets, since it might prevent the founding companies from entering the market of the joint venture.

Also considered problematic are cases in which the joint venture is not or is no longer exclusively controlled by the founding companies but continues to compete with them and to share competitively sensitive information.

Other than in these circumstances, however, and in gun-jumping matters particularly, there are no cases under German law in which the potentially anticompetitive pre-closing conduct of merging parties (e.g. exchanging competitively sensitive information during the due diligence phase), was examined or challenged under substantive antitrust laws (Chapter I of the ARC), as opposed to the standstill provisions of Chapter VII.

5. Are the substantive antitrust laws more likely to apply at specific stages of the transaction – i.e. at an early stage, or prior to closing (or does it not make a difference)? Do companies face ongoing risk following the consummation (or failure) of their transaction for conduct that allegedly occurred pre-closing (pre-failure)?

German antitrust law is generally applicable at any stage of the transaction if the transaction or the behavior of the parties involved pursues an anticompetitive object or effect pursuant to section 1 ARC. The BKartA has the power to open a separate investigation concerning a possible antitrust violation at any time before, during or after the merger control process.

In principle, there is a so-called "double control", i.e. merger control and antitrust review are subject to separate proceedings. The clearing of a transaction by the BKartA does not cover possible violations of antitrust law unless explicitly stated in the decision. In particular, joint ventures may come under close antitrust scrutiny in separate proceedings during or after merger clearance.

6. Please explain how the relevant authority enforces (or could enforce) the substantive antitrust laws in an M&A context. How would the investigation occur, and what timing constraints would apply?

See Question 5.

7. **Is private enforcement of the substantive antitrust laws possible in an M&A context, and has it occurred?**

Whoever violates antitrust law is obliged to the person affected by the violation to rectify the infringement and, where there is a risk of recurrence, to desist from further infringements. A claim for injunction also exists if an infringement is likely. Affected persons are competitors or other market participants impaired by the infringement, section 33(1) and (2) ARC.

Such claims may also be asserted by certain associations with the legal capacity for the promotion of commercial or independent professional interests or other entities named in section 33(4) ARC.

8. **Could behavior subject to the substantive antitrust laws also be caught under the merger control rules/standstill obligation? (Please also refer to the Annex.)**

The anticompetitive pre-closing conduct of merging parties (e.g. exchanging competitively sensitive information during the due diligence phase) could be investigated and sanctioned by the BKartA pursuant to section 1 ARC/Article 101 TFEU (cartel prohibition). In addition, if such conduct were to qualify as "putting the concentration into effect" within the meaning of section 41(1) ARC (see above Question 2 of Part 1) the BKartA could investigate and sanction it pursuant to the standstill provision of Chapter VII (section 41(1) ARC). However, this would be done in one and the same administrative offense proceeding since the conduct under investigation would be one and the same. Such proceeding would be different from the merger control proceeding dealing with the clearance or prohibition of the concentration. There are no decisions in which the BKartA did find a violation of section 1 ARC/Article 101 TFEU in such a case.

9. **Please describe the penalties for infringing the substantive antitrust laws. Please indicate whether these include criminal penalties, including individual criminal penalties. As a practical matter, how have these been applied in the context of an M&A transaction?**

An intentional or negligent violation of antitrust law by any person is considered an administrative offense, which may be punished by a fine of up to €1 million (section 81(2) sentence 1). If a fine is imposed on an undertaking or an association of undertakings, the fine for each undertaking or association of undertakings participating in the infringement may not, beyond the abovementioned amount, exceed 10% of its total turnover in the preceding business year (section 81(4) sentence 2 ARC). The law does not provide for criminal sanctions, unless the impugned conduct qualifies as bid-rigging in (public or private) tenders pursuant to section 298 of the Criminal Code.

10. **Please describe policy and enforcement trends in your jurisdiction.**

With the ninth Amendment to the ARC, the German government has adopted the EU's Directive on Antitrust Damages Actions after which it has become significantly easier for those harmed by antitrust violations to pursue their claims. Companies that face such claims may be obliged to disclose certain documents if they are necessary for proving the claim (section 33g ARC). Details are still largely unclear. The Higher Regional Court of Düsseldorf recently held that section 33g ARC is not applicable to violations committed prior to the entry into force of the new law on 9 June 2017 (Case VI-W (*Kart*) 2/18, order of 3 April 2018).

German Competition Authority, "The German Competition Authority fines an undertaking specialized in organic dairies for providing incorrect information in a merger notification (Bongrain Europe)" 7 January 2016, e-Competitions Bulletin January 2016, Art. N° 77370

Carsten Gromotke, "The German Cartel Office imposes 'Gun Jumping' fine against a leading US candy manufacturer for failure to comply with German premerger notification (Mars, Nutro Products)" 15 December 2008, e-Competitions Bulletin December 2008, Art. N° 32014

Silke Heinz, "The German Bundeskartellamt fines an undertaking operating in the metal recycling market for having implemented a concentration without merger approval (Interseroh)" 10 May 2011, e-Competitions Bulletin May 2011, Art. N° 36337

Porter Elliott, "The German FCO fines publishing company €4.13m for gun-jumping (DuV)" 13 February 2009, e-Competitions Bulletin February 2009, Art. N° 43785

Annex

Table 1: Actual Enforcement of Specific Conduct under the Relevant Merger Control Rules and Substantive Antitrust Laws

Please identify whether the following type of conduct has been subject to investigation/enforcement in your jurisdiction, under the merger control laws or substantive antitrust laws. Please cite any such case(s) and provide a brief description in the table below.

Specific Conduct	Actual Enforcement under Merger Control Laws	Actual Enforcement under Substantive Antitrust Laws
Pre-signing due diligence	No	No
Post-signing/pre-approval due diligence	No	No
Post-approval/pre-closing due diligence	No	No
Use of "clean teams"	No	No
Restrictions on the target in an M&A agreement, e.g. buyer approval required for: Investments above a certain level; New business above a certain level; Other obligations to consult/obtain approval from the buyer before closing.	In *EDEKA/Kaiser's Tengelmann*, two of Germany's biggest chains of grocery stores wanted to merge. The transaction was notified to the BKartA but certain measures were taken before the BKartA had authorized the transaction. Among these, the target (Kaiser's Tengelmann (**KT**)) was obliged to devaluate/ shut down certain branches ("carve-out branches") which were not cost efficient. Other problematic measures included the devaluation/shut down of storage units and meat production sites, and the reduction of administrative staff within KT.	No

Specific Conduct	Actual Enforcement under Merger Control Laws	Actual Enforcement under Substantive Antitrust Laws
	The BGH considered this an infringement of s 41 (1) ARC.[16]	
Joint marketing	No	No
Joint presentations (e.g. industry fairs)	No	No
Joint communications	No	No
Strategy/planning regarding customers	No	No
Strategy/planning regarding suppliers	In *EDEKA/Kaiser's Tengelmann*,[17] EDEKA gave KT the opportunity to buy supplies through their supply system at rates which were lower than those normally granted to KT by other suppliers before the merger was fully accomplished; furthermore, certain product categories had to be sourced through EDEKA. The BGH reasoned that this would have had massive consequences for the concerned markets because KT would essentially not be an active buyer anymore. Even though the obligation to buy through EDEKA was only applied for certain product categories, it would have led KT not to rely on their existing supply system because of the lower rates. The BGH concluded that this behavior anticipated the effects of the merger significantly and constituted an infringement of s 41 (1) ARC.	No
Third party contract novation	No	No

---

11 Decision of 14 November 2017, case KVR 57/16.

12 ibid.

Specific Conduct	Actual Enforcement under Merger Control Laws	Actual Enforcement under Substantive Antitrust Laws
Personnel Issues: Secondments Retention Strategies	In *EDEKA/Kaiser's Tengelmann*, KT had been obliged by EDEKA to reduce administrative staff prior to closing.	No
IT Planning/Database Migration	No	No
Other	No	No

Table 2: Hypothetical Enforcement of Specific Conduct under the Relevant Merger Control Rules and Substantive Antitrust Laws

For any conduct that is *not* the subject of actual enforcement (Table 1), please indicate in the Table below whether the conduct identified *could potentially* be enforced under the merger control laws and/or substantive antitrust laws.

Specific Conduct	Hypothetical Enforcement under Merger Control Laws	Hypothetical Enforcement under Substantive Antitrust Laws
Pre-signing due diligence	For all categories below please see Table 1 and the assessments made by the BGH in *EDEKA/Kaiser's Tengelmann.*	For the exchange of information during the due diligence process in general: the exchange of such information is permitted as long as it is limited to the necessary data. Still, the parties should keep in mind antitrust law when exchanging information. There is no exception from antitrust law (especially Article 101 TFEU/s 1 ARC) while preparing a merger.
Post-signing/pre-approval due diligence		
Post-approval/pre-closing due diligence		
Use of "clean teams"		The usage of clean teams can further aid when "sensitive" information has to be exchanged.

▶

Specific Conduct	Hypothetical Enforcement under Merger Control Laws	Hypothetical Enforcement under Substantive Antitrust Laws
Restrictions on the target in an M&A agreement, e.g. buyer approval required for: – Investments above a certain level; – New business above a certain level; – Other obligations to consult/obtain approval from the buyer before closing.		
Joint marketing		
Joint presentations (e.g. industry fairs)		Should not be done: even "informing" customers of impending changes could be misconstrued.
Joint communications		One should not leave the impression that the merger has been completed before the authorities responsible for permitting this have done so.
Strategy/planning regarding customers		No allocation of customers; arrangements concerning pricing must not be made.
Strategy/planning regarding suppliers		Before the transaction, offers must not be coordinated.
Third party contract novation		
Personnel Issues: – Secondments – Retention Strategies		
IT Planning/Database Migration		

Specific Conduct	Hypothetical Enforcement under Merger Control Laws	Hypothetical Enforcement under Substantive Antitrust Laws
Other	Generally speaking, the acquiring company cannot undertake any measures which at least partly anticipate the effects of the merger. This is especially the case when the acquiring party gains power which they would only get after acquiring shares. Furthermore, measures which anticipate the integration of the two parties are not permitted. (see: Case *KVR 57/16 EDEKA/Kaiser's Tengelmann*)	All measures which are taken before the actual merger need to be examined with regard to the compatibility with antitrust law.

INDIA

Arshad (Paku) Khan, Anisha Chand[1]
and Sakshi Agarwal[2]
(Khaitan & Co)

1 The authors would like to thank Pranjal Prateek, Anmol Awasthi, Soham Banerjee, and Vasudhaa Ahuja at Khaitan & Co for their contributions.

2 At the time of printing, Sakshi Agarwal was no longer with Khaitan & Co.

Part 1: Merger Control and the "Standstill Obligation"

1. **Please identify the relevant merger control legislation in your jurisdiction. Please provide a link to the relevant legislation (if possible, in English) and also indicate:**
   - **whether the merger control system is mandatory or voluntary,**
   - **the relevant authority, and**
   - **the duration of the review period.**

Sections 5 and 6 of the Competition Act 2002, as amended (**Competition Act**),[3] deal with the substantive provisions regarding notifying "combinations" to the Indian competition authority, namely the Competition Commission of India (**CCI**). A combination is a merger, acquisition or amalgamation which satisfies the asset- or turnover-based financial thresholds provided under section 5 of the Competition Act (**Jurisdictional Thresholds**).

The CCI promulgated the Competition Commission of India (Procedure in regard to the transaction of business relating to combinations) Regulations 2011 (**Combination Regulations**)[4] on 11 May 2011, setting in place the framework for review of pre-merger notifications by the CCI. The Combination Regulations came into effect on 1 June 2011. These regulations have subsequently been amended by the CCI in February 2012, April 2013, March 2014, July 2015, 7 January 2016 and, most recently, 9 October 2018.[5]

Criteria

India is a mandatory and suspensory merger control regime. A transaction which meets the Jurisdictional Thresholds and does not qualify for any exemptions provided under the Combination Regulations or the notifications issued by the Ministry of Corporate Affairs, Government of India (**MCA**), must be notified to the CCI. There is no concept of voluntary notification to the CCI. Therefore, if the Jurisdictional Thresholds are not met, no merger notification can be filed with the CCI.

---

3 <https://www.cci.gov.in/sites/default/files/cci_pdf/competitionact2012.pdf>.

4 <https://www.cci.gov.in/sites/default/files/regulation_pdf/Combination%20Regulations%202016%20-%20FINAL_0.pdf>.

5 The recent amendments to the Combination Regulations dated 9 October 2018 can be accessed here <https://www.cci.gov.in/sites/default/files/whats_newdocument/Comb.%20Amend%20Regl.2018.pdf>.

Review timelines

Before June 2017, parties only had 30 calendar days after the occurrence of the triggering event to file the merger notification with the CCI. However, this deadline has been abolished by the MCA, provisionally until 28 June 2022, bringing India into line with jurisdictions such as the European Union, where the obligation is simply to secure a merger control clearance prior to consummating the notified transaction.

Once the merger notification has been filed, the CCI has 30 working days from the date of filing the merger notification to form a prima facie opinion as to whether the proposed combination would result in an appreciable adverse effect on competition (**AAEC**) in India. This is generally known as a "Phase I" investigation. The time taken by the parties to the combination to respond to the CCI's requests for additional information is excluded from the 30 working-day period. Additionally, the Combination Regulations allow for an additional 15 working days for the CCI to reach out to third parties for its assessment of the proposed merger.

If the CCI's prima facie opinion is that the transaction does not (or is not likely to) cause an AAEC in India, it issues a formal order approving the proposed combination.

However, if the CCI forms a prima facie opinion that the combination is likely to cause an AAEC within the relevant market(s) in India, it issues a show cause notice to the parties under section 29(1) of the Competition Act, seeking their views on why a detailed investigation into the proposed combination should not be initiated. If the parties are successful in addressing the CCI's concerns (including offering structural or behavioral remedies, if necessary), the CCI does not initiate a formal inquiry and approves the transaction. However, if the CCI is not satisfied, it initiates a formal "Phase II" investigation.

The CCI's review process (for both Phase I and Phase II reviews) could take up to 210 calendar days from the date of filing the merger notification (to which a period of up to 60 working days may statutorily be added in certain circumstances for evaluating remedies). This deadline is subject to further exceptions depending on the circumstances of each case. However, in our experience, the CCI is committed to the 30 working days deadline for issuing its approval in "no-issues" Phase I transactions.

2. Does the merger control system in your jurisdiction impose a "standstill obligation" – meaning, that the transaction cannot be implemented prior to completing the merger control process? (Please cite the relevant legislation.) Please also indicate the legal scope of the standstill obligation according to the relevant legislation (e.g. the parties to the transaction cannot effect a change of control, cannot take steps towards implementation, etc.).

Yes, section 6(2A) of the Competition Act imposes a standstill obligation. A notified transaction cannot be completed until the CCI has given its approval or 210 calendar days have passed from the date of notification, whichever is earlier.

If CCI clearance has not been obtained, taking any step towards the full or part consummation of the transaction, for example, closing the foreign leg of the transaction, depositing part consideration, even if the same is refundable, putting shares in an escrow, is considered as gun-jumping by the CCI (see Table 1 below).

3. **Have the relevant authorities in your jurisdiction issued internal or external guidelines concerning the scope of the standstill obligation, and/or their authority to enforce it? Please provide a copy/link of such guidance, if possible in English.**

The CCI has not issued any specific guidelines concerning the scope of the standstill obligation.

4. **Are there any exceptions to the standstill obligation – for example, through derogation or "carve out"? Please describe the circumstances in which this is possible. Please also describe the relevant process, e.g. do parties need to apply to the authority for a derogation from the standstill obligation? If so, how long is the approval process? If there are specific cases addressing these issues, please identify them.**

There are no exceptions to the standstill obligation under the Competition Act, including by way of "carve-out" provisions.

5. **Does a public bid exception exist in your jurisdiction? (For example, under the EU Merger Regulation it is possible to acquire shares as part of a public bid, provided that the shares are not exercised until the acquisition is cleared by the Commission.) If such an exception exists in your jurisdiction, please describe how it is applied.**

There is no public bid exception under the Indian merger control regime.

6. **What powers does the relevant authority have to investigate and enforce violations of the standstill obligation? Are dawn raids possible? What timing applies to investigation/enforcement proceedings?**

The CCI can regulate its own procedure under section 36(1) of the Competition Act. Additionally, for the purposes of discharging its functions under the Competition Act, section 36(2) confers upon the CCI the same powers that are vested in an Indian Civil Court under the Code of Civil Procedure 1908, while trying a suit. This means that the CCI has sufficient powers for search and seizure, requiring discovery and production of documents, and summoning evidence.

The CCI also has the power to conduct dawn raids under section 41 of the Competition Act. As of the date of writing, the CCI has conducted five dawn raids in the context of abuse of dominance and cartelization in India. The CCI has not yet conducted a dawn raid in the context of an M&A transaction; however, generally speaking, in a non-adversarial regulatory *ex ante* procedure, it is unlikely that the CCI would exercise this power.

7. **What are the possible penalties for violating the standstill obligation? Are there criminal sanctions, including on individuals? Have these been applied in practice? Is there a difference in enforcement between transactions involving domestic companies and "foreign-to-foreign" transactions? Does the authority have the power to unwind transactions implemented in breach of the standstill obligation? If so, has the authority made use of that power in practice? If yes, please provide examples.**

Section 43A of the Competition Act provides for the imposition of a monetary penalty in a case of contravention of the standstill obligation. While there are no criminal sanctions for violating the standstill obligation (either on the entity or the concerned individuals), it is pertinent to note that monetary penalties can be imposed on both the concerned individuals and the parties to the combination.

The maximum penalty that the CCI can impose under section 43A of the Competition Act is 1% of the total turnover or the value of the assets, whichever is higher, of the parties to the combination. There is no difference in enforcement between transactions involving domestic companies and foreign-to-foreign transactions. Given that the Competition Act contemplates a suspensory regime, global transactions cannot be consummated in part or in full prior to receiving approval from the CCI.

Further, section 20(1) of the Competition Act is the "claw-back" provision which empowers the CCI to inquire whether a combination implemented in breach of the standstill obligation, has caused or is likely to cause an AAEC in India. However, this investigatory power of the CCI only extends for a period of one year from the date on which such combination has taken effect or is consummated. If the CCI concludes that the combination has resulted in an AAEC in India, it can declare it to be void and can impose penalties on the parties as well as on the concerned individuals. However, the CCI's power to impose a monetary penalty is not restricted by the expiry of the one-year time period.

As of the date hereof, the CCI has not passed any order resulting in voiding or unwinding of a combination.

8. How does the relevant authority typically learn of potential violations of the standstill obligation? Does the authority actively monitor the trade press?

The CCI has a strong media research wing which actively monitors business and trade media. Typically, the CCI will learn of a potential contravention of the standstill obligation through media reports or through an information/complaint filed by a third-party with the CCI.

9. Please describe the relevant authority's enforcement of the standstill obligation. If there have been cases, please describe the specific conduct that was found to violate the standstill provision and the criteria applied by the relevant authority or court. Has the relevant authority considered the market impact of the conduct? (Please refer to the Annex.)

The details regarding the CCI's enforcement of the standstill obligation have been provided in the Annex below. Thus far, the CCI has found conduct such as consummation of the foreign leg of a transaction, consummation of other legs of a composite transaction, payment of part consideration, good faith deposits, depositing shares in an escrow account and conditions precedent which can amount to disincentivizing the need to compete independently, to amount to a step towards implementing the transaction and, hence, a violation of the standstill obligation.

To date, a maximum penalty of INR 50 million (approx. US$720,000) has been imposed for gun-jumping in the case of *GE Energy Europe BV/GE/GEIF Alstom India Limited/Alstom T&D India Limited*,[6] for failing to notify the CCI and filing the merger notification with a delay of 203 days.

---

6 Order of the CCI under Section 43A of the Competition Act dated 16 February 2016 in Combination Registration C-2015/01/241.

A fine of INR 50 million (approx. US$720,000) was also imposed in *Piramal Enterprises Limited/Shriram Transport Finance Company/Shriram Capital Limited/Shriram City Union Finance Limited*,[7] for consummating the transaction without prior notification to the CCI.

Prior to the 29 June 2017 MCA notification (see Question 1, under "Review timelines"), gun-jumping included both (i) part and/or full consummation of a notifiable transaction before receiving the CCI approval; and (ii) filing a belated merger notification after the expiry of the 30-day period. However, following the MCA notification, gun-jumping refers to only part and/or full consummation of a notifiable transaction before receiving the CCI's approval (including non-notification of an otherwise notifiable transaction).[8]

Recently, two of the CCI's decisions on gun-jumping have been confirmed on appeal by the Supreme Court of India. In *Thomas Cook*,[9] the Supreme Court held that where a series of steps is envisaged to accomplish a combination, consummation of even a single step, prior to CCI approval, would violate the standstill obligation. All the steps of the transaction were held to be intrinsically connected and interdependent with each other and formed part of one composite business transaction. In *SCM Solifert*,[10] the Supreme Court found that the transfer of shares in escrow before CCI approval amounted to gun-jumping, and the non-exercise of voting rights by the acquirer was, at best, a self-imposed contractual obligation.

10. In cases involving alleged violations of the standstill obligation under the relevant merger control laws, has the relevant authority (or court) also considered the substantive antitrust laws? (Please refer to the Annex.)

As of the date of writing, the CCI has not applied substantive antitrust provisions in cases involving violation of the standstill obligation.

11. Is private enforcement of the standstill obligation possible?

The Competition Act does not have an enabling provision for a third party to file an objection relating to a possible breach of the standstill obligation. Therefore, private enforcement of the standstill obligation is not possible. However, a third party could alert the CCI to such a breach.

The CCI decides whether there has been a breach of the standstill obligation.

12. Please describe the private law risks/consequences (i.e. contractual/validity consequences) for transactions that are subject to notification, but which are completed without notification/approval. Please identify any relevant cases and describe them.

Combinations that have not been notified to the CCI are not automatically void. Thus, the validity of any private law arrangements would not be affected automatically. Only combinations which have been determined to cause or are likely

---

7 Order of the CCI under Section 43A of the Competition Act dated 2 May 2016 in Combination Registration C-2015/02/249.

8 *Intellect Design Arena Limited/Polaris Financial Technology Limited*, Order of the CCI under Section 43A of the Competition Act dated 7 May 2018 in Combination Registration C-2015/12/348.

9 *Competition Commission of India v Thomas Cook (India) Ltd & Anr* [2018] 6 SCC 549 (17 April 2018).

10 *SCM Solifert Limited & Anr v Competition Commission of India* [2018] 6 SCC 631 (17 April 2018).

to cause an AAEC in India, after a thorough competition assessment, can be modified/voided, consequently resulting in a modification/voiding of the contracts/ private law arrangements.

As stated in Question 7, section 20(1) of the Competition Act sets forth the CCI's "claw-back" power to inquire into combinations which were not notified and that have already been consummated. This power only extends for a one-year period from the date on which the combination took effect.

The CCI can declare the combination void if it causes or is likely to cause an AAEC in any relevant market(s) in India. This would also include any private law arrangements such as contracts. To date, the CCI has not declared a transaction void while exercising its power under the "claw-back" provision.

13. Please describe policy and enforcement trends in your jurisdiction.

In the last eight years of the Indian merger control regime, the CCI has played a proactive role in shaping merger control jurisprudence, including in gun-jumping cases. The past few years have witnessed several multijurisdictional filings and divestments in key sectors such as agro-chemicals, where the CCI was also required to cooperate with its global counterparts.

Additionally, in September 2018, the Competition Law Review Committee (**CLRC**) was set up by the MCA to review the Competition Act in view of the changing business environment and to better handle cross-border competition issues in line with international best practices. The key amendments likely to be introduced by the CLRC could include provisions for settlement of antitrust disputes, buyer cartels, certain merger control exemptions, creation of a separate bench with the National Company Law Appellate Tribunal (**NCLAT**) to hear appeals from competition matters.

Part 2: Substantive Antitrust Law in an M&A Context

1. **Please identify the relevant substantive antitrust laws in your jurisdiction that can potentially apply in an M&A context (e.g. for the EU, this would include Article 101 of the Treaty on the Functioning of the European Union). Please provide a link to the relevant legislation (if possible, in English).**

Section 3 (which applies to anticompetitive horizontal and vertical agreements) and section 4 (which applies to abuse of dominant position) of the Competition Act are the relevant substantive provisions of the Competition Act.[11]

Typically, sections 3 and 4 (substantive enforcement provisions) and sections 5 and 6 (substantive merger control provisions) of the Competition Act are applied independently. As such, it has been held by the NCLAT that section 4 (pertaining to abuse of dominance) cannot be applied in the M&A context.[12] However, given the lack of guidance on the subject, it is possible for section 3 to be applicable in an M&A context.

2. **Do any guidelines exist in your jurisdiction concerning the application of the substantive antitrust laws in an M&A context – whether internal to the relevant authority, or external, formal or informal (e.g. speeches)? If so, please provide a copy/link to such guidance.**

The CCI has published a Guidance Note on non-compete restrictions in transactions.[13]

The CCI has also published frequently asked questions and answers for combinations.[14]

3. **As a general matter (not limited to M&A), how are the substantive antitrust laws enforced with respect to the exchange of competitively sensitive information between competing firms? Please also indicate the relevance of anticompetitive effects or intent in such enforcement.**

As a general matter, any exchange of competitively/commercially sensitive information between competing firms will be regarded as a horizontal arrangement and may constitute a breach of section 3(3) of the Competition Act. Section 3(3) of the Competition Act specifically provides that the following arrangements (including cartels), between enterprises/persons which are horizontally placed,

---

11 The Competition Act is available at <https://www.cci.gov.in/sites/default/files/cci_pdf/competitionact2012.pdf>.

12 *Piyush Joshi v Competition Commission of India*, Competition Appeal No. 32 of 2017 (Old Appeal No. 43 of 2016) (2 July 2019).

13 <https://www.cci.gov.in/sites/default/files/Non-Compete/Guidance_Note.pdf>.

14 <https://www.cci.gov.in/node/2847>.

will be presumed to cause an AAEC in India (except for joint venture agreements resulting in efficiency gains):

a) direct/indirect determination of purchase or sale prices;

b) limiting or controlling production, supply, markets, technical development, investment or provision of services;

c) market-sharing or allocation; and

d) big-rigging or collusive bidding.

There is a rebuttable presumption of AAEC for these agreements.

4. Have there been any cases in your jurisdiction in which the substantive antitrust laws were enforced in an M&A context? Please describe/explain and cite any such cases. (See also Annex.)

As of the date of writing, the CCI has not enforced substantive antitrust provisions (i.e. sections 3 and 4) in an M&A context.

5. Are the substantive antitrust laws more likely to apply at specific stages of the transaction – i.e. at an early stage, or prior to closing (or does it not make a difference)? Do companies face ongoing risk following the consummation (or failure) of their transaction for conduct that allegedly occurred pre-closing (pre-failure)?

In a recent appeal decision where there was an allegation of abuse of dominance arising out of a merger control approval of the CCI, it was observed that question of abuse of dominant position cannot arise at the time of assessing a transaction/combination for AAEC. It is only after the combination has come into effect and an actual abuse has occurred that an assessment of abuse of dominant position can take place. Accordingly, the allegation of abuse of dominant position cannot be looked into at the stage of assessment for approval of the combination.[15]

Since there is no precedent in the context of appling section 3 to M&A transactions, it is difficult to state at what specific stage of a transaction the CCI would apply the provision in an M&A context. However, it is likely that it may be applied at any stage of the transaction. Further, the Competition Act does not prescribe a limitation period for filing claims for infringement of the Competition Act.

The CCI has also reserved the right in the Combination Regulations to accept delayed merger notifications without prejudice to its powers of imposing penalties for failure to file under section 43A of the Competition Act. Further, as stated above in Question 7 of Part 1, the CCI can initiate an enquiry into the effects of a transaction that has not been notified for a period of up to one year from the transaction completion date.

6. Please explain how the relevant authority enforces (or could enforce) the substantive antitrust laws in an M&A context. How would the investigation occur, and what timing constraints would apply?

As a general matter, while there is yet no precedent in India, it would likely be a hybrid of an enforcement action relating to anti-competitive agreements and a

---

15 n 10.

merger control notification, with many of the questions from the merger notification forming part of the investigation.

The CCI is likely to follow the same procedure for investigation followed in enforcement matters (i.e. calling for production of documents, conducting depositions, oral examination on oath by enforcing summons and possibly dawn raids). While there are no timing constraints, if the matter is referred to the CCI's investigative arm (i.e. the office of the Director General (**DG**)), then the DG will be required to complete the investigation within 60 days of the date of the CCI's directions, which is extendable.

7. Is private enforcement of the substantive antitrust laws possible in an M&A context, and has it occurred?

There is no private enforcement of competition law in the M&A context in India. However, a private/third party can theoretically file a complaint/information against a merger for substantive breach of the Competition Act based on the plain language of the damages provision in the Competition Act (subject to proof of loss as a result of the contravention).

There has been no case to date where the private enforcement provision has been tested in the context of M&A.

8. Could behavior subject to the substantive antitrust laws also be caught under the merger control rules/standstill obligation? (Please also refer to the Annex.)

There are no provisions to this effect in the Competition Act.

9. Please describe the penalties for infringing the substantive antitrust laws. Please indicate whether these include criminal penalties, including individual criminal penalties. As a practical matter, how have these been applied in the context of an M&A transaction?

The Competition Act is civil legislation and, accordingly, it does not provide for criminal penalties either on the concerned entities or individuals. However, under section 42(3) of the Competition Act, criminal liability may arise when the contravening entity, in non-compliance with the CCI's directions/orders, continues to engage in the sanctioned misconduct or fails to pay the penalty imposed upon it. In such a scenario, further enforcement is pursued through a criminal complaint filed by the CCI.

The penalties for infringing the substantive provisions of the Competition Act (i.e. sections 3 and 4) are levied under section 27 of the Competition Act. The CCI can direct an enterprise in breach of the Competition Act to cease and desist from any activity of entering into anticompetitive agreements or abuse of a dominant position. In addition, the CCI can also impose a monetary penalty of up to 10% of such enterprise's relevant turnover for the preceding three financial years.

For cartels, the CCI can impose a monetary penalty upon an enterprise involved in the cartel, up to the higher of three times the relevant profit or 10% of its relevant turnover for each year of the cartel's continuance.

Further, section 28 of the Competition Act also empowers the CCI to order division of a dominant enterprise to ensure it does not abuse its dominant position.

Additionally, section 48 of the Competition Act provides for imposition of a penalty on individuals who are officers in charge of the conduct of business of the responsible enterprise.

As of the date hereof, these provisions have not been applied in an M&A context.

10. Please describe policy and enforcement trends in your jurisdiction.

While the Competition Act has been relatively new in India, in the last 10 years of its enforcement work, the CCI's progressive and proactive approach has made a tremendous impact in evolving competition jurisprudence in India and also on how businesses are conducted in India.

On the enforcement side, cartel enforcement has been a priority area for the CCI. Severe penalties have been imposed on contravening parties to leave a strong message of deterrence. For example, in the cement cartel case,[16] the CCI imposed a hefty penalty of INR 67 billion (approx. US$1 billion) on 11 cement companies in India. Additionally, the CCI has also used its "lesser penalty" (i.e. cartel leniency) provisions to encourage entities/individuals to come forward and cooperate in cartel investigations. This is evidenced by the increased number of leniency applications being filed with the CCI.

In addition to the scrutiny of anticompetitive agreements, abuse of dominance enforcement has also been on the CCI's radar. Recently, the CCI imposed a penalty of INR 136 million (approx. US$19.56 million) on Google, Inc for abuse of a dominant position.[17]

An analysis of the CCI enforcement trends shows that the focus has been on the technology and digital sector, airline sector, automotive sector, telecommunication sector, cement sector, pharmaceutical sector, film and movie distribution sector, etc. Recently, the CCI has also initiated a market study into the Indian e-commerce sector.

Kalyani Singh, "The Competition Commission of India approves an acquisition in the power and grid sector (GE/Alstom)" 5 May 2015, e-Competitions Bulletin May 2015, Art. N° 75465

Gauri Chhabra, Suhail Nathani," The Competition Commission of India directs a company to file a merger notification following several minority stakes acquisitions (Piramal)" 18 February 2015, e-Competitions Bulletin February 2015, Art. N° 77564

Suhail Nathani, "The Supreme Court of India applies a strict interpretation to the requirement of notifying the Competition Commission prior to the implementation of a merger (Thomas Cook/Sterling)" 17 April 2018, e-Competitions Bulletin April 2018, Art. N° 86822

---

16 *Builders Association of India v Cement Manufacturers' Association*, 2016 SCC OnLine CCI 46 (31 August 2016). The appeal by the cement companies to the National Company Law Appellate Tribunal (NCLAT) was dismissed on 25 July 2018 in Competition Appeal No. 22-26 of 2017.

17 *Matrimony.com Limited v Google LLC* [2018] SCC OnLine CCI 1 (8 February 2018). The matter is currently under appeal to NCLAT and the penalty has been stayed by way of the NCLAT's order dated 27 April 2018, see *Google LLC & Ors v Competition Commission of India & Ors* (Competition Appeal No. 18 of 2018).

Man Mohan Sharma, "The Indian National Company Law Appellate Tribunal (NCLAT) upholds the Indian Competition Authority's record fine imposed in the cement cartel case (Builders Association of India/Cement Manufacturers' Association)" 25 July 2018, e-Competitions Bulletin July 2018, Art. N° 87865

Man Mohan Sharma, "The Indian Competition Authority fines a global tech company for abuse of dominance in the market for online search and related advertising services (Matrimony.com/Consumer Unity & Trust Society/Google)" 8 February 2018, e-Competitions Bulletin February 2018, Art. N° 87477

Man Mohan Sharma, "The Indian Competition Authority clears structural separation of global pharmaceutical company's bioscience business into separate new pharmaceutical company (Baxter India/Baxalta India)" 8 September 2015, e-Competitions Bulletin September 2015, Art. N° 87760

Man Mohan Sharma, "The Indian Competition Authority fines 7 cement manufacturers for bid rigging (State of Haryana/Cement Manufacturers)" 19 January 2017, e-Competitions Bulletin January 2017, Art. N° 87593

Annex

Table 1: Actual Enforcement of Specific Conduct under the Relevant Merger Control Rules and Substantive Antitrust Laws

Please identify whether the following type of conduct has been subject to investigation/enforcement in your jurisdiction, under the merger control laws or substantive antitrust laws. Please cite any such case(s) and provide a brief description in the table below.

Specific Conduct	Actual Enforcement under Merger Control Laws	Actual Enforcement under Substantive Antitrust Laws
Pre-signing due diligence	No	No
Post-signing/pre-approval due diligence	No	No
Post-approval/pre-closing due diligence	No	No
Use of "clean teams"	No	No
Restrictions on the target in an M&A agreement, e.g. buyer approval required for: – Investments above a certain level; – New business above a certain level; – Other obligations to consult/obtain approval from the buyer before closing.	In *LT Foods Limited/ Hindustan Unilever Limited*,[18] the CCI, inter alia, found that the acquirer had imposed restrictions on promotional spending. Further, the CCI also found that there was a restriction on the seller to enter/exit any geographic territories. This, among other reasons, formed the basis for the CCI to penalize the acquirer with INR 500,000 (approx. US$7,500).	No

18 Order of the CCI under Section 43A of the Competition Act dated 11 May 2018 in Combination Registration C-2016/04/387.

Specific Conduct	Actual Enforcement under Merger Control Laws	Actual Enforcement under Substantive Antitrust Laws
Joint marketing	No	No
Joint presentations (e.g. industry fairs)	No	No
Joint communications	No	No
Strategy/planning regarding customers	No	No
Strategy/planning regarding suppliers	In *LT Foods,*[19] the CCI also found that there were requirements on the seller to hand over certain inventories to the acquirers, the acquirer's introduction to and interaction with the suppliers of the seller.	No
Third party contract novation	No	No
Personnel Issues: – Secondments – Retention Strategies	No	No
IT Planning/Database Migration	No	No
Other	In *Hindustan Colas Private Limited/Shell India Markets Private Limited,*[20] the CCI held that payment of consideration in a refundable deposit account prior to obtaining CCI clearance constituted contravention of the standstill obligation under the Competition Act. A penalty of INR 500,000 (approx. US$7,500) was imposed.[21]	No

▶

19 ibid.

20 Order of the CCI under Section 43A of the Competition Act dated 14 September 2016 in Combination Registration No. C-2015/08/299.

21 In addition to *Hindustan Colas* and *LT Foods*, there have been a number of other cases with similar instances of pre-payment of consideration. See *Chhatwal Group Trust/Dilip Builcon Limited*, Order of the CCI under Section 43A of the Competition Act dated 8 August 2018 in Combination Registration C-2018/01/544.

Specific Conduct	Actual Enforcement under Merger Control Laws	Actual Enforcement under Substantive Antitrust Laws
Other	In *LT Foods,*[22] another aspect was that the acquirer had prepaid the consideration, in contravention of the standstill obligation. In *SCM Solifert Limited/ Mangalore Chemicals and Fertilizers Limited,*[23] the CCI held that depositing shares in an escrow account prior to obtaining CCI clearance would constitute contravention of the standstill obligation under the Competition Act. A penalty of INR 20 million (approx. US$300,000) was imposed. In *Baxalta Incorporated/ Baxter International Inc,*[24] the CCI held that in cases of global combinations, the combination must not be consummated at the global level before the CCI's approval. The trigger document was the global agreement, and not the local agreement. A penalty of INR 10 million (approx. US$150,000) was imposed.	No

22 n 16.

23 Order of the CCI under Section 43A of the Competition Act dated 10 February 2015 in Combination Registration C-2014/05/175.

24 Order of the CCI under Section 43A of the Competition Act dated 8 March 2016 in Combination Registration C-2015/07/297.

Specific Conduct	Actual Enforcement under Merger Control Laws	Actual Enforcement under Substantive Antitrust Laws
Other	In *Eli Lilly & Company/ Novartis AG*,[25] the CCI held that in cases of global combinations, the combination must not be consummated at the global level before the CCI's approval. The trigger document was the global agreement, and not the local agreement. A penalty of INR 10 million (approx. US$150,000) was imposed. In *UltraTech Cement/ Jaiprakash Associates Limited*,[26] the CCI held that the extension of a corporate guarantee pursuant to the combination constituted prepayment of consideration leading to consummation of a part of the combination before the approval of the CCI. A penalty of INR 1 million (approx. US$14,000) was imposed. In *Adani Transmission Limited/Reliance Electric Generation and Supply Limited*,[27] the CCI held that advancement of a loan against the consideration	No

25 Order of the CCI under Section 43A of the Competition Act dated 14 July 2016 in Combination Registration C-2015/07/289.

26 Order of the CCI under Section 43A of the Competition Act dated 12 March 2018 in Combination Registration C-2015/02/246.

27 Order of the CCI under Section 43A of the Competition Act dated 30 July 2018 in Combination Registration C-2018/01/547.

Specific Conduct	Actual Enforcement under Merger Control Laws	Actual Enforcement under Substantive Antitrust Laws
Other	payable for the combination is in contravention of the standstill obligation under the Competition Act. A penalty of INR 1 million (approx. US$14,000) was imposed. In *Bharti Airtel Limited/ Tata Teleservices Limited,*[28] the transaction agreement contained a customary "ER clause" which contained an appointed date or notional date agreements to ensure that parties had a definitive basis for computation of liabilities or assets from a particular date. However, the CCI noted that it was incumbent on the acquirer entity to ensure that the form and scope of such customary arrangements imposed on the target entity were inherent and proportionate to the objective of ensuring certainty and preservation of business valuation and that such conditions did not violate the standstill obligation under the Competition Act. Accordingly, the CCI held that merely stating that the clause was subject to regulatory (including CCI)	No

28 Order of the CCI under Section 43A of the Competition Act dated 14 July 2016 in Combination Registration C-2015/07/289.

Specific Conduct	Actual Enforcement under Merger Control Laws	Actual Enforcement under Substantive Antitrust Laws
Other	approval, did not absolve the acquirer of its obligations. The clause was required to be assessed for its competitive effects and the question of whether it was notional or otherwise was irrelevant to the findings of gun-jumping. Therefore, it was concluded that the clause was an "anteriority clause" and had the potential to cause AAEC in the interim period i.e. the clause was indeed disincentivizing Tata from competing with Airtel. The CCI imposed a penalty of INR 1 million (approx. US$14,000) on Airtel.	No

Table 2: Hypothetical Enforcement of Specific Conduct under the Relevant Merger Control Rules and Substantive Antitrust Laws

For any conduct that is *not* the subject of actual enforcement (Table 1), please indicate in the Table below whether the conduct identified *could potentially* be enforced under the merger control laws and/or substantive antitrust laws.

Specific Conduct	Hypothetical Enforcement under Merger Control Laws	Hypothetical Enforcement under Substantive Antitrust Laws
Pre-signing due diligence	It is customary for parties to engage in pre-signing due diligence. It is advisable to implement clean teams, otherwise, there may be a contravention of the standstill obligation under the Competition Act.	Any exchange of commercially or competitively sensitive information between two independent enterprises engaged in identical or similar trade of goods or provision of services at any time can constitute a violation of s 3 of the Competition Act.

▶

Specific Conduct	Hypothetical Enforcement under Merger Control Laws	Hypothetical Enforcement under Substantive Antitrust Laws
Post-signing/ pre-approval due diligence	While it is not common in India for the parties to engage in post-signing due diligence, the parties do commonly work towards an integration plan which covers specific issues, such as employee transfer, specific movable assets/ stock-in trade transfers etc. However, the parties to the combination are required to not engage in discussions pertaining to commercially or competitively sensitive information.	Any exchange of commercially or competitively sensitive information between two independent enterprises engaged in identical or similar trade of goods or provision of services at any time can constitute a violation of s 3 of the Competition Act.
Post-approval/pre-closing due diligence	No	Any exchange of commercially or competitively sensitive information between two independent enterprises engaged in identical or similar trade of goods or provision of services at any time can constitute a violation of s 3 of the Competition Act.
Use of "clean teams"	Use of clean teams is not always required. For example, a transaction involving a pure financial investment where the investor has no prior interests in a competing business may not require implementing clean teams.	Any exchange of commercially or competitively sensitive information between two independent enterprises engaged in identical or similar trade of goods or provision of services at any time can constitute a violation of s 3 of the Competition Act.

Specific Conduct	Hypothetical Enforcement under Merger Control Laws	Hypothetical Enforcement under Substantive Antitrust Laws
Restrictions on the target in an M&A agreement, e.g. buyer approval required for: – Investments above a certain level; – New business above a certain level; – Other obligations to consult/obtain approval from the buyer before closing.	Certain restrictions on the target, which could be justified as minority protection for protecting investments that the buyer is making, should not raise concerns. However, restrictions without justification, which are more blanket in nature, will attract scrutiny. In *LT Foods*, restrictions on the seller to enter/exit any geographic territories was considered a contravention of the standstill obligation under the Competition Act.	Such restrictions prior to consummation of the transaction may be seen as amounting to influence over the target. Hence, it could lead to potential concerns relating to horizontal or vertical agreements.
Joint marketing	Joint marketing could potentially be a part of a standstill obligation and implementing this before approval could potentially lead to an adverse finding.	Joint marketing can constitute a violation of s 3(3) of the Competition Act if the parties are engaged in identical or similar trade of goods or provision of services.
Joint presentations (e.g. industry fairs)	This could be seen as projecting the parties as a single entity that could potentially lead to adverse consequences.	Depending on the content, such presentations can constitute a violation of s 3(3) of the Competition Act if the parties are engaged in identical or similar trade of goods or provision of services.
Joint communications	This could be seen as projecting the parties as a single entity that could potentially lead to adverse consequences, unless it were clearly disclosed that the parties were awaiting CCI merger control approval.	Depending on the content, joint communications may be construed as a violation of s 3(3) of the Competition Act if the parties are engaged in identical or similar trade of goods or provision of services.

Specific Conduct	Hypothetical Enforcement under Merger Control Laws	Hypothetical Enforcement under Substantive Antitrust Laws
Strategy/planning regarding customers	The standstill obligation could cover decisions regarding strategy and planning with respect to customers. For example, if the parties to a notifiable transaction agreed to cease serving a customer prior to obtaining CCI clearance, that would almost certainly be seen as gun-jumping. By contrast, integration planning, without sharing commercially sensitive information, might be permissible, but care needs to be taken.	Such strategies/planning can constitute a violation of s 3(3) of the Competition Act if the parties are engaged in identical or similar trade of goods or provision of services.
Strategy/planning regarding suppliers	The standstill obligation could cover decisions regarding strategy and planning with respect to suppliers. For example, if the parties to a notifiable transaction agreed to cease dealing with a supplier prior to obtaining CCI clearance, that would be seen as gun-jumping.	Such strategies/planning can constitute a violation of s 3(3) of the Competition Act if the parties are engaged in identical or similar trade of goods or provision of services.
Third party contract novation	This could be seen as projecting the parties as a single entity that could potentially lead to adverse consequences.	Such conduct can constitute a violation of s 3(3) of the Competition Act if the parties are engaged in identical or similar trade of goods or provision of services
Personnel Issues: – Secondments – Retention Strategies	Subject to the nature of information shared among the personnel (i.e. whether any commercially sensitive information becomes a part of such discussions), such a step may constitute a violation of the standstill obligation under the Competition Act.	Depending on the nature of information being shared among personnel, the conduct of the personnel may be construed as contravention of substantive antitrust laws.

Specific Conduct	Hypothetical Enforcement under Merger Control Laws	Hypothetical Enforcement under Substantive Antitrust Laws
IT Planning/Database Migration	The standstill obligation could cover IT integration and/or database migration. However, IT integration and/ or database migration may be relatively less risky as long as it does not entail exchange of commercial information.	Any exchange of commercially or competitively sensitive information between two independent enterprises engaged in identical or similar trade of goods or provision of services at any time can constitute a violation of s 3 of the Competition Act.
Other	–	–

ISRAEL

Eytan Epstein, Mazor Matzkevich
and Inbal Rosenblum Brand
(M Firon & Co)

Part 1: Merger Control and the "Standstill Obligation"

1. **Please identify the relevant merger control legislation in your jurisdiction. Please provide a link to the relevant legislation (if possible, in English) and also indicate:**
   - **whether the merger control system is mandatory or voluntary,**
   - **the relevant authority, and**
   - **the duration of the review period.**

   Merger control is regulated under the Economic Competition Law 5748-1988 (**Competition Law**) and the regulations thereunder. The Israeli Competition Authority (**ICA**) is the agency in charge of the enforcement of the Competition Law. The ICA, headed by the General Director, is mandated to prevent the attainment of market power through merger control and anti-cartel enforcement, to restrain abuse by dominant firms and to preserve competition in the various markets. The Competition Tribunal, sitting with the District Court in Jerusalem, has an exclusive jurisdiction over non-criminal administrative antitrust proceedings. The administrative actions and decisions of the General Director are subject to judicial review by the Competition Tribunal and some decisions are subject to review by other courts. Criminal proceedings for violations of the Competition Law may be launched by the General Director on behalf of the state attorney general, and are conducted exclusively before the District Court in Jerusalem.[1]

   If any of the thresholds mentioned in the Competition Law is met, the filing of a pre-merger notification form is *mandatory*. In such a case the parties to the merger must obtain the approval of the General Director prior to the implementation of the transaction.

   The General Director must render a decision within 30 days from the submission of complete pre-merger notification forms by all parties to the transaction. If no decision is made within this period, the merger is deemed to be cleared.

   The 30-day period may be extended either with the consent of the parties, or by the Competition Tribunal on application of the General Director. A merger that must be notified under the Competition Law must not be implemented prior to its clearance.

2. **Does the merger control system in your jurisdiction impose a "*standstill obligation*" – meaning, that the transaction cannot be implemented prior to completing the merger control process? (Please cite the relevant legislation.)**

---

1 Merger Control Legislation <http://www.antitrust.gov.il/eng/Antitrustlaw.aspx>.

Please also indicate the *legal scope* of the standstill obligation according to the relevant legislation (e.g. the parties to the transaction cannot effect a change of control, cannot take steps towards implementation, etc.).

Once an acquisition transaction has come within the scope of the merger provisions of the Competition Law, the parties are subject to special requirements, which the ICA strictly observes. The source of these requirements is in section 19 of the Competition Law, which states the following:

> Companies may not merge unless a merger notice is filed and the consent of the General Director to the merger is obtained and, if such consent is conditional, the merger must be consummated in accordance with such conditions, all as provided in this section.

Two primary and extensive requirements for parties to a merger are derived from the language of this section. The first requirement is the *advance reporting requirement*, i.e. the review process is a condition *ex ante* for the merger. The second requirement is *the waiting requirement*, and the main part of it is the *absolute prohibition* imposed on the parties against any consolidation whatsoever of their activities, against any initiation of a merger act until the General Director's decision is issued and against taking any action other than in accordance with that ruling.

The prohibition applies to any act which on some level gives the acquirer a foothold in the target company, a full or partial combination of activity, or an act which is expected to have a significant effect on the behavior of the target corporation. Among these acts are: the transfer of consideration to a seller or on its behalf; the transfer of securities to a buyer or to a party acting on its behalf; the transfer of economic risk involved in the holding of securities; the transfer of a right to benefit from the increased value of a corporation; the transfer of the right to vote at the corporation's general meeting; the appointment of officers in the corporation – all these, whether in theory or in practice, are covered.

3. **Have the relevant authorities in your jurisdiction issued internal or external guidelines concerning the scope of the standstill obligation, and/or their authority to enforce it? Please provide a copy/link of such guidance, if possible in English.**

The ICA addressed this issue (directly and indirectly) in two guidelines published on the ICA website.[2]

In section b of the *Guidelines for Reporting and Evaluating Mergers*, the ICA refers to the requirement of prior notification and the requirement to wait for a response before consummating the merger (i.e. the standstill obligation). The ICA states that the waiting requirement is an absolute prohibition imposed on the parties against any consolidation whatsoever of their activities, and against any initiation of a merger act until the General Director's decision is issued. The ICA notes that a failure to comply with the reporting and waiting requirements

---

2 <http://www.antitrust.gov.il//files/site/Merger%20Guidelines.pdf>.

(a "de facto merger") may lead to (and has in fact led to) the initiation of criminal proceedings alongside the General Director's request for a civil remedy consisting of a request to have the companies separated. The ICA mentioned two cases in which it brought criminal proceedings against companies that had violated the waiting and reporting requirements.[3]

The ICA also published guidelines regarding the disclosure of information in a due diligence process.[4] According to the guidelines, the disclosure of information, inter alia in a merger process, may cause damage to competition and constitute a restrictive arrangement under the Competition Law, if not conducted appropriately.

4. **Are there any exceptions to the standstill obligation – for example, through derogation or "carve out"? Please describe the circumstances in which this is possible. Please also describe the relevant process, e.g. do parties need to apply to the authority for a derogation from the standstill obligation? If so, how long is the approval process? If there are specific cases addressing these issues, please identify them.**

In general, the "standstill obligation" under the Competition Law is absolute and does not contain exceptions.

That being said, while in the context of the advance reporting requirement and the waiting requirement (mentioned above), there is a prohibition against a potential acquirer injecting funds or appointing directors (whatever titles are actually given to them) for the target corporation, there is no prohibition against transferring shares and consideration funds to an *external trustee*, as long as these transfers are not accompanied by additional rights given to an acquirer wishing to merge with the target corporation, and so long as the trusteeship mechanism creates a complete and real buffer between the transferred rights and the acquirer, and the acquirer does not have, because of the trusteeship, any actual link to the transferred shares.

Parties to a merger executed outside Israel, that wish to "carve out" Israel until such time as the merger is cleared by the General Director, may do so, provided that the "foreign" merger will not affect competition in the Israeli market.

5. **Does a public bid exception exist in your jurisdiction? (For example, under the EU Merger Regulation it is possible to acquire shares as part of a public bid, provided that the shares are not exercised until the acquisition is cleared by the Commission.) If such an exception exists in your jurisdiction, please describe how it is applied.**

In general, the public bid exception does not exist directly, but rather derives from the definition of a corporate merger under the Competition Law. The purpose of the legislature is to include all transactions that may establish an affinity or significantly strengthen the relationship between the business decision-making mechanisms of two or more entities.

Therefore, a public bid, which does not grant an additional corporate right apart from the right to profits, does not usually constitute a merger under the Competition

---

3 Criminal Case 300/95 *The State of Israel v Electrochemical Industries (Protrom) Ltd et al.* (9 June 1996); Criminal Case 1268/01 *The State of Israel v Ehud Friedlander* (published in Nevo, 5 September 2004).

4 <http://www.antitrust.gov.il/subject/130/item/33144.aspx>.

Law, since the transaction does not grant the acquiring company a foothold in the decision-making process of the acquired company. Otherwise, acquisition of shares or a significant part of the business as part of a public bid, that amounts to a "merger" under the Competition Law, (including a bid or similar process as part of a court-supervised winding-up or insolvency of a corporation), will be conditioned by the clearance of the ICA.

6. **What powers does the relevant authority have to investigate and enforce violations of the standstill obligation? Are dawn raids possible? What timing applies to investigation/enforcement proceedings?**

Any person is obliged, upon the order of the General Director, to provide all information, documents, ledgers and other certificates that, in the opinion of the General Director, would ensure or facilitate the implementation of the Competition Law. The ICA makes extensive use of this power.

The General Director (or any authorized person from the civil service) may, if they have reasonable grounds to believe it is necessary to ensure implementation of the Competition Law or to prevent its contravention:

- enter into any business premises and conduct a search without a search warrant – however, entry into residential premises is only permissible in accordance with a search warrant handed down by a court of competent jurisdiction; and
- seize any article or document (including computer material), if they have reasonable grounds for believing that it may serve as evidence in the hearing of an offense.

Furthermore, in the event that suspicion arises regarding a possible breach of the Competition Law, the General Director or any authorized person may investigate any person related to such contravention, or any person who may have information regarding such contravention, and may order any such person to accompany the investigation and provide any details, documents or information relevant to such contravention. An investigator is authorized to compel oral testimony, and the person under investigation is obliged to answer any question except for potentially self-incriminating ones. Such testimony may be used against the provider thereof.

In addition, wiretapping is also permissible in certain circumstances, subject to the approval of the president of a district court.

In general, it takes between several months and several years from the commencement of an investigation until the file is closed.

7. **What are the possible penalties for violating the standstill obligation? Are there criminal sanctions, including on individuals? Have these been applied in practice? Is there a difference in enforcement between transactions involving domestic companies and "foreign-to-foreign" transactions? Does the authority have the power to unwind transactions implemented in breach of the standstill obligation? If so, has the authority made use of that power in practice? If yes, please provide examples.**

The implementation of a notifiable merger prior to its clearance or without an approval is a criminal offense.

The criminal sanctions determined in the Competition Law are up to three years' imprisonment (five years in aggravating circumstances). In addition, fines may be imposed – up to about NIS 2.2 million for an individual, plus NIS 14,000 for each day the offense persists. In the case of a corporation, the fine or additional fine, as applicable, will be doubled. Moreover, the Competition Law includes a strict liability offense for managers, under which any person serving in a corporation at the same time as an antitrust offense is being committed, in the role of an active director, a partner (other than a limited partner) or a senior administrative employee with responsibilities in the relevant field, has a criminal liability for the offense, unless it can be shown that the offense was committed without the manager's knowledge and that the manager took all reasonable measures to ensure compliance with the Competition Law.

In addition, the following administrative sanctions are available under the Competition Law:

- The General Director may issue an administrative declaration, thereby exposing the parties to civil lawsuits, since such declaration constitutes prima facie evidence in any judicial proceedings.
- The General Director and parties may agree the framework of a consent decree, inter alia, on an amount of money to be paid to the State Treasury in lieu of criminal procedures or an administrative declaration. The consent decree may include a provision according to which the parties do not admit responsibility.
- Under article 50D of the Competition Law (added to the Competition Law in an amendment from 2012), the General Director is authorized to impose a monetary sanction of up to NIS 1 million on an individual. As for corporations, if in the year preceding the fiscal year in which the infringement took place, the corporation turnover exceeded NIS 10 million, the General Director may impose a monetary sanction of up to 8% of the turnover, up to NIS 100 million.
- The Competition Tribunal may order the separation of an entity merged in violation of the Competition Law on the application of the General Director. According to the Competition Law, the Competition Tribunal is entitled to use this approach only upon showing a reasonable likelihood of significant harm to competition or injury to the public in respect of the product's price, quality, quantity, or regularity or terms of supply.

The main considerations that guide the ICA in determining the penalty (criminal or administrative), are the degree or likelihood of harm to competition caused by the unlawfully implemented merger, and whether the violation of the standstill obligation was committed in good faith. In the vast majority of cases, the ICA will take administrative action in lieu of criminal action.

When determining the amount of the monetary sanction, the ICA will examine, inter alia, the following criteria: the duration of the violation, the extent of the damage to competition, the existence or absence of previous violations, and actions taken to prevent recurrence of the violation.

In practice, the General Director has taken action against allegedly unlawful mergers in only a few cases, two of which resulted in criminal sanctions (see n

3). The Competition Tribunal has considered only two cases in Israel brought by the General Director to separate an allegedly illegally merged entity: one in 2007 – *Prinir (Hadas 1987) Ltd and Milos (1989) Ltd* and the other in 2003 – *Baron-Fishman Communication Ltd and Yedioth Achronot Ltd.* In these cases, the Competition Tribunal ultimately accepted the ICA's position and determined that the effective and appropriate penalty would be the separation of the merged entities, mainly because the merger in *Prinir* immediately created a monopoly in six different markets, and *Baron-Fishman* created an essential structural link between two daily newspapers, one of which was a declared monopoly at the time of the merger.

As for foreign-to-foreign mergers, in general, if a foreign-to-foreign merger constitutes a merger according to the criteria of the Israeli Competition Law, all the sanctions listed above are applicable. Nevertheless, we are unaware of any case in which the General Director has sanctioned a foreign entity for unlawfully implementing a merger.

8. **How does the relevant authority typically learn of potential violations of the standstill obligation? Does the authority actively monitor the trade press?**

The ICA's sources of information regarding actions that violate the standstill obligation are varied: for instance, in *Prinir*, which dealt with Prinir's takeover of the decision-making mechanisms of Milos, the companies' activity was exposed following a criminal investigation and search warrants that were executed at the companies' offices. Another relevant source is information provided by third parties – thus, for example, in *Koor and Bank Hapoalim*, the "Committee of Examination of the Aspects of the Holdings of Banks in Real Corporations", drew the ICA's attention to the transaction. The ICA also actively monitors the trade press, which qualifies a legitimate source of information.

9. **Please describe the relevant authority's enforcement of the standstill obligation. If there have been cases, please describe the specific conduct that was found to violate the standstill provision and the criteria applied by the relevant authority or court. Has the relevant authority considered the market impact of the conduct? (Please refer to the Annex.)**

Over the past year, the Competition Tribunal approved three consent decrees – the first involved two construction companies, El Har Ltd and Taan Ltd, who made a transfer of shares according to a share purchase agreement, prior to the submission of pre-merger notification forms. The companies agreed to pay an amount of NIS 250,000, and the General Director undertook not to take additional enforcement measures in the matter. The second consent decree involved a share purchase agreement between Tal Hel Yasca Ltd and Fresh and Smooth Part 2 Ltd. Prior to the submission of pre-merger notification forms by either party, the companies informed the General Director that Tal Hel had transferred a sum of NIS 5 million to the acquired company, in order to enable its continued operation in light of its financial problems. According to the General Director, the provision of finance was part of the merger transaction, and therefore constituted an implementation of the transaction before approval. The parties agreed to pay the State Treasury sums of NIS 170,000 and NIS 40,000, pursuant to an agreement that they would not admit to a violation of the provisions of the law and the General

Director undertook not to take additional enforcement measures against them in this matter. The third consent decree dealt with the implementation of a share purchase agreement without prior approval of the General Director. Pursuant to the transaction, SOS Energy Express Ltd purchased 100% of the shares of Gas Station "Shaarei Holon" Ltd.

The General Director indeed takes the market impact into consideration. For instance, in the Tal Hel case, the General Director specifically stated that the penalty in that case (i.e. consent decree in lieu of enforcement measures), was preferable in light of the fact that the merger was eventually approved, as it did not entail significant damage to competition, thus saving litigation costs and prolonged proceedings and enabling the General Director to direct resources to deal with matters of public importance.

10. **In cases involving alleged violations of the standstill obligation under the relevant merger control laws, has the relevant authority (or court) *also* considered the substantive antitrust laws? (Please refer to the Annex.)**

The sections of the Competition Law that prohibit restrictive arrangements do not allow for any premature implementation of a merger, and such conduct is not the subject matter of any other section. Thus, any violation of the standstill obligation will be treated as a violation of the Competition Law.

Any pre-closing conduct of merging parties that may per se harm competition (for example, exchanging competitively sensitive information during the due diligence phase, or a buyer exercising operational control over a target's decisions pre-closing) will be examined and sanctioned as a violation of the rules of Competition Law that prohibit restrictive horizontal agreements/arrangements between competitors.

The severity of harm to competition resulting from such violation of the Competition Law will be taken into consideration in determining criminal liability and the financial sanctions that are to be imposed on the parties.

We are not aware of actual enforcement activities in which parties were sanctioned under the restrictive arrangements section of the Competition Law, for their pre-merger activities (Although we cannot rule out that there have been unpublicized investigations regarding such activities that did not develop into actual sanctions procedures.)

11. **Is private enforcement of the standstill obligation possible?**

Every individual or corporation is entitled to claim civil remedies for violation of the Competition Law. Violation of the provisions of the Competition Law (and the standstill obligation included) is a tort under the Torts Ordinance. The Competition Law grants individuals and corporations that have been damaged by a violation of the provisions of the law the possibility of repaying their damages through a regular tort claim.

See section 50(a) of the Competition Law:

> An act or omission contrary to the provisions of this Law has the legal standing of a tort in accordance with the Civil Wrongs Ordinance [New Version].

In addition, the Competition Law permits those who meet certain conditions to file a class action in respect of a violation of the provisions of the law. Some of the class actions are filed after the General Director has exercised their authority and determined that a certain matter is in violation of the Competition Law. This determination allows the class action plaintiffs to use it as prima facie evidence within the framework of the claim, thus effectively assisting the plaintiffs to meet the complex burden of proving the claim.

We are not aware of any cases where third parties have sued merging parties for violation of the standstill obligation.

12. **Please describe the private law risks/consequences (i.e. contractual/validity consequences) for transactions that are subject to notification, but which are completed without notification/approval. Please identify any relevant cases and describe them.**

This issue has been discussed in the context of restrictive arrangements, however the conclusions are applicable also to the implementation of a notifiable merger prior to its clearance or without an approval.

For example, in *Tivall (1993) Ltd v Chef Hayam (1994) Ltd*, the question discussed was whether the stipulation of a non-competition clause constitutes an illegal and unenforceable restrictive arrangement. The Court held that:

> My opinion, therefore, is that the restrictive arrangement between the litigants before us is an illegal and invalid arrangement, that we are not permitted to enforce.

Similarly, in application for permission to appeal *Akstel Ltd v Kalma v Industry Ltd*, the Court stated:

> Indeed, a restrictive arrangement that has been approved, temporarily approved, or exempted under the Antitrust Law is not an illegal contract.

And therefore vice versa – a restrictive arrangement, or a merger (as in our case) that has not been approved by the General Director, or the implementation of a merger prior to an approval of the such, constitutes an illegal contract.

13. **Please describe policy and enforcement trends in your jurisdiction.**

In most cases involving closing or integrating the activities of the merging businesses before clearance, i.e. in violation of the standstill obligation (and depending on the degree of harm to competition), the General Director imposes administrative penalties in lieu of criminal indictment.

As described in detail above, an amendment to the Competition Law (from 2012) enables the General Director to impose *monetary sanctions* in lieu of criminal indictment. Additionally, the Competition Law enables the General Director and parties to an unlawful merger to agree in the framework of a *consent decree*, inter alia, on an amount of money to be paid to the State Treasury instead of criminal procedures.

Part 2: Substantive Antitrust Law in an M&A Context

1. **Please identify the relevant *substantive antitrust laws* in your jurisdiction that can potentially apply in an M&A context (e.g. for the EU, this would include Article 101 of the Treaty on the Functioning of the European Union). Please provide a link to the relevant legislation (if possible, in English).**

   The restrictive arrangement section of the Competition Law could potentially apply to the pre-closing conduct of merging parties.

   Section 2(a) of the Competition Law defines a "restrictive arrangement" as an arrangement made between two or more persons conducting business that restricts at least one party to the arrangement in a manner that may prevent or reduce competition.

   In the guidelines regarding the disclosure of information in a due diligence process (mentioned above), the ICA stated that classification of the disclosure of information between competitors as a restrictive arrangement depends on a number of parameters. Thus, for example, if the information disclosed makes it easier to predict the conduct of the information owner in the arena of competition, there is greater risk of harm to competition. On the other hand, if measures taken by the parties reduce the fear of reduction of competition, it may be possible that the disclosure of information will not qualify as a restrictive arrangement under the Competition Law.

2. **Do any guidelines exist in your jurisdiction concerning the application of the substantive antitrust laws in an M&A context – whether internal to the relevant authority, or external, formal or informal (e.g. speeches)? If so, please provide a copy/link to such guidance.**

   As stated above, the ICA has published guidelines regarding the disclosure of information in a due diligence process.[5] In these guidelines, the ICA noted that companies are in a state of uncertainty regarding the capabilities of their competitors, their business policies and their plans for the future. The uncertainty about the state of the market stimulates competition. The exposure of competitively sensitive information between competitors reduces this uncertainty in a way that may reduce their competitive efforts and increase the risk of coordinated behavior, and facilitates the existence of cartelistic arrangements.

---

5 <http://www.antitrust.gov.il/subject/130/item/33144.aspx>.

In these guidelines, the ICA specifies types of information considered competitively sensitive, and outlines appropriate rules of conduct in a due diligence process, which reduces the concern of harm to competition.

3. **As a general matter (not limited to M&A), how are the substantive antitrust laws enforced with respect to the exchange of competitively sensitive information between competing firms? Please also indicate the relevance of anticompetitive effects or intent in such enforcement.**

In 2014, the ICA published a public statement regarding the exchange of information prior to a transaction between competitors. According to the ICA, when in a transaction between competitors, if any of the parties is exposed to information that is sensitive from a competitive standpoint, there may be a fear of harm to competition. The disclosure of this sensitive information may constitute a restrictive arrangement as defined in the Competition Law. In the statement, the ICA outlined the rules of conduct that would help reduce possible harm to competition stemming from the exchange of competitively sensitive information between competitors. Inter alia, the ICA stated that information may be transferred to employees of the receiving party who are not involved in the pricing, marketing or sales of products that are at the core of competition between the parties, who will be part of a "clean team" composed of a few specific employees.

Classification of information disclosure between competitors as a restrictive arrangement depends on a number of parameters, including the quality of the information exposed, the exposure procedure and the state of competition in the relevant market. If the exposure of sensitive information is likely to lead to a more significant reduction in competition among competitors, it is more likely that the ICA will determine that the arrangement is a restrictive arrangement.

The intention of the parties is not examined directly, but the ICA will examine whether, in disclosing the information, the parties acted in accordance with the rules of conduct outlined by the ICA. For example, the parties are required to document the transmission of information and to review the information provided, if possible, by an external party.

4. **Have there been any cases in your jurisdiction in which the substantive antitrust laws were enforced in an M&A context? Please describe/explain and cite any such cases. (See also Annex.)**

We are not aware of actual enforcement activities in which parties were sanctioned for their pre-merger activities under the restrictive arrangements section of the Competition Law. (Although we cannot rule out that there have been unpublicized investigations regarding such activities that did not develop into actual sanctions procedures.)

5. **Are the substantive antitrust laws more likely to apply at specific stages of the transaction – i.e. at an early stage, or prior to closing (or does it not make a difference)? Do companies face ongoing risk following the consummation (or failure) of their transaction for conduct that allegedly occurred pre-closing (pre-failure)?**

The stage of the transaction does not have an impact on the application of the law. That being said, the stage of the transaction will be taken into consideration in assessing the extent of harm to competition, and as a result also in the choice of the appropriate penalty.

Whether or not the transaction has been fully consummated, or whether information has only been transferred between the parties in a due diligence process, the parties are exposed to ongoing risks in an M&A context, as well as to restrictive arrangement accusations.

The statute of limitations is based on the general criminal code. As aforementioned, pre-closing conduct may constitute a restrictive arrangement under the Competition Law. Due to a recent amendment to the Competition Law, restrictive arrangements are felony-level crimes, and therefore have a limitation period of 10 years. In comparison, the limitation period regarding implementation of a merger in violation of the standstill obligation, depends on the severity of the offense. There is a standard limitation period of five years. However, if aggravating circumstances are involved, the offense will have a limitation period of 10 years. It should be emphasized that the limitation periods mentioned above are relevant to an offense that has been ceased (for instance, from the moment the parties ceased to transfer competitively sensitive information between them in a due diligence process). However, violation of the standstill obligation is an ongoing offense and therefore the limitation period will not commence, as long as the merger of the parties is still in effect.

6. **Please explain how the relevant authority enforces (or could enforce) the substantive antitrust laws in an M&A context. How would the investigation occur, and what timing constraints would apply?**

Two enforcement institutions were established under the Competition Law: the ICA and the Competition Tribunal.

The ICA is an independent government enforcement agency. The ICA employs about 100 staff members and is divided into three professional departments: legal, economic and investigations. Therefore, the ICA conducts both investigations and prosecution of cartel matters, and uses other enforcement measures as well.

The Competition Tribunal, sitting with the District Court of Jerusalem, has exclusive jurisdiction over non-criminal governmental antitrust proceedings. The District Court of Jerusalem has exclusive jurisdiction over criminal antitrust matters.

An investigation may take the form of an open or a concealed investigation.

An open investigation is conducted mainly by demanding documents and information that may assist in examining whether an offense has been (or is being) committed. This type of investigation has been extensively used by the General Director, either through the legal department or the investigations department of the ICA.

The investigations department mostly investigates activities that may result in criminal charges, and is vested with extensive investigatory powers, including the right to enter any business premises and conduct a search, seize any article or document, or question any relevant suspect or witness, and arrest and detention powers. During an investigation, the investigations department usually consults with the legal department of the ICA, inter alia, with respect to the sufficiency of the evidentiary material. Later, the legal department reviews the material collected by the investigations department and either invites the suspects to a hearing or requests the investigations department to carry out additional investigatory actions. The decision whether to prosecute or not is made by the General Director following the termination of the hearing proceedings. A criminal investigation in which findings indicate that the Competition Law has been breached does not necessarily lead to criminal indictment but may end up with an administrative enforcement measure. The appropriate measure is determined on a case-by-case basis.

In general, it takes between several months and several years from the commencement of an investigation until the file is closed.

7. **Is private enforcement of the substantive antitrust laws possible in an M&A context, and has it occurred?**

See Question 11 above.

To the best of our knowledge, as at the time of writing, civil claims or class actions have not been filed in an M&A context. Generally, antitrust class action suits dealt with restrictive arrangements or violations of monopoly restrictions.

8. **Could behavior subject to the substantive antitrust laws also be caught under the merger control rules/standstill obligation? (Please also refer to the Annex.)**

Yes, this is possible in certain situations. For example, exchange of competitively sensitive information or when a CEO attends management meeting of the competing entity before the merger is approved, when the companies are still operating separately.

9. **Please describe the penalties for infringing the substantive antitrust laws. Please indicate whether these include criminal penalties, including individual criminal penalties. As a practical matter, how have these been applied in the context of an M&A transaction?**

A recent amendment to the Competition Law raised the maximum penalty for restrictive arrangement offenses to up to five years' imprisonment. Up until then, the Competition Law did not distinguish between the offenses, and stipulated a maximum sentence of up to three years' imprisonment for all offenses set forth in the Competition Law, and up to five years' imprisonment when committed under aggravated circumstances, i.e. in circumstances in which there could be significant harm to competition.

Note, that the distinction between the offenses relates only to the criminal sanctions. The administrative sanctions set out in Question 7 of Part 1 remain the same and may apply to restrictive arrangements.

10. **Please describe policy and enforcement trends in your jurisdiction.**

See Question 13 above.

Despite the authority vested to it, the Competition Tribunal has considered only two cases in Israel brought by the General Director to separate an allegedly illegally merged entity: one in 2007 – *Prinir (Hadas 1987) Ltd and Milos (1989) Ltd* and the other in 2003 – *Baron-Fishman Communication Ltd and Yedioth Achronot Ltd.*

Annex

Table 1: Actual Enforcement of Specific Conduct under the Relevant Merger Control Rules and Substantive Antitrust Laws

Please identify whether the following type of conduct has been subject to investigation/enforcement in your jurisdiction, under the merger control laws or substantive antitrust laws. Please cite any such case(s) and provide a brief description in the table below.

Specific Conduct	Actual Enforcement under Merger Control Laws	Actual Enforcement under Substantive Antitrust Laws
Pre-signing due diligence	No	No
Post-signing/pre-approval due diligence	No	No
Post-approval/pre-closing due diligence	In general, the issue is not problematic according to the ICA, and it is difficult to say that it is illegal under the relevant legislation.	
Use of "clean teams"	No	No
Restrictions on the target in an M&A agreement, e.g. buyer approval required for: – Investments above a certain level; – New business above a certain level; – Other obligations to consult/obtain approval from the buyer before closing.	No	No
Joint marketing	No	No
Joint presentations (e.g. industry fairs)	No	No
Joint communications	No	No
Strategy/planning regarding customers	No	No
Strategy/planning regarding suppliers	No	No
Third party contract novation	No	No
Personnel Issues: – Secondments – Retention Strategies	No	No

Specific Conduct	Actual Enforcement under Merger Control Laws	Actual Enforcement under Substantive Antitrust Laws
IT Planning/Database Migration	No	No
Other		

Additional Explanation:

To the best of our knowledge, there exists no public information suggesting that any of the conducts in the table have been investigated or enforced by the ICA.

There are only a few decisions of the ICA regarding gun-jumping (detailed in the answers to Questions 9–10 of Part 1 above).

There is significant enforcement regarding illegal restraints of trade, and gun-jumping may be reviewed under this framework.

Table 2: Hypothetical Enforcement of Specific Conduct under the Relevant Merger Control Rules and Substantive Antitrust Laws

For any conduct that is *not* the subject of actual enforcement (Table 1), please indicate in the Table below whether the conduct identified *could potentially* be enforced under the merger control laws and/or substantive antitrust laws.

<table>
<tr><th>Specific Conduct</th><th>Hypothetical Enforcement under Merger Control Laws</th><th>Hypothetical Enforcement under Substantive Antitrust Laws</th></tr>
<tr><td>Pre-signing due diligence</td><td>Yes</td><td>Yes</td></tr>
<tr><td>Post-signing/pre-approval due diligence</td><td>Yes</td><td>Yes</td></tr>
<tr><td>Post-approval/pre-closing due diligence</td><td colspan="2">In general, the issue is not problematic according to the ICA, and it is difficult to say that it is illegal under the relevant legislation.</td></tr>
<tr><td>Use of “clean teams”</td><td>Yes</td><td>Yes</td></tr>
<tr><td>Restrictions on the target in an M&A agreement, e.g. buyer approval required for:
– Investments above a certain level;
– New business above a certain level;
– Other obligations to consult/obtain approval from the buyer before closing.</td><td></td><td></td></tr>
<tr><td>Joint marketing</td><td>Yes</td><td>Yes</td></tr>
<tr><td>Joint presentations (e.g. industry fairs)</td><td>Yes</td><td>Yes</td></tr>
</table>

Specific Conduct	Hypothetical Enforcement under Merger Control Laws	Hypothetical Enforcement under Substantive Antitrust Laws
Joint communications	Yes	Yes
Strategy/planning regarding customers	Yes	Yes
Strategy/planning regarding suppliers	Yes	Yes
Third party contract novation	Yes	Yes
Personnel Issues: – Secondments – Retention Strategies	Yes	Yes
IT Planning/Database Migration	Yes	Yes
Other		

JAPAN

Atsushi Yamada and Etsuko Hara
(Anderson Mori & Tomotsune)

Part 1:
Merger Control and the "Standstill Obligation"

1. **Please identify the relevant merger control legislation in your jurisdiction. Please provide a link to the relevant legislation (if possible, in English) and also indicate:**
   - **whether the merger control system is mandatory or voluntary,**
   - **the relevant authority, and**
   - **the duration of the review period.**

In Japan, merger control is governed by the Act on Prohibition of Private Monopolization and Maintenance of Fair Trade (**AMA**).[1]

According to Chapter IV of the AMA, it is mandatory to notify certain types of transactions to the Japan Fair Trade Commission (**JFTC**) that fall within relevant statutory thresholds.

The five types of transactions provided by the AMA are as follows: (i) share acquisitions (Article 10), (ii) mergers (Article 15), (iii) joint incorporation-type company splits (an incorporation-type company split that a company effects jointly with another company (Article 15-2)), (iv) joint share transfers (a share transfer carried out by a company jointly with another company (Article 15-3), and (v) accepting an assignment of the whole or a substantial part of the business of another company, including asset transfers (Article 16).

The statutory thresholds are generally based on domestic turnover and vary depending on the type of transaction, as mentioned above. Chapter IV of the AMA sets out details of the thresholds for each type of transaction.[2]

The JFTC's review is characterized by a two-step approach. The Phase I review starts from the date of the JFTC's acceptance of the notification form. A 30-day waiting period commences from this acceptance date, during which the parties are not allowed to proceed with the transaction. During the Phase I review, the JFTC will decide to either clear the transaction or request the parties to submit necessary reports, information or materials for further review (the Phase II review). The AMA provides that the Phase II review period shall continue until the later of either (i) the end of a period of 120 days starting from the date of acceptance of the notification form, or (ii) the end of a period of 90 days starting from the date of acceptance of all the reports or additional information or materials that the JFTC has requested. However, in practice the latter 90-day review period is

1 A translation of the AMA can be found at <https://www.jftc.go.jp/en/legislation_gls/amended_ama09/index.html>.
2 See <https://www.jftc.go.jp/en/legislation_gls/amended_ama09/amended_ama15_04.html>.

the norm as parties usually require some time to respond to all the information requests made by the JFTC.

Given that the 30-day waiting period for the Phase I review starts once the notification form is accepted by the JFTC, it is common practice for parties to start engaging with the JFTC prior to filing the notification form. The period of this pre-notification discussion varies on a case-by-case basis but, according to the JFTC, consultations in a typical case last between two weeks and one month.

2. **Does the merger control system in your jurisdiction impose a "*standstill obligation*" – meaning, that the transaction cannot be implemented prior to completing the merger control process? (Please cite the relevant legislation.) Please also indicate the *legal scope* of the standstill obligation according to the relevant legislation (e.g. the parties to the transaction cannot effect a change of control, cannot take steps towards implementation, etc.).**

There is a standstill obligation imposed by the AMA for notifiable transactions, prohibiting parties from proceeding with the transaction during the 30-day waiting period. For example, Article 10(8) AMA provides that no company may acquire the target shares until the expiration of the 30-day waiting period. This paragraph applies *mutatis mutandis* to other types of transactions, such as mergers, joint incorporation-type company splits, joint share transfers, accepting assignments of the whole or a substantial part of the business of another company (Article 15–16 AMA).

With respect to the legal scope of the standstill obligation, the AMA merely prohibits the parties from proceeding with the relevant transaction and does not provide any further details. Even when a review moves to Phase II, the 30-day waiting period will not be extended, meaning that the parties may close the transaction. However, the launch of a Phase II review also means that the transaction raises substantial competition issues and so, if the parties were to proceed with the relevant transaction without solving the issues, the JFTC could issue a cease and desist order or make a petition to seek an order to stop engaging in the action.

3. **Have the relevant authorities in your jurisdiction issued internal or external guidelines concerning the scope of the standstill obligation, and/or their authority to enforce it? Please provide a copy/link of such guidance, if possible in English.**

There are no such internal or external guidelines publicly available that specifically refer to the scope of the standstill obligation.

The JFTC has issued *Guidelines to the Application of the Antimonopoly Act Concerning Review of Business Combination* to provide general guidance on its merger review.[3] These *Guidelines*, however, do not provide guidance concerning the scope of the standstill obligation and/or the JFTC's authority to enforce it. It only provides for the possibility of shortening the waiting period (see Question 4).

4. **Are there any exceptions to the standstill obligation – for example, through derogation or "carve out"? Please describe the circumstances in which this**

---

3 A translation of the Guidelines can be found at <https://www.jftc.go.jp/en/legislation_gls/imonopoly_guidelines_files/110713.2.pdf>.

is possible. Please also describe the relevant process, e.g. do parties need to apply to the authority for a derogation from the standstill obligation? If so, how long is the approval process? If there are specific cases addressing these issues, please identify them.

There are no exceptions to the standstill obligation, except for the possibility of shortening the waiting period.

Article 10(8) AMA provides that whenever the JFTC finds it necessary, it may shorten the 30-day waiting period. Further, the *Guidelines* referred to in Question 3 above state that the shortening of the waiting period may be granted when: (i) it is evident that the effect of the transaction may not be substantially to restrain competition in any particular field of trade; and (ii) the notifying company requests in writing to shorten the waiting period. As mentioned in Question 1, in practice it is common for parties to engage in pre-notification discussions with the JFTC and, therefore, parties seeking to shorten the waiting period would usually file the notification form after they think they have had sufficient pre-notification discussions with the JFTC.

It is generally not possible for parties to "carve out" Japan, i.e. to close the transaction in other jurisdictions but not in Japan, pending receipt of the JFTC's clearance.

5. **Does a public bid exception exist in your jurisdiction? (For example, under the EU Merger Regulation it is possible to acquire shares as part of a public bid, provided that the shares are not exercised until the acquisition is cleared by the Commission.) If such an exception exists in your jurisdiction, please describe how it is applied.**

There is no such public bid exception in Japan. Regardless of the method used to acquire shares, the parties have to notify to the JFTC prior to closing the transaction and to comply with the applicable standstill obligation.

6. **What powers does the relevant authority have to investigate and enforce violations of the standstill obligation? Are dawn raids possible? What timing applies to investigation/enforcement proceedings?**

The JFTC can order persons concerned with a case or third-party witnesses to appear before it for interrogation, or obtain their opinions or reports (Article 47(1)(i) AMA). It can also order persons holding books and documents or other objects to submit such objects (Article 47(1)(iii) AMA). Furthermore, dawn raids may technically be possible if the JFTC deems it necessary for its investigation (Article 47(1)(iv) AMA). To date, however, the JFTC has not carried out a dawn raid to investigate possible violations of the standstill obligation.

If the JFTC were to suspect a breach of the standstill obligation, it would start its investigation by requesting the relevant parties to cooperate, without initially using its enforcement powers under Article 47 AMA. There are no limitations on the length of investigations or enforcement proceedings carried out by the JFTC.

7. **What are the possible penalties for violating the standstill obligation? Are there criminal sanctions, including on individuals? Have these been applied in practice? Is there a difference in enforcement between transactions involving domestic companies and "foreign-to-foreign" transactions? Does the**

authority have the power to unwind transactions implemented in breach of the standstill obligation? If so, has the authority made use of that power in practice? If yes, please provide examples.

Parties closing a notifiable transaction in violation of the standstill obligation, may be subject to a criminal fine of up to JPY 2 million (Articles 91, 92 and 95 AMA). Individuals such as a representative, an agent or an employee of the company can also be subject to a criminal fine of up to JPY 2 million (Articles 91, 92 and 95 AMA). To the best of our knowledge, however, these penalties have never been imposed in practice.

Although the AMA makes no distinction between domestic companies and foreign companies, there is uncertainty as to whether the above penalties can apply to foreign-to-foreign transactions.

In addition, when companies implement a notifiable transaction in violation of the standstill obligation, the JFTC may bring an action to have the merger, the joint incorporation-type company split, the absorption-type split or the joint share transfer declared invalid (Article 18(1) – (3) AMA) irrespective of the transaction's impact on the market. The JFTC's action must be filed within a period of six months from the day on which the transaction became effective. To the best of our knowledge, however, the authority has so far never made use of that power.

Moreover, upon petition by the JFTC, if the court finds there to be an urgent necessity of doing so, the court may order the person engaging in an act suspected of resulting in substantial restraint of competition in any particular field of trade, to temporarily stop implementing the transaction, to stop exercising voting rights or to stop doing business as an officer of a company, or may rescind or modify such order (however, the authority has made use of that power in an M&A context only once, in 1969).

8. **How does the relevant authority typically learn of potential violations of the standstill obligation? Does the authority actively monitor the trade press?**

The JFTC usually monitors the trade press through the internet or other tools. Such monitoring would be a typical way for the JFTC to learn of potential violations of the standstill obligation.

9. **Please describe the relevant authority's enforcement of the standstill obligation. If there have been cases, please describe the specific conduct that was found to violate the standstill provision and the criteria applied by the relevant authority or court. Has the relevant authority considered the market impact of the conduct? (Please refer to the Annex.)**

There are no court cases yet discussing the standstill obligation and only one JFTC decision on the issue (*Canon/TMSC*, discussed below). In that case, the JFTC did not make any formal order but merely issued a caution (the JFTC issues a "caution" when it does not find sufficient evidence to support the existence of an illegal conduct but finds that such a conduct may lead to a possible violation).

In *Canon/TMSC*, which concerned the acquisition of shares of Toshiba Medical Systems Corporation (**TMSC**) by Canon Inc, the JFTC cautioned Canon, the acquirer, against conducting any action that could be inconsistent with the spirit of the merger notification system.[4] The JFTC noted that before submitting the notification to the JFTC, Canon had acquired share options whose underlying shares were common shares of TMSC. As consideration for such share options, Canon had paid to Toshiba Corporation (**Toshiba**) an amount equal to the value of the underlying common shares. Furthermore, a third party had acquired voting shares of TMSC until Canon exercised its share options. This series of actions was seen as likely to give rise to the formation of a certain joint relationship between Canon and TMSC through the abovementioned third party, forming part of a structure premised on Canon ultimately acquiring the voting shares of TMSC, subject to approval under the AMA. In its decision, the JFTC seems to have focused its analysis on identifying the point at which the series of actions amounted to a transaction that required notification and did not consider the market impact of the conduct.

10. **In cases involving alleged violations of the standstill obligation under the relevant merger control laws, has the relevant authority (or court) *also* considered the substantive antitrust laws? (Please refer to the Annex.)**

In *Canon/TMSC*, the JFTC cautioned that the inconsistency of the parties' conduct with the spirit of the prior notification system could lead to a violation of Article 10(2) AMA (which sets out the prior notification requirements applicable to share acquisitions) and does not seem to have considered the application of substantive antitrust laws.

11. **Is private enforcement of the standstill obligation possible?**

Technically, it would be possible to bring a private damages suit if someone suffered damages as a result of a breach of the standstill obligation. However, we are not aware of any such cases in Japan. In our view, bringing a private action based on a breach of the standstill obligation is likely to be challenging, especially given the difficulty in proving the damages resulting from the breach.

12. **Please describe the private law risks/consequences (i.e. contractual/validity consequences) for transactions that are subject to notification, but which are completed without notification/approval. Please identify any relevant cases and describe them.**

From a Japanese contract law perspective, notifiable transactions which are closed prior to obtaining clearance from the JFTC (and therefore implemented in breach of the standstill obligation) remain contractually valid.

If the JFTC finds, however, that the transaction substantially restrains competition in the relevant market, it may issue a cease and desist order and enjoin the concerned party to dispose of all or some of its shares, to transfer a part of its business or to take any other measures necessary to eliminate the act that caused a substantial restraint of competition (Article 17-2(1) AMA). Depending on the content of the JFTC's cease and desist order, private lawsuits could be brought by private parties.

---

4 See <https://www.jftc.go.jp/en/pressreleases/yearly-2016/June/160630.html>.

In addition, when companies complete a proposed transaction in violation of the standstill obligation, the JFTC is entitled, within a period of six months from the day on which the transaction became effective, to bring an action to have the merger, the joint incorporation-type company split, the absorption-type split or the joint share transfer declared invalid (Article 18(1) – (3) AMA) irrespective of the transaction's impact on the market. Thus, if the JFTC brings this action and the court grants it, the transaction becomes invalid.

13. **Please describe policy and enforcement trends in your jurisdiction.**

In Japan, the JFTC only recently started to take a more rigorous approach to possible violations of the standstill obligation. As mentioned above (see Question 9), in 2016 the JFTC issued a first "caution" pertaining to a breach of the standstill obligation and, since then, it has paid a much closer attention to the issue.

Part 2:
Substantive Antitrust Law in an M&A Context

1. **Please identify the relevant *substantive antitrust laws* in your jurisdiction that can potentially apply in an M&A context (e.g. for the EU, this would include Article 101 of the Treaty on the Functioning of the European Union). Please provide a link to the relevant legislation (if possible, in English).**

   Article 3 AMA provides that an enterprise must not effect a private monopolization or an unreasonable restraint of trade.[5]

   The term "private monopolization", as used in the AMA, means such business activities by which any enterprise, individually or by combination, in conspiracy with other enterprises or by any other manner, excludes or controls the business activities of other enterprises, thereby causing, contrary to the public interest, a substantial restraint of competition in any particular field of trade (Article 2(5) AMA).[6]

   The term "unreasonable restraint of trade", as used in the AMA, means such business activities by which any enterprise, by contract, agreement or any other means irrespective of its name, in concert with other enterprises, mutually restrict or conduct their business activities in such a manner as to fix, maintain or increase prices, or to limit production, technology, products, facilities or counterparties, thereby causing, contrary to the public interest, a substantial restraint of competition in any particular field of trade (Article 2(6) AMA). This paragraph is applicable to horizontal agreements such as price-fixing and bid-rigging.

2. **Do any guidelines exist in your jurisdiction concerning the application of the substantive antitrust laws in an M&A context – whether internal to the relevant authority, or external, formal or informal (e.g. speeches)? If so, please provide a copy/link to such guidance.**

   There are no such guidelines in Japan.

3. **As a general matter (not limited to M&A), how are the substantive antitrust laws enforced with respect to the exchange of competitively sensitive information between competing firms? Please also indicate the relevance of anticompetitive effects or intent in such enforcement.**

   The exchange of competitively sensitive information between competing firms does not in itself constitute a violation of the AMA. However, such activity

---

5 An English translation of the provision can be found at <https://www.jftc.go.jp/en/legislation_gls/amended_ama09/amended_ama15_02.html>.

6 An English translation can be found at <https://www.jftc.go.jp/en/legislation_gls/amended_ama09/amended_ama15_01.html>.

could be considered an important factor for inferring the existence of a conduct amounting to an unreasonable restraint of trade in breach of Article 3 AMA. When assessing unreasonable restraints of trade, the JFTC examines whether the parties engaged in commercial conduct that "mutually restrict[s] or conduct[s] their business activities" and results in a "substantial restraint of competition in any particular field of trade". The parties' intent is not a required element of the offense, but it would be considered a relevant factor during the analysis. As for the conduct's market impact, the language of Article 2(6) AMA makes it clear that proof of the anticompetitive effect is necessary to establish the offense. In practice, however, such effect is presumed for hard core cartels.

4. **Have there been any cases in your jurisdiction in which the substantive antitrust laws were enforced in an M&A context? Please describe/explain and cite any such cases. (See also Annex.)**

In an M&A context, there have not been any cases to date regarding the exchange of competitively sensitive information or any other pre-closing conduct of merging parties, which served as a basis for inferring a breach of Article 3 AMA, which prohibits unreasonable restraints of trade.

5. **Are the substantive antitrust laws more likely to apply at specific stages of the transaction – i.e. at an early stage, or prior to closing (or does it not make a difference)? Do companies face ongoing risk following the consummation (or failure) of their transaction for conduct that allegedly occurred pre-closing (pre-failure)?**

The application of the private monopolization and unreasonable restraint of trade provisions (Article 3 and Article 2(5) and (6)) is not limited to a specific stage of a transaction. Therefore, the likelihood of the substantive antitrust laws being applied remains the same, regardless of the stage that the transaction has reached.

With respect to the issue of ongoing risk following consummation (or failure) of a transaction, this risk will remain in cases where the parties did not receive clearance from the JFTC (i.e. either the transaction was not notifiable, or the transaction was notified but not cleared). On the other hand, with respect to transactions that are notifiable and were cleared by the JFTC, the likelihood of the JFTC enforcing substantive antitrust laws would be low so long as all relevant facts were reviewed by the JFTC.

In the case of a breach of the provisions on private monopolization and unreasonable restraint of trade, the JFTC may issue a cease and desist order and a surcharge payment order within a period of five years from the day of discontinuance of the relevant act (Article 7(2) and Article 7-2(27) AMA). This compares with a limitation period of six months, as stated in Questions 7 and 12 of Part 1, applicable to enforcement actions of the JFTC in case of violation of the standstill obligation under the merger control rules (Article 18(1) – (3) AMA).

6. **Please explain how the relevant authority enforces (or could enforce) the substantive antitrust laws in an M&A context. How would the investigation occur, and what timing constraints would apply?**

When companies breach the substantive antitrust laws as stated in Question 1, dawn raids are possible (Article 47(1)(iv) AMA). Also, the JFTC can order persons concerned with a case or third-party witnesses to appear before it for interrogation, or to submit their opinions or reports (Article 47(1)(i) AMA). It can also order persons holding books and documents or other objects to submit such objects (Article 47(1)(iii) AMA). For private monopolization and unreasonable restraint of trade, if the JFTC finds that there was indeed a violation of the AMA, it can order a cease and desist order and surcharge payment order (Articles 7 and 7-2 AMA).

7. **Is private enforcement of the substantive antitrust laws possible in an M&A context, and has it occurred?**

Technically, it would be possible to bring a private damages suit to compensate for damage suffered as a result of a breach of the substantive antitrust laws in an M&A context, however, we are not aware of any such cases of private enforcement.

8. **Could behavior subject to the substantive antitrust laws also be caught under the merger control rules/standstill obligation? (Please also refer to the Annex.)**

The standstill obligation provision (Article 10(8) AMA) prohibits merging companies from completing their proposed transaction. It would not necessarily cover a mere exchange of competitively sensitive information or other types of pre-closing conduct (such as the buyer exercising a decisive influence on the target's market conduct prior to closing). Such conduct would rather fall to be examined under the substantive antitrust laws prohibiting unreasonable restraints of trade.

9. **Please describe the penalties for infringing the substantive antitrust laws. Please indicate whether these include criminal penalties, including individual criminal penalties. As a practical matter, how have these been applied in the context of an M&A transaction?**

As discussed in Question 6, in a case of private monopolization and unreasonable restraint of trade, the JFTC can issue a cease and desist order and a surcharge payment order (Article 7 and 7-2 AMA). Furthermore, pursuant to Article 89(1)(i) AMA, persons found in violation of the provisions of Article 3 who have effected a private monopolization or an unreasonable restraint of trade can be subject to jail sentences of up to five years, or to criminal fines of not more than JPY five million.

In practice, however, we are not aware of any cases to date in which these provisions have been applied in an M&A context.

10. **Please describe policy and enforcement trends in your jurisdiction.**

The JFTC generally reviews M&A transactions under the merger control regime and has so far not applied the provisions on private monopolization or unreasonable restraint of trade in an M&A context. We are not aware of any recent change or expected change to such practice.

Annex

Table 1: Actual Enforcement of Specific Conduct under the Relevant Merger Control Rules and Substantive Antitrust Laws

Please identify whether the following type of conduct has been subject to investigation/enforcement in your jurisdiction, under the merger control laws or substantive antitrust laws. Please cite any such case(s) and provide a brief description in the table below.

Specific Conduct	Actual Enforcement under Merger Control Laws	Actual Enforcement under Substantive Antitrust Laws
Pre-signing due diligence	No	No
Post-signing/pre-approval due diligence	No	No
Post-approval/pre-closing due diligence	No	No
Use of "clean teams"	No	No
Restrictions on the target in an M&A agreement, e.g. buyer approval required for: – Investments above a certain level; – New business above a certain level; – Other obligations to consult/obtain approval from the buyer before closing.	No	No
Joint marketing	No	No
Joint presentations (e.g. industry fairs)	No	No
Joint communications	No	No
Strategy/planning regarding customers	No	No
Strategy/planning regarding suppliers	No	No
Third party contract novation	No	No
Personnel Issues: – Secondments – Retention Strategies	No	No
IT Planning/Database Migration	No	No
Other	No	No

Table 2: Hypothetical Enforcement of Specific Conduct under the Relevant Merger Control Rules and Substantive Antitrust Laws

For any conduct that is *not* the subject of actual enforcement (Table 1), please indicate in the Table below whether the conduct identified *could potentially* be enforced under the merger control laws and/or substantive antitrust laws.

Specific Conduct	Hypothetical Enforcement under Merger Control Laws	Hypothetical Enforcement under Substantive Antitrust Laws
Pre-signing due diligence	No	All of the specific types of pre-closing conduct listed below could theoretically be examined under the substantive antitrust laws of the AMA prohibiting unreasonable restraints of trade.
Post-signing/pre-approval due diligence	No	
Post-approval/pre-closing due diligence	No	
Use of "clean teams"	No	
Restrictions on the target in an M&A agreement, e.g. buyer approval required for: – Investments above a certain level; – New business above a certain level; – Other obligations to consult/obtain approval from the buyer before closing.	No	
Joint marketing	No	
Joint presentations (e.g. industry fairs)	No	
Joint communications	No	
Strategy/planning regarding customers	No	
Strategy/planning regarding suppliers	No	
Third party contract novation	No	
Personnel Issues: – Secondments – Retention Strategies	No	

Specific Conduct	Hypothetical Enforcement under Merger Control Laws	Hypothetical Enforcement under Substantive Antitrust Laws
IT Planning/Database Migration	No	
Other Implementing a series of steps in a transaction that trigger a notification requirement, without having notified.	The JFTC could rule such transaction as illegal, as it warned it would do in *Canon/ TMSC* (see Question 9 of Part 1).	

KOREA

Cecil Saehoon Chung
(Yulchon LLC)

Part 1: Merger Control and the "Standstill Obligation"

1. **Please identify the relevant merger control legislation in your jurisdiction. Please provide a link to the relevant legislation (if possible, in English) and also indicate:**
   - **whether the merger control system is mandatory or voluntary,**
   - **the relevant authority, and**
   - **the duration of the review period.**

   Relevant Legislation:[1] The Monopoly Regulation and Fair Trade Act (**MRFTA**) is the primary antitrust statute and governs the merger control process in Korea. With respect to merger filing and review, the applicable statutes, regulations and guidelines are as follows:
   - MRFTA and the Enforcement Decree of the MRFTA;
   - *Guidelines on Methods of Business Combination Notification*;
   - *Guidelines on Standards of Business Combination Examination*;
   - *Guidelines on Standards of Imposition of Fines for Violation of Rules on Business Combination Notification*;
   - *Guidelines on Standards of Imposition of a Corrective Order Regarding a Business Combination*; and
   - *Guidelines on Imposition of Fines for Non-Performance of a Corrective Order Regarding a Business Combination.*

   Mandatory Filing: A transaction that satisfies the jurisdictional and local nexus tests must be reported to the KFTC unless it qualifies for an exemption under the MRFTA. The three most notable exemptions are for an interlocking directorate between affiliates, a share acquisition of which the parties are all specially related persons (e.g. affiliates), and a transaction where either the acquirer or the target is an investment company or a fund that satisfies certain conditions.

   Relevant authority: Under the MRFTA, the Korea Fair Trade Commission (**KFTC**) is the government agency that oversees the merger control process in Korea.[2]

---

1 The unofficial translation provided by the KFTC of the relevant legislation and its amendments can be accessed at <http://ftc.go.kr/eng/cop/bbs/selectBoardList.do?key=526&bbsId=BBSMSTR_000000002411&bbsTyCode=BBST11>.

2 The mergers and acquisitions division of the KFTC is in charge of merger control matters.

Duration of Review: The waiting period for the ordinary pre-merger filing is initially 30 days from the date of filing of notification, but the KFTC may, on its own initiative, extend the waiting period for an additional 90 days, if necessary. In addition, the clock stops whenever the KFTC issues a formal written request for information, until all questions have been sufficiently answered by the merging parties. There is no limit as to how often and how many times the KFTC may issue such official requests for information.

2. **Does the merger control system in your jurisdiction impose a "*standstill obligation*" – meaning, that the transaction cannot be implemented prior to completing the merger control process? (Please cite the relevant legislation.) Please also indicate the *legal scope* of the standstill obligation according to the relevant legislation (e.g. the parties to the transaction cannot effect a change of control, cannot take steps towards implementation, etc.).**

Article 12(8) of the MRFTA imposes a standstill obligation by mandating that where a pre-merger filing is required, the Notifying Company to the pending transaction cannot (i) own shares of the target, (ii) file for merger registration, (iii) transfer business assets, or (iv) acquire shares of the target before the KFTC renders a decision one way or another. It is also important to note that, pursuant to Article 12(8) of the MRFTA, the mere expiration of the applicable waiting period is not sufficient to allow the merging parties to consummate the transaction. They can only do so after receiving an official written clearance decision from the KFTC, either upon the expiration of the applicable waiting period or on completion of the KFTC's substantive merger review.

Specifically, the legal scope of each standstill obligation can be further described as follows:

(1) **Acquisition of Shares**: The standstill obligation would be breached in case of delivery of a stock certificate or full payment for the stock. This includes the de facto transfer of right over the stocks (including the right to vote) *before* the stock certificate is delivered or before full payment is made.

(2) **Merger Registration**: There would be a breach of the standstill obligation in case of merger registration, i.e. a registration before the relevant governmental body of the notifying company's certified copy of corporate registration reflecting the completed merger.

(3) **Business Transfer**: In this case, the prohibited conduct is the full advance payment for the transferred assets. Even if payment has not been made in full, the prohibition encompasses the handover or delivery of movable assets, and the registration of immovable assets (in cases where such registration is required).

3. **Have the relevant authorities in your jurisdiction issued internal or external guidelines concerning the scope of the standstill obligation, and/or their authority to enforce it? Please provide a copy/link of such guidance, if possible in English.**

The KFTC's *Guidelines on Methods of Business Combination Notification* detail the specific legal scope of each standstill obligation as described above. In addition, the KFTC's Merger Review Division has published a *Guidebook on Business*

Combination Notification, which presents the KFTC's position on the standstill obligation.[3]

4. **Are there any exceptions to the standstill obligation – for example, through derogation or "carve out"? Please describe the circumstances in which this is possible. Please also describe the relevant process, e.g. do parties need to apply to the authority for a derogation from the standstill obligation? If so, how long is the approval process? If there are specific cases addressing these issues, please identify them.**

The Korean merger control regime does not recognize any exceptions to the standstill obligation, including by way of carve-out. The KFTC's *Guidebook on Business Combination Notification (2019)* explicitly states that there are no exceptions.[4]

5. **Does a public bid exception exist in your jurisdiction? (For example, under the EU Merger Regulation it is possible to acquire shares as part of a public bid, provided that the shares are not exercised until the acquisition is cleared by the Commission.) If such an exception exists in your jurisdiction, please describe how it is applied.**

There is no such public bid exception to the standstill obligation recognized in Korea. Note that in Korea the acquisition of stocks through a competitive bidding process on a securities exchange[5] is only subject to a post-merger filing (see the proviso to Article 12(6) MRFTA and Article 18(9)(1) of the Enforcement Decree thereof) and, accordingly, the standstill obligation is inapplicable to such a situation.

6. **What powers does the relevant authority have to investigate and enforce violations of the standstill obligation? Are dawn raids possible? What timing applies to investigation/enforcement proceedings?**

The KFTC enjoys very broad investigative powers over alleged violations of the MRFTA. When the KFTC deems it necessary to enforce the MRFTA, it is empowered to summon a relevant person for interrogation, request the submission of information and conduct a field investigation (or dawn raid), among other things. In practice, however, it would be extremely rare for the KFTC to conduct a field investigation (or dawn raid) for an alleged violation of the standstill obligation.

Normally, the KFTC's investigation of an alleged violation of the standstill obligation lasts three to six months from the time the KFTC becomes aware of the issue (for instance, when a company makes a post-merger filing after having consummated a pre-notifiable transaction). After the KFTC completes its investigation, it issues an Examiner's Report (or Statement of Objections). Thereafter, the KFTC (the Commission rather than its staff investigators) reviews the matter,

---

3 The KFTC Merger Notification Guidebook (July 2019 edition) (in Korean only) <http://www.ftc.go.kr/solution/skin/doc.html?fn=0edaec68341d45b1afa8202a3908f3dc87f39b7bbc5e9a2939aa4d1aff89b570&rs=/fileupload/data/result/BBSMSTR_000000002342/>.

4 See p79 of the The KFTC Merger Notification Guidebook (July 2019).

5 This excludes situations where stocks are acquired in such a manner that parties to the transaction have predetermined the quantity, price and other terms of the transaction by means of contract or agreement, and execute on this by merely using the securities exchange as the place for conducting the transaction.

deliberates and determines (i) whether to impose an administrative penalty and, if so, (ii) the amount of the penalty.

7. **What are the possible penalties for violating the standstill obligation? Are there criminal sanctions, including on individuals? Have these been applied in practice? Is there a difference in enforcement between transactions involving domestic companies and "foreign-to-foreign" transactions? Does the authority have the power to unwind transactions implemented in breach of the standstill obligation? If so, has the authority made use of that power in practice? If yes, please provide examples.**

A violation of the standstill obligation subjects the company to an administrative fine. The KFTC may impose a fine not exceeding KRW 100 million on a business entity and not exceeding KRW 10 million on an individual, such as the company's executives or employees (Article 69-2(1)(2) MRFTA). In practice, the KFTC often imposes fines on companies for violation of the standstill obligation. The KFTC may also impose an uplift of 30% on the fine depending on the effects of the breach of the standstill obligation (see Question 9 below).

There are no criminal sanctions for violations of the standstill obligation.

In principle, there is no difference in enforcement between transactions involving domestic companies and foreign-to-foreign transactions. However, in practice, most of the cases where the KFTC imposed fines involved business combinations between domestic companies. Cases where foreign-to-foreign transactions were subject to late filing fines often involve a situation where the merging parties already undertook or consummated preparatory steps in multi-step transactions without knowing that in Korea such preparatory steps might be separately and independently reportable.

Where companies are merged, or a new company is established in violation of the standstill obligation, the KFTC may file a lawsuit to nullify the consummated merger or establishment of the new company (Article 16(2) MRFTA). To date, however, the KFTC has never filed an action to have the transaction annulled. As a matter of law, the KFTC is entitled to bring such an action even if the merger itself does not raise antitrust issues. In practice, however, it would be highly unlikely for the KFTC to try to unwind a consummated transaction for purely technical reasons.

8. **How does the relevant authority typically learn of potential violations of the standstill obligation? Does the authority actively monitor the trade press?**

In addition to actively monitoring the trade press, another and more practical source of information is the KFTC's review of lists of affiliates or subsidiaries which merging parties need to submit when filing their proposed transaction. This could reveal that the merging parties never properly filed merger notifications in the past to acquire affiliates or to establish JVs mentioned on the lists.

9. **Please describe the relevant authority's enforcement of the standstill obligation. If there have been cases, please describe the specific conduct that was found to violate the standstill provision and the criteria applied by the relevant authority or court. Has the relevant authority considered the market impact of the conduct? (Please refer to the Annex.)**

As stated in Question 7, the KFTC enforces the standstill obligation by:
(i) imposing a fine not exceeding KRW 100 million on a business entity; or
(ii) imposing a fine not exceeding KRW 10 million on executives, employees and other interested parties of the business entity concerned.

As noted above in Question 2, the KFTC considers four specific types of conduct as violations of the standstill obligation (i.e. conduct which amounts to the premature consummation of the merger transaction, before receiving a written clearance notice from the KFTC, at the expiration of the applicable waiting period or the completion of the KFTC's substantive merger review). For a list of KFTC's actual cases, please refer to Table 1 below.

Note that Article IV.3 B(3) of the *Guidelines on Standards of Imposition of Fines for Violation of Rules on Business Combination Notification* provides that the KFTC may at its discretion increase the applicable fine by up to 30% if the business combination at issue is found by the KFTC to produce illegal anticompetitive effects. However, in most gun-jumping cases the parties acknowledged their wrongdoings and, therefore, the KFTC's findings are drafted in a simple concise manner, without explicit consideration of the impact of the conduct.

10. **In cases involving alleged violations of the standstill obligation under the relevant merger control laws, has the relevant authority (or court) *also* considered the substantive antitrust laws? (Please refer to the Annex.)**

The authors have not found any gun-jumping cases in which the KFTC considered the substantive antitrust laws.

11. **Is private enforcement of the standstill obligation possible?**

No, private enforcement of the standstill obligation is not possible in Korea.

12. **Please describe the private law risks/consequences (i.e. contractual/validity consequences) for transactions that are subject to notification, but which are completed without notification/approval. Please identify any relevant cases and describe them.**

There are no MRFTA provisions regarding the private law effect of the transactions that are subject to notification, but which are completed without notification/approval.

Parties can, however, obviously agree in the relevant contract on the private law effects of their transaction, if it is subject to notification or approval under the relevant antitrust laws. For example, the parties can agree that the transaction will not take effect until it has been properly notified or approved.

13. **Please describe policy and enforcement trends in your jurisdiction.**

While the authors have seen a number of minor gun-jumping cases in which the KFTC imposed a small fine (e.g. KRW 30 million, approx. US$28,000), there have been no major gun-jumping cases in Korea. Such an enforcement record may indicate a relatively passive enforcement trend with respect to gun-jumping cases in Korea, or that there have not yet been any major transactions which breached the standstill obligation.

Part 2: Substantive Antitrust Law in an M&A Context

1. **Please identify the relevant *substantive antitrust laws* in your jurisdiction that can potentially apply in an M&A context (e.g. for the EU, this would include Article 101 of the Treaty on the Functioning of the European Union). Please provide a link to the relevant legislation (if possible, in English).**

   Article 19 of the MRFTA, which covers cartels (or anticompetitive joint conduct), is the relevant provision of substantive antitrust law in Korea that could potentially apply in an M&A context. Note that certain M&A transactions such as a contractual JV agreement and other types of collaborations between two or more independent entities are technically not subject to the merger control regime in Korea and are instead analyzed under the provision of Article 19.[6]

2. **Do any guidelines exist in your jurisdiction concerning the application of the substantive antitrust laws in an M&A context – whether internal to the relevant authority, or external, formal or informal (e.g. speeches)? If so, please provide a copy/link to such guidance.**

   The MRFTA Enforcement Decree provides guidance on the application of the substantive antitrust laws in an M&A context.[7]

3. **As a general matter (not limited to M&A), how are the substantive antitrust laws enforced with respect to the exchange of competitively sensitive information between competing firms? Please also indicate the relevance of anticompetitive effects or intent in such enforcement.**

   The MRFTA governs anticompetitive conduct in Korea. Specifically, Article 19(1) prohibits "unfair collaborative acts" (or agreements which unfairly restricts competition).

   According to Article 19(1) of the MRFTA, an unfair collaborative act is established only when an "anticompetitive agreement" exists. In this context, the term "agreement" includes not only an "explicit agreement," but also an "implicit agreement," such as a tacit understanding between business entities. In particular, according to Article 19(5) of the MRFTA, even in the absence of direct evidence establishing the existence of an agreement between business

---

6 The unofficial translation of the MRFTA provided by the KFTC (for reference only) can be accessed at <http://ftc.go.kr/eng/cop/bbs/selectBoardList.do?key=526&bbsId=BBSMSTR_000000002411&bbsTyCode=BBST11>.

7 The unofficial translation of the Enforcement Decree of the MRFTA (for reference only) can be accessed at <http://ftc.go.kr/eng/cop/bbs/selectBoardList.do?key=526&bbsId=BBSMSTR_000000002411&bbsTyCode=BBST11>.

entities, such an agreement can be legally presumed in light of all relevant circumstances.

Under the MRFTA, price-related information exchanges are not prohibited as such but can be used as circumstantial evidence of the existence of an agreement which unfairly restricts competition in a relevant market.

On 9 April 2009, the KFTC revised its *Enforcement Guideline for Concerted Acts* by reinforcing the role of circumstantial evidence as a means of presuming the existence of an illegal collusive agreement. With respect to information exchange on prices and output in particular, the revised *Guidelines* provide that such information exchanges can be used as circumstantial evidence of agreements among competitors.

A landmark ruling of 24 December 2015 from the Korean Supreme Court in the so-called *Ramen Cartel Case*[8] has reaffirmed the position in Korean antitrust law that price-related information exchange alone is not sufficient to constitute a price-fixing agreement.

4. **Have there been any cases in your jurisdiction in which the substantive antitrust laws were enforced in an M&A context? Please describe/explain and cite any such cases. (See also Annex.)**

To the best of the authors' knowledge, there are no decisions where the KFTC applied Article 19(1), the anti-cartel or anti-illegal concerted conduct provision, to an exchange of information or other types of anticompetitive concerted conduct in an M&A context.

5. **Are the substantive antitrust laws more likely to apply at specific stages of the transaction – i.e. at an early stage, or prior to closing (or does it not make a difference)? Do companies face ongoing risk following the consummation (or failure) of their transaction for conduct that allegedly occurred pre-closing (pre-failure)?**

There is no specific timing for the application of the substantive antitrust laws. Therefore, companies may face ongoing risk following the consummation (or failure) of their transaction for their allegedly illicit conduct that occurred pre-closing (or pre-failure) until the applicable time limit for enforcement action has expired. Currently, the limitation period can last up to 12 years, i.e. seven years after the end of the illegal conduct at issue for the KFTC to open an investigation and then up to an additional five years for enforcement actions to follow. This rule applies to all types of infringements of the MRFTA, including violations of the standstill agreement and breaches of the anti-cartel provisions.

6. **Please explain how the relevant authority enforces (or could enforce) the substantive antitrust laws in an M&A context. How would the investigation occur, and what timing constraints would apply?**

Investigations may occur at any point in time, subject to information that would justify dawn raids. No particular timing constraints apply.

---

8 Case No 2013du25924, decided 24 December 2015 (Korean Supreme Court).

7. **Is private enforcement of the substantive antitrust laws possible in an M&A context, and has it occurred?**

   Private enforcement of the substantive antitrust laws is possible and has increased significantly in recent years. The amended MRFTA has introduced a provision that alleviates the plaintiff's burden of demonstrating the amount of damages arising from competition law violations. However, the authors are not aware of any cases yet where private parties have sought private enforcement of substantive antitrust law violations in an M&A context.

8. **Could behavior subject to the substantive antitrust laws also be caught under the merger control rules/standstill obligation? (Please also refer to the Annex.)**

   The *Guidelines on Methods of Business Combination Notification* do not specifically identify specific types of conduct subject to the substantive antitrust laws which could also form part of the standstill obligation. That being said, neither primary nor secondary legislation excludes such a situation. In theory, therefore, anticompetitive conduct subject to the substantive laws could also be caught under the merger control/standstill obligations, although this has not been the case in practice so far.

9. **Please describe the penalties for infringing the substantive antitrust laws. Please indicate whether these include criminal penalties, including individual criminal penalties. As a practical matter, how have these been applied in the context of an M&A transaction?**

   Practices contrary to the substantive antitrust laws are subject to administrative sanctions by the KFTC and to criminal prosecution if the KFTC files a complaint with the Prosecutor's Office against business entities or individuals, in cases of violations that seriously restrain competition.

   For cartels, the KFTC imposes an administrative fine under which companies can be fined a sum not exceeding the equivalent of 10% of the turnover generated by the sale of the relevant goods or services during the period of the violation. For criminal penalties, companies can be subject to a criminal fine of up to KRW 200 million.

10. **Please describe policy and enforcement trends in your jurisdiction.**

    There is no specific enforcement trend regarding the application of substantive antitrust laws to the pre-closing conduct of merging parties.

Annex

Table 1: Actual Enforcement of Specific Conduct under the Relevant Merger Control Rules and Substantive Antitrust Laws

Please identify whether the following type of conduct has been subject to investigation/enforcement in your jurisdiction, under the merger control laws or substantive antitrust laws. Please cite any such case(s) and provide a brief description in the table below.

Specific Conduct	Actual Enforcement under Merger Control Laws	Actual Enforcement under Substantive Antitrust Laws
Pre-signing due diligence	No	No
Post-signing/pre-approval due diligence	No	No
Post-approval/pre-closing due diligence	No	No
Use of "clean teams"	No	No
Restrictions on the target in an M&A agreement, e.g. buyer approval required for: – Investments above a certain level; – New business above a certain level; – Other obligations to consult/obtain approval from the buyer before closing.	No	No
Joint marketing	No	No
Joint presentations (e.g. industry fairs)	No	No
Joint communications	No	No
Strategy/planning regarding customers	No	No

Specific Conduct	Actual Enforcement under Merger Control Laws	Actual Enforcement under Substantive Antitrust Laws
Strategy/planning regarding suppliers	No	No
Third party contract novation	No	No
Personnel Issues: – Secondments – Retention Strategies	No	No
IT Planning/Database Migration	No	No
Other	***2005kigyul0765*** (Interlocking Directorate) Pursuant to Article 69-2(1)(2) MRFTA, the KFTC imposed an administrative fine of KRW 18 million on Kolon Corp for failing to notify its formation of a new company and interlocking directorate in violation of Articles 12(6) and (7) MRFTA ***2006gyulhap4610*** (Merger Registration) Pursuant to Article 69-2(1)(2) MRFTA, the KFTC imposed an administrative fine of KRW 15 million on Korail Tourism Development Co Ltd for its pre-approval merger registration in violation of Articles 12(6) and (7) MRFTA. ***2007jei2562*** (Merger Registration) Pursuant to Article 69-2(1)(2) MRFTA, the KFTC imposed an administrative fine of KRW 15 million on GE Medical Holding AB for its pre-approval merger registration in violation of Articles 12(6) and (7) MRFTA.	No

Specific Conduct	Actual Enforcement under Merger Control Laws	Actual Enforcement under Substantive Antitrust Laws
Other	***2006gyulhap0154*** (Share Acquisition) Pursuant to Article 69-2(1)(2) MRFTA, the KFTC imposed an administrative fine of KRW 7.5 million on Mittal Steel Germany GmbH for its pre-approval merger registration (filed for merger two weeks after acquiring the target's shares) in violation of Article 12(1), proviso to 12(6) and 12(7) MRFTA, as well as Article 18(8) of the Enforcement Decree. ***2005kigyul 0774*** (Share Acquisition) Pursuant to Article 69-2(1)(2) MRFTA, the KFTC imposed an administrative fine of KRW 15 million on SK Chemicals for its pre-approval share acquisition in violation of Articles 12(6) and (7) MRFTA. ***2007jeil2879*** (Business Transfer) Pursuant to Article 69-2(1)(2) MRFTA, the KFTC imposed an administrative fine of KRW 2 million on DI Semicon for its pre-approval business transfer (filed for approval 266 days after closing the transaction) in violation of Articles 12(1), (6), and (7) MRFTA.	No
Other	***2008jijang2118*** (Formation of a New Company) Pursuant to Article 69-2(1)(2) MRFTA, the KFTC imposed an administrative fine of KRW 30 million on Shinhan Card Co Ltd for its pre-approval	No

Specific Conduct	Actual Enforcement under Merger Control Laws	Actual Enforcement under Substantive Antitrust Laws
Other	contribution to the newly formed company and share acquisition (notified to the KFTC 44 days after the last date on which such notification should have been made under the MRFTA) in violation of Article 12(1), proviso to 12(6) and 12(7) MRFTA, as well as Article 18(9) of the Enforcement Decree. ***2008jei0129*** (Formation of a New Company) Pursuant to Article 69-2(1)(2) MRFTA, the KFTC imposed an administrative fine of KRW 7.5 million on Techno Semichem Co Ltd for its pre-approval contribution to the newly formed company and share acquisition (notified the KFTC 11 days after the last date on which such notification should have been made under the MRFTA) in violation of Articles 12(6) and (7) MRFTA, as well as Article 18(8) of the Enforcement Decree. Simultaneously, pursuant to Article 69-2(1)(2) MRFTA, the KFTC imposed an administrative fine of KRW 15 million on Mitsubishi Chemical Co Ltd for its pre-approval contribution to the newly formed company and share acquisition (notified to the KFTC 159 days after the last date on which such notification should have been made under the MRFTA) in violation of Articles 12(6) and (7) MRFTA, as well as Article 18(8) of the Enforcement Decree.	No

Additional Explanation:

To date, the KFTC's enforcement record has been confined to the types of "failure to file" or "premature implementation" situations mentioned in the table. However, this does not eliminate the possibility that the KFTC could someday begin considering other types of conduct listed above as a violation of the standstill obligation or of the substantive antitrust laws.

Table 2: Hypothetical Enforcement of Specific Conduct under the Relevant Merger Control Rules and Substantive Antitrust Laws

For any conduct that is *not* the subject of actual enforcement (Table 1), please indicate in the Table below whether the conduct identified *could potentially* be enforced under the merger control laws and/or substantive antitrust laws.

Specific Conduct	Hypothetical Enforcement under Merger Control Laws	Hypothetical Enforcement under Substantive Antitrust Laws
Pre-signing due diligence	Yes, potentially possible	Yes, potentially possible
Post-signing/pre-approval due diligence	Yes, potentially possible	Yes, potentially possible
Post-approval/pre-closing due diligence	Yes, potentially possible	Yes, potentially possible; there is no specific guidance in this respect, but merging parties are likely allowed to exchange information necessary to close the deal, however, it is potentially possible that excessive due diligence could be challenged.
Use of "clean teams"	Yes, potentially possible	Yes, potentially possible; there is no specific guidance in this respect, but the use of "clean teams" is probably favored although it does not provide blanket immunity.

Specific Conduct	Hypothetical Enforcement under Merger Control Laws	Hypothetical Enforcement under Substantive Antitrust Laws
Restrictions on the target in an M&A agreement, e.g. buyer approval required for: – Investments above a certain level; – New business above a certain level; – Other obligations to consult/obtain approval from the buyer before closing.	Yes, potentially possible	Yes, potentially possible
Joint marketing	Yes, potentially possible	Yes, potentially possible
Joint presentations (e.g. industry fairs)	Yes, potentially possible	Yes, potentially possible
Joint communications	Yes, potentially possible	Yes, potentially possible
Strategy/planning regarding customers	Yes, potentially possible	Yes, potentially possible
Strategy/planning regarding suppliers	Yes, potentially possible	Yes, potentially possible
Third party contract novation	Yes, potentially possible	Yes, potentially possible
Personnel Issues: – Secondments – Retention Strategies	Yes, potentially possible	Yes, potentially possible
IT Planning/Database Migration	Yes, potentially possible	Yes, potentially possible
Other		

MEXICO

Amilcar Peredo Rivera
(Basham, Ringe y Correa)

Part 1: Merger Control and the "Standstill Obligation"

1. **Please identify the relevant merger control legislation in your jurisdiction. Please provide a link to the relevant legislation (if possible, in English) and also indicate:**
   - **whether the merger control system is mandatory or voluntary,**
   - **the relevant authority, and**
   - **the duration of the review period.**

Antitrust merger control in Mexico is regulated by the Federal Economic Competition Law (**Law**).[1]

If the threshold requirements for filing are met and no exemption is available, filing and clearance is mandatory; however, there is also a voluntary procedure available to review transactions that do not exceed these thresholds (e.g. when a transaction poses some competition concerns and parties want to avoid the risk of being challenged by the Commission, which can occur up to a year following closing).

The relevant authorities responsible for enforcing the Law and clearing transactions from an antitrust perspective are (i) the Federal Economic Competition Commission (**Commission**), for general matters, and (ii) the Federal Telecom Institute (**IFT**), only for the telecom and broadcasting sectors.

The maximum review period to clear a transaction is 60 business days, counted from the filing date or from the filing of any basic and/or additional information requested by the relevant antitrust agency; in extraordinary complex cases, the Commission or IFT may extend this period for another 40 business days.

2. **Does the merger control system in your jurisdiction impose a "*standstill obligation*" – meaning, that the transaction cannot be implemented prior to completing the merger control process? (Please cite the relevant legislation.) Please also indicate the *legal scope* of the standstill obligation according to the relevant legislation (e.g. the parties to the transaction cannot effect a change of control, cannot take steps towards implementation, etc.).**

Yes, the transaction cannot be carried out until the relevant agency has issued antitrust clearance under articles 86 and 87 of the Law; any actions infringing this rule will be null and void, without prejudice to the parties' administrative,

1 An English translation of the Law is available at <https://www.cofece.mx/wp-content/uploads/2018/03/Federal_Economic_Competition_Law.pdf>. Although translated by the agency, this version is for reference only. The origin al version of the Law, published in the Official Gazette in Spanish, should guide all legal interpretations.

civil or criminal liability and that of the individuals who ordered or contributed to the execution.

Furthermore, the legal acts pertaining to the concentration may not be registered in the corporate ledgers, formalized under a public deed or registered in the Public Commercial Registry until the relevant agency has issued its authorization.

More specifically, pursuant to article 87 of the Law, companies must refrain from: (i) perfecting the legal act; (ii) acquiring or exercising direct or indirect, factual or legal control over another economic agent; (iii) executing the merger agreement; (iv) in a sequence of transactions, completing the one that triggers the thresholds; or (v) allowing agreements executed abroad to have any legal or material effects in Mexico, before clearance is issued and served in Mexico.

3. **Have the relevant authorities in your jurisdiction issued internal or external guidelines concerning the scope of the standstill obligation, and/or their authority to enforce it? Please provide a copy/link of such guidance, if possible in English.**

There are no guidelines issued by the Commission specifically on the standstill obligation, nevertheless, the Commission has issued general guidelines regarding the concentration notices.[2]

4. **Are there any exceptions to the standstill obligation – for example, through derogation or "carve out"? Please describe the circumstances in which this is possible. Please also describe the relevant process, e.g. do parties need to apply to the authority for a derogation from the standstill obligation? If so, how long is the approval process? If there are specific cases addressing these issues, please identify them.**

The Law does not provide for exceptions, but in multijurisdictional filings a carve-out of the Mexican part of the deal may be negotiated, allowing the parties to close the part outside the Mexican jurisdiction. The carve-out must be implemented in such a way that the transaction will not have effect in Mexico until clearance is granted. The Law does not provide for a specific authorization to proceed with the carve-out.

5. **Does a public bid exception exist in your jurisdiction? (For example, under the EU Merger Regulation it is possible to acquire shares as part of a public bid, provided that the shares are not exercised until the acquisition is cleared by the Commission.) If such an exception exists in your jurisdiction, please describe how it is applied.**

Such an exception is not provided by Law.

6. **What powers does the relevant authority have to investigate and enforce violations of the standstill obligation? Are dawn raids possible? What timing applies to investigation/enforcement proceedings?**

---

2 Guidelines (Spanish only) are available at <https://www.cofece.mx/wp-content/uploads/2017/12/guia-0042015_not_concentraciones.pdf>.

In order to provide a complete answer, it is necessary to clarify that the obligation in the Law not to carry out or consummate a notifiable transaction before it is cleared can lead to different types of violations and legal consequences:

(i) When filing is not made at all or when filing is extemporary (i.e. submitted after the transaction was executed),[3] the Commission will impose fines ranging from 5,000 times the measurement unit (**MU**)[4] (Mex$422,450 in 2019 figures, approx. US$22,117)[5] and up to 5% of the parties' annual accruable income, while all actions carried out before clearance will be null and void. This type of violation is analyzed in a summary proceeding.

(ii) When filing is made before closing but the parties do not observe the standstill obligation, the fine described in (i), above, would not strictly apply. Further to the breach, all actions would be null and void, but no administrative penalty would be triggered and, as such, there would be no direct power to initiate an investigation or to enforce such violations. However, note that during a merger review the antitrust agency has the power to request information and documents, not only from the parties involved but also from third parties participating in the relevant market, thus it is possible in fact for the agency to "investigate" or gain knowledge of a violation to the standstill obligation. Moreover, the current accepted criterion of the Commission is that only *ex ante* operations can be approved; accordingly, the agency could try to dismiss the parties' notification (on the grounds that the transaction is no longer *ex ante*), forcing the parties to follow the extemporary notice proceeding, with the consequences described in (i) above as a result of violating the standstill obligation.

In addition, note that during the pre-clearance period, parties must remain independent market players, and actions violating the standstill obligation could denote the existence of more serious antitrust infringements, such as absolute monopolistic practices (cartels and collusions), relative monopolistic practices (abuse of dominance) or illegal mergers (e.g. if the transaction is ultimately rejected and parties had initiated the integration process). In this scenario, the process will be that of a full investigation, in which the Chief Enforcer has all powers to conduct dawn raids, request written information or request depositions.

7. **What are the possible penalties for violating the standstill obligation? Are there criminal sanctions, including on individuals? Have these been applied in practice? Is there a difference in enforcement between transactions involving domestic companies and "foreign-to-foreign" transactions? Does the authority have the power to unwind transactions implemented in breach of the standstill obligation? If so, has the authority made use of that power in practice? If yes, please provide examples.**

For a general explanation on penalties please refer to Question 6 above. Furthermore: (i) there are no criminal penalties for any type of infringement regarding

---

3 Please refer to Question 2 for details on when a transaction can be considered as executed.

4 The MU is the economic reference in Mexico, expressed in Mexican pesos, to calculate the amount to be paid for obligations and payments established by laws and regulations.

5 According to Mexico's Central Bank, the exchange rate applicable on 11 June 2019 is 19.1 pesos per US Dollar.

the notification filing. A possible criminal sanction could be imposed if parties make false statements or submit false information, or if the merging parties act as one company since this could be viewed as cartel conduct; (ii) there is no difference in enforcement between transactions involving domestic companies and foreign-to-foreign transactions; (iii) the authority has the power to unwind non-reportable transactions, but in the case of a violation of the standstill obligation, the authority does not strictly need to unwind the transaction, since it is considered null and void.

The Commission has challenged a number of cases for late filing or for complete failure to file.

8. **How does the relevant authority typically learn of potential violations of the standstill obligation? Does the authority actively monitor the trade press?**

It is common for the Commission to learn of this type of violation due to a subsequent filing made by either of the parties involved. When filing is made to the Commission with respect to a subsequent transaction (unrelated to the first one which wasn't notified), the parties will need to submit financial and corporate information which could disclose the previous non-reported transaction. The Commission also monitors press releases.

9. **Please describe the relevant authority's enforcement of the standstill obligation. If there have been cases, please describe the specific conduct that was found to violate the standstill provision and the criteria applied by the relevant authority or court. Has the relevant authority considered the market impact of the conduct? (Please refer to the Annex.)**

As generally discussed in Questions 6 and 7 above, the Commission has so far generally investigated and enforced cases of (i) extemporary notice (i.e. filings made after closing) and (ii) complete lack of notice. To the best of our knowledge, there are no cases so far under Mexican Law where parties were sanctioned for having violated the standstill obligation i.e. for implementing the transaction prior to approval.

(i) To date the Commission has handled and concluded three cases of extemporary notice of a merger and has imposed the following sanctions:

- File *VCN-001-2017*:[6] In relation to a transaction concerning asset transfer through the cession or acquisition of trustees' rights, the Commission imposed a penalty of Mex$365,200 (approx. US$18,060) on each party who failed to notify on time and an additional penalty of Mex$8,545,680 (approx. US$422,600) on the notary public who executed the transaction.
- File *VCN-002-2017*:[7] The Commission imposed a penalty of Mex$14,020,000 (approx. US$693,315) on four parties who failed to notify on time and

---

6 The parties involved were: i) Mexico Multifamily Fund VIII (Cayman) LP; ii) Banco INVEX, Sociedad Anónima, Institución de Banca Múltiple, INVEX Grupo Financiero; iii) CIBANCO, Sociedad Anónima, Institución de Banca Múltiple, División Fiduciaria; iv) Banco Monex, sociedad anónima, Institución de Banca Múltiple, Monex Grupo Financiero; and v) HSBC México, Sociedad Anónima, Institución de Banca Múltiple, Grupo Financiero HSBC, División Fiduciaria.

7 The parties involved were: i) Panasonic Corporation; ii) Ficosa Inversión SL, iii) Panasonic Europe Ltd, iv) Pertacol Holding SL; and v) Pindro Holding SL.

of Mex$183,310.25 (approx. US$9,065) on another party. The transaction concerned was the acquisition by Panasonic Corporation of a 49% interest in Ficosa International, SA.

- File *VCN-003-2017*:[8] The Commission imposed a penalty of Mex$377,450 (approx. US$18,666) on each party who failed to notify on time. The transaction concerned was the acquisition by Banco Santander SA of 100% of the shares of Banco Popular Español and, indirectly, of 24.99% of the shares of Grupo Financiero Ve por Más SA de CV.

(ii) The Commission has not recently issued any decisions imposing sanctions in cases of complete lack of notice.

However, there are five ongoing cases in which the Commission is currently analyzing transactions that were not notified (files *VCN-001-2018*, *VCN-002-2018*, *IO-003-2016*, *IO-004-2016* and *DE-018-2017*). According to public information on the Commission's website, the first four files concern investigations as to whether illegal mergers in the milk and dairy products market were carried out. The Commission made clear that it learned about the possible transactions through public information on the internet. The last file (*DE-018-2017*) concerns an investigation initiated as a result of a complaint, which seeks to determine whether there was an illegal merger in the market for the marketing, distribution and sale to the public of gasoline and diesel.

Note that the Commission can also review transactions that are not executed in accordance with the exact terms of the clearance given. In this case, as well as in the case of failure to file or filing following closing, the Commission will open a summary proceeding to investigate the facts and decide on the fine.

According to the Law, the market impact of the transaction should be considered when assessing the fine. Nevertheless, recent decisions of the Commission (supported by some court precedents) consider that in gun-jumping cases there is no need to analyze the market impact.

10. **In cases involving alleged violations of the standstill obligation under the relevant merger control laws, has the relevant authority (or court) *also* considered the substantive antitrust laws? (Please refer to the Annex.)**

No.

11. **Is private enforcement of the standstill obligation possible?**

This is an unexplored area, but since conduct carried out in breach of the standstill obligation is considered null and void, private enforcement would be technically possible.

12. **Please describe the private law risks/consequences (i.e. contractual/validity consequences) for transactions that are subject to notification, but which are completed without notification/approval. Please identify any relevant cases and describe them.**

If merging parties close a transaction and such transaction was subject to the Commission's approval, the acts carried out are considered null and void without

8 The parties involved were: i) Santander SA; and ii) Banco Popular Español SA.

prejudice to the parties' administrative, civil or criminal liability and that of the persons who ordered or contributed to the execution.

Furthermore, legal acts pertaining to the concentration may not be registered in the corporate ledgers, formalized under a public deed or registered in the Public Commercial Registry until the Commission has issued its authorizations.

The Commission may also order a partial or total divestiture where the merger transaction itself is considered an unlawful concentration.

13. **Please describe policy and enforcement trends in your jurisdiction.**

The Commission is active in the enforcement of gun-jumping cases, particularly in case of late filing or failure to file.

In 2017, for example, the Commission fined Panasonic, Ficosa and other companies Mex$14,020,00 (approx. US$693,315) and of Mex$183,310.25 (approx. US$9,065) for failure to file an operation which took place in 2015, in which Panasonic Europe acquired more than 35% of Ficosa Internacional shares (including Ficosa Mexico).

Part 2: Substantive Antitrust Law in an M&A Context

1. **Please identify the relevant *substantive antitrust laws* in your jurisdiction that can potentially apply in an M&A context (e.g. for the EU, this would include Article 101 of the Treaty on the Functioning of the European Union). Please provide a link to the relevant legislation (if possible, in English).**

   Antitrust merger control in Mexico is regulated by the Federal Economic Competition Law (**Law**).[9]

   The Law (articles 53 and 88) also covers the prohibition of unlawful horizontal agreements between competitors and exchange of competitively sensitive information.

2. **Do any guidelines exist in your jurisdiction concerning the application of the substantive antitrust laws in an M&A context – whether internal to the relevant authority, or external, formal or informal (e.g. speeches)? If so, please provide a copy/link to such guidance.**

   Yes, there are two relevant guidelines (a) the concentration notice guidelines,[10] which provide general assistance as to when a transaction may be subject to the competition authority review and related matters, and (b) the guidelines for the exchange of information between competitors,[11] which provide general assistance as to what type of information may be shared and under what terms.

3. **As a general matter (not limited to M&A), how are the substantive antitrust laws enforced with respect to the exchange of competitively sensitive information between competing firms? Please also indicate the relevance of anti-competitive effects or intent in such enforcement.**

   The Law prohibits as cartel conduct any exchange of sensitive information among competitors made for the purpose, or having the effect, of:

   - Fixing prices
   - Restraining production
   - Dividing the market
   - Coordinating bids or abstentions from tenders.

---

9 An English translation of the Law is available at <https://www.cofece.mx/wp-content/uploads/2018/03/Federal_Economic_Competition_Law.pdf>. Although translated by the agency, this version is for reference only. The original version of the Law, published in the Official Gazette in Spanish, should guide all legal interpretations.

10 Guidelines (Spanish only): <https://www.cofece.mx/wp-content/uploads/2017/12/guia-0042015_not_concentraciones.pdf>.
Amendments (Spanish only): <https://www.cofece.mx/wp-content/uploads/2017/12/mod_guia_not_concentraciones.pdf>.

11 Guidelines for the exchange of information between competitors (Spanish only): <https://www.cofece.mx/wp-content/uploads/2018/01/guia-0072015_intercambioinf.pdf#pdf%3E>.

Such conduct may be incur administrative fines of up to 10% of the economic agent's annual income or 1,500,000 times the MU. Additionally, criminal fines and criminal liability may be imposed on participating individuals.

Note that Article 88 of the Law explicitly indicates that parties subject to a notified transaction are not excluded from this obligation but rather explicitly covered by it.

4. **Have there been any cases in your jurisdiction in which the substantive antitrust laws were enforced in an M&A context? Please describe/explain and cite any such cases. (See also Annex.)**

As discussed above, since 2014, the Commission has been actively investigating gun-jumping conduct, but so far has only sanctioned merging parties for their failure to notify the concentration (or for having filed late). Sanctions, however, have been more aggressive in recent years.

To the best of our knowledge, there are no cases in which the potentially anti-competitive pre-closing conduct of merging parties was examined or sanctioned pursuant to the substantive antitrust rules (articles 53 and 88 of the Law) in an M&A context.

5. **Are the substantive antitrust laws more likely to apply at specific stages of the transaction – i.e. at an early stage, or prior to closing (or does it not make a difference)? Do companies face ongoing risk following the consummation (or failure) of their transaction for conduct that allegedly occurred pre-closing (pre-failure)?**

Exchanges of information that may be considered a cartel practice must be avoided at any stage up to closing.

The Commission has 10 years to initiate an investigation in relation to any conduct that may result in liability and imposition of sanction, pursuant to the Law.

6. **Please explain how the relevant authority enforces (or could enforce) the substantive antitrust laws in an M&A context. How would the investigation occur, and what timing constraints would apply?**

In the M&A context, substantive antitrust laws would be typically enforced (a) if a non-reportable transaction has an anticompetitive impact, (b) if during the pre-closing period the merging parties in effect cease to act as independent market players (most commonly, by illegally exchanging information between them), or (c) if the parties fail to file a reportable transaction.

The limitation period for the initiation of an investigation into possible infringements in situations (b) and (c) above is 10 years; one year in the case of (a).

The limitation period for the Commission to bring proceedings alleging that parties failed to notify a merger or filed after closing is 10 years.

7. **Is private enforcement of the substantive antitrust laws possible in an M&A context, and has it occurred?**

No.

8. **Could behavior subject to the substantive antitrust laws also be caught under the merger control rules/standstill obligation? (Please also refer to the Annex.)**

An illegal exchange of information between competitors can be caught under the standstill obligation as well as the substantive antitrust Law.

In addition, note that during the pre-clearance period, parties must remain independent market players, and conduct violating the standstill obligation could denote the existence of more serious antitrust infringements, such as absolute monopolistic practices (cartels and collusions), relative monopolistic practices (abuse of dominance) or illegal concentrations (e.g. if the transaction is ultimately rejected and parties had initiated the integration process). In this scenario, the process will be that of a full investigation, in which the Chief Enforcer has all powers to conduct dawn raids, request written information or request depositions.

9. **Please describe the penalties for infringing the substantive antitrust laws. Please indicate whether these include criminal penalties, including individual criminal penalties. As a practical matter, how have these been applied in the context of an M&A transaction?**

Penalties for infringing antitrust laws in Mexico may be classified depending on the conduct.

- Cartel conduct:
  - administrative fines of up to 10% of the annual income of the economic agent.
  - criminal fines and criminal liability up to 10 years' imprisonment.
  - civil liabilities enforceable by third parties.
- Abuse of dominance:
  - administrative fines of up to 8% of the annual income of the economic agent.
  - civil liabilities enforceable by third parties.
- Unlawful concentrations:
  - administrative fines of up to 8% of the annual income of the economic agent.
  - civil liabilities enforceable by third parties.
  - order of correction measures.

10. **Please describe policy and enforcement trends in your jurisdiction.**

N/A

Annex

Table 1: Actual Enforcement of Specific Conduct under the Relevant Merger Control Rules and Substantive Antitrust Laws

Please identify whether the following type of conduct has been subject to investigation/enforcement in your jurisdiction, under the merger control laws or substantive antitrust laws. Please cite any such case(s) and provide a brief description in the table below.

Specific Conduct	Actual Enforcement under Merger Control Laws	Actual Enforcement under Substantive Antitrust Laws
Pre-signing due diligence	No	No
Post-signing/pre-approval due diligence	No	No
Post-approval/pre-closing due diligence	No	No
Use of "clean teams"	No	No
Restrictions on the target in an M&A agreement, e.g. buyer approval required for: – Investments above a certain level; – New business above a certain level; – Other obligations to consult/obtain approval from the buyer before closing.	No	No
Joint marketing	No	No
Joint presentations (e.g. industry fairs)	No	No
Joint communications	No	No
Strategy/planning regarding customers	No	No
Strategy/planning regarding suppliers	No	No
Third party contract novation	No	No
Personnel Issues: – Secondments – Retention Strategies	No	No
IT Planning/Database Migration	No	No
Other	No	No

Note: To the best of our knowledge, there are no cases so far which have sanctioned the categories of conduct listed above. As discussed above, all gun-jumping cases in Mexico so far involve situations in which the merging parties either failed to file a reportable transaction or filed it late (after closing).

Table 2: Hypothetical Enforcement of Specific Conduct under the Relevant Merger Control Rules and Substantive Antitrust Laws

For any conduct that is *not* the subject of actual enforcement (Table 1), please indicate in the Table below whether the conduct identified *could potentially* be enforced under the merger control laws and/or substantive antitrust laws.

Specific Conduct	Hypothetical Enforcement under Merger Control Laws	Hypothetical Enforcement under Substantive Antitrust Laws
Pre-signing due diligence	Yes. Sensitive strategic information should not be shared. Use of clean teams recommended.	Yes
Post-signing/pre-approval due diligence	Idem	Yes
Post-approval/pre-closing due diligence	Yes	Yes.
Use of "clean teams"	Reduced number of members. Members should not belong to the commercial/marketing/ sales department.	–
Restrictions on the target in an M&A agreement, e.g. buyer approval required for: – Investments above a certain level; – New business above a certain level; – Other obligations to consult/obtain approval from the buyer before closing.	No	No
Joint marketing	Yes	The exchange of information among competitors can be considered as an absolute monopolistic practice.

Specific Conduct	Hypothetical Enforcement under Merger Control Laws	Hypothetical Enforcement under Substantive Antitrust Laws
Joint presentations (e.g. industry fairs)	Idem	Idem
Joint communications	Yes. Communications should be carefully reviewed to avoid violations.	Yes. Communications should be carefully reviewed to avoid violations.
Strategy/planning regarding customers	Yes	No
Strategy/planning regarding suppliers	Yes	No
Third party contract novation	Yes	No
Personnel Issues: – Secondments – Retention Strategies	Secondments are subject to the guidelines re: exchange of information between competitors.	No
IT Planning/Database Migration	Generally permitted but subject to the Guidelines re: exchange of information.	Generally permitted but subject to the Guidelines re: exchange of information.
Other	–	–

SOUTH AFRICA

Jean Meijer and Sandhya Foster
(Herbert Smith Freehills)

Part 1: Merger Control and the "Standstill Obligation"

1. **Please identify the relevant merger control legislation in your jurisdiction. Please provide a link to the relevant legislation (if possible, in English) and also indicate:**
   - **whether the merger control system is mandatory or voluntary,**
   - **the relevant authority, and**
   - **the duration of the review period.**

The Competition Act, No. 89 of 1998, as amended (**Act**) regulates merger control in South Africa.[1] The merger control regime is mandatory in relation to intermediate[2] and large mergers.[3] The Competition Commission (**Commission**) may request notification of small mergers within six months of implementation.

The decision to approve small and intermediate mergers is made by the Commission. The initial review period for an intermediate merger is 20 business days from receipt of a complete notification. The Commission can (and in practice, often does) extend the initial period by 40 business days. The maximum time period is 60 business days.

In the case of a large merger, the Commission makes a recommendation to the Competition Tribunal (**Tribunal**) to approve, approve with conditions or prohibit a merger. The Commission has an initial review period of 40 business days from receipt of a complete notification. This period may be extended on application to the Tribunal by 15 business days at a time. On receipt of the Commission's recommendation, the Tribunal must set a date for a hearing or pre-hearing within 10 business days. This period may be extended by 10 business days by the Chairperson of the Tribunal or by a further period with the consent of the merging parties. Most large mergers are approved within 50 to 70 business days, but in complex cases the cumulative extensions by the Commission and process before the Tribunal may take a year or more.

---

1 <https://www.comptrib.co.za/legislation-and-forms/competition-act>.

2 A merger will qualify as an intermediate merger if (i) the acquiring group and the target firm have combined assets or turnover (whichever combination is higher) in South Africa greater than or equal to R600 million; and (ii) the target firm has assets or turnover (whichever is the higher) in South Africa greater than or equal to R100 million.

3 A merger will qualify as a large merger if (i) the acquiring group and the target firm have combined assets or turnover (whichever combination is the higher) in South Africa greater than or equal to R6.6 billion; and (ii) the target firm has assets or turnover (whichever is the higher) in South Africa greater than or equal to R190 million.

2. **Does the merger control system in your jurisdiction impose a "*standstill obligation*" – meaning, that the transaction cannot be implemented prior to completing the merger control process? (Please cite the relevant legislation.) Please also indicate the *legal scope* of the standstill obligation according to the relevant legislation (e.g. the parties to the transaction cannot effect a change of control, cannot take steps towards implementation, etc.).**

A party to an intermediate or large merger may not implement a merger, i.e. effect a change of control, until the merger is approved (with or without conditions) by the relevant competition authority.[4] The merging parties may, however, plan the post-merger integration (provided the plans are not implemented prior to merger clearance).

In April 2019, the Commission issued *Guidelines for the Determination of Administrative Penalties for Failure to Notify Mergers and Implementation of Mergers Contrary to the Competition Act* (**Penalty Guidelines**) which makes the distinction between a failure to notify and prior implementation: "failure to notify" means the failure to notify a notifiable transaction and "prior implementation" means the premature implementation of a notifiable merger prior to obtaining the necessary approval of the competition authorities. In the context of this chapter, prior or premature implementation is a violation of the standstill obligation.

The Commission may consider inter alia the following scenarios as premature implementation or failure to notify:

(i) a senior executive of the acquiring firm engaging in the day-to-day operations of the target firm;

(ii) the merging parties marketing themselves as a single entity prior to approval being obtained;

(iii) the acquiring firm changing the name of the target firm;

(iv) premature integration and consolidation of the merging firms; or

(v) the acquiring firm becoming involved in the making and/or executing of strategic decisions regarding the future of the target firm, including identifying markets for the target firm to pursue, developing new products or services for the target firm, taking charge of ordering the target firm's raw materials, amending the target firm's procurement policies or becoming involved in its customer relations.[5]

3. **Have the relevant authorities in your jurisdiction issued internal or external guidelines concerning the scope of the standstill obligation, and/or their authority to enforce it? Please provide a copy/link of such guidance, if possible in English.**

Yes, the Penalty Guidelines referred to above.

---

4 See Act s 13A(1) and (3).

5 Competition Commission "Guidelines for the Determination of Administrative Penalties for Failure to Notify Mergers and Implementation of Mergers contrary to the Competition Act" (March 2019).

4. **Are there any exceptions to the standstill obligation – for example, through derogation or "carve out"? Please describe the circumstances in which this is possible. Please also describe the relevant process, e.g. do parties need to apply to the authority for a derogation from the standstill obligation? If so, how long is the approval process? If there are specific cases addressing these issues, please identify them.**

The Act does not provide for carve-out or ring-fencing arrangements and there is no formal procedure to follow.

In practice, however, it may be possible to ring-fence depending on the nature of the target firm. The parties would have to be able to satisfy the Commission that, as a consequence of the arrangement, there has been no establishment or acquisition of control over the target.

5. **Does a public bid exception exist in your jurisdiction? (For example, under the EU Merger Regulation it is possible to acquire shares as part of a public bid, provided that the shares are not exercised until the acquisition is cleared by the Commission.) If such an exception exists in your jurisdiction, please describe how it is applied.**

A public bid exception does not exist in South Africa.

However, in a matter involving a hostile takeover, the South African Competition Appeal Court (**CAC**) held that the Act[6] does not seek to prohibit completion of a merger. Rather, the Act seeks to ensure that notifiable mergers are not implemented prior to authorization being granted by the relevant competition authorities. As a result, the CAC allowed the acquisition of the shares but prevented the acquiring firm from voting prior to merger clearance.[7]

6. **What powers does the relevant authority have to investigate and enforce violations of the standstill obligation? Are dawn raids possible? What timing applies to investigation/enforcement proceedings?**

The Act confers extensive investigative powers upon the Commission including the power to conduct a dawn raid on any premises (business or private dwelling).[8]

A judge or magistrate may issue a warrant to enter and search premises if there are reasonable grounds to believe that (i) a prohibited practice has taken place or is likely to take place on or in those premises, or (ii) anything connected with an investigation in terms of the Act is in the possession of or under the control of a person who is on or in those premises.[9]

---

6 Particularly s 13A(3) of the Act which provides that parties to an intermediate or large merger may not implement that merger until it has been approved.

7 *Harmony Gold Mining Company Ltd v Gold Fields and others* [2005] ZACAC 4; see also: *Murray & Roberts Holdings Ltd v Aton Holdings GmbH; Aton Austria Holdings GmbH and the Competition Commission* Case No: IDT079Jun18, Competition Tribunal.

8 See *SOS Support Public Broadcasting Coalition and Others v South African Broadcasting Corporation (SOC) Limited and Others* [2018] ZACC 37, paras 46–50.

9 s 46(1) of the Act.

The Commission will usually request information from the parties by way of a letter. However, the Commissioner has the power to summon any person who is believed to be able to furnish any information on the subject of the investigation or to have possession or control of any book, document or other object that has bearing on the subject.

The person summonsed is required to:

(i) appear before the Commissioner or a person authorized by the Commissioner to be interrogated; and

(ii) deliver or produce to the Commissioner or a person authorized by the Commissioner any book, document or other object specified in the summons, at a time and place specified in the summons.[10]

A person questioned must answer each question truthfully and to the best of that person's ability, but the person is not obliged to answer any question if the answer is self-incriminating.[11]

There are no time limits applicable to investigations or enforcement proceedings in relation to pre-implementation or a failure to notify.

7. **What are the possible penalties for violating the standstill obligation? Are there criminal sanctions, including on individuals? Have these been applied in practice? Is there a difference in enforcement between transactions involving domestic companies and "foreign-to-foreign" transactions? Does the authority have the power to unwind transactions implemented in breach of the standstill obligation? If so, has the authority made use of that power in practice? If yes, please provide examples.**

Implementation of a merger without approval may attract an administrative penalty of up to 10% of the firm's annual turnover in, and its exports from, South Africa during the firm's preceding financial year.[12]

Set out below is a table reflecting examples of penalties imposed on firms by the competition authorities for *premature implementation*:

No.	Case	Conduct	Penalty
	Competition Commission v Dunlop Industrial Products (Pty) Ltd & Another (Case No 018689) **Date of decision:** 9 July 2014	The CEO of Nenana Management Services (Pty) Ltd (**Nenana**) engaged in the day-to-day operations of Dunlop Industrial Products (Pty) Ltd (**Dunlop**), and Nenana and Dunlop marketed themselves as a single entity	R250,000 each

10 s 49A(1) of the Act.

11 s 49A(2) of the Act.

12 s 59(1)(d) read with s 59(2) of the Act.

No.	Case	Conduct	Penalty
	Competition Commission v Macsteel Services Centre SA (Pty) Ltd & Unique Ventilation and Support Systems (Pty) Ltd (Case No FTN154Nov16) **Date of decision:** 21 February 2018	Macsteel Services Centres SA (Pty) Ltd (**Macsteel**) implemented a merger without approval by involving itself in the operations and affairs of Unique Ventilation and Support Systems (Pty) Ltd (**UVSS**), including: – appointing directors to the board of Ricoco (Pty) Ltd (**Ricoco**) which later changed its name to UVSS; – providing recommendations in relation to changing the name of Ricoco; and – providing administrative services including company secretarial duties.	R1 million

Set out below is a table reflecting a range of penalties imposed on firms by the competition authorities for *failure to notify*:

No.	Case	Conduct	Penalty
	Competition Commission v WBHO Construction (Pty) Ltd & Another (69/AM/Oct10) **Date of decision:** 10 November 2010	The acquisition of 49% of the issued share capital of a company coupled with control in the form of the right to appoint the majority of the directors in the company	WBHO: R1 million Edwin: R100,000
	Competition Commission v Pangbourne Properties Limited and others (16246) **Date of decision:** 13 March 2013	The mistaken belief that the transactions amounted to two small mergers	R75,000

No.	Case	Conduct	Penalty
	Competition Commission v Life Healthcare Group (Pty) Ltd & Joint Medical Holdings Ltd (FTN229Feb16) **Date of decision:** 4 February 2016	The agreement to set prices jointly	R10 million
	Competition Commission v Deican Investments (Pty) Ltd and New Seasons Investments Holding (Pty) Ltd (FTN151Aug15) *Competition Commission v Dickerson Investments (Pty) Ltd & Nodus Equity (Pty) Ltd* (FTN127Aug15) **Date of decision:** 3 June 2016	The acquisition of the right to veto strategic decisions	(FTN151Aug15): R150,000 each (FTN127Aug15): Dickerson Investments: R250,000 Nodus Equity: R150,000

According to the Penalty Guidelines, the minimum penalty (or base amount, as it is referred to in the Penalty Guidelines) for premature implementation or a failure to notify in relation to an intermediate merger is double the application filing fee for an intermediate merger.[13] For premature implementation or a failure to notify in relation to large mergers, the minimum penalty is double the applicable filing fee for a large merger.[14]

The Penalty Guidelines further provide that once the Commission has established the base amount, it will take into account the duration of the merging parties' contravention. In doing so, the Commission will add to the relevant base amount a proportion of the relevant base amount for each month of the contravention according to the following formulae:

(i) for contraventions not exceeding a year, the additional amount will be (50% × base amount) × number of months of contravention;

(ii) for contraventions exceeding a year but less than two years, the additional amount will be (75% × base amount) × number of months of contravention; and

(iii) for contraventions exceeding two years, the additional amount will be (100% × base amount) × number of months of contravention.

Once the amount is determined according to the above formulae, the Commission will adjust this figure based on the relevant aggravating and mitigating factors.

---

13 The filing fee for an intermediate merger is R150,000 and so the minimum penalty would be R300,000. With effect from 1 January 2019, the filing fee will increase to R165,000.

14 The filing fee for a large merger is R500,000 and so the minimum penalty would be R1 million. With effect from 1 January 2019, the filing fee will increase to R550,000.

However, the Commission is not bound by these guidelines. Indeed, the Commission has discretion to seek a lower penalty or the maximum penalty of 10% of turnover in exceptional circumstances. Exceptional circumstances may include intentional disregard of the Act.[15]

There are no criminal sanctions for implementing a merger without clearance.

The Act applies to all economic activity within, or having an effect within, South Africa. As a result, there is no difference in enforcement between transactions involving domestic companies and foreign-to-foreign transactions.

In addition to imposing an administrative penalty, the Tribunal may (i) order a party to the merger to sell any shares, interest or other assets it has acquired pursuant to the merger; or (ii) declare void any provision of an agreement to which the merger was subject (see section 60 of the Act).

In the *Distillers* case, following the implementation of a merger without clearance, the Tribunal (i) found that a substantial lessening of competition was likely in the proprietary spirits market; and (ii) ordered the termination of distribution agreements (which resulted in control of certain brands reverting to their owners).[16] This was in essence a divestiture order.[17]

8. **How does the relevant authority typically learn of potential violations of the standstill obligation? Does the authority actively monitor the trade press?**

The Commission actively monitors the press. It may learn of potential contraventions of section 13A of the Act through the press, subsequent merger notifications involving the same parties or where a third party (such as a trade union) notifies the Commission of an act of premature implementation or failure to notify.

9. **Please describe the relevant authority's enforcement of the standstill obligation. If there have been cases, please describe the specific conduct that was found to violate the standstill provision and the criteria applied by the relevant authority or court. Has the relevant authority considered the market impact of the conduct? (Please refer to the Annex.)**

There have been instances where the competition authorities have enforced the standstill obligation (see Question 7 above).

There have also been instances (in addition to those set out in Question 7 above) where the competition authorities have enforced the provisions of the Act in relation to a failure to notify, including:[18]

- Failure by a bank to notify the Commission when it had not disposed of shares acquired from a debtor within the required 12-month period.[19] The

15 The factors that will be taken into account are set out in s 59(3) of the Act.

16 *Distillers Corporation (SA) Ltd v Stellenbosch Farmers Winery Group Ltd* (08/LM/Feb02) [2003] ZACT 15 (CT).

17 See s 60 of the Act which states that the Tribunal may make an order for divestiture if a merger is implemented in contravention of Chapter 3 of the Act (which contains all merger control provisions).

18 The Penalty Guidelines provide that this list is not an exhaustive list of instances of prior implementation but merely serves as guidance on instances where the Commission will find that certain conduct constitutes a prior implementation of a merger.

19 *Competition Commission v Standard Bank of South Africa Ltd* (FTN228Feb16) [2016] ZACT 56 (CT).

Commission has issued a Practitioner Update which allows a financial services institution to establish control of the business or assets of a debtor without filing a merger notification, provided that the financial services institution disposes of the business or assets within a period of 12 months (now 24 months).[20]

- Failure to notify the Commission of the acquisition of a 50% share in a company due to the mistaken belief that the transaction amounted to a small merger because the wrong financial statements were used in determining whether the requisite thresholds were met.[21]
- Acquisition of 49% of the issued share capital of a company coupled with the right to appoint the majority of the directors in the company.[22]
- Acquisition of a company's book debt (including customer information) where the book debt was found to be a part of a business.[23]

10. **In cases involving alleged violations of the standstill obligation under the relevant merger control laws, has the relevant authority (or court) *also* considered the substantive antitrust laws? (Please refer to the Annex.)**

In *Netcare Hospital Group/Community Hospital Group*[24] (where the merging parties had failed to notify an acquisition of joint control) the Tribunal held that not all unlawful implementations of a merger involve a prohibited practice. A vertical merger or a conglomerate merger, or a merger between firms in the same line of production who were not competitors in the same market would typically not give rise to conduct prohibited under the substantive antitrust laws, even if implemented unlawfully.

The merging parties argued that because the merger related to joint control, had the merger been approved Netcare and Community Hospital Group would have been considered as a single economic entity and accordingly it would be artificial to say that it had both failed to notify and contravened section 4(1)(b) (the section prohibiting cartel conduct).[25]

Netcare and Community Hospital Group settled with the Commission on the basis that a fine was imposed for the following conduct: (i) implementing a merger without clearance and (ii) cartel conduct, i.e. Netcare's involvement in the pricing of Community Hospital Group prior to merger clearance.

11. **Is private enforcement of the standstill obligation possible?**

No, but a private individual can notify the Commission if it believes that a firm has implemented a merger without clearance.

---

[20] See Commission's Practitioner Update, "The application of merger provisions of the Competition Act 89 of 1998, as amended, to risk mitigation transactions" Issue 4 (as amended) (10 April 2015).

[21] *Competition Commission v Structa Technology (Pty) Ltd and others* (83/LM/Nov02) [2003] ZACT 18 (CT).

[22] *Competition Commission v WBHO Construction (Pty) Ltd and Edwin Construction (Pty) Ltd* (69/AM/Oct10) [2010] ZACT 77 (CT).

[23] *Competition Commission v Edgars Consolidated Stores Limited and another* (Case No 95/FN/Dec02).

[24] *Netcare Hospital Group (Pty) Ltd/Community Hospital Group (Pty) Ltd* (27/CR/Mar07) [2008] ZACT 19 (CT).

[25] See text of s 4 (1)(b)(i) to (iii) of the Act at Part 2 Question 1 below.

12. **Please describe the private law risks/consequences (i.e. contractual/validity consequences) for transactions that are subject to notification, but which are completed without notification/approval. Please identify any relevant cases and describe them.**

    Please refer to the response to Question 7 above.

13. **Please describe policy and enforcement trends in your jurisdiction.**

    There has been an increased focus in the past few years on the monitoring and prosecution of premature implementation and failure to notify. This has resulted in the Penalty Guidelines.

Part 2: Substantive Antitrust Law in an M&A Context

1. **Please identify the relevant *substantive antitrust laws* in your jurisdiction that can potentially apply in an M&A context (e.g. for the EU, this would include Article 101 of the Treaty on the Functioning of the European Union). Please provide a link to the relevant legislation (if possible, in English).**

   The substantive antitrust laws that can potentially apply in an M&A context in South Africa are set out in the Act.[26]

   Section 4(1) of the Act prohibits an agreement between, or concerted practice by, firms, or a decision by an association of firms, if it is between parties in a horizontal relationship which (a) has the effect of substantially preventing or lessening competition in the market; or (b) involves the following restrictive horizontal practices:

   (i) directly or indirectly fixing a purchase or selling price or any other trading condition;

   (ii) dividing markets by allocating customers, suppliers, territories, or specific types of goods or services; or

   (iii) collusive tendering.

   Conduct that is prohibited by section 4(1)(b) of the Act is generally referred to as "cartel conduct" and is per se prohibited.

2. **Do any guidelines exist in your jurisdiction concerning the application of the substantive antitrust laws in an M&A context – whether internal to the relevant authority, or external, formal or informal (e.g. speeches)? If so, please provide a copy/link to such guidance.**

   The Commission has issued draft guidelines on information exchange between competitors[27] which would be applicable in the context of due diligence performed by a prospective purchaser in anticipation of a merger.

3. **As a general matter (not limited to M&A), how are the substantive antitrust laws enforced with respect to the exchange of competitively sensitive information between competing firms? Please also indicate the relevance of anti-competitive effects or intent in such enforcement.**

---

26 See <https://www.comptrib.co.za/legislation-and-forms/competition-act>.

27 Competition Commission, "Draft Guidelines on the Exchange of Information between Competitors under the Competition Act" (14 July 2017) <http://www.compcom.co.za/wp-content/uploads/2015/01/Competition-Commission-draft-guidelines-on-information-exchange-between-....pdf>.

The exchange of competitively sensitive information is not in itself a contravention of the Act. However, there are certain types of information exchange between competitors which the Commission considers likely to result in cartel conduct, including the exchange of competitively sensitive information intimately related to price and which forms part of the price – quantity – quality nexus.

Cartel conduct is per se prohibited and the effect of the conduct is therefore not relevant. However, a process of characterization is required to determine whether the character of the conduct complained of coincides with the character of the prohibited conduct. In *American Natural Soda Ash Corporation and Another v Competition Commission of South Africa*,[28] the Supreme Court of Appeal held that this entails a two-step process: (i) determining the scope of the prohibition through statutory interpretation; and (ii) determining the nature of the conduct complained of through a factual enquiry.

4. **Have there been any cases in your jurisdiction in which the substantive antitrust laws were enforced in an M&A context? Please describe/explain and cite any such cases. (See also Annex.)**

See the case referred to in Part 1, Question 10 above.

5. **Are the substantive antitrust laws more likely to apply at specific stages of the transaction – i.e. at an early stage, or prior to closing (or does it not make a difference)? Do companies face ongoing risk following the consummation (or failure) of their transaction for conduct that allegedly occurred pre-closing (pre-failure)?**

The primary risk is in respect of conduct that occurs pre-closing or pre-failure.

If a merger filing arises from a cooperation agreement, for example, and the post-merger cooperation extends beyond that which was cleared by the competition authorities, there is a risk of prosecution under the substantive antitrust laws.

6. **Please explain how the relevant authority enforces (or could enforce) the substantive antitrust laws in an M&A context. How would the investigation occur, and what timing constraints would apply?**

The Commission can initiate a complaint if it believes that a firm has engaged in a prohibited practice.

Following the complaint, the Commission will investigate and, where it considers that the complaint has merit, refer the complaint to the Tribunal for adjudication. Where the Commission does not consider that a complaint has merit, it will issue a notice of non-referral.

A complaint in respect of a prohibited practice may not be initiated more than three years after the practice has ceased.[29]

7. **Is private enforcement of the substantive antitrust laws possible in an M&A context, and has it occurred?**

---

28 *American Natural Soda Ash Corporation and Another v Competition Commission of South Africa* [2005] ZASCA 42; [2005] 3 All SA 1 (SCA).

29 s 67(1) of the Act.

A private individual can file a complaint with the Commission where it believes that a firm has engaged in a prohibited practice.

If the Commission issues a notice of non-referral or fails to refer the complaint to the Tribunal within a year (or such extended period as may be agreed with the complainant), the complainant may refer the complaint directly to the Tribunal for adjudication.

8. **Could behavior subject to the substantive antitrust laws also be caught under the merger control rules/standstill obligation? (Please also refer to the Annex.)**

Yes, please see the Annex attached.

9. **Please describe the penalties for infringing the substantive antitrust laws. Please indicate whether these include criminal penalties, including individual criminal penalties. As a practical matter, how have these been applied in the context of an M&A transaction?**

Where a firm engages in cartel conduct, the Tribunal may impose an administrative penalty of up to 10% of the firm's annual turnover in South Africa and its exports from South Africa during the firm's preceding financial year. The Act allows for an administrative penalty of up to 25% of the firm's annual turnover in South Africa and its exports from South Africa for conduct that is substantially a repeat by the same firm of conduct previously found by the Tribunal to be a prohibited practice.

In May 2016, criminal sanctions were introduced for directors or persons in a position of management authority who cause a firm to engage in or who knowingly acquiesce to a firm engaging in cartel conduct.[30] A fine of up to R500,000 and/or imprisonment for a period not exceeding 10 years may be imposed. There has not yet been a criminal prosecution in South Africa.

A person who has suffered harm as a result of a prohibited practice (even in the context of M&A transactions) may institute proceedings for civil damages in a civil court. To our knowledge, this has not occurred in the context of an M&A transaction.

10. **Please describe policy and enforcement trends in your jurisdiction.**

The Commission actively enforces the prohibitions on cartel conduct, including in instances where there have been exchanges of competitively sensitive information.

---

30 Competition Amendment Act 2009, s 12.

Annex

Table 1: Actual Enforcement of Specific Conduct under the Relevant Merger Control Rules and Substantive Antitrust Laws

Please identify whether the following type of conduct has been subject to investigation/enforcement in your jurisdiction, under the merger control laws or substantive antitrust laws. Please cite any such case(s) and provide a brief description in the table below.

Specific Conduct	Actual Enforcement under Merger Control Laws	Actual Enforcement under Substantive Antitrust Laws
Pre-signing due diligence	No	No
Post-signing/pre-approval due diligence	No	No
Post-approval/pre-closing due diligence	No	No
Use of "clean teams"	No	No
Restrictions on the target in an M&A agreement, e.g. buyer approval required for: – Investments above a certain level; – New business above a certain level; – Other obligations to consult/obtain approval from the buyer before closing.	No	No
Joint marketing	*Competition Commission v Dunlop Industrial Products (Pty) Ltd & Another* (Case No 018689) Nenana and Dunlop marketed themselves as a single entity.	No

Specific Conduct	Actual Enforcement under Merger Control Laws	Actual Enforcement under Substantive Antitrust Laws
Joint marketing	In addition, the CEO of Nenana engaged in the day-to-day operations of Dunlop. *Competition Commission v Trade Call Investments Apparel (Pty) Ltd and Seardel Group Trading (Pty) Ltd* (Case No FTN114Jul18) Trade Call Investments Apparel (Pty) Ltd (TCIA) and Seardel Apparel had joint marketing and signage.	No
Joint presentations (e.g. industry fairs)	No	No
Joint communications	No	No
Strategy/planning regarding customers	No[29]	No
Strategy/planning regarding suppliers	No[30]	No
Third party contract novation	No	No
Personnel Issues: – Secondments – Retention Strategies	No[31]	No
IT Planning/Database Migration	No	No

1 In *Trade Call Investments Apparel (Pty) Ltd/Seardel Group Trading (Pty) Ltd* (Case No FTN114Jul18), TCIA went beyond planning and inter alia negotiated certain customer arrangements in order to ensure that the business would be able to continue operating going forward. The Commission considered this, together with a number of factors, to amount to prior implementation.

2 In *Trade Call Investments/Seardel* (n 31), TCIA had access to the strategic information and interacted with suppliers of Seardel Apparel. The Commission considered this, together with a number of factors, to amount to prior implementation.

3 In *Trade Call Investment/Seardel* (n 31) TCIA was involved in the employment contracts of Seardel staff. The Commission considered this, together with a number of factors, to amount to prior implementation.

Specific Conduct	Hypothetical Enforcement under Merger Control Laws	Hypothetical Enforcement under Substantive Antitrust Laws
Other	*Competition Commission v Macsteel Services Centre SA (Pty) Ltd & Unique Ventilation and Support Systems (Pty) Ltd* (Case No FTN154Nov16) In 2018, the Commission accused Macsteel of implementing a merger without approval by involving itself in the operations and affairs of UVSS, including: – appointing directors to the board of Ricoco, which later changed its name to UVSS; – providing recommendations in relation to changing the name of Ricoco; and – providing administrative services including company secretarial duties. – Macsteel settled on the basis that this conduct may constitute prior implementation and agreed to pay a fine of R1 million.	No

Table 2: Hypothetical Enforcement of Specific Conduct under the Relevant Merger Control Rules and Substantive Antitrust Laws

For any conduct that is *not* the subject of actual enforcement (Table 1), please indicate in the Table below whether the conduct identified *could potentially* be enforced under the merger control laws and/or substantive antitrust laws.

Specific Conduct	Hypothetical Enforcement under Merger Control Laws	Hypothetical Enforcement under Substantive Antitrust Laws
Pre-signing due diligence	No	Potentially
Post-signing/pre-approval due diligence	No	Potentially
Post-approval/pre-closing due diligence	No	Potentially
Use of "clean teams"	No	No
Restrictions on the target in an M&A agreement, e.g. buyer approval required for: – Investments above a certain level; – New business above a certain level; – Other obligations to consult/obtain approval from the buyer before closing.	Potentially	Potentially
Joint marketing	Yes	Yes
Joint presentations (e.g. industry fairs)	Yes	Yes
Joint communications	Potentially	Potentially
Strategy/planning regarding customers	Potentially	Potentially
Strategy/planning regarding suppliers	Potentially	Potentially
Third party contract novation	Yes	Yes
Personnel Issues: – Secondments – Retention Strategies	Potentially	Potentially
IT Planning/Database Migration	Potentially	Potentially
Other		

SWEDEN

Kristian Hugmark and Kristin Heilborn[1]

(Roschier)

1 The authors would like to express their gratitude to Måns Gottfries and Sebastian Uddgren for their assistance in preparing this chapter.

Part 1: Merger Control and the "Standstill Obligation"

1. **Please identify the relevant merger control legislation in your jurisdiction. Please provide a link to the relevant legislation (if possible, in English) and also indicate:**
   - **whether the merger control system is mandatory or voluntary,**
   - **the relevant authority, and**
   - **the duration of the review period.**

The merger control rules are set out in Chapter 4 of the Swedish Competition Act (**Act**). According to Chapter 4, section 6 of the Act, it is mandatory to notify a concentration to the Swedish Competition Authority (**SCA**) if:

(i) the combined aggregate turnover in Sweden of all undertakings involved in the preceding financial year exceeds SEK 1 billion; and

(ii) at least two of the undertakings involved had a turnover in Sweden in the preceding financial year exceeding SEK 200 million for each of the undertakings.

According to Chapter 4, section 7 of the Act, the following applies if the combined turnover threshold in (i) above is met, but not the threshold in (ii):

(i) the SCA may *ex officio* request a notification if there is special cause to do so; or

(ii) a party or other participant in the concentration may voluntarily notify the concentration.

According to Chapter 4, section 11 of the Act, within 25 business days of receipt of a complete notification the SCA must decide whether to carry out a special investigation of the concentration or decline to take any further action (Phase 1). If, within the review period of 25 days, the SCA has received an offer with commitments from a party to the concentration for the purpose of obtaining a decision by the SCA that it will decline to take any further action, the review period is extended to 35 business days.

According to the SCA's merger control guidelines,[2] the SCA aims to complete its review of "simple" concentrations (i.e. concentrations that have no horizontal or vertical effect or where it is apparent that the concentration will not substantially impede competition on any market), and to deliver a decision within 15 business days.

---

2 The merger control guidelines are currently only available in Swedish (<http://www.konkurrensverket.se/globalassets/konkurrens/pm/vagledning_foretagskoncentrationer.pdf>).

According to Chapter 4, section 13 of the Act, if the SCA decides to initiate an in-depth investigation (Phase 2), the SCA must announce a decision within three months from the date on which the investigation was initiated. This period can be extended by one month at a time, provided that the parties grant their consent to an extension. According to Chapter 4, section 14 of the Act, the SCA can extend the review period without the parties' consent if there is special cause to do so.[3]

2. **Does the merger control system in your jurisdiction impose a "*standstill obligation*" – meaning, that the transaction cannot be implemented prior to completing the merger control process? (Please cite the relevant legislation.) Please also indicate the *legal scope* of the standstill obligation according to the relevant legislation (e.g. the parties to the transaction cannot effect a change of control, cannot take steps towards implementation, etc.).**

Yes. Pursuant to Chapter 4, section 12 of the Act, and section 13(a) with respect to Phase 2 investigations, a party or any other participant in the notified concentration may not take any measures to carry out the concentration before the review period has expired. This standstill obligation ceases to apply if the SCA has decided not to take any further measures against the concentration before the review period has expired. The decision not to take any further action is notified to the parties in a formal decision issued by the SCA.

3. **Have the relevant authorities in your jurisdiction issued internal or external guidelines concerning the scope of the standstill obligation, and/or their authority to enforce it? Please provide a copy/link of such guidance, if possible in English.**

The SCA has not issued guidelines specifically relating to the standstill obligation. However, new general merger control guidelines were issued on 1 January 2018 which contain a brief section regarding the standstill obligation.[4] The guidelines state that a concentration may not be either fully or partially completed until the SCA has announced its decision as to whether or not it will decline to take any action against the concentration.

According to the guidelines,[5] the parties to the concentration must pay particular attention to the fact that certain measures carried out before the completion of the concentration, such as exchanging sensitive information or coordinating market behavior, may infringe the Act and the EU's prohibition on anticompetitive cooperation regardless of whether or not it is mandatory to notify the concentration.

With respect to public bids, see Question 5 below.

4. **Are there any exceptions to the standstill obligation – for example, through derogation or "carve out"? Please describe the circumstances in which this is possible. Please also describe the relevant process, e.g. do parties need to**

---

3 <http://www.konkurrensverket.se/globalassets/english/publications-and-decisions/the-swedish-competition-act.pdf>. Please note that the SCA's translation of the Act does not include the latest amendments to the Act that entered into force in January 2018, such as Chapter 4, s 13(a), which is referred to in the answer to Question 2.

4 Dnr. 617/2017, 11 January 2018, paras 51–4.

5 n 1.

apply to the authority for a derogation from the standstill obligation? If so, how long is the approval process? If there are specific cases addressing these issues, please identify them.

There are no exceptions specifically relating to a derogation or "carve out". However, pursuant to Chapter 4, section 12 (Phase 1) and section 13(a) (Phase 2) of the Act, the SCA may grant an exemption from the standstill obligation if there is special cause to do so. According to the preparatory works to the Act, the purpose of such an exemption is to allow the parties to the concentration to take measures which prevent or decrease the risk of financial loss or other negative consequences during Phase 1.

The parties need to apply to the SCA for an exemption. To our knowledge, there are no cases at the SCA concerning exemptions from the standstill obligation. Accordingly, it is not clear how long the approval process would take. In one case at the SCA, a request for an exemption was submitted, but, since the SCA approved the concentration within six business days, there was no need to consider the request.[6]

5. **Does a public bid exception exist in your jurisdiction? (For example, under the EU Merger Regulation it is possible to acquire shares as part of a public bid, provided that the shares are not exercised until the acquisition is cleared by the Commission.) If such an exception exists in your jurisdiction, please describe how it is applied.**

In practice, yes, although there is no specific exception in the Act. The merger control guidelines specifically state that when an acquisition of control takes place on a regulated market (stock market) or a multi-trading facility in such a way that it is not possible to notify the concentration before it is completed, the SCA's view is that the parties are entitled to acquire the securities. However, the standstill obligation covers all other forms of exercising rights related to the securities (e.g. voting rights) before the review period has expired.

6. **What powers does the relevant authority have to investigate and enforce violations of the standstill obligation? Are dawn raids possible? What timing applies to investigation/enforcement proceedings?**

If it is necessary for the SCA to fulfill its duties under the Act (including, but not limited to, merger control), the SCA may impose an obligation on a company or any other legal entity to provide information and documents (for example), and it may also impose an obligation on an individual to be subject to a hearing. Failure to comply with these obligations may result in the imposition of a fine.

The SCA does not have the authority to conduct dawn raids in order to investigate violations of the standstill obligation. The authority to do so is limited to investigating violations of Articles 101 and 102 TFEU and the equivalents in the Act.

7. **What are the possible penalties for violating the standstill obligation? Are there criminal sanctions, including on individuals? Have these been applied in practice? Is there a difference in enforcement between transactions invol-**

---

6 *Carnegie Investment Bank AB* Dnr. 480/2010, 23 September 2010.

ving domestic companies and "foreign-to-foreign" transactions? Does the authority have the power to unwind transactions implemented in breach of the standstill obligation? If so, has the authority made use of that power in practice? If yes, please provide examples.

There are no penalties for violating the standstill obligation unless coupled with a finding of infringement of general antitrust rules. However, the SCA may impose an obligation on a party to notify the transaction or issue a hold separate order, under penalty of a fine. There is no statutory maximum fine, but it is expected to be set at an amount that is prohibitive for the parties.

There are no differences between transactions involving domestic companies and foreign-to-foreign transactions.

Pursuant to the Act, the implication of a prohibition of a concentration is that any legal act constituting a component of the concentration or taken for the purpose of carrying out the transaction will be void. Thus, if the SCA prohibits a transaction carried out in breach of the standstill obligation, the transaction (including all steps involved in carrying it out) will be void, which in principle means that the parties need to "unscramble the egg".

That complex legal consequence and related gun-jumping issues were subject to the scrutiny of the courts in a case concerning a concentration between two real estate agent franchises.[7] Since the threshold for a mandatory notification was not met, the parties signed and closed simultaneously after a very brief pre-notification discussion with the SCA. After closing, the purchaser appointed a new board of directors of the target company and significant integration took place. Following concerns raised by the SCA, the parties chose to voluntarily file the concentration post-closing. The notification triggered a standstill period during which the parties were not permitted to implement the concentration any further. The merger was eventually prohibited by the Stockholm District Court in 2014 (the SCA did not at the time have the power to block concentrations). The legal consequence of the prohibition was that the concentration was considered void. The court thus clarified that even when it is not mandatory to notify a concentration and thereby no legal impediments to implement the transaction exist at the time of the signing and closing, the concentration may nevertheless be rendered void. It should be noted that the parties may, in any event, voluntarily submit a notification to the SCA, or the SCA may request such notification.

8. How does the relevant authority typically learn of potential violations of the standstill obligation? Does the authority actively monitor the trade press?

The SCA actively monitors the trade press, and companies and individuals may also (anonymously) inform the SCA.

9. Please describe the relevant authority's enforcement of the standstill obligation. If there have been cases, please describe the specific conduct that was found to violate the standstill provision and the criteria applied by the relevant

---

7 T 3629-14, *SCA v Swedbank Franchise/Svensk Fastighetsförmedling* Decision of 16 December 2014.

authority or court. Has the relevant authority considered the market impact of the conduct? (Please refer to the Annex.)

To our knowledge, there have been no cases where parties were found to have been in breach of the standstill obligation.

In the Swedbank case (summarized in Question 7), after the parties had voluntarily filed the concentration, the SCA imposed an obligation on Swedbank Franchise (**SF**) to comply with the standstill rule during the Phase 1 investigation by not acting as an owner of Svensk Fastighetsförmedling (**SFM**), under penalty of a fine of SEK 20 million. After Phase 2 had been initiated, the SCA applied to the Stockholm District Court for an interim injunction prohibiting SF from directly or indirectly exercising certain rights of SFM and from representing SFM's franchisees in the Swedish real estate agent association. SF conceded, and the court imposed the injunction under penalty of a fine of SEK 20 million. Shortly before the proceedings concerning the prohibition of the merger were initiated, the SCA once again applied to the Stockholm District Court for an interim injunction against SF under penalty of a fine. This time, the SCA sought an injunction to prohibit SF from directly or indirectly using information about business or operational conditions received from SFM, unless legally obligated to use such information and provided that the SF Group informed the SCA within five business days of the type of information that had been transferred. The court found that the SCA's claim was too general and lacked the clarity and concreteness necessary for SF to have the actual and legal ability to comply with the injunction, and therefore dismissed the SCA's claim. To our knowledge, the SCA never sought to impose any fines.

For related gun-jumping issues, please see Question 7 and the *Scandorama* case, which related to an infringement of antitrust rules, described in Part 2, Question 4.

10. In cases involving alleged violations of the standstill obligation under the relevant merger control laws, has the relevant authority (or court) also considered the substantive antitrust laws? (Please refer to the Annex.)

The substantive antitrust laws may apply in the context of concentrations. Please see *Scandorama* in Part 2, Question 4. However, to our knowledge there has not been any case where both the merger control rules and the substantive antitrust rules have been applied simultaneously. In principle, the substantive antitrust rules do not apply if a transaction results in a concentration of undertakings. However, if the parties take measures during the standstill period that are not necessary to carry out the transaction, such measures may simultaneously be in violation of both the substantive antitrust rules and the standstill obligation.

11. Is private enforcement of the standstill obligation possible?

No, it is not possible. Private enforcement would be limited to damages claims for loss caused indirectly by the violation of the standstill obligation.

12. Please describe the private law risks/consequences (i.e. contractual/validity consequences) for transactions that are subject to notification, but which are completed without notification/approval. Please identify any relevant cases and describe them.

See the response to Question 7 above.

13. Please describe policy and enforcement trends in your jurisdiction.

The standstill obligation was recently expanded to apply during Phase 2 as well.

In addition, the absence of a firm sanction for infringements is likely to be discussed in the foreseeable future. Before such a legislative change is enacted, it is unlikely that the SCA will focus its enforcement activities on violations of the standstill obligation, other than to order filings in cases of a failure to notify and to enforce general antitrust rules where such apply.

Part 2: Substantive Antitrust Law in an M&A Context

1. **Please identify the relevant *substantive antitrust laws* in your jurisdiction that can potentially apply in an M&A context (e.g. for the EU, this would include Article 101 of the Treaty on the Functioning of the European Union). Please provide a link to the relevant legislation (if possible, in English).**

Chapter 2, section 1 of the Act, which prohibits anticompetitive cooperation between undertakings, states:

> Agreements between undertakings shall be prohibited if they have as their object or effect, the prevention, restriction or distortion of competition in the market to an appreciable extent, if not otherwise regulated in this act. This shall apply, in particular, to agreements which
>
> 1. directly or indirectly fix purchase or selling prices or any other trading conditions;
> 2. limit or control production, markets, technical development, or investment;
> 3. share markets or sources of supply,
> 4. apply dissimilar conditions to equivalent transactions with other trading parties, thereby placing them at a competitive disadvantage; or
> 5. make the conclusion of contracts subject to acceptance by the other parties of supplementary obligations, which by their nature or according to commercial usage have no connection with the subject of such contracts.[8]

It is essentially identical to Article 101 TFEU (save for the trade between Member States criterion).

As a general rule, the prohibition against anticompetitive cooperation only applies if the transaction is not considered a concentration of undertakings. If the transaction results in such a concentration – irrespective of whether the transaction must be notified to the SCA or not – the prohibition is not applicable. However, if the SCA prohibits the concentration for any reason, measures can be subject to sanctions under the prohibition against anticompetitive cooperation. Measures that are not necessary for carrying out of the transaction can still be caught by the prohibition, even if the transaction results in a concentration of undertakings.

---

8 n 2.

2. Do any guidelines exist in your jurisdiction concerning the application of the substantive antitrust laws in an M&A context – whether internal to the relevant authority, or external, formal or informal (e.g. speeches)? If so, please provide a copy/link to such guidance.

There are no specific guidelines concerning the application of substantive antitrust laws in an M&A context. However, the SCA's general merger control guidelines refer to the situation in which the exchange of sensitive information between companies in the context of a transaction could violate the prohibition against anticompetitive cooperation.[9]

3. As a general matter (not limited to M&A), how are the substantive antitrust laws enforced with respect to the exchange of competitively sensitive information between competing firms? Please also indicate the relevance of anti-competitive effects or intent in such enforcement.

If the exchange of competitively sensitive information is part of an anticompetitive agreement between competing undertakings, e.g. a cartel agreement, the exchange of information is considered to constitute part of the same violation of Chapter 2, section 1 of the Act. However, exchanging competitively sensitive information may also in itself violate the prohibition against anticompetitive cooperation. Receiving strategic information from a competitor can constitute an agreement or a concerted practice between undertakings, which could have as its object or effect the restriction of competition.

The SCA may conduct dawn raids, order parties to supply information, and require individuals who are likely to be in a position to provide relevant information to appear at a hearing to investigate potentially illegal exchange of information. If the SCA finds alleged violations of the prohibition against anticompetitive cooperation, it can take the case to the Swedish Patent and Market Court. The power to impose fines rests with the courts in Sweden.

4. Have there been any cases in your jurisdiction in which the substantive antitrust laws were enforced in an M&A context? Please describe/explain and cite any such cases. (See also Annex.)

The *Scandorama* case is of relevance.[10] The case concerned the merger between two companies on the market for coach tours to Europe. Scandorama was to acquire Ölvemarks through a three-step procedure: (i) the acquisition of 10% of the shares, (ii) the acquisition of a further 10% of the shares, and (iii) the acquisition of the remaining 80% of the shares. However, only the first two steps were completed due to Scandorama undergoing financial difficulties. The shares were returned, and instead Ölvemarks acquired Scandorama. During the period in which the first two steps were being carried out, as well as before the first step took place, the parties undertook an extensive synergy program. The court found that, by doing so, the parties had breached the prohibition against anticompetitive cooperation and imposed fines.

---

9 See paragraph 54 in the guidelines (n 1).

10 T 19974-10, *SCA v Scandorama AB & Ölvemarks Holiday AB*, Decision of 24 February 2012.

The case is interesting since it highlights the relationship between Swedish merger control laws and substantive antitrust laws. The court found that there had not been a concentration of undertakings, since the planned third step of the transaction (which would have entailed the actual change of control) was abandoned by the parties. Accordingly, the court considered the case under substantive antitrust law. Had a concentration been created, it would have fallen below the filing thresholds and no notification would have been required. In other words, the parties would have been "safe" with respect to behavior post-concentration, given that mergers below the threshold are also evaluated under the merger control rules.

Another case worth mentioning, although it was outside the scope of gun-jumping but within the scope of M&A and antitrust, is the *Alfa* case.[11] The SCA deemed a five-year non-compete clause in a concentration falling below the filing threshold to be restrictive of competition by object and sued for fines. The court and the appeal court both disagreed with the SCA and no fines were imposed.

5. Are the substantive antitrust laws more likely to apply at specific stages of the transaction – i.e. at an early stage, or prior to closing (or does it not make a difference)? Do companies face ongoing risk following the consummation (or failure) of their transaction for conduct that allegedly occurred pre-closing (pre-failure)?

It does not make any difference. Companies do face an ongoing risk following the consummation of their transaction since the SCA may prohibit a concentration for up to two years after the concentration "arose".[12] If the parties to a concentration start to implement the transaction in a manner that infringes antitrust rules, without a concentration having occurred or before the concentration has closed, the substantive antitrust laws are applicable.

6. Please explain how the relevant authority enforces (or could enforce) the substantive antitrust laws in an M&A context. How would the investigation occur, and what timing constraints would apply?

In practice, enforcement and investigation in an M&A context would probably not be that different from a normal investigation of anticompetitive conduct on the market. That investigation would be conducted independently and separately from the assessment of the concentration under merger control rules.

7. Is private enforcement of the substantive antitrust laws possible in an M&A context, and has it occurred?

Private enforcement of substantive antitrust laws is not limited to certain contexts. Thus, at least in theory, private enforcement is possible in an M&A context. However, to the best of our knowledge it has not occurred in practice.

8. Could behavior subject to the substantive antitrust laws also be caught under the merger control rules/standstill obligation? (Please also refer to the Annex.)

---

11 PMT 7498-16, *SCA v Alfa Quality Moving AB*, Decision of 29 November 2017.

12 The actual time when a concentration arises has not been tested. The most likely relevant date is that of the signing of the relevant sale and purchase agreement.

Behavior such as coordination between the merging parties or the exchange of information before the transaction is closed could violate both the merger control standstill obligation and the antitrust laws.

9. Please describe the penalties for infringing the substantive antitrust laws. Please indicate whether these include criminal penalties, including individual criminal penalties. As a practical matter, how have these been applied in the context of an M&A transaction?

The main penalty for infringing substantive antitrust law in Sweden is the imposition of an administrative fine. The SCA does not have the authority to impose fines, but must apply to the Swedish Patent and Market Court.

The administrative fine is determined based on the sanction value of the infringement and account must be taken of the gravity of the infringement and its duration. When assessing the gravity of the infringement, particular account must be taken of three factors: the nature of the infringement, the size and significance of the market, and the infringement's actual or potential impact on the competition on the market. The administrative fine may not exceed 10% of the annual turnover of the undertaking in the preceding business year.

Criminal penalties cannot be imposed under Swedish law, either on companies or on individuals. There is a theoretical possibility of individuals being banned from carrying on business, but it has never been applied in practice.

For an example of how the penalties have been applied in the context of an M&A transaction, please see the *Scandorama* case under Question 4 above. The companies in that case were fined a total of SEK 11 million (approx. €1.1 million) for infringing the prohibition against anticompetitive cooperation.

10. Please describe policy and enforcement trends in your jurisdiction.

There are no particular policy or enforcement trends related to substantive antitrust laws in an M&A context in Sweden.

Swedish Competition Authority, "The Swedish Competition Authority forwards an application for a prohibition order against the acquisition of the franchisors of two largest national real estate chains (Swedbank Franchise/Svensk Fastighetsförmedling)" 17 June 2014, e-Competitions Bulletin June 2014, Art. N° 67241

European Competition Network Brief, "A Swedish Court imposes fines on bus company cartel (Ölvemarks and Scandorama)" 24 February 2012, e-Competitions Bulletin February 2012, Art. N° 47065

European Competition Network Brief, "The Swedish Patent and Market Court upholds decision by Stockholm District Court that excessively long non-compete clauses in share purchase agreements do not constitute infringement of competition rules by object (Alfa Quality Moving)" 29 November 2017, e-Competitions Bulletin November 2017, Art. N° 86359

ANNEX

Table 1: Actual Enforcement of Specific Conduct under the Relevant Merger Control Rules and Substantive Antitrust Laws

Please identify whether the following type of conduct has been subject to investigation/enforcement in your jurisdiction, under the merger control laws or substantive antitrust laws. Please cite any such case(s) and provide a brief description in the table below.

Specific Conduct	Actual Enforcement under Merger Control Laws	Actual Enforcement under Substantive Antitrust Laws
Pre-signing due diligence	No	No
Post-signing/pre-approval due diligence	No	No
Post-approval/pre-closing due diligence	No	No
Use of "clean teams"	No	No
Restrictions on the target in an M&A agreement, e.g. buyer approval required for: – Investments above a certain level; – New business above a certain level; – Other obligations to consult/obtain approval from the buyer before closing.	No	No
Joint marketing	No	No
Joint presentations (e.g. industry fairs)	No	No
Joint communications	No	No
Strategy/planning regarding customers	No	Yes, *Scandorama*
Strategy/planning regarding suppliers	No	No

Specific Conduct	Actual Enforcement under Merger Control Laws	Actual Enforcement under Substantive Antitrust Laws
Third party contract novation	No	No
Personnel Issues: – Secondments – Retention Strategies	No	No
IT Planning/Database Migration	No	Yes, *Scandorama*
Other	No	No

Table 2: Hypothetical Enforcement of Specific Conduct under the Relevant Merger Control Rules and Substantive Antitrust Laws

For any conduct that is *not* the subject of actual enforcement (Table 1), please indicate in the Table below whether the conduct identified *could potentially* be enforced under the merger control laws and/or substantive antitrust laws.

Specific Conduct	Hypothetical Enforcement under Merger Control Laws	Hypothetical Enforcement under Substantive Antitrust Laws
Pre-signing due diligence	No	Yes
Post-signing/pre-approval due diligence	Yes, although enforcement only possible through a cease and desist order under penalty of a fine.	Yes
Post-approval/pre-closing due diligence	No	Yes
Use of "clean teams"	No	Yes

Specific Conduct	Hypothetical Enforcement under Merger Control Laws	Hypothetical Enforcement under Substantive Antitrust Laws
Restrictions on the target in an M&A agreement, e.g. buyer approval required for: – Investments above a certain level; – New business above a certain level; – Other obligations to consult/obtain approval from the buyer before closing.	Yes, although enforcement only possible through a cease and desist order under penalty of a fine.	Yes
Joint marketing	Yes, although enforcement only possible through a cease and desist order under penalty of a fine.	Yes
Joint presentations (e.g. industry fairs)	Yes, although enforcement only possible through a cease and desist order under penalty of a fine.	Yes
Joint communications	Yes, although enforcement only possible through a cease and desist order under penalty of a fine.	Yes
Strategy/planning regarding customers	Yes, although enforcement only possible through a cease and desist order under penalty of a fine.	Yes
Strategy/planning regarding suppliers	Yes, although enforcement only possible through a cease and desist order under penalty of a fine.	Yes
Third party contract novation	Yes, although enforcement only possible through a cease and desist order under penalty of a fine.	Yes

Specific Conduct	Hypothetical Enforcement under Merger Control Laws	Hypothetical Enforcement under Substantive Antitrust Laws
Personnel Issues: – Secondments – Retention Strategies	Yes, although enforcement only possible through a cease and desist order under penalty of a fine.	Yes
IT Planning/Database Migration	Yes, although enforcement only possible through a cease and desist order under penalty of a fine.	Yes
Other		

SWITZERLAND

David Mamane and Amalie Wijesundera
(Schellenberg Wittmer)

Part 1: Merger Control and the "Standstill Obligation"

1. **Please identify the relevant merger control legislation in your jurisdiction. Please provide a link to the relevant legislation (if possible, in English) and also indicate:**
   - **whether the merger control system is mandatory or voluntary,**
   - **the relevant authority, and**
   - **the duration of the review period.**

Merger control in Switzerland is regulated by the Federal Act on Cartels and other Restraints of Competition (**Cartel Act**, **CartA**)[1] and the Ordinance on the Control of Concentrations of Undertakings (**Merger Control Ordinance**, **MCO**).[2]

The merger control system is mandatory. If the turnover achieved on a world-wide level and in Switzerland reaches certain thresholds, the transaction must be notified to the Swiss competition authority. Prior to formal notification the parties may submit a draft notification. Filing a draft notification is voluntary but strongly recommended.

The relevant authority is the Swiss Competition Commission (**ComCo**). Should a concentration be prohibited by the ComCo, the undertakings concerned may request a special authorization based on public interest reasons from the Swiss Federal Council. However, such an authorization has, to date, never been granted.

The overall review time for the competition authority is limited to five months. Following the notification, the ComCo has one calendar month (Phase I) to decide whether the transaction raises any competition concerns and whether an investigation procedure should be initiated. The subsequent in-depth investigation procedure (Phase II) must be completed within four months.

2. **Does the merger control system in your jurisdiction impose a "*standstill obligation*" – meaning, that the transaction cannot be implemented prior to completing the merger control process? (Please cite the relevant legislation.) Please also indicate the *legal scope* of the standstill obligation according to the relevant legislation (e.g. the parties to the transaction cannot effect a change of control, cannot take steps towards implementation, etc.).**

Art. 32 para 2 CartA provides for a standstill obligation. If a transaction has to be notified, this has the effect that the undertakings concerned are prohibited from closing and implementing the transaction during Phase I and Phase II, if

[1] See <https://www.admin.ch/opc/en/classified-compilation/19950278/index.html>.

[2] See <https://www.admin.ch/opc/en/classified-compilation/19960295/index.html>.

applicable. The transaction is deemed to be implemented when the change of control has taken place. This is the case if the undertaking acquiring control is able to exercise decisive influence over another undertaking based on ownership or similar rights, as well as contractual agreements, which allow decisive influence on key governance areas. It may even be based on a significant loan, combined with additional contractual rights.

3. **Have the relevant authorities in your jurisdiction issued internal or external guidelines concerning the scope of the standstill obligation, and/or their authority to enforce it? Please provide a copy/link of such guidance, if possible in English.**

The ComCo has not issued specific guidelines regarding the standstill obligation. However, the authority has issued an explanatory note on the merger control notification form. This note merely states that as a general rule the undertakings concerned are prohibited from closing and implementing the transaction during Phase I, if the ComCo has not granted an exception (para 29).[3]

4. **Are there any exceptions to the standstill obligation – for example, through derogation or "carve out"? Please describe the circumstances in which this is possible. Please also describe the relevant process, e.g. do parties need to apply to the authority for a derogation from the standstill obligation? If so, how long is the approval process? If there are specific cases addressing these issues, please identify them.**

At the request of the undertakings concerned, the ComCo may grant permission to complete the transaction prior to the end of the standstill period for important reasons, such as the reorganization of companies facing imminent insolvency or a pending public takeover bid. Furthermore, once the ComCo initiates the Phase II investigation, it must render a decision as to whether the transaction may be carried out provisionally.

In the following cases ComCo waived the standstill obligation in order to allow the reorganization in case of failing companies: *Schweizerische Post/BEVO* RPW 1998/2, 268; *Ernst & Emmi Gruppe/Swiss Dairy Food* RPW 2003/3, 529; *NZZ-Espace-Der Bund: Vorläufiger Vollzug* RPW 2004/1, 152. In one case, the ComCo has allowed a preliminary closing of a pending public takeover bid (*Schaeffler/Continental* RPW 2009/1, 85).

It generally takes the authority approx. 10–25 days to waive the standstill obligation. In *Schweizerische Post/BEVO*, the authority waived the standstill obligation within 10 days, in *Ernst & Emmi Gruppe/Swiss Dairy Food*, within 15 days, in *NZZ-Espace-Der Bund: Vorläufiger Vollzug*, within 21 days and in *Schaeffler/Continental*, within 23 days.

Note that it is generally not possible to unilaterally carve out Switzerland and close the transaction outside Switzerland pending clearance by the ComCo.

5. **Does a public bid exception exist in your jurisdiction? (For example, under the EU Merger Regulation it is possible to acquire shares as part of a public**

---

[3] The explanatory note can be found under <https://www.weko.admin.ch/weko/de/home/dienstleistungen/melde-formulare.html> (German, French and Italian only).

bid, provided that the shares are not exercised until the acquisition is cleared by the Commission.) If such an exception exists in your jurisdiction, please describe how it is applied.

There is no general exception for public bids. However, at the request of the undertaking(s) concerned, the ComCo may grant an exemption from the prohibition to complete the transaction prior to its clearance. As at the time of writing, such an exception has only been granted in one case (*Schaeffler/Continental* RPW 2009/1, 85; see Question 4). Under the exception granted, the buyer was entitled to exercise its voting and election rights prior to clearance, solely for the purpose of maintaining the full value of its investment.

6. **What powers does the relevant authority have to investigate and enforce violations of the standstill obligation? Are dawn raids possible? What timing applies to investigation/enforcement proceedings?**

The ComCo may use all regular powers of investigation, including dawn raids. Such proceedings are not subject to specific timing constraints.

7. **What are the possible penalties for violating the standstill obligation? Are there criminal sanctions, including on individuals? Have these been applied in practice? Is there a difference in enforcement between transactions involving domestic companies and "foreign-to-foreign" transactions? Does the authority have the power to unwind transactions implemented in breach of the standstill obligation? If so, has the authority made use of that power in practice? If yes, please provide examples.**

Closing a transaction that should have been notified or breaching the standstill obligation can lead to administrative fines for companies of up to CHF 1 million (approx. US$984,600) and criminal fines for individuals of up to CHF 20,000 (approx. US$19,700).

There is no risk of criminal liability for companies or imprisonment for individuals for closing a transaction that should have been notified and for infringing of the standstill obligation.

As at the time of writing, ComCo has imposed the following administrative fines on companies for failure to file a notifiable transaction or for implementing a concentration prior to its clearance: CHF 68,400 (approx. US$67,350, *Curti & Co AG,* RPW 1998/4, 613), CHF 60,000 (approx. US$59,100, *Rhône-Poulenc SA/ Merck & Co* – this decision was overturned on appeal but upheld by the Swiss Federal Supreme Court by decision of 24 April 2001: RPW 2001/2, 443), CHF 35,000 (approx. US$34,500, *Verfügung in Sachen Übernahme der ProVAG Versicherungen AG und der PROVITA Gesundheitsversicherung AG* RPW 2013/2, 222) and CHF 15,000 (approx. US$14,750, *BKW-AEK/Comtop* RPW 1997/2, 237).

There is no difference in enforcement between transactions involving domestic companies and foreign-to-foreign transactions. The ComCo has issued fines in two cases due to closing a foreign-to-foreign transaction without clearance.

The ComCo does not have the power to unwind transactions where there has been a violation of the standstill obligation. However, if the transaction is carried out without clearance, the ComCo will initiate the merger proceedings *ex officio* and it may order (among other measures) divestments if it ultimately prohibits the transaction.

8. **8. How does the relevant authority typically learn of potential violations of the standstill obligation? Does the authority actively monitor the trade press?**

The authority may learn of possible violations of the standstill obligations in a number of ways, such as media coverage, third-party complaints, its own investigations.

9. **Please describe the relevant authority's enforcement of the standstill obligation. If there have been cases, please describe the specific conduct that was found to violate the standstill provision and the criteria applied by the relevant authority or court. Has the relevant authority considered the market impact of the conduct? (Please refer to the Annex.)**

All fines imposed so far by ComCo relate to the closing of a concentration that the parties failed to notify (see Question 7).

In *Rhône-Poulenc SA/Merck & Co*, the founders of a joint venture closed the transaction and failed to notify the concentration. This decision was overturned on appeal by the first instance, but was upheld by the Swiss Federal Supreme Court.

In *BNP/Paribas*, the buyer acquired 65.2% of the voting rights and closed the transaction in the context of a public takeover bid without prior notification. The transaction in question was also a foreign-to-foreign transaction.

In *ProVAG Versicherungen AG und der PROVITA Gesundheitsversicherung AG*, the proposed concentration was intended to be implemented in two steps, namely (i) to acquire the shares in ProVAG Versicherungen AG and at a later time (ii) to acquire the shares in PROVITA Gesundheitsversicherung AG. The transaction was notified only after the buyer had already acquired the shares in ProVAG Versicherungen AG. The ComCo held that the planned transactions were closely related and were therefore to be treated as one single concentration. As a result, the ComCo held that the acquirer had failed to notify the concentration, since it should have submitted a filing prior to implementing the first step of the transaction.

In *BKW-AEK/Comtop*, the founders were fined for closing and not notifying the establishment of a joint venture by means of a participation agreement.

In *X/C-AG und D-AG*, the acquirer did not take into account all Swiss turnover of the companies concerned and mistakenly believed the turnover thresholds were not met, and closed the transaction without notifying the concentration prior to closing.

In *Schweizerische National-Versicherungs-Gesellschaft/Coop Leben*, the buyer closed the acquisition of the majority of the shares in the target (by way of exchange of shares) without prior notification.

In *Phm Holding, der Simon et Membrez SA und der Termiboîtes SA*, the acquirer closed the transaction without prior notification to the ComCo due to the fact that the turnover thresholds were not met. However, since in a past decision a subsidiary of the acquirer was considered to be dominant, the ComCo affirmed an obligation of notification on the basis of Art. 9 para 4 CartA, according to which dominant companies are obliged to notify all concentrations, irrespective of turnover. Upon appeal, the ComCo's decision was overturned by the Swiss Federal Administrative Court.

10. In cases involving alleged violations of the standstill obligation under the relevant merger control laws, has the relevant authority (or court) *also* considered the substantive antitrust laws? (Please refer to the Annex.)

No (see Question 9).

11. Is private enforcement of the standstill obligation possible?

In *Etablissements Ed Cherix et Filanosa SA/Edipresse SA*, the Swiss Federal Supreme Court has confirmed that third parties do not have any party rights in merger control procedures. In addition, third parties have no legal standing to appeal the merger control decisions of the ComCo.

12. Please describe the private law risks/consequences (i.e. contractual/validity consequences) for transactions that are subject to notification, but which are completed without notification/approval. Please identify any relevant cases and describe them.

From a civil law perspective, the validity of a transaction completed before clearance is suspended until the deadline for Phase I and (if applicable) Phase II has expired. If the ComCo ultimately prohibits the transaction it may order (among other measures) divestments.

13. Please describe policy and enforcement trends in your jurisdiction.

The last proposed reform of the CartA, which included changes to the merger control regime, was rejected by the Swiss Parliament in 2014. The current intention is to introduce the uncontested changes of the failed revision, in particular, the introduction of the SIEC test ("significant impediment to effective competition"). Currently, the merger control regime is based on a "qualified dominance" test. Therefore, the assessment consists of determining whether a proposed concentration will (i) create or strengthen a dominant position, which (ii) is liable to eliminate effective competition.

Part 2: Substantive Antitrust Law in an M&A Context

1. **Please identify the relevant *substantive antitrust laws* in your jurisdiction that can potentially apply in an M&A context (e.g. for the EU, this would include Article 101 of the Treaty on the Functioning of the European Union). Please provide a link to the relevant legislation (if possible, in English).**

   The ComCo can apply the CartA (see Part 1, Question 1). It may in particular apply Art. 5 CartA (on agreements that significantly restrict competition), for instance in the event of joint ventures that do not qualify as full-function or if sensitive information between the undertakings concerned is exchanged during the suspensive period or in case of ancillary restraints with excessive reach, such as non-compete obligations.

2. **Do any guidelines exist in your jurisdiction concerning the application of the substantive antitrust laws in an M&A context – whether internal to the relevant authority, or external, formal or informal (e.g. speeches)? If so, please provide a copy/link to such guidance.**

   The ComCo has issued an explanatory note regarding merger notifications (see Part 1, Question 2). Furthermore, it has published a notice on certain notification issues under the Swiss merger control procedure. However, the application of the substantive antitrust laws in an M&A context is not further discussed in the notice.

3. **As a general matter (not limited to M&A), how are the substantive antitrust laws enforced with respect to the exchange of competitively sensitive information between competing firms? Please also indicate the relevance of anti-competitive effects or intent in such enforcement.**

   In general, the exchange of sensitive information between competitors may be considered an unlawful agreement under the meaning of Art. 5 CartA. This is the case (i) if the exchange of such information significantly restricts competition and cannot be justified on grounds of economic efficiency, or (ii) if the exchange of such information eliminates effective competition. According to Art. 4 CartA, the exchange of information may restrict competition by object or by effect. However, the ComCo considers the anticompetitive effects, which also depend on the market structure and the nature of the information being exchanged (e.g. current information, aggregated information), as well as the conduct in question, in particular the frequency of the information exchange.

4. **Have there been any cases in your jurisdiction in which the substantive antitrust laws were enforced in an M&A context? Please describe/explain and cite any such cases. (See also Annex.)**

As at the time of writing, there have been no such cases in Switzerland.

5. **Are the substantive antitrust laws more likely to apply at specific stages of the transaction – i.e. at an early stage, or prior to closing (or does it not make a difference)? Do companies face ongoing risk following the consummation (or failure) of their transaction for conduct that allegedly occurred pre-closing (pre-failure)?**

During the pre-signing phase (in particular within the framework of due diligence), there is the risk of an exchange of sensitive information. Therefore, the due diligence process should be monitored and access to sensitive information restricted as much as possible. While the authority has not to date given any guidance on the issue, it may be necessary to set up clean teams. The same applies for the phase between signing and closing. There is also a risk following the failure of closing the transaction and it must be ensured that sensitive information will no longer be available to the potential buyer.

6. **Please explain how the relevant authority enforces (or could enforce) the substantive antitrust laws in an M&A context. How would the investigation occur, and what timing constraints would apply?**

The authority may initiate investigations at any given time and it may use all regular powers of investigation, including dawn raids. Proceedings are not subject to specific timing constraints.

7. **Is private enforcement of the substantive antitrust laws possible in an M&A context, and has it occurred?**

Contrary to merger control proceedings, private enforcement of the substantive antitrust laws in an M&A context would be possible. As at the time of writing there has been no such case in Switzerland.

8. **Could behavior subject to the substantive antitrust laws also be caught under the merger control rules/standstill obligation? (Please also refer to the Annex.)**

As at the time of writing, there is no established practice of the Swiss competition authorities according to which behavior subject to the substantive antitrust laws (e.g. the exchange of sensitive information prior to clearance) would be considered a breach of the standstill obligation. According to Swiss legal doctrine, such behavior could be treated as an infringement of the substantive antitrust laws (in particular Art. 5 and 7 CartA) and not as an infringement of the standstill obligation. However, it cannot be excluded that the competition authorities may come to a different conclusion, in particular, if the EU practice would consider that such behavior is caught by the EU merger control rules.

9. **Please describe the penalties for infringing the substantive antitrust laws. Please indicate whether these include criminal penalties, including individual criminal penalties. As a practical matter, how have these been applied in the context of an M&A transaction?**

Sanctions for infringing certain provisions of the substantive antitrust laws can reach up to a maximum of 10% of the turnover that the respective undertaking has achieved in Switzerland in the preceding three years.

Art. 54 *et seq.* CartA provides for criminal sanctions for individuals. The conduct subject to such sanctions is limited to (i) cases of intentional violations of decisions of the competition authorities or amicable settlements, and (ii) failure to fully comply with information requests. The maximum sanction amounts up to CHF 100,000 (approx. US$98,450).

As at the time of writing, these sanctions have never been applied in the context of an M&A transaction. Regarding fines imposed for the failure to notify a transaction, reference is made to Part 1, Question 8.

10. Please describe policy and enforcement trends in your jurisdiction.

There are currently no specific enforcement trends related to substantive antitrust laws in the context of an M&A transaction.

ANNEX

Table 1: Actual Enforcement of Specific Conduct under the Relevant Merger Control Rules and Substantive Antitrust Laws

Please identify whether the following type of conduct has been subject to investigation/enforcement in your jurisdiction, under the merger control laws or substantive antitrust laws. Please cite any such case(s) and provide a brief description in the table below.

Specific Conduct	Actual Enforcement under Merger Control Laws	Actual Enforcement under Substantive Antitrust Laws
Pre-signing due diligence	No	No
Post-signing/pre-approval due diligence	No	No
Post-approval/pre-closing due diligence	No	No
Use of "clean teams"	No	No
Restrictions on the target in an M&A agreement, e.g. buyer approval required for: Investments above a certain level; – New business above a certain level; – Other obligations to consult/obtain approval from the buyer before closing.	No	No
Joint marketing	No	No
Joint presentations (e.g. industry fairs)	No	No
Joint communications	No	No
Strategy/planning regarding customers	No	No

Specific Conduct	Actual Enforcement under Merger Control Laws	Actual Enforcement under Substantive Antitrust Laws
Strategy/planning regarding suppliers	No	No
Third party contract novation	No	No
Personnel Issues: – Secondments – Retention Strategies	No	No
IT Planning/Database Migration	No	No
Other	No	No

All sanctions so far have been imposed on parties who closed a transaction that should have been notified without having done so on time. See Question 9 of Part 1.

Table 2: Hypothetical Enforcement of Specific Conduct under the Relevant Merger Control Rules and Substantive Antitrust Laws

For any conduct that is *not* the subject of actual enforcement (Table 1), please indicate in the Table below whether the conduct identified *could potentially* be enforced under the merger control laws and/or substantive antitrust laws.

Specific Conduct	Hypothetical Enforcement under Merger Control Laws	Hypothetical Enforcement under Substantive Antitrust Laws
Pre-signing due diligence	Potentially – however, it seems more likely that such behavior, in particular an information exchange, would be enforced under the substantive antitrust laws (Art. 5 CartA)	Yes
Post-signing/pre-approval due diligence	Potentially	Yes
Post-approval/pre-closing due diligence	/	Yes
Use of "clean teams"	Yes	Yes

Specific Conduct	Hypothetical Enforcement under Merger Control Laws	Hypothetical Enforcement under Substantive Antitrust Laws
Restrictions on the target in an M&A agreement, e.g. buyer approval required for: – Investments above a certain level; – New business above a certain level; – Other obligations to consult/obtain approval from the buyer before closing.	Yes, the undertaking acquiring control must not exercise decisive influence. This may be the case if a contractual agreement provides for the obligation to obtain approval of the buyer as regards certain decisions (e.g. to invest/divest etc.).	Yes
Joint marketing	Yes	Yes
Joint presentations (e.g. industry fairs)	Yes	Yes
Joint communications	Yes, depending on the content of the communication. If this implies that the buyer is already controlling, this might be problematic.	Yes, depending on the content.
Strategy/planning regarding customers	Yes	Yes
Strategy/planning regarding suppliers	Yes	Yes
Third party contract novation	Yes	Yes
Personnel Issues: – Secondments – Retention Strategies	Depends on circumstances: the mere planning of strategies or reassignments will likely not change the market structure but implementing certain transfers could be problematic.	Depends on circumstances: discussions/coordination, e.g. on income levels etc., could be seen as problematic behavior.
IT Planning/Database Migration	Depends on circumstances: the mere planning of the integration will likely not be problematic.	Depends on circumstances: the mere planning of the integration will likely not be problematic.

Specific Conduct	Hypothetical Enforcement under Merger Control Laws	Hypothetical Enforcement under Substantive Antitrust Laws
IT Planning/Database Migration	The implementation of the migration could, however, already change the market structure if this cannot be undone or it relates to the productive system.	The implementation of the migration could, however, already lead to an exchange of sensitive information.
Other	/	/

TURKEY

Gönenç Gürkaynak
(ELIG Gürkaynak Attorneys-at-Law)

Part 1: Merger Control and the "Standstill Obligation"

1. **Please identify the relevant merger control legislation in your jurisdiction. Please provide a link to the relevant legislation (if possible, in English) and also indicate:**
   - **whether the merger control system is mandatory or voluntary,**
   - **the relevant authority, and**
   - **the duration of the review period.**

Relevant Legislation: The Turkish merger control regime is primarily regulated by the Law on Protection of Competition No. 4054 (**Law No. 4054**) dated 13 December 1994, and Communiqué No. 2010/4 on Mergers and Acquisitions Requiring the Approval of the Competition Board (**Communiqué No. 2010/4**) published on 7 October 2010.

Mandatory Filing: Once the jurisdictional turnover thresholds set in the Communiqué No. 2010/4 are exceeded, there is no exception for filing a notification, filing is mandatory.

Relevant authority: The relevant authority overseeing the enforcement of Law No. 4054 and relevant secondary legislation is the Turkish Competition Authority (**Authority**). The Authority is the enforcement authority and the Turkish Competition Board (**Competition Board**) is its decision-making body.

Duration of Review: The Competition Board, upon its preliminary review of the notification (Phase I), will decide either to approve or to investigate the transaction further (Phase II). It notifies the parties of the outcome within 30 calendar days of a complete filing. In the absence of any such notification, the decision is deemed to be an "approval" through an implied approval mechanism. Moreover, any written request by the Competition Board for missing information will stop the review process and restart the 30-calendar-day period anew from the date of receipt of such additional information request.

If a notification leads to a Phase II review, it turns into a full-fledged investigation. Under Turkish competition law, Phase II investigations take about six months. If necessary, the Competition Board may extend this period once by up to six months.

Access to Legislation: The links to the unofficial translations provided by the Turkish Competition Authority of the relevant legislation and its amendments:

- Law No. 4054: <http://www.rekabet.gov.tr/Dosya/geneldosya/kanuning.pdf>.
- Communiqué No. 2010/4 : <http://www.rekabet.gov.tr/Dosya/communiques/43-pdf>.

- Communiqué No. 2017/2 Amending the Communiqué on Mergers and Acquisitions Calling for the Authorization of the Competition Board (Communiqué No: 2010/4): <http://www.rekabet.gov.tr/Dosya/communiques/54-pdf>.

2. **Does the merger control system in your jurisdiction impose a "*standstill obligation*" – meaning, that the transaction cannot be implemented prior to completing the merger control process? (Please cite the relevant legislation.) Please also indicate the *legal scope* of the standstill obligation according to the relevant legislation (e.g. the parties to the transaction cannot effect a change of control, cannot take steps towards implementation, etc.).**

Standstill Obligation: Under the Turkish merger control regime, the closing of a notifiable transaction before obtaining the required approval of the Competition Board constitutes a violation of a suspension requirement (i.e. a standstill obligation) as regulated under Article 11 of Law No. 4054. Therefore, the parties will need to get the Competition Board's approval before the closing of the transaction. According to Article 16 of Law No. 4054, failure to do so can trigger monetary fines and legal status risks.

Scope of the Standstill Obligation: The mergers or acquisitions that are subject to notification must be notified to the Competition Board before the realization of the transactions. Under Article 10(7) of Communiqué No. 2010/4, a transaction is deemed to be "realized" (i.e. closed) on the date when the change in control occurs. In other words, the realization occurs with the closing.

In this regard, "control" is understood to be the right to exercise decisive influence over day-to-day management or on long-term strategic business decisions, and it can be exercised de jure or de facto. Therefore, changes to minority and other interests that do not lead to a change of control do not trigger a filing requirement and thus a standstill obligation. However, if minority interests acquire certain negative control elements (such as veto rights) that may influence management of the company, then the nature of control could be deemed to be changed and the transaction could be subject to filing and the standstill obligation.

3. **Have the relevant authorities in your jurisdiction issued internal or external guidelines concerning the scope of the standstill obligation, and/or their authority to enforce it? Please provide a copy/link of such guidance, if possible in English.**

Body Authorized to Enforce the Standstill Obligation: If a notifiable transaction is closed prior to the approval of the Competition Board, and the Authority becomes aware of such situation, it *ex officio* reviews the transaction and imposes a monetary fine. Along with its assessment of the parties' compliance with the standstill obligation, the Competition Board also reviews the transaction on the merits using the dominance test.

Relevant Legislation: The Authority has not issued internal or external guidelines concerning the scope of the standstill obligation. On the other hand, since the standstill obligation under the Turkish merger control regime is closely related to a change of control, the Authority issued detailed guidelines (*Guideline on Cases Considered as Mergers and Acquisitions and the Concept of Control*) on the conditions upon which a change of control can be said to occur. The English version of these Guidelines can be accessed via <http://www.rekabet.gov.tr/Dosya/guide-lines/10-pdf>.

4. Are there any exceptions to the standstill obligation – for example, through derogation or "carve out"? Please describe the circumstances in which this is possible. Please also describe the relevant process, e.g. do parties need to apply to the authority for a derogation from the standstill obligation? If so, how long is the approval process? If there are specific cases addressing these issues, please identify them.

Carve-out in Turkey: There is no normative regulation allowing or disallowing carve-out arrangements. Carve-out arrangements have been rejected by the Competition Board (e.g. *Total SA* 06-92/1186-355, 20.12.2006, and *CVR Inc/Inco Limited* 07-11/71-23, 07.02.2007) so far arguing that a closing is sufficient for the suspension violation fine to be imposed and that a further analysis of whether a change in control actually took effect in Turkey is unwarranted. The wording of the Competition Board's reasoned decisions does not analyze the merits of the carve-out arrangements and takes the position that the "carve-out" concept is unconvincing. Therefore, methods like carve-out or hold separate would not eliminate the filing requirement and cannot authoritatively be advised as safe for early closing mechanisms recognized by the Competition Board. Finally, it should be noted that Turkish merger control rules do not provide the possibility of derogations from the suspension obligation.

Nonetheless, there are highly exceptional cases where concentrations were closed/implemented prior to the approval of the Competition Board and were not fined due to the specific circumstances surrounding the transactions.[1] However, none of the cases cited in this regard points to the establishment of a de facto precedent concerning a Competition Board-accepted derogation from the suspension obligation, due to the exceptional characteristics of the cited cases.

Other exceptions: Article 3 of Communiqué No. 2017/2 introduced a new paragraph to be included in Article 10 of Communiqué No. 2010/4, which reads as follows:

> If the control is acquired from various sellers by way of a series of transactions in terms of securities on the stock exchange, the concentration could be notified to the Turkish Competition Board after the realization of the transaction provided that the following conditions are satisfied:
>
> (a) the concentration should be notified to the Turkish Competition Board without delay; and
>
> (b) the voting rights attached to the acquired securities are not exercised or exercised solely to maintain the full value of its investments based on a derogation granted by the Turkish Competition Board. For the sake of completeness, the Turkish

1 *Prysmian* 11-15/259-87 and dated 10 March 2011; *APMT/Grup Maritim* 16-16/267-118 and dated 11 May 2016

> Competition Board may impose conditions and obligations in terms of such derogation in order to ensure conditions of effective competition.

This newly introduced provision is similar to Article 7(2) of the European Commission Merger Regulation. At any rate, although there was no similar specific statutory rule in Turkey on this matter, even before the promulgation of Communiqué No. 2017/2, the Competition Board had already judicially recognized this exception. In the *Camargo* decision (*Camargo Corrêa SA* 12-24/665-187, 03.05.2012), the Competition Board recognized that the parties can close a public bid on a listed company before the Competition Board's approval, subject to the condition that: (i) the transaction is notified to the Competition Board without any delay; and (ii) the acquirer does not exercise the control over the target pending the Competition Board's approval decision.

5. Does a public bid exception exist in your jurisdiction? (For example, under the EU Merger Regulation it is possible to acquire shares as part of a public bid, provided that the shares are not exercised until the acquisition is cleared by the Commission.) If such an exception exists in your jurisdiction, please describe how it is applied.

There are no exceptions to the standstill obligation regarding public bids under Turkish merger control regime aside from the exception derived from Article 10(6) of Communiqué No. 2010/4 (see Question 4).

6. What powers does the relevant authority have to investigate and enforce violations of the standstill obligation? Are dawn raids possible? What timing applies to investigation/enforcement proceedings?

The Authority can send written information requests to the parties, any other party related to the transaction, or third parties such as competitors, customers or suppliers, and thus conduct an extensive market investigation within the legal period and possible extensions. Article 15 of Law No. 4054 authorizes the Competition Board to conduct on-site investigations in order to carry out the duties assigned to it by Law No. 4054. Therefore, dawn raids are possible to investigate and enforce violations of the standstill obligation. For example, in the *Cegedim* and *Ajans Press* cases, the Authority conducted on-site inspections (dawn raids) in the premises of the relevant undertakings. The decisions are not clear as to whether the on-site inspections were conducted in order to detect the violation of the standstill requirement or to collect other information, but they demonstrate at the very least that evidence can be found concerning a possible violation of the standstill requirement during on-site inspections.

Timing: The Authority, after becoming aware of a violation of the standstill obligation, will immediately initiate its review. In the case of a failure to file, the Competition Board, on its preliminary review (Phase I), will decide either to approve or to investigate the transaction further (Phase II) within the timeline explained under Question 1. Although there is no case on point, it is expected that if the breach of the standstill obligation also amounts to a substantial violation of competition rules, the Competition Board would likely initiate separate investigations (with different timelines) to look into the matters. It could approve the transaction and impose an administrative monetary fine for the violation of the standstill obligation, and then continue a separate investigation of the possible substantial violation of competition rules. See Question 6 of Part 2 for a discussion of the timing of the Competition Board's investigation process.

7. **What are the possible penalties for violating the standstill obligation? Are there criminal sanctions, including on individuals? Have these been applied in practice? Is there a difference in enforcement between transactions involving domestic companies and "foreign-to-foreign" transactions? Does the authority have the power to unwind transactions implemented in breach of the standstill obligation? If so, has the authority made use of that power in practice? If yes, please provide examples.**

Penalties: Article 16 of Law No. 4054 states that if the parties to a notifiable transaction violate the suspension requirement, a monetary fine based on the local turnover generated in the financial year preceding the date of the fining decision at a rate of 0.1% will be imposed on the incumbent firms (acquirer(s) in the case of an acquisition; both merging parties in the case of a merger).

A monetary fine imposed as a result of a violation of a suspension requirement shall in any event not be less than TRY 21,036 (approx. €5,118) for 2018. Moreover, the wording of Article 16 of Law No. 4054 does not give the Competition Board discretion on whether to impose a monetary fine in case of a violation of the suspension requirement. In other words, once the violation of the suspension requirement is detected, the monetary fine will be imposed automatically.

If, at the end of its review of a notifiable transaction that was not notified, the Competition Board decides that the transaction falls within the prohibition of Article 7 under the "dominance test" applicable in Turkey, the undertakings could be subject to fines of up to 10% of their turnover generated in the financial year preceding the date of the fining decision. Employees and managers (of the undertakings concerned) that had a determinant impact on the violation may also be fined up to 5% of the fine imposed on the undertakings as a result of implementing a problematic transaction without the Competition Board's approval.

In such a case, in addition to the monetary sanction, the Competition Board is authorized under Article 11(b) of Law No. 4054 to take all necessary measures to terminate the transaction, remove all de facto legal consequences of every action that has been taken unlawfully, return all shares and assets (if possible) to the places they were or persons who owned them before the transaction or, if such measure is not possible, assign them to third parties; and, meanwhile, to forbid participation in control of these undertakings until this assignment takes place and to take all other necessary measures.

Foreign-to-foreign Transactions: Foreign-to-foreign transactions, even if the undertakings concerned do not have local subsidiaries, branches, sales outlets, etc. in Turkey, are caught under the Law No. 4054 to the extent that they affect the relevant markets within the territory of the Republic of Turkey. Mere sales into Turkey may thus trigger the notification requirement to the extent the thresholds are met. Article 2 of the Law No. 4054 establishes the "effects criteria", pursuant to which the criterion to apply is whether the undertakings concerned affect the goods and services markets in Turkey.

Furthermore, the legal consequences of a violation of the standstill obligation also apply to foreign-to-foreign transactions. In other words, when it comes to the violation of the suspension requirement, the Competition Board does not treat these transactions differently in terms of sanctions. The Competition Board's decisions in *Fairless-Simsmetal* (16.09.2009, 09-42/1057-269) and *Longsheng* (02.06.2011, 11-33/723-226) are examples where the Competition Board imposed a turnover-based monetary fine for the violation of the suspension requirement in a foreign-to-foreign transaction, as both of the transactions above were closed prior to mandatory filing.

Individual Charges and Fines: There is no criminal sanction for the violation of the standstill obligation in Turkey. As discussed above, unless the transaction is viewed as problematic under the dominance test under Article 7, there is also no individual fine for the violation of standstill obligation under Law No. 4054.

8. How does the relevant authority typically learn of potential violations of the standstill obligation? Does the authority actively monitor the trade press?

The Competition Board usually becomes aware that parties to a notifiable merger failed to comply with the standstill obligation upon complaint or on an *ex officio* basis.

The Competition Board may also become aware of the unlawful closing of a notifiable transaction as it delves into a market investigation in the course of another case or, on a much more irregular and infrequent basis, from publicly available sources, such as business magazines and newspapers and financial news portals, particularly for transactions where very well-known entities are involved.

9. Please describe the relevant authority's enforcement of the standstill obligation. If there have been cases, please describe the specific conduct that was found to violate the standstill provision and the criteria applied by the relevant authority or court. Has the relevant authority considered the market impact of the conduct? (Please refer to the Annex.)

In the *Boyner/YKM* decision, which was rendered as a result of a complaint,[2] the Competition Board confirmed that administrative fines may be imposed in cases where a notifiable merger and acquisition is implemented without clearance, though the decision does not include a finding of a violation. The Competition Board evaluated whether the parties had actually implemented the transaction prior to clearance by examining matters such as: (i) cancellation of orders of the target entity; (ii) integration of organizational structures between stores, (iii) obtaining of résumés of the other parties' employees and executives; (iv) dismissal of other parties' employees; (v) the target refraining from renting a store in an area where the acquirer and the target competed with each other because the acquirer undertaking was de facto included in the management of the target; and (vi) the acquirer informing shopping malls about the acquisition and requesting

---

2 *Boyner/YKM* 12-44/1359-M and dated 20 September 2012

oral commitments to change store signboards. The Competition Board, however, could not find any evidence that Boyner (the acquirer) had played a decisive role in YKM's business decisions. It must be noted that the elements examined by the Competition Board were newly established precedents and thus could have been overlooked by the undertakings.

In *Cegedim*,[3] a different set of factors were examined by the Competition Board, which suggested that the transaction had closed prior to the Competition Board's consent. The Competition Board noted that (i) the vice chairman of Cegedim (the acquirer) had been appointed to the board of directors of Ultima (the target) as the representative of Cegedim based on a board of directors' resolution of 8 February 2008 (the transaction was cleared on 28 August 2008), and (ii) Cegedim's 2008 interim annual report and the press review of April 2009 indicated that Ultima was purchased on 2 August 2008. The Competition Board also indicated that the following elements led to the impression that the acquisition had been de facto realized before the closing: Cegedim's (i) intervention in Ultima's invoicing procedures, (ii) review of the agreements of its employees, (iii) collecting of employee information, and (iv) considering printing business cards for them. Again, this precedent discloses a whole different set of practices to avoid, for example, the preparation of business cards that could have been easily mistaken for a step in the preparation for the closing of the transaction.

Similarly, in *Ajans Press*,[4] the Competition Board found that Ajans Press actually controlled PR Net for a certain period of time before the share transfer. The Competition Board listed the following factors as indicative of a de facto transfer of control to Ajans Press: (i) PR Net moved to the same building as Ajans Press, (ii) Ajans Press intervened in matters such as choosing PR Net's telephone numbers and broadcast subscriptions, (iii) PR Net network worked within Ajans Press' network, (iv) PR Net personnel had a meeting at a specific time upon the direction of the owner of Ajans Press, Mehmet Ali Özkan, (v) shared customer lists had been prepared and joint studies had been arranged, and (vi) production sources had been shared.

In *Tekno Ray*,[5] the Competition Board concluded that holding the right to exercise decisive influence over day-to-day management or long-term strategic business decisions de jure or de facto is sufficient to infer a change of control. Furthermore, the articles of association of the joint venture were published in the trade registry. The Competition Board rejected the parties' defense that the undertaking had not started its activities before the clearance and imposed a monetary fine.

Under similar circumstances, in *Anayurt*,[6] the Competition Board again rejected the argument that the greenfield joint venture in question had not yet undertaken any commercial activities (and thus had not yet gained full-function status), that

---

3 *Cegedim* 10-56/1089-411 and dated 26 August 2010

4 *Ajans Press* 10-66/1402-523 and dated 21 October 2010; appeal decision of the Council of State dated 29 December 2017 (E:2011/961; K:2017/4523)

5 *Tekno Ray* 12-08/224-55 and dated 23 February 2012

6 *Anayurt* 14-22/422-186 and dated 25 June 2014

it had generated no turnover or had no market share, and decided to penalize the parties for having established the joint venture prior to clearance.

It should be noted that each transaction has different dynamics and there may be new elements indicative of a change of control which may be considered as gun-jumping by the Competition Board. One must be careful not to overlook practices which, even though regarded as standard commercial behavior within a specific sector, could be construed as implying a change of control in light of the existence of the general principles pertaining to the suspension requirement and the foregoing precedents.

Furthermore, as the de minimis exception is not applicable in the Turkish merger control regime, the market impact of a concentration would be irrelevant if minimal. However, due to the application of the dominance test (see Question 11), the market impact of the concentration, if it creates or strengthens a dominant position, will be taken into consideration by the Competition Board.

10. In cases involving alleged violations of the standstill obligation under the relevant merger control laws, has the relevant authority (or court) *also* considered the substantive antitrust laws? (Please refer to the Annex.)

The Competition Board's jurisprudence does not contain a specific case that reflects these circumstances. Having said that, there are no provisions in Turkish competition law which prevent the Competition Board from assessing a transaction from an Article 4 or Article 6 perspective, either through a separate administrative proceeding on the matter or in conjunction with an administrative proceeding which also examines possible violations of the standstill obligation.

11. Is private enforcement of the standstill obligation possible?

Private enforcement: According to Article 57 of Law No. 4054, any person injured in their business or property by reason of a conduct that prevents, distorts or restricts competition via practices, decisions, contracts or agreements contrary to Law No. 4054 or abuses the dominant position in a particular market for goods or services, is entitled to sue the violators for three times their damages plus litigation costs and attorney fees.

Therefore, a violation of the standstill obligation under Article 11 of Law No. 4054 cannot, in and of itself, be subject to a private enforcement if the transaction is cleared by the Competition Board under Article 7 of Law No. 4054 (i.e. if the merger or acquisition does not create or strengthen a dominant position). The undertakings in question would be fined for their violation of the suspension requirement, but the transaction itself would not create competition law concerns under Article 7 of Law No. 4054. However, if the violation of the standstill obligation also amounts to a substantial breach of competition law, those who suffer as a result of the breach could have a distinct claim for damages, since it is expected that the investigation of the substantial violation of competition law would be carried out separately from the assessment of the notified transaction itself (see Part 2, Question 7).

12. Please describe the private law risks/consequences (i.e. contractual/validity consequences) for transactions that are subject to notification, but which are

completed without notification/approval. Please identify any relevant cases and describe them.

In terms of the legal standing of a notifiable concentration that was closed prior to receiving the approval of the Competition Board, said transaction would be invalid with all its legal consequences, unless and until approval is granted by the Competition Board. However, in practice, and to the best of our knowledge, there is no example of the Competition Board unwinding a transaction in its entirety to the degree that private law consequences occur.

13. Please describe policy and enforcement trends in your jurisdiction.

The Competition Board has a rather strict approach to gun-jumping issues, as there are no derogations recognized under the law. Even the technical closing of a transaction, without the acquirer having exerted any degree of influence on the business of the target, can be regarded as a violation of the standstill obligation and lead to the imposition of an administrative monetary fine.

More generally, it must be noted that until 2013, the Competition Board dealt with a significant number of merger control cases. Since the notification threshold was increased by Communiqué 2012/3 on the Amendment of Communiqué 2010/4 on the Mergers and Acquisitions Subject to the Approval of the Competition Board, this trend has changed and the number of transactions reviewed by the Authority has gradually decreased. As expected, the Competition Board shifted its focus from merger control cases to concentrate on the fight against cartels and abuse of dominance. The Competition Board finalized 303 merger control cases in 2012 – this fell to 213 in 2013, 215 in 2014, 159 in 2015 and 209 in 2016.

According to the Merger and Acquisition Insight Report of the Turkish Competition Authority for 2017, the Competition Board finalized 184 merger control cases. Four cases were taken into Phase-II review.

Part 2: Substantive Antitrust Law in an M&A Context

1. **Please identify the relevant *substantive antitrust laws* in your jurisdiction that can potentially apply in an M&A context (e.g. for the EU, this would include Article 101 of the Treaty on the Functioning of the European Union). Please provide a link to the relevant legislation (if possible, in English).**

Articles 4 and 6 of Law No. 4054 provide the substantive background to the Turkish competition law. The unofficial translations provided by the Turkish Competition Authority of Law No. 4054 can be accessed from: <http://www.rekabet.gov.tr/Dosya/geneldosya/kanuning.pdf>.

Article 4 is akin to and closely modelled on Article 101(1) of the Treaty on the Functioning of the European Union (**TFEU**). It prohibits all agreements between undertakings, decisions by associations of undertakings and concerted practices that have (or may have) as their object or effect the prevention, restriction or distortion of competition within a Turkish product or services market or a part thereof.

Article 6 is the main legislation applying specifically to the behavior of dominant firms. It provides that "any abuse on the part of one or more undertakings, individually or through joint agreements or practices, of a dominant position in a market for goods or services within the whole or part of the country is unlawful and prohibited". Article 6 of Law No. 4054 does not define what constitutes "abuse" per se but it provides a non-exhaustive list of specific forms of abuse which is, to some extent, similar to Article 102 TFEU.

2. **Do any guidelines exist in your jurisdiction concerning the application of the substantive antitrust laws in an M&A context – whether internal to the relevant authority, or external, formal or informal (e.g. speeches)? If so, please provide a copy/link to such guidance.**

There are no guidelines that specifically discuss the extent to which the merging parties' pre-closing conduct would potentially violate Article 4 of Law No 4054.

3. **As a general matter (not limited to M&A), how are the substantive antitrust laws enforced with respect to the exchange of competitively sensitive information between competing firms? Please also indicate the relevance of anti-competitive effects or intent in such enforcement.**

The exchange of commercially sensitive information between competitors could be considered a violation of Article 4 of Law No 4054. The Competition Board considers that an exchange of information is mainly carried out in three ways:

directly among parties, through third parties or via publicly available platforms.[7] Depending on the specific circumstances surrounding each case, the exchange of sensitive information between competitors or via third parties (such as customers, distributors or market research companies) may or may not raise competition law concerns. The Competition Board's *Guidelines on Horizontal Cooperation Agreements* (13-24/326-RM(6)) (**Horizontal Cooperation Guidelines**) provide detailed principles on information exchange practices.

According to the Guidelines, the analysis depends mainly on the nature and scope of the exchanged information. Paragraph 58 of the Guidelines reads as follows: "in order to determine anticompetitive effects of information exchanges, the relevant markets structure and the nature of the information exchange have to be taken into account". To that end, exchange of (i) competition-sensitive (strategic), (ii) comprehensive (comprising the whole market), (iii) company-specific, (iv) current, (v) detailed (broken-down) and (vi) not publicly available information may raise questions for the Authority. In particular, in cases where the exchange is systematic and/or frequent, the potential risks might be higher. Furthermore, an exchange of competition-sensitive information within a merger/acquisition process prior to the approval of the Competition Board would be examined under Article 4 of Law No 4054.

4. **Have there been any cases in your jurisdiction in which the substantive antitrust laws were enforced in an M&A context? Please describe/explain and cite any such cases. (See also Annex.)**

To the best of our knowledge, there are no cases that articulate that merging parties' pre-closing conduct violated Article 4 or Article 6 of Law No. 4054, rather than Articles 7 and 11. However, in theory, there is no legal obstacle to the Competition Board conducting such an assessment, depending on the dynamics of the case, although this is unprecedented.

5. **Are the substantive antitrust laws more likely to apply at specific stages of the transaction – i.e. at an early stage, or prior to closing (or does it not make a difference)? Do companies face ongoing risk following the consummation (or failure) of their transaction for conduct that allegedly occurred pre-closing (pre-failure)?**

There is no specific timing for the application of the substantive antitrust laws. Therefore, companies may face ongoing risk following the consummation (or failure) of their transaction for their allegedly illicit conduct that occurred pre-closing (pre-failure) until the expiry of the limitation period applying to acts that violate Law No. 4054, which is generally eight years (including violations of Article 4).

6. **Please explain how the relevant authority enforces (or could enforce) the substantive antitrust laws in an M&A context. How would the investigation occur, and what timing constraints would apply?**

It should be noted that the Turkish antitrust regime does not recognize de minimis exceptions and there is currently no threshold for opening an investigation into

---

7 *PETDER II* 11-48/1215-428 and dated 22 September 2011

a violation of Article 4 or Article 6 of Law No 4054. The Competition Board is entitled to launch an investigation *ex officio* or in response to a notice or complaint.

The Competition Board will decide to conduct a pre-investigation if it finds the notice or complaint to be serious. At this preliminary stage, unless there is a dawn raid, the undertakings concerned are not notified that they are under investigation. Dawn raids and other investigatory tools (e.g. formal information request letters) are used both during the pre-investigation and investigation process.

The preliminary report of the Authority experts will be submitted to the Competition Board within 30 days of the pre-investigation decision. The Competition Board will then decide within 10 days whether to launch a formal investigation or not. If it decides to initiate an investigation, it will send a notice to the undertakings concerned within 15 days.

Once the notice has been formally served, the investigated undertakings have 30 days to prepare and submit their first written defense. Subsequently, the main investigation report is issued by the Authority within six months (if deemed necessary, this period may be extended by the Competition Board only once, for an additional period of up to six months). Once this is served on the defendants, they have 30 calendar days to respond, extendable for a further 30 days (second written defense). The investigation committee will then have 15 days to prepare an additional opinion concerning the second written defense. The defending parties will have another 30-day period to reply to the additional opinion (third written defense). When this reply is served on the Authority, the investigation process will be completed (i.e. the written phase of investigation involving the claim or defense exchange will close with the submission of the third written defense). An oral hearing may be held upon request by the parties. The Competition Board may also *ex officio* decide to hold an oral hearing. Oral hearings are held between 30 and 60 days of the completion of the investigation process under the provisions of Communiqué No. 2010/2 on Oral Hearings before the Competition Board. The Competition Board will render its final decision within 15 days from the hearing, if an oral hearing is held; otherwise, the decision is rendered 30 days from the completion of the investigation process.

7. Is private enforcement of the substantive antitrust laws possible in an M&A context, and has it occurred?

Enforcement can also be supplemented with private lawsuits which are entitled to recover treble damages. Pursuant to Article 57 of Law No. 4054, any person injured in their business or property by reason of anything forbidden by the antitrust laws is entitled to sue the violators for three times their damages plus litigation costs and fees. Owing to the entitlement to treble damages, private antitrust litigations are increasing in the cartel enforcement arena. Most courts wait for the decision of the Competition Board and build their own decision on that finding.

Note that Turkish procedural law does not allow for class actions or procedures. Class certification requests would not be granted by Turkish courts. Antitrust-based private lawsuits are rare but increasing in practice.

We are not aware of any cases under Turkish law of private enforcement of Article 4 or 6 in an M&A context.

8. Could behavior subject to the substantive antitrust laws also be caught under the merger control rules/standstill obligation? (Please also refer to the Annex.)

Neither primary nor secondary legislation includes a clause that prevent such a situation. Therefore, theoretically speaking, competition infringing behavior that is assessed under Articles 4 and/or 6 of Law No 4054 can also be caught under the merger control regime depending on the dynamics and timing of the behavior.

9. Please describe the penalties for infringing the substantive antitrust laws. Please indicate whether these include criminal penalties, including individual criminal penalties. As a practical matter, how have these been applied in the context of an M&A transaction?

The sanctions that may be imposed under Law No. 4054 are administrative in nature. Therefore, Law No. 4054 leads to administrative fines (and civil liability), but not to criminal sanctions. Violations such as cartel conduct will not result in imprisonment of the individuals implicated. That said, there have been cases where the matter was referred to a public prosecutor before and after the investigation under Law No. 4054 was complete. On that note, bid-rigging activity may be criminally prosecutable under section 235 *et seq.* of the Criminal Code. Illegal price manipulation (manipulation through disinformation or other fraudulent means) may also be punished by up to two years' imprisonment and a judicial monetary fine under section 237 of the Criminal Code.

In cases of violation of Article 4 and 6, the undertakings concerned will be separately subject to fines of up to 10% of their turnover generated in Turkey in the financial year prior to the date of the decision (if this is not calculable, the turnover generated in the financial year nearest to the date of the decision will be considered). The fines for individuals, such as employees or members of the executive bodies of undertakings or associations that had a determining effect on the creation of the violation, are also applicable to substantive antitrust laws.

The Regulation on Fines applies to both cartel activity and abuse of dominance. According to the Regulation on Fines, fines are calculated by first determining the basic level, which, in the case of cartels, is between 2 and 4% of the company's turnover in the financial year preceding the date of the decision (if this is not calculable, the turnover in the financial year nearest to the date of the decision); for other violations, the fine is between 0.5% and 3% of the company's turnover in the financial year preceding the date of the decision. It should be noted that aggravating and mitigating factors are then factored in. The Regulation on Fines applies also to managers or employees that had a determining effect on the violation (such as participating in cartel meetings and making decisions that would involve the company in cartel activity), and provides for certain reductions in their favor.

In addition to monetary sanctions, the Competition Board is authorized to take all necessary measures to terminate the restrictive agreement, to remove all de facto and legal consequences of every action that has been taken unlawfully, and to take all other measures necessary to restore the level of competition and status to that existing prior to the infringement. Furthermore, such a restrictive agreement will be deemed legally invalid and unenforceable with all its legal consequences. Similarly, Law No. 4054 authorizes the Competition Board to take interim measures until the final resolution on the matter in cases where there is a possibility of serious and irreparable damages.

We are not aware of any cases under Turkish law of sanctions being imposed for violations of Article 4 or 6 in an M&A context.

10. Please describe policy and enforcement trends in your jurisdiction.

Over the past five years, the Competition Board has shifted its focus from merger control cases to concentrate more on the fight against cartels and cases of abuse of dominance.

Eren Gönen, Alper Koç, "The Turkish Competition Board clears without remedies an acquisition in the fuel sector (Total/CEPSA)" 20 December 2006, e-Competitions Bulletin December 2006, Art. N° 13301

Ercüment Erdem, "The Turkish Competition Board Imposes fine for failing to notify of the establishment of a joint venture (Anayurt)" 25 June 2014, e-Competitions Bulletin June 2014, Art. N° 78808

ANNEX

Table 1: Actual Enforcement of Specific Conduct under the Relevant Merger Control Rules and Substantive Antitrust Laws

Please identify whether the following type of conduct has been subject to investigation/ enforcement in your jurisdiction, under the merger control laws or substantive antitrust laws. Please cite any such case(s) and provide a brief description in the table below.

Specific Conduct	Actual Enforcement under Merger Control Laws	Actual Enforcement under Substantive Antitrust Laws
Pre-signing due diligence	No*	No*
Post-signing/pre-approval due diligence	No*	No*
Post-approval/pre-closing due diligence	No*	No*
Use of "clean teams"	No*	No*
Restrictions on the target in an M&A agreement, e.g. buyer approval required for: – Investments above a certain level; – New business above a certain level; – Other obligations to consult/ obtain approval from the buyer before closing.	No*	No*
Joint marketing	Joint marketing was considered as an element in *Boyner/YKM*, although the Competition Board eventually decided that there were no violations of the suspension requirement. Nevertheless, joint marketing was listed as an indication that gun-jumping could have occurred.	No*

Specific Conduct	Actual Enforcement under Merger Control Laws	Actual Enforcement under Substantive Antitrust Laws
Joint presentations (e.g. industry fairs)	No*	No*
Joint communications	*Ajans Press* (21.10.2010, 10-66/1402-523) took into consideration the market perception of the two entities as an indication that a change in control occurred (i.e. the acquisition took place). In *Ajans Press,* it was found that the buyer (i) interfered in the assignment of telephone numbers for the target; (ii) interfered in subscriptions to publications; (iii) started integrating the target company into the buyer's network; (iv) called meetings that were attended by the target's staff; (v) prepared shared customer lists; and (vi) shared production sources. Additionally, in *Cegedim* (26.08.2010, 10-56/1089-411) the fact that the buyer considered printing business cards for the target employees was considered as a factor. (See Question 10, Part I for a brief explanation of the cases.)	No*
Strategy/planning regarding customers	*Ajans Press* (21.10.2010, 10-66/1402-523) explains that shared customer lists had been prepared, joint studies had been arranged and the buyer interfered in the publishing and broadcasting subscriptions of the target. (See Question 10, Part I for a brief explanation of the case.)	No*
Strategy/planning regarding suppliers	No*	No*

Specific Conduct	Actual Enforcement under Merger Control Laws	Actual Enforcement under Substantive Antitrust Laws
Third party contract novation	No*	No*
Personnel Issues: – Secondments – Retention Strategies	*Cegedim* (26.08.2010, 10-56/1089-411) references the fact that the buyer (i) reviewed the agreements of the target's employees (ii) collected employee information and (iii) considered printing business cards for them. (See Question 10, Part I for a brief explanation of the case.)	No*
IT Planning/Database Migration	*Ajans Press* (21.10.2010, 10-66/1402-523) mentioned that the buyer interfered in the broadcast subscriptions of the target as well as the target being integrated and working in the buyer's network. (See Question 10, Part I for brief explanation of the case.)	No*
Other	The Competition Board has considered various elements indicative of a change of control: In *Ajans Press* the physical integration of the target and the acquirer, and an obvious change in command for personnel were considered as indications that the concentration was implemented prior to the approval of the Competition Board. In *Cegedim*, the Competition Board noted that the (i) vice-chairman of the buyer had been appointed to the target's board of directors, and (ii) the buyer's 2008 interim annual report and press review of April 2009 indicated that the target was purchased on 2 August 2008. In addition, the buyer had interfered in the invoicing procedures of the target.	X

Specific Conduct	Actual Enforcement under Merger Control Laws	Actual Enforcement under Substantive Antitrust Laws
Other	In *Tekno Ray*, the articles of association of the joint venture had been published in the trade registry. The Competition Board therefore imposed a fine, rejecting the parties' defense that the undertaking had not started its activities prior to clearance. Note that the factors listed above are generally assessed collectively in order to determine whether a change of control has occurred; depending on the circumstances, each of these factors taken individually may not be sufficient to conclude that the standstill obligation has been breached.	X

* To the best of our knowledge, there are no precedents relating to the behavior listed above and marked with an asterisk. The fact that the listed conduct was not yet taken into consideration in antitrust proceedings before the Authority does not eliminate the possibility that the Authority could consider the relevant behavior as a violation of standstill obligation.

Table 2: Hypothetical Enforcement of Specific Conduct under the Relevant Merger Control Rules and Substantive Antitrust Laws

For any conduct that is *not* the subject of actual enforcement (Table 1), please indicate in the Table below whether the conduct identified *could potentially* be enforced under the merger control laws and/or substantive antitrust laws.

Specific Conduct	Hypothetical Enforcement under Merger Control Laws	Hypothetical Enforcement under Substantive Antitrust Laws
Pre-signing due diligence	Although this will depend on the specific dynamics of the conduct, a normal due diligence process on its own would not be a violation of Article 11 of Law No. 4054 as long as the scope of the due diligence is not extended	Although this will depend on the specific dynamics of the conduct, a normal due diligence process on its own would not be a violation of Articles 4 and 6 of Law No. 4054 as long as the scope of the due diligence
Pre-signing due diligence		

Specific Conduct	Hypothetical Enforcement under Merger Control Laws	Hypothetical Enforcement under Substantive Antitrust Laws
Pre-signing due diligence Post-signing/ pre-approval due diligence	from what could commonly be expected of a due diligence process, or the due diligence process is not used as a cover of some other illicit behavior.	is not extended from what could commonly be expected of a due diligence process, or diligence process is not used as a cover of some other illicit behavior.
Post-approval/ pre-closing due diligence	After the approval of the transaction by the Competition Board it is expected that there will be no risk of violating the standstill obligation, since the Competition Board has already approved the transaction to be implemented.	After the approval of the transaction by the Competition Board it is expected that there will be no risk of violating the standstill obligation, since the Competition Board has already approved the transaction to be implemented.
Use of "clean teams"	Use of clean teams and Chinese walls could be a method to mitigate the competitive concerns that arise from the suspension obligation. However, if the clean teams' authority exceeds what is necessary to implement the transaction and allows the clean teams to interfere in the business decisions of the other party, there is a hypothetical risk of a violation of the standstill obligation.	Use of clean teams and Chinese walls could be a method to mitigate the competitive concerns that arise from the suspension obligation. However, if the clean teams' authority exceeds what is necessary to implement the transaction and allows the clean teams to interfere in the business decisions of the other party, there is a hypothetical risk of a violation of Articles 4 and 6 of Law No. 4054.
Restrictions on the target in an M&A agreement, e.g. buyer approval required for: Investments above a certain level; New business above a certain level; Other obligations to consult/obtain approval from the buyer before closing.	Although this will depend on the specific dynamics of the conduct, possible restrictions imposed by the buyer on the target such as those listed here would not be violations of Article 7 of Law No. 4054, as long as (i) the conduct is reasonable in that it is limited to what is necessary to protect the value of the target and (ii) the duration of such conduct is until closing.	Although this will depend on the specific dynamics of the conduct, possible restrictions imposed by the buyer on the target such as those listed here would not be violations of Articles 4 and 6 of Law No 4054, as long as (i) the conduct is reasonable in that it is limited to what is necessary to protect the value of the target and (ii) the duration of such conduct is until closing.

Specific Conduct	Hypothetical Enforcement under Merger Control Laws	Hypothetical Enforcement under Substantive Antitrust Laws
Joint marketing	Depending on the specific dynamics of the conduct, joint marketing prior to the approval of the Competition Board could be an indication of the implementation of the transaction, therefore could lead to a merger control review by the Authority for the evaluation of gun-jumping issues.	Depending on the specific dynamics of the conduct, joint marketing could indicate the existence of a concerted practice or an agreement contrary to Articles 4 and 6 of Law No. 4054.
Joint presentations (e.g. industry fairs)	Depending on the specific dynamics of the conduct, joint presentations prior to the approval of the Competition Board could be an indication of the implementation of the transaction, therefore could lead to a merger control review by the Authority for the evaluation of gun-jumping issues.	Depending on the specific dynamics of the conduct, joint presentations could indicate the existence of a concerted practice or an agreement contrary to Articles 4 and 6 of Law No. 4054.
Joint communications	Depending on the specific dynamics of the conduct, joint communications prior to the approval of the Competition Board could be an indication of the implementation of the transaction, therefore could lead to a merger control review by the Authority for the evaluation of gun-jumping issues.	Depending on the specific dynamics of the conduct, joint communications could indicate the existence of a concerted practice or an agreement contrary to Articles 4 and 6 of Law No. 4054.
Strategy/planning regarding customers	Depending on the specific dynamics of the conduct, strategy/planning regarding customers prior to the approval of the Competition Board could be an indication of the implementation of the transaction, therefore could lead to a merger control review by the Authority for the evaluation of gun-jumping issues.	Depending on the specific dynamics of the conduct, strategizing by competitors on the matter of customers could be evaluated as an agreement or concerted practice, and therefore would be subjected to an assessment under Articles 4 and 6 of Law No. 4054.

Specific Conduct	Hypothetical Enforcement under Merger Control Laws	Hypothetical Enforcement under Substantive Antitrust Laws
Strategy/planning regarding suppliers	Depending on the specific dynamics of the conduct, strategy/planning regarding suppliers prior to the approval of the Competition Board could be an indication of the implementation of the transaction, therefore could lead to a merger control review by the Authority for the evaluation of gun-jumping issues.	Depending on the specific dynamics of the conduct, strategizing by competitors on the matter of suppliers could be evaluated as an agreement or concerted practice, and therefore would be subjected to an assessment under Articles 4 and 6 of Law No. 4054.
Third party contract novation	Depending on the specific dynamics of the conduct, third party contract novation prior to the approval of the Competition Board could be an indication of the implementation of the transaction, therefore could lead to a merger control review by the Authority for the evaluation of gun-jumping issues.	Depending on the specific dynamics of the conduct, third party contract novation could be considered under Articles 4 and 6 of Law No. 4054 as either an agreement or concerted practice.
Personnel Issues: Secondments Retention Strategies	Depending on the specific dynamics of the conduct, addressing personnel issues prior to the approval of the Competition Board could be an indication of the implementation of the transaction, therefore could lead to a merger control review by the Authority for the evaluation of gun-jumping issues.	Depending on the specific dynamics of the conduct, personnel issues could be considered under Articles 4 and 6 of Law No. 4054 as either an agreement or concerted practice.
IT Planning/ Database Migration	Depending on the specific dynamics of the conduct, IT planning/database migration prior to the approval of the Competition Board could be an indication of the implementation of the transaction, therefore could lead to a merger control review by the Authority for the evaluation of gun-jumping issues.	Depending on the specific dynamics of the conduct, IT planning/database migration could be considered under Articles 4 and 6 of Law No. 4054 as either an agreement or concerted practice.
Other		

UKRAINE

Anastasia Usova
(Redcliffe Partners)

Part 1: Merger Control and the "Standstill Obligation"

1. Please identify the relevant merger control legislation in your jurisdiction. Please provide a link to the relevant legislation (if possible, in English) and also indicate:

- **whether the merger control system is mandatory or voluntary,**
- **the relevant authority, and**
- **the duration of the review period.**

A merger notification to the Antimonopoly Committee of Ukraine (**AMC**) is mandatory in any cases where the transaction qualifies as a concentration and the jurisdictional thresholds are met.

The AMC is the primary state authority responsible for enforcement of merger control rules in Ukraine. In particular, the AMC has powers to review notifications on concentrations and to issue clearance/prohibition decisions, launch investigations, issue individual guidance and impose penalties for violations of competition laws.

The standard review procedure takes up to 45 calendar days and includes:

- Preview period: 15 days for the AMC to decide whether the application is (i) complete and may be accepted for review on substance (Phase I) or (ii) incomplete and should be rejected and resubmitted;
- Phase I: 30 days for the AMC to decide whether (i) the concentration should be cleared or (ii) in-depth analysis is required due to competition concerns (Phase II).

The AMC opens a Phase II investigation before the end of Phase I if there are grounds to consider that a transaction may lead to monopolization (reaching of monopoly (dominant) position on product market, maintaining or strengthening such position) or substantial restriction of competition in the Ukrainian market or a significant part thereof.

Phase II lasts up to 135 calendar days unless extended upon the parties' written request in order to provide the information requested by the AMC.

There is also a fast-track procedure of up to 25 calendar days if:

(i) only one party is active in Ukraine;

(ii) the combined market share of the parties does not exceed 15% on the same product markets; or

(iii) the individual or combined market share of the parties do not exceed 20% on vertically related markets.

As a matter of practice, the eligibility for the fast-track procedure is quite straightforward under criterion (i) above. However, the application of criteria (ii) and (iii) is rather problematic, since the AMC often requests that additional information be provided on the parties' activities in Ukraine, including on those markets which are not relevant to the transaction. In particular, according to the AMC's recent practice, criterion (ii) would not apply if the market share of any party to the transaction based on market share data before closing (including a seller losing any links with a target post-closing) exceeds 15% on any product market in Ukraine, even if another party to the transaction is not active on such a market.

The Law of Ukraine On Protection of Economic Competition (2001) (**Competition Law**)[1] is the main competition legislation in Ukraine.

2. **Does the merger control system in your jurisdiction impose a "*standstill obligation*" – meaning, that the transaction cannot be implemented prior to completing the merger control process? (Please cite the relevant legislation.) Please also indicate the *legal scope* of the standstill obligation according to the relevant legislation (e.g. the parties to the transaction cannot effect a change of control, cannot take steps towards implementation, etc.).**

Article 24 of the Competition Law provides for a standstill obligation. If the jurisdictional thresholds are met, the implementation of the transaction which constitutes a "concentration" is prohibited until a merger clearance is obtained. The parties should refrain from any actions that may result in restriction of competition and make impossible the restoration of the pre-transaction state.

According to a standstill obligation, the parties to the transaction are not allowed to close the transaction by effecting a change of control prior to merger clearance. A transaction is deemed to be closed when ownership over the shares or the target's asset is transferred to the buyer or if the parties' pre-closing conduct in effect allows the acquirer to obtain a decisive influence over the business activity of the target (e.g. through the appointment by the acquirer of target's management).

3. **Have the relevant authorities in your jurisdiction issued internal or external guidelines concerning the scope of the standstill obligation, and/or their authority to enforce it? Please provide a copy/link of such guidance, if possible in English.**

The AMC has not issued any specific guidelines on this issue.

4. **Are there any exceptions to the standstill obligation – for example, through derogation or "carve out"? Please describe the circumstances in which this is possible. Please also describe the relevant process, e.g. do parties need to apply to the authority for a derogation from the standstill obligation? If so, how long is the approval process? If there are specific cases addressing these issues, please identify them.**

No possibilities for derogation or carve-out are provided in Ukraine. Therefore, it is prohibited to implement a transaction even outside Ukraine prior to receiving the AMC's merger control clearance.

---

[1] Competition Law is available in Ukrainian: <http://zakon.rada.gov.ua/laws/show/2210-14>.

5. **Does a public bid exception exist in your jurisdiction? (For example, under the EU Merger Regulation it is possible to acquire shares as part of a public bid, provided that the shares are not exercised until the acquisition is cleared by the Commission.) If such an exception exists in your jurisdiction, please describe how it is applied.**

Implementation of any notifiable transaction (including public bids) must be suspended until the AMC grants the merger clearance.

6. **What powers does the relevant authority have to investigate and enforce violations of the standstill obligation? Are dawn raids possible? What timing applies to investigation/enforcement proceedings?**

The AMC may use all of its regular powers of investigation, including dawn raids, to determine whether companies have complied with the requirements of the competition laws, including the standstill obligation. The statute of limitations for violations of the standstill obligation is five years from closing of the transaction.

The Competition Law does not provide any statutory deadlines regarding the length of gun-jumping investigations. In practice, investigations of violations of the standstill obligation may last from a couple of months to more than one year. The timing largely depends on the willingness of the parties to cooperate with the AMC and to provide all the information requested by the authority on a timely basis. In cases where the violation of the standstill obligation arose from a failure to notify the transaction, the submission of a retrospective merger control filing may significantly accelerate the investigation process and normally serves as a mitigating circumstance in determining the amount of the fine.

The AMC intends to introduce statutory deadlines for the length of investigations. In particular, draft law No. 6746 provides for a one-year statutory deadline for investigations of violations of the standstill obligation. The draft was blocked by the presidential veto, and the updated version, which includes amendments suggested by the President of Ukraine, is pending the consideration by the Parliament of Ukraine.

7. **What are the possible penalties for violating the standstill obligation? Are there criminal sanctions, including on individuals? Have these been applied in practice? Is there a difference in enforcement between transactions involving domestic companies and "foreign-to-foreign" transactions? Does the authority have the power to unwind transactions implemented in breach of the standstill obligation? If so, has the authority made use of that power in practice? If yes, please provide examples.**

There are no criminal sanctions for violating the standstill obligation in Ukraine.

Failure to notify, late notification of a notifiable concentration or other forms of gun-jumping are subject to a maximum fine of up to 5% of the group's worldwide turnover for the preceding financial year in which the fine is imposed. (A maximum fine can be imposed only in exceptional circumstances to ensure a deterrent effect.) According to the *Guidelines on Calculation of Fines*, a basic amount of fine is calculated based on the group's turnover on the relevant and adjacent markets in Ukraine as follows:

(i) 10% of the infringer's turnover – if a concentration resulted in a monopoly or substantial restriction of competition;

(ii) UAH 510,000 (approx. €15,900) to 5% of the infringer's turnover on the relevant and adjacent product markets in Ukraine during the period of the violation – if a concentration did not (a) result in a monopoly or substantial restriction of competition and/or (b) affect any product markets; and

(iii) UAH 170,000 (approx. €5,300) to UAH 510,000 (approx. €15,900) – if parties are active on the different and non-adjacent markets.

The basic amounts in (i) and (ii) above may be adjusted by coefficients from 5% to 200% depending on the effect of violation on competition, the social importance of the products and the profitability of the relevant business. Mitigating and aggravating circumstances may further reduce or increase the amount of the fine up to 50% from the basic amount. In addition to the fine, the parties may also face the following negative consequences:

(i) unwinding of the transaction. The AMC may initiate unwinding of the transaction by filing a claim to the court if the transaction leads or may lead to monopolization or substantive restriction of competition in the market or a significant element of it. Based on publicly available information, we are not aware of any cases where the AMC has applied for unwinding the transaction;

(ii) a temporary ban on the undertaking's cross-border activities with Ukraine by the Ministry of Economy of Ukraine upon the AMC's request if the parties refuse to pay the imposed fine;

(iii) third-party claims for double recovery of damages;

(iv) reputational issues due to publication on the AMC's website of the decision on the violation; and

(v) complications with clearances in Ukraine in future transactions, as the AMC is likely to scrutinize them more closely.

As a matter of practice, the risks of the above negative consequences (i) – (iii) appear to be quite remote.

There is no difference in penalties for violating the standstill obligation between transactions involving domestic companies and foreign-to-foreign transactions.

8. How does the relevant authority typically learn of potential violations of the standstill obligation? Does the authority actively monitor the trade press?

It is common for the AMC to identify violations of the standstill obligation through regular monitoring of the press and the decisions on merger control clearances in the EU and other jurisdictions, especially in relation to undertakings which have had Ukrainian filings in the past.

Furthermore, the AMC has recently created a new department on EU integration and international cooperation, which is to monitor and analyze the enforcement of competition laws in the EU and other countries, including in relation to merger control violations. Thus, more attention from the AMC regarding failure to notify concentrations in other jurisdictions can be expected.

In addition, the AMC often compares information on the corporate structures of the applicants as well as the percentage of shareholdings in entities related by control relations to the applicants with information from previous filings of the respective corporate groups. If the AMC notices changes in the group structure or increases in percentage of the voting rights that may qualify as notifiable transactions, it normally requests confirmation that such acquisition did not require a merger control clearance and the provision of respective justifications. If such confirmation cannot be provided, the AMC will normally open a case on violation of the standstill obligation.

9. Please describe the relevant authority's enforcement of the standstill obligation. If there have been cases, please describe the specific conduct that was found to violate the standstill provision and the criteria applied by the relevant authority or court. Has the relevant authority considered the market impact of the conduct? (Please refer to the Annex.)

Most cases so far are either cases where the parties failed to file a transaction that met the notification thresholds or closed a notified transaction prior to obtaining clearance. Normally, a technical failure to notify a concentration which meets the established financial thresholds is sufficient to support a finding of breach by the AMC, even in the absence of an actual market impact of the transaction. However, the market impact of the concentration influences the size of the fine imposed, as reflected in the *Guidelines on Calculation of Fines* (see Question 7).

Below are several examples of typical cases of standstill violation, based on the enforcement practice of the AMC.

Acquisition of control through interlocking directorship. In *Infox LLC, Brociti Investments Ltd/KUB-GAZ LLC*, an individual who owned 100% of shares in Brociti Investments Ltd and more than 50% of shares in Infox LLC also held a position of thc CEO at Infox LLC. On 14 June 2016, Brociti Investments Ltd filed an application for a merger control clearance for the acquisition of more than 50% of shares in KUB-GAZ LLC. The AMC found that clearance should have been obtained earlier, before 11 February 2016, when the individual was appointed as a Head of Supervisory Board of KUB-GAZ LLC, since such appointment resulted in the individual obtaining control over KUB-GAZ LLC. In this case the AMC imposed the second largest fine for violation of the standstill obligation (approx. €110,000).[2] The fine was imposed on a group of undertakings including the individual, Infox LLC and Brociti Investments Ltd.

Closing of the notified transaction before the clearance. In *Cisco Systems Inc/One Mainstream Inc*, the transaction was notified to the AMC on 5 November 2015. On 19 November 2015, during the review of the application, the parties informed the AMC that due to business reasons the transaction had to be completed by 23 November 2015. This was before they had obtained clearance, which was

---

2 Case No 24-26.13/142-16 – *Infox LLC, Brociti Investments Ltd/KUB-GAZ LLC*, Decision of the Anti-Monopoly Committee of Ukraine of 27 December 2016.

subsequently issued by the AMC on 1 December 2015. Cisco Systems Inc was fined approximately €4,200.[3]

Acquisition of control over single property complex through lease agreement. In *PJSC Kirovogradavtotrans* (**KTrans**)*/Dominion-Kirovograd LLC*, KTrans leased a part of a non-residential building, used as a bus station from November 2011 until September 2013. The AMC opened a case in October 2014 after the lease agreement was terminated. According to the AMC, as the bus station had features of a single property complex which generated income from the provision of bus services and the financial thresholds were met, the lease of the bus station constituted a notifiable concentration. The AMC imposed a fine on KTrans in the amount of approximately €1,800.[4]

Acquisition of control via a financial institution before the shares were further resold by such institution. The second largest fine in the history of the Ukrainian merger control (€1.8 million) was imposed in April 2019 for the acquisition of control by the TAS Group over Private Joint Stock Company Dniprometyz (**Dniprometyz**), one of the largest Ukrainian manufacturers of low-carbon metal products, from the Russian Severstal group.[5]

In November 2017, the AMC received the application from Devisal Limited, a Cyprus subsidiary of the TAS Group, to approve the acquisition of a controlling stake in Dniprometyz. During the review the AMC discovered that earlier the same year – on 26 October 2017 – Blossom Investments OÜ (**Blossom**), an Estonian subsidiary of the TAS Group, the normal activities of which include conducting transactions and dealing in securities, acquired 100% of the shares in Dialzone Holding Ltd (British Virgin Islands) (**Dialzone**), which owned 98.6578% of the shares in Dniprometyz, with a view to reselling them within one year of the date of acquisition.

The Competition Law bears some similarity to the EU Merger Regulation because it exempts from the obligation to notify transactions where financial institutions, the normal activities of which include transactions and dealing in securities, hold securities on a temporary basis that they have acquired with a view to reselling them. This exception requires that the financial institution (i) does not exercise voting rights in the highest or other management bodies of the target, and (ii) the disposal of the securities takes place within one year of the date of acquisition.

In this case, however, the AMC established that:

- on the same day, when Blossom acquired 100% in Dialzone, there had been changes to the composition of the Dniprometyz's Supervisory Board (**SB**), as a result of which two out of three SB members had been appointed by the TAS Group representing Dialzone;

3 Case No 24-26.13/20-16 – *Cisco Systems Inc/One Mainstream Inc*, Decision of the Anti-Monopoly Committee of Ukraine of 31 May 2016.

4 Case No 24-26.13/97-14 – *PJSC Kirovogradavtotrans/Dominion-Kirovograd LLC*, Decision of the Anti-Monopoly Committee of Ukraine of 1 December 2015.

5 Case No 24-26.13/50-18 – *Blossom Investments OÜ (TAS Group)/PrJSC Dniprometyz*, Decision of the Anti-Monopoly Committee of Ukraine of 25 April 2018.

- according to Dniprometyz's Articles of Association, the SB manages the activity of the company, controls and regulates the activity of the general director and has exclusive powers to approve significant transactions;
- at the general shareholders' meeting of Dniprometyz, which had taken place in April 2018, the representatives of Dialzone had voted on commercial decisions of Dniprometyz regarding purchase of raw materials, procurement of energy source materials and sale of products.

Having analyzed these facts, the AMC concluded that the above-mentioned exemption from the obligation to notify could not apply to Blossom since it indirectly exercised decisive influence over Dniprometyz, in particular, due to 1) the appointment by the TAS Group and Dialzone of their representatives to the SB of Dniprometyz (more than 50% of SB members); and 2) Dialzone's voting at the Dniprometyz shareholders' meeting, including in relation to dismissal and appointment of the members of the SB and approval of the significant transactions. According to public announcements, the TAS Group intends to challenge the AMC decision in the courts.

10. In cases involving alleged violations of the standstill obligation under the relevant merger control laws, has the relevant authority (or court) *also* considered the substantive antitrust laws? (Please refer to the Annex.)

Based on publicly available information, we are not aware of such cases.

11. Is private enforcement of the standstill obligation possible?

Private enforcement of the standstill obligation is possible. According to the Ukrainian Civil Code, the transaction may be invalidated upon a claim to the commercial court by one of the parties to the transaction or any other interested third party whose rights might be violated if legal requirements applicable to the transaction have not been fulfilled. In view of this, failure to obtain merger control clearance prior to the completion of the transaction can serve as one of the grounds for invalidation.

There were a few cases where the parties to the transaction filed claims to the court on invalidation of the transaction. However, none of the cases resulted in invalidation since based on the facts of the cases there was no violation of standstill obligation, e.g. the transaction did not appear to be a notifiable concentration.

12. Please describe the private law risks/consequences (i.e. contractual/validity consequences) for transactions that are subject to notification, but which are completed without notification/approval. Please identify any relevant cases and describe them.

In case of private enforcement of standstill obligation violation, the transaction may be invalidated by the commercial court. In such case the parties to the transaction will have to act according to the restitution order, e.g. the transferred shares or assets should be returned to the previous owners.

Furthermore, there is a risk of third-party claims for double recovery of damages incurred as a result of the competition law violation. Both pecuniary damages (including the actual losses and loss of profits) and non-pecuniary (moral) damages can be claimed.

13. Please describe policy and enforcement trends in your jurisdiction.

According to the requirements of the EU – Ukraine Association Agreement, the AMC is going to change the rules of calculation of the merger control thresholds for the target group so that only the assets/turnover of the target and entities controlled by the target are counted. This will change the current approach, according to which the turnover/assets of the controlling seller or shareholder need to be counted in relation to the target, which often results in a formal triggering of the filing requirement only based on the turnover/assets of the seller, which loses control over the target post-closing.

The following priority developments are currently in the AMC's pipeline:

- new guidelines on the definition of the relevant market and assessment of market power;
- new guidelines on the definition of control;
- changes to the AMC's *Guidelines on Calculation of Fines for Competition Law Violations* in order to add more legal certainty, increase transparency in calculation of fines and remove certain practical shortcomings in its application.

Part 2: Substantive Antitrust Law in an M&A Context

1. **Please identify the relevant *substantive antitrust laws* in your jurisdiction that can potentially apply in an M&A context (e.g. for the EU, this would include Article 101 of the Treaty on the Functioning of the European Union). Please provide a link to the relevant legislation (if possible, in English).**

   The relevant legislation is the Competition Law.[6] Article 6 of the Competition Law is in essence equivalent to Article 101 of the Treaty on the Functioning of the European Union (**TFEU**) and may also apply in an M&A context, in particular, in cases of exchange of competitively sensitive information or coordination of competitive behavior.

   The substantive antitrust rules may also apply to the establishment of a newly-formed joint venture which may qualify as concerted practice if it results in coordination of the competitive behavior of either: (i) the founding parents among themselves or (ii) the founding parents and the joint venture. Should it be the case, such transactions may require preliminary approval for concerted practices by the AMC if relevant financial thresholds are exceeded.

   Also, ancillary restraints are not covered by merger clearance in Ukraine and may require a separate antitrust clearance for non-compete clauses, non-solicitation or similar restraints which may be formalistically treated by the AMC as anticompetitive concerted practices. If the agreement contains such kind of restraints, normally an application for concerted practices should be filed with the AMC in parallel with merger control application.

2. **Do any guidelines exist in your jurisdiction concerning the application of the substantive antitrust laws in an M&A context – whether internal to the relevant authority, or external, formal or informal (e.g. speeches)? If so, please provide a copy/link to such guidance.**

   There are no specific guidelines on the substantive antitrust laws in an M&A context. The AMC has issued guidelines on assessment of horizontal and non-horizontal concentrations which are largely based on the principles of the respective EU guidelines. These guidelines provide criteria for the assessment of potential coordination effects from the concentrations in the context of a merger control review.

3. **As a general matter (not limited to M&A), how are the substantive antitrust laws enforced with respect to the exchange of competitively sensitive infor-**

---

6 Competition Law (Ukrainian only) <http://zakon.rada.gov.ua/laws/show/2210-14>.

mation between competing firms? Please also indicate the relevance of anti-competitive effects or intent in such enforcement.

There are no comprehensive guidelines on the exchange of competitively sensitive information between competing firms, except for the *Standard Requirements of the AMC to Establishment of Business Associations for Exemption from Notification of Concerted Practices* (2007). The *Standard Requirements* set out the rules on the collection and exchange of information among the members of business associations. In particular, only aggregated and historical (i.e. at least one month after its collection) information can be distributed among members of business associations. Most importantly, such information should not contain any data that might facilitate the coordination of competitive behavior, or facilitate understanding of future behavior of the other members of the association, competitors or customers, such as information on pricing, commercial strategies and other key commercial terms.

In the absence of relevant general guidance on information exchange, in 2015 the AMC decided one of the landmark cases on the alleged coordination of competitive behavior. The case involved alleged coordination among Kiev-based retailers based on information from a marketing research agency. In its decision, the AMC made direct reference to the Guidelines on the Applicability of Article 101 of the Treaty on the Functioning of the European Union to horizontal cooperation agreements[7] in assessing competition concerns related to exchange of information. In this particular case, the AMC accused 15 retailers of Kiev of having coordinated their competitive behavior based on the marketing reports of ACNielsen Ukraine, which provided historical aggregated marketing data such as historical average market prices. The AMC concluded that obtaining information on the historical market trends facilitated coordination of competitive conduct and assumed that an alleged similarity in the dynamics of pricing, sales volumes and average bill of the retailers had been caused by anticompetitive concerted practices among the retailers based on such alleged "information exchange".[8] On appeal, the AMC's allegations were, however, proved to be erroneous, and the AMC's decision was fully revoked by the court.

4. **Have there been any cases in your jurisdiction in which the substantive antitrust laws were enforced in an M&A context? Please describe/explain and cite any such cases. (See also Annex.)**

Based on publicly available information, there have been no such cases.

5. **Are the substantive antitrust laws more likely to apply at specific stages of the transaction – i.e. at an early stage, or prior to closing (or does it not make a difference)? Do companies face ongoing risk following the consummation (or**

---

7 European Commission, Guidelines on the applicability of Article 101 of the Treaty on the Functioning of the European Union to horizontal cooperation agreements [2011] OJ C 11.

8 Case No 242-26.13/150-12 – *ACNielsen Ukraine LLC, Auchan Ukraine Hypermarket LLC, Metro Cash and Carry LLC, Fozzy-Food LLC, Novus Ukraine LLC, Enterprise with 100% foreign investment "BILLA-UKRAINE" and others*, Decision of the Anti-Monopoly Committee of Ukraine of 29 April 2015.

failure) of their transaction for conduct that allegedly occurred pre-closing (pre-failure)?

Substantive antitrust laws apply at any stage of the transaction. The companies face ongoing risk following the consummation (or failure) of their transaction for conduct that allegedly occurred pre-closing (pre-failure) within a limitation period of five years after the violation was terminated.

6. **Please explain how the relevant authority enforces (or could enforce) the substantive antitrust laws in an M&A context. How would the investigation occur, and what timing constraints would apply?**

The investigation of the substantive antitrust laws in an M&A context is held based on general investigation rules on violation of the competition laws. In particular, the AMC may send requests for documents and information to the respondents or to any third parties, carry out dawn raids and hearings with the respondents, etc. The statute of limitation is five years from termination of the infringement. The statute of limitation is suspended for the period of the AMC's investigation of the alleged violation. The AMC can launch an investigation of an alleged violation of substantive antitrust rules based on a complaint or on its own initiative.

7. **Is private enforcement of the substantive antitrust laws possible in an M&A context, and has it occurred?**

Private enforcement of the substantive antitrust laws is generally possible, including in an M&A context. In particular, the following types of claims may be brought before the commercial court: (i) third-party claims for award of double damages incurred as a result of anticompetitive conduct (it is more efficient to claim follow-up damages after the fact of violation is established in the AMC's decision); (ii) claims for invalidation of the transaction; and (iii) claims for putting an end of unlawful practice violating the rights of the claimant or forcing the defendant to perform certain actions.

Based on publicly available information, however, there are no cases on private enforcement of the substantive antitrust laws in an M&A context so far.

8. **Could behavior subject to the substantive antitrust laws also be caught under the merger control rules/standstill obligation? (Please also refer to the Annex.)**

Potentially yes, the AMC may learn about violations of substantive antitrust laws within the context of a merger control review, however, based on publicly available information we are not aware of any such cases. If the AMC finds signs of infringement of substantive antitrust laws, such as coordination of competitive behavior or exchange of competitively sensitive information, a separate investigation under Article 6 of the Competition Law (equivalent of Article 101 TFEU) may be launched.

9. **Please describe the penalties for infringing the substantive antitrust laws. Please indicate whether these include criminal penalties, including individual criminal penalties. As a practical matter, how have these been applied in the context of an M&A transaction?**

There are no criminal penalties for infringing the substantive antitrust laws in Ukraine.

Anticompetitive concerted practices (equivalent to Article 101 TFEU) are subject to administrative fines of up to 10% of the annual turnover of the undertaking in the year immediately preceding the year when the fine is imposed. However, this maximum fine can be imposed only in exceptional circumstances to ensure deterrence.

According to the *Guidelines on Calculation of Fines*, the basic amount of a fine is calculated as 10% of the group's turnover of the products directly or indirectly related to the infringement in Ukraine (except for hard-core violations such as price-fixing, market-sharing, fixing volumes of production, purchase or sales, where 15% applies instead). The basic amount is further adjusted by coefficients from 5% to 200% depending on the effect of the violation on competition, social importance and profitability of the services in question. The above amount may be further decreased or increased by up to 50% based on mitigating and aggravating circumstances.

10. Please describe policy and enforcement trends in your jurisdiction.

There are no particular policy or enforcement trends related to substantive antitrust laws in an M&A context in Ukraine.

Anastasia Usova, Nataliya Kovalyova, "The Ukrainian Competition Authority imposes a fine of EUR 1.8 million for 'gun jumping' in a merger in the heavy industry sector, and does not clear the transaction due to economic sanctions on the seller's beneficiary (TAS group/Dniprometyz)" 25 April 2019, e-Competitions Bulletin April 2019, Art. N° 90748

ANNEX

Table 1: Actual Enforcement of Specific Conduct under the Relevant Merger Control Rules and Substantive Antitrust Laws

Please identify whether the following type of conduct has been subject to investigation/enforcement in your jurisdiction, under the merger control laws or substantive antitrust laws. Please cite any such case(s) and provide a brief description in the table below.

Specific Conduct	Actual Enforcement under Merger Control Laws	Actual Enforcement under Substantive Antitrust Laws
Pre-signing due diligence	No	No
Post-signing/pre-approval due diligence	No	No
Post-approval/pre-closing due diligence	No	No
Use of "clean teams"	No	No
Restrictions on the target in an M&A agreement, e.g. buyer approval required for: Investments above a certain level; New business above a certain level; Other obligations to consult/ obtain approval from the buyer before closing.	No	No
Joint marketing	No	No
Joint presentations (e.g. industry fairs)	No	No
Joint communications	No	No
Strategy/planning regarding customers	No	No
Strategy/planning regarding suppliers	No	No
Third party contract novation	No	No

Specific Conduct	Actual Enforcement under Merger Control Laws	Actual Enforcement under Substantive Antitrust Laws
Personnel Issues: – Secondments – Retention Strategies	No	No
IT Planning/Database Migration	No	No
Other	No	No

Please note that since the AMC only started to publish its decisions on July 2015, it cannot be ruled out that some cases dealing with the topics mentioned in the above table were issued before July 2015. Based on publicly available information, most cases so far are either cases where the parties failed to file a transaction that met the notification thresholds or closed a notified transaction prior to obtaining clearance.

Table 2: Hypothetical Enforcement of Specific Conduct under the Relevant Merger Control Rules and Substantive Antitrust Laws

For any conduct that is *not* the subject of actual enforcement (Table 1), please indicate in the Table below whether the conduct identified *could potentially* be enforced under the merger control laws and/or substantive antitrust laws.

Specific Conduct	Hypothetical Enforcement under Merger Control Laws	Hypothetical Enforcement under Substantive Antitrust Laws
Pre-signing due diligence	No	Yes (Information exchange, horizontal coordination)
Post-signing/pre-approval due diligence	No	Yes (Information exchange, horizontal coordination)
Post-approval/pre-closing due diligence	No	Yes (Information exchange, horizontal coordination)
Use of "clean teams"	No	Yes (Information exchange, horizontal coordination)

Specific Conduct	Hypothetical Enforcement under Merger Control Laws	Hypothetical Enforcement under Substantive Antitrust Laws
Restrictions on the target in an M&A agreement, e.g. buyer approval required for: Investments above a certain level; New business above a certain level; Other obligations to consult/obtain approval from the buyer before closing.	Yes	Yes (Information exchange, horizontal coordination)
Joint marketing	Yes	Yes (Information exchange, horizontal coordination)
Joint presentations (e.g. industry fairs)	Yes	Yes (Information exchange, horizontal coordination)
Joint communications	Yes	Yes (Information exchange, horizontal cooperation)
Strategy/planning regarding customers	Yes	Yes (Information exchange; horizontal cooperation)
Strategy/planning regarding suppliers	Yes	Yes (Information exchange; horizontal cooperation)
Third party contract novation	Yes	Yes (Information exchange; horizontal cooperation)

UNITED KINGDOM

David Cardwell
(Baker Botts LLP)

Part 1: Merger Control and the "Standstill Obligation"

1. **Please identify the relevant merger control legislation in your jurisdiction. Please provide a link to the relevant legislation (if possible, in English) and also indicate:**
   - **whether the merger control system is mandatory or voluntary,**
   - **the relevant authority, and**
   - **the duration of the review period.**

Legislation

The key piece of legislation applicable to merger control in the UK is the Enterprise Act 2002 (**EA02**).[1] The EA02 has been amended significantly by changes introduced under the Enterprise and Regulatory Reform Act 2013 (**ERRA13**).[2] Among other changes, the ERRA13 abolished both the Office of Fair Trading (**OFT**) and the Competition Commission, replacing them with a single competition authority – the Competition and Markets Authority (**CMA**).[3]

Voluntary system

The submission of merger filings under the UK regime is voluntary only. The CMA retains the right to open an investigation on its own initiative (when certain prescribed thresholds allowing the CMA to establish jurisdiction over a transaction are met),[4] and in practice a large number of transactions are notified prior to completion in order to give the merging parties legal certainty in respect of their transaction.

Waiting period

The duration of a Phase I review is 40 working days from the time of notification, after which the CMA must decide whether to approve the transaction or make a reference for a Phase II review. If a Phase II review is begun, the CMA has 24 weeks from the time of making the Phase II reference to take a decision, and may extend that by a further eight weeks. The overall timeline of the review period may be extended for consideration of undertakings in lieu (essentially an offer of

---

1 <https://www.legislation.gov.uk/ukpga/2002/40/contents>.
2 <http://www.legislation.gov.uk/ukpga/2013/24/contents/enacted>.
3 <https://www.gov.uk/government/organisations/competition-and-markets-authority>.
4 EA02, s 23.

undertakings by the merging parties in lieu of a reference of the case to a Phase II investigation), or Phase II remedies.

2. **Does the merger control system in your jurisdiction impose a "*standstill obligation*" – meaning, that the transaction cannot be implemented prior to completing the merger control process? (Please cite the relevant legislation.) Please also indicate the *legal scope* of the standstill obligation according to the relevant legislation (e.g. the parties to the transaction cannot effect a change of control, cannot take steps towards implementation, etc.).**

Although merging parties are entitled to close transactions without submitting a notification to the CMA, once a notification has been submitted by the parties (or the CMA has begun an investigation on its own initiative), there can be constraints on the parties from integrating their businesses before the CMA issues a clearance decision.

Initial undertakings

The CMA may accept initial undertakings offered by the merging parties.[5] Initial undertakings are not sought or offered in all cases; the CMA sees initial undertakings as particularly important in cases where it has reason to believe that a particular transaction could potentially qualify for a Phase II reference. Initial undertakings tend to specify that the merging parties will not engage in further integration until a clearance decision is issued by the CMA (or suitable remedial action is taken in response to the CMA's qualified decision). Initial undertakings list specific types of conduct from which the parties agree to refrain, e.g. integration of IT systems, employment decisions being taken by the acquirer over the target business, etc.

The CMA maintains a template set of initial undertakings for use in most transactions where they are sought.[6]

Initial enforcement orders

The CMA is also entitled to impose initial enforcement orders (**IEOs**) to prevent any further integration by the merging parties. It may also use such orders to unwind any integration that has already taken place. The CMA does not regularly use IEOs – it tends to threaten to use them only in cases where merging parties refuse to enter into initial undertakings, and the threat to impose an IEO is normally sufficient to ensure that the merging parties agree to initial undertakings.[7]

If a Phase II review is opened, the CMA prohibits any party to a completed merger from engaging in any further integration or any party to an anticipated merger from acquiring an "interest in shares" of another company, by way of IEOs.[8]

---

5 EA02, s 71 (see also s 80).

6 <https://assets.publishing.service.gov.uk/government/uploads/system/uploads/attachment_data/file/642070/guidance-initial-enforcement-orders-and-derogations-merger-investigations.pdf>.

7 EA02, s 72.

8 EA02, s 78.

Interim undertakings

The CMA may accept "interim" undertakings from an acquirer in a situation where a merger is subject to a Phase II reference; it may do so where neither initial undertakings nor an IEO has yet been used in that particular case.[9]

3. Have the relevant authorities in your jurisdiction issued internal or external guidelines concerning the scope of the standstill obligation, and/or their authority to enforce it? Please provide a copy/link of such guidance, if possible in English.

There are two key sets of guidelines which are relevant. *Guidance on the CMA's jurisdiction and procedure* (**Procedural Guidance**)[10] and *Interim measures in merger investigations* (**Interim Measures Guidance**).[11]

The main parts of the Procedural Guidance which are relevant are:

- paragraphs 7.28–7.31 which set out some explanation of the CMA's approach to the use of IEOs;
- paragraphs 11.8–11.10 which provide details on the CMA's approach to using IEOs in mergers which are subject to a reference for a Phase II investigation (and for the CMA's practice in potentially accepting interim undertakings under section 80 of the EA02); and
- Annexe C, where the CMA sets out detailed guidance on the types of cases where it will typically seek to secure IEOs in respect of anticipated mergers, and the mechanics for enforcing such IEOs.

The Interim Measures Guidance sets out detailed guidance on the CMA's likely practice in respect of IEOs and interim measures more generally. The guidance is specifically designed to give merging parties insight into the CMA's likely practice based on previous cases and precedents. Overall, the Interim Measures Guidance emphasizes the CMA's focus on preventing integration activities by merging parties, rather than preventing actual completion of a transaction (it underlines that the CMA's chief concern is to preserve its ability to implement effective remedies if necessary).[12]

The CMA maintains a standard form template for an IEO which it expects merging parties to use in most circumstances.[13] It will entertain proposed tailoring of the

---

9 EA02, s 80.

10 CMA, *Guidance on the CMA's jurisdiction and procedure* (CMA2) (January 2014) <https://assets.publishing.service.gov.uk/government/uploads/system/uploads/attachment_data/file/384055/CMA2__Mergers__Guidance.pdf>.

11 CMA, *Interim Measures in merger investigations* (CMA108) (28 June 2019) <https://assets.publishing.service.gov.uk/government/uploads/system/uploads/attachment_data/file/813144/Interim_Measures_in_Merger_Investigations_June_2019.pdf>. These guidelines updated and replaced the previous set of guidelines in place, *Guidance on initial enforcement orders and derogations in merger investigations* (CMA60).

12 See e.g. *Interim Measures Guidance* (CMA 108), para 1.7.

13 <https://assets.publishing.service.gov.uk/government/uploads/system/uploads/attachment_data/file/642072/initial-enforcement-order-template.pdf>.

standard form template – particularly where an IEO is being used in respect of an anticipated merger rather than a completed merger.[14]

4. **Are there any exceptions to the standstill obligation – for example, through derogation or "carve out"? Please describe the circumstances in which this is possible. Please also describe the relevant process, e.g. do parties need to apply to the authority for a derogation from the standstill obligation? If so, how long is the approval process? If there are specific cases addressing these issues, please identify them.**

Availability of derogations

Derogations from IEOs are possible. The CMA may grant a derogation that gives consent to the merging parties to undertake certain actions that would otherwise be prohibited by an IEO.

The CMA has typically shown a willingness to accede to derogation requests (where sufficiently specified, reasoned and evidenced) in respect of:

- the provision of back-office support services by the acquirer to the target;[15]
- the exclusion from the scope of an IEO of parts of one party's business that are not engaged in activities that are related to the other party's business;[16]
- the exclusion from the scope of an IEO of parts of either party's business that have no relevance to the merging parties' relevant activities in the UK;[17] and
- the replacement of specified key staff at the target or substantive changes to the merging parties' relevant activities in the UK.[18]

Procedural aspects

Derogation requests are most likely to be accepted by the CMA where the parties are able to demonstrate that allowing the derogation would not create a risk of pre-emptive action that would be costly or difficult to reverse, and/or is necessary for the effective continuation of the acquired business.

Any request to the CMA must:

- include a full explanation, with a description of the action that the party wishes to take;
- explain that granting the derogation would create no risk of pre-emptive action that would be costly/difficult to reverse;
- explain whether the request is urgent, and if so how urgent.

The CMA considers derogation requests as quickly as possible, and a monitoring trustee may be appointed in order to assist the CMA in assessing and providing a prompt response to derogation requests.[19]

---

14 *Interim Measures Guidance*, paras 2.29–2.33.
15 ibid, paras 3.26–3.31.
16 ibid, paras 3.43–3.48.
17 ibid, paras 3.49–3.56.
18 ibid, paras 3.57–3.62.
19 *Jurisdictional Guidance* (CMA 2), Annex C, paras C.19 – C.23.

The CMA maintains a standard template for derogation requests which merging parties are encouraged to use.[20]

5. Does a public bid exception exist in your jurisdiction? (For example, under the EU Merger Regulation it is possible to acquire shares as part of a public bid, provided that the shares are not exercised until the acquisition is cleared by the Commission.) If such an exception exists in your jurisdiction, please describe how it is applied.

There is no provision in the UK under the relevant legislation linked specifically to the mechanics of IEOs or interim undertakings and the launch of a public bid. In practice, the CMA tends not to impose an IEO or seek "obstructive" interim undertakings in a public bid situation.

6. What powers does the relevant authority have to investigate and enforce violations of the standstill obligation? Are dawn raids possible? What timing applies to investigation/enforcement proceedings?

The CMA normally requires the CEOs (or other agreed individuals) of the companies providing initial or interim undertakings to provide a compliance statement which supports the terms agreed upon. The CMA typically requires a compliance statement to be provided every two weeks during Phase I and every month during a Phase II investigation. The CMA may require further information on an ad hoc basis, and it may also require a representative of the acquired business to prepare a periodic report to the CMA for the purpose of monitoring compliance with any IEO or other interim measures.[21]

A monitoring trustee may be appointed (more usually at the beginning of Phase II investigations), to first assess how well any existing interim measures/orders have been complied with, and to make recommendations on any further measures that may be necessary (and to continue to monitor compliance).[22]

Dawn raids are not used to monitor compliance with the terms of existing interim measures.

7. What are the possible penalties for violating the standstill obligation? Are there criminal sanctions, including on individuals? Have these been applied in practice? Is there a difference in enforcement between transactions involving domestic companies and "foreign-to-foreign" transactions? Does the authority have the power to unwind transactions implemented in breach of the standstill obligation? If so, has the authority made use of that power in practice? If yes, please provide examples.

Since there is no formal standstill obligation under the UK's voluntary merger filing regime, discussion of sanctions for non-compliance in this context needs

---

20 <https://assets.publishing.service.gov.uk/government/uploads/system/uploads/attachment_data/file/642074/initial-enforcement-order-derogation-template.pdf>.

21 *Jurisdictional Guidance*, Annex C, para C.39.

22 For further detail, see *Jurisdictional Guidance* paras C.27 – C.32.

to focus on failure to comply with any initial undertakings given to the CMA or with any IEO imposed by the CMA, if such arrangements have been put in place.

If a party fails to comply with any undertakings that it has given or with any order imposed on it by the CMA, compliance may be enforced by means of civil proceedings brought by the CMA – for an injunction, interdict or any other appropriate relief or remedy – in the UK courts. Financial (civil) penalties may be imposed as part of any eventual court-based enforcement.[23] Section 94A of the EA02 also gives the CMA the power to impose a financial penalty of up to 5% of total global turnover of a party whom it judges to have failed to comply with an interim measure (initial/interim undertaking, or IEO) imposed under section 80 of the EA02.[24]

It is also worth noting that it is a criminal offense under section 117 of the EA02 for parties to provide misleading information to the CMA without reasonable excuse, and this provision is specifically mentioned in the CMA's Jurisdictional Guidance in respect of CEOs providing compliance statements to the CMA in order to confirm that the terms of an IEO or other interim measure have been/are being complied with.[25]

See Table 1 below with respect to the CMA's enforcement against merging parties for breach of an IEO.

There is, in theory, no distinction made between enforcement against a UK-based party and a foreign party.

The failure to comply with an interim measure cannot in itself give rise to an unwinding order. The CMA does have the power to issue an order unwinding a merger which has already closed or that has already involved some form of integration, but only if the transaction or its partial implementation is likely to cause or has already caused a substantial lessening of competition.

8. How does the relevant authority typically learn of potential violations of the standstill obligation? Does the authority actively monitor the trade press?

In the context of the giving of initial undertakings to the CMA, or the imposition of an IEO by the CMA, the CMA may become aware of a potential violation through ongoing monitoring of arrangements that have been put in place (see Question 6 in respect of CMA requirements for CEOs or comparable individuals to provide regular compliance statements). This is the means by which the CMA became aware of alleged breaches of IEOs in the cases of both *Electro Rent* and *Ausurus/MWR*, both discussed in further detail below at Table 1.

In cases where a hold separate manager has been appointed, this represents an additional layer of monitoring that can be used by the CMA to ensure compliance with any agreed hold separate arrangements.

There is a connection also with the CMA's merger intelligence function. The authority's merger intelligence unit maintains a considerable media/trade press-monitoring team who pay attention to any public reports (e.g. deal announcements,

---

23 EA02, s 94; CMA *Jurisdictional Guidance*, para 14.8 *et seq.*

24 s 80 provides for interim undertakings to be offered by parties to a merger which is subject to a Phase II reference, where no initial undertakings or IEO have been used.

25 *Jurisdictional Guidance*, Annex C, para C.39.

etc.) that indicate that a merger is in progress or has been completed which in all likelihood is one with which the CMA may find substantive competition law issues. In that case, the CMA may investigate the merger *ex officio*. Even if the CMA were to open a full merger investigation, there would be no enforcement against the relevant parties for "gun-jumping" since there is no formal standstill obligation. However, initial undertakings may then be requested or an IEO issued.[26]

9. Please describe the relevant authority's enforcement of the standstill obligation. If there have been cases, please describe the specific conduct that was found to violate the standstill provision and the criteria applied by the relevant authority or court. Has the relevant authority considered the market impact of the conduct? (Please refer to the Annex.)

Not applicable, given lack of standstill obligation in the UK. Note, however, cases such as *Electro Rent* and *Ausurus/MWR*, in which the CMA has imposed financial penalties on merging parties for breaches of IEOs which were in place in respect of both transactions. These cases are discussed in Table 1 below.

10. In cases involving alleged violations of the standstill obligation under the relevant merger control laws, has the relevant authority (or court) *also* considered the substantive antitrust laws? (Please refer to the Annex.)

Not applicable, given lack of standstill obligation in the UK.

11. Is private enforcement of the standstill obligation possible?

Not applicable, given lack of standstill obligation in the UK. It is worth noting that private litigation in respect of any damages suffered by private parties as a result of an infringement is generally permitted, but there is no formal ability for a private party to litigate to enforce any standstill arrangements.

12. Please describe the private law risks/consequences (i.e. contractual/validity consequences) for transactions that are subject to notification, but which are completed without notification/approval. Please identify any relevant cases and describe them.

Not applicable, given lack of standstill obligation in the UK.

13. Please describe policy and enforcement trends in your jurisdiction.

There are no policy trends as such, given the lack of a formal standstill obligation. However, it is worth noting that the CMA continues to lend considerable resources to its mergers intelligence function – the part of its organization that monitors trade/transaction developments in order to help it in determining about which anticipated or completed acquisitions it may conduct enquiries. The CMA published updated guidelines on its mergers intelligence function in September 2017 and clearly continues to treat this as an integral part of its overall merger review operations.[27]

---

26 Further details of the CMA's merger intelligence function is available in CMA, *Guidance on the CMA's merger intelligence function* (CMA56) (5 September 2017) <https://assets.publishing.service.gov.uk/government/uploads/system/uploads/attachment_data/file/648247/CMA56.pdf>.

27 CMA, *Guidance on the CMA's mergers intelligence function* (CMA56) (5 September 2017).

The CMA's decision in February 2019 to impose a fine for breach of an IEO in the *Ausurus* case (see Table 1 for further information) came swiftly after the CMA's imposition of a fine for the same type of infringement in the *Electro Rent* case (see Table 1). The imposition of a considerable financial penalty so swiftly after the imposition of the first ever fine for such a breach could be taken as a clear indication by the CMA that it intends to pursue rigidly any perceived breaches of IEOs or other orders which require merging parties to hold their respective businesses separate.

The UK's withdrawal from the European Union, previously scheduled for March 2019 and now tentatively scheduled for end of October 2019 (as at time of writing) will inevitably lead to certain changes in competition law policy and enforcement in the UK. The UK government and the CMA have both issued various statements in respect of potential changes to the law affecting the competition rules in the UK. Most recently, the Chairman of the CMA, Andrew Tyrie, wrote to the UK government proposing some sweeping changes to the enforcement of competition law in the UK, including in respect of the merger regime. Among his suggestions was the introduction of a hybrid system of merger control in which larger, cross-border transactions would be subject to mandatory – suspensory – notifications, while small transactions would continue to fall under a voluntary regime. Any such change would have important implications for the rules on gun-jumping in the UK, though it is far from clear at the time of writing whether the CMA Chairman's proposal will gather traction in the near term. It seems likely that any switch from an entirely voluntary notification regime to a mixed mandatory/voluntary system will take a substantial amount of time and political willpower.

Part 2: Substantive Antitrust Law in an M&A Context

1. **Please identify the relevant *substantive antitrust laws* in your jurisdiction that can potentially apply in an M&A context (e.g. for the EU, this would include Article 101 of the Treaty on the Functioning of the European Union). Please provide a link to the relevant legislation (if possible, in English).**

The main piece of legislation in this regard is the Competition Act 1998 (**CA98**), which sets out Article 101 TFEU-style prohibitions on competition law restrictions. Chapter I of the CA98 prohibits agreements between undertakings that may affect trade in the UK and which have as their object or effect the prevention, restriction or distortion of competition within the UK.[28]

In the M&A context, this can be particularly relevant to joint venture arrangements which fall short of the jurisdictional tests set out in the EA02 – for example in respect of information exchanges between the parties – and also relevant in particular in respect of possible ancillary arrangements set up in connection with a transaction.

2. **Do any guidelines exist in your jurisdiction concerning the application of the substantive antitrust laws in an M&A context – whether internal to the relevant authority, or external, formal or informal (e.g. speeches)? If so, please provide a copy/link to such guidance.**

There are no specific guidelines that deal with the application of the substantive competition law (Chapter I prohibition under the CA98, etc.) in the M&A context, outside the more general merger control guidance (e.g. Jurisdictional Guidance, etc.).

3. **As a general matter (not limited to M&A), how are the substantive antitrust laws enforced with respect to the exchange of competitively sensitive information between competing firms? Please also indicate the relevance of anti-competitive effects or intent in such enforcement.**

As a general matter, exchanges of information between competing firms can be considered to be Chapter I-prohibited conduct. Under Chapter I and section 9 of the CA98, an exchange of information can be either a by object or by effect infringement – it is not necessary for the CMA to prove anticompetitive effect where anticompetitive object is established. The key test for assessing whether an exchange of information has a collusive object/effect for the purposes of Chapter I of the CA98 is whether or not the flow of information reduces the strategic uncertainty of competitors, consequently diminishing their incentives to compete against one another. The UK's practice in this

[28] Competition Act 1998, s 1–16 <http://www.legislation.gov.uk/ukpga/1998/41/contents>.

regard is closely aligned with the EU approach, and the CMA (currently) has regard to the EU's horizontal information-sharing guidelines and case law.

4. **Have there been any cases in your jurisdiction in which the substantive antitrust laws were enforced in an M&A context? Please describe/explain and cite any such cases. (See also Annex.)**

None.

5. **Are the substantive antitrust laws more likely to apply at specific stages of the transaction – i.e. at an early stage, or prior to closing (or does it not make a difference)? Do companies face ongoing risk following the consummation (or failure) of their transaction for conduct that allegedly occurred pre-closing (pre-failure)?**

Application of substantive antitrust law at specific stages

Substantive antitrust laws – (arguably) mainly those which may catch potential exchanges of competitively sensitive information – may be most relevant during the earlier stages of transaction planning (e.g. due diligence), and during the period between notification of a transaction and formal clearance by the CMA, followed by closing.

As regards the former (due diligence), the UK's Chapter I prohibition of anticompetitive agreements (including exchanges of competitively sensitive information) applies to a company's conduct as it receives information from the target company in order to assess the viability of its intended transaction. Proper safeguards (possible use of information-sharing protocols, clean teams, etc.) may be merited.

As regards the latter, companies are prohibited from pre-closing conduct that could be seen as anticompetitive while the two sides remain, technically, competitors. The scope for permitted conduct may be defined under any agreed interim undertakings (see Part 1).

Ongoing risk

At whatever time the CMA may become aware of a potential Chapter I infringement, it may investigate that and take action as appropriate. In this sense, companies face ongoing risk following the consummation (or failure) of their transaction for conduct that occurred pre-closing.

6. **Please explain how the relevant authority enforces (or could enforce) the substantive antitrust laws in an M&A context. How would the investigation occur, and what timing constraints would apply?**

The CMA is entitled to investigate any suspected infringement of Chapter I of the CA98 when it becomes aware of such a potential infringement. Once it becomes aware of a suspected infringement, the CMA's Enforcement Directorate conducts an initial assessment as to whether it has solid grounds for suspecting an infringement of Chapter I, and then a formal investigation would be opened. The CMA's procedures and overall approach to enforcement of such infringements is set out in some detail in its Investigation Procedures Guidance.[29] Close cooperation between the Enforcement Directorate and the relevant merger review team members can be expected in cases concerning mergers which have been notified to the CMA.

7. Is private enforcement of the substantive antitrust laws possible in an M&A context, and has it occurred?

Private enforcement is certainly possible: section 60 of the CA98 makes it clear that damages for infringement of the CA98 are available in UK courts where damages would be available for infringements of EU competition law.[30] Section 47A of the CA98 also gives the Competition Appeal Tribunal (**CAT**) jurisdiction to hear damages claims following on from an infringement decision by the CMA.

We are not aware of any instances of cases in the UK involving the private enforcement of substantive antitrust laws in an M&A context.[31]

8. Could behavior subject to the substantive antitrust laws also be caught under the merger control rules/standstill obligation? (Please also refer to the Annex.)

Due to the nature of the UK regime (no formal standstill obligation) this has limited applicability. If parties have entered into or been made subject to any of the interim measures referenced in Part 1 of the survey, then conduct by the parties which contravenes a term agreed or imposed under a particular interim measure could be subject to enforcement as part of the CMA's merger control regime. See also Annex.

9. Please describe the penalties for infringing the substantive antitrust laws. Please indicate whether these include criminal penalties, including individual criminal penalties. As a practical matter, how have these been applied in the context of an M&A transaction?

The CMA has the power to impose financial penalties of up to 10% of turnover of an undertaking found to have infringed a Chapter I/Chapter II prohibition.[32] Under the ERRA13, the CMA applies penalty guidelines which can result in the increase or decrease of the basic amount of a financial penalty due to various considerations such as mitigating or aggravating factors.[33]

Individual criminal liability for infringement of the substantive antitrust laws is possible under an offense introduced in the EA02 – the cartel offense (this is arguably of less relevance in the M&A context). A finding of guilt in respect of this offense can lead to a criminal fine or to imprisonment (or both). We are not aware of application of these types of penalties in the context of M&A.

---

29 CMA, *Competition Act 1998: Guidance on the CMA's investigation procedures in Competition Act 1998 cases* (CMA8) (18 January 2019) <https://assets.publishing.service.gov.uk/government/uploads/system/uploads/attachment_data/file/771970/CMA8_CA98_guidance.pdf>.

30 <http://www.legislation.gov.uk/ukpga/1998/41/section/60>

31 See also CMA, *Competition Law Redress* (CMA55) (May 2016), para 1.4 *et seq.* <https://assets.publishing.service.gov.uk/government/uploads/system/uploads/attachment_data/file/520423/competition-law-redress-a-guide-to-taking-action-cma55.pdf>

32 CA98, s 36.

33 ERRA13, s 44.

10. Please describe policy and enforcement trends in your jurisdiction.

There are no major policy/enforcement trends in this respect in the UK. See also Question 13 in Part 1 above – the UK's withdrawal from the European Union, currently expected to take place at the end of October 2019, will inevitably lead to certain changes in competition law policy and enforcement in the UK. The UK government and the CMA have both issued various statements in respect of potential changes to the law affecting competition law in the UK. Most recently, the Chairman of the CMA, Andrew Tyrie, has written to the UK government suggesting significant changes to the CMA's enforcement powers in respect of both antitrust (e.g. cartel enforcement) and the merger regime. It is likely that any proposed changes to the regime in the UK will take a substantial amount of time to gain traction and to eventually become law.

Porter Elliott, "The UK Competition Authority fines a company for breach of an interim order during a merger review (Electro Rent)" 11 June 2018, e-Competitions Bulletin June 2018, Art. N° 87350

Robert Bell, "The UK Competition Appeal Tribunal announces an appeal against the first decision fining a party for gun jumping (Electro Rent)" 13 August 2018, e-Competitions Bulletin August 2018, Art. N° 88524

ANNEX

Table 1: Actual Enforcement of Specific Conduct under the Relevant Merger Control Rules and Substantive Antitrust Laws

Please identify whether the following type of conduct has been subject to investigation/enforcement in your jurisdiction, under the merger control laws or substantive antitrust laws. Please cite any such case(s) and provide a brief description in the table below.

Specific Conduct	Actual Enforcement under Merger Control Laws	Actual Enforcement under Substantive Antitrust Laws
Pre-signing due diligence	See *Electro Rent* and *Ausurus* cases referred to below.	n/a
Post-signing/pre-approval due diligence		
Post-approval/pre-closing due diligence		
Use of "clean teams"		
Restrictions on the target in an M&A agreement, e.g. buyer approval required for: Investments above a certain level; New business above a certain level; Other obligations to consult/obtain approval from the buyer before closing.		
Joint marketing	n/a	n/a
Joint presentations (e.g. industry fairs)		
Joint communications		
Strategy/planning regarding customers		
Strategy/planning regarding suppliers		
Third party contract novation		
Personnel Issues: – Secondments – Retention Strategies		
IT Planning/Database Migration		

Specific Conduct	Actual Enforcement under Merger Control Laws	Actual Enforcement under Substantive Antitrust Laws
Other	*Electro Rent* In June 2018 the CMA issued its first ever penalty on a company for breach of an initial order. Electro Rent, a company that had completed its acquisition of a competing business – Microlease – had been subject to an IEO from the CMA as of February 2017, while the CMA opened a merger investigation into the completed merger. The CMA subsequently opened a Phase II investigation, having found reason to believe that the transaction would lead to a substantial lessening of competition, and having not received a satisfactory remedy offer from the merging parties. Upon opening a Phase II investigation, the CMA issued an Interim Order, effectively continuing the obligations placed on the merging parties during Phase I under the original IEO. The Interim Order essentially required Electro Rent to continue to operate the two businesses separately and to obtain	n/a

Specific Conduct	Actual Enforcement under Merger Control Laws	Actual Enforcement under Substantive Antitrust Laws
Other	the CMA's permission if it were to take certain actions in respect of its own business (designed to cover actions which could have a material impact on the Electro Rent business). In April 2018, the CMA became aware that Electro Rent had served notice to terminate a commercial lease for one of its business premises, without consulting the CMA. Although Electro Rent argued that it had consulted with the Monitoring Trustee, the CMA dismissed this argument and found that Electro Rent had contravened the terms of the Initial Order by seeking to terminate the lease without obtaining permission. While the action by Electro Rent did not involve the premature exercise of control over the target business as such, the lease in question had in fact been discussed with the CMA as part of a potential remedy package to resolve the CMA's competition concerns, meaning that termination of the lease constituted a material change to the merging parties' businesses.	n/a

Specific Conduct	Actual Enforcement under Merger Control Laws	Actual Enforcement under Substantive Antitrust Laws
Other	The CMA imposed a fine of £100,000, representing the first case in which the CMA has taken action to impose a penalty for infringement of an Initial Order. The CMA's decision to impose a penalty was appealed by Electro Rent to the CAT; the CAT heard the appeal in October 2018 and issued its judgment in February 2019, finding that Electro Rent's appeal was unmerited. It found in particular that any reasonable person would have seen Electro Rent's decision in respect of lease termination as a breach of the Interim Order that was in place, and further found that the level of fine imposed by the CMA was proportionate given the flagrant nature of the infringement. *Ausurus/MWR* In January 2019 the CMA announced that it had issued another fine for breach of an IEO, this time in respect of Ausurus, the parent company of a metal recycling company, EMR.	n/a

Specific Conduct	Actual Enforcement under Merger Control Laws	Actual Enforcement under Substantive Antitrust Laws
	EMR had been subject to an IEO in respect of its acquisition of a rival scrap metal company, MWR. Having been made subject to the IEO in September 2017, the CMA established at a later stage – March 2018 (while a Phase 2 investigation was ongoing) – that EMR may have breached the terms of the IEO. Specifically, the CMA alleged that EMR had directed MWR's customers to make payments into Ausurus's bank account, with Ausurus itself also making payments directly to some of MWR's suppliers. The CMA also alleged that EMR had failed to give MWR's existing managing director a clear indication that decisions could be taken without first consulting or obtaining permission from Ausurus/EMR in advance. The CMA concluded that Ausurus'/EMR's actions had infringed the terms of the IEO, and issued a fine of £300,000.	

Table 2: Hypothetical Enforcement of Specific Conduct under the Relevant Merger Control Rules and Substantive Antitrust Laws

For any conduct that is *not* the subject of actual enforcement (Table 1), please indicate in the Table below whether the conduct identified *could potentially* be enforced under the merger control laws and/or substantive antitrust laws.

<table>
<tr><th>Specific Conduct</th><th>Hypothetical Enforcement under Merger Control Laws</th><th>Hypothetical Enforcement under Substantive Antitrust Laws</th></tr>
<tr><td>Pre-signing due diligence</td><td rowspan="2">Not applicable as such</td><td rowspan="4">Yes – if information exchange between parties or other collaborative conduct could fall under prohibited collusive/ cartel practices under Chapter I of the Competition Act 1998.</td></tr>
<tr><td>Post-signing/pre-approval due diligence</td></tr>
<tr><td>Post-approval/pre-closing due diligence</td><td rowspan="11">Yes – if in contravention of agreed initial undertakings (or IEO imposed by CMA).</td></tr>
<tr><td>Use of “clean teams”</td></tr>
<tr><td>Restrictions on the target in an M&A agreement, e.g. buyer approval required for:
– Investments above a certain level;
– New business above a certain level;
– Other obligations to consult/obtain approval from the buyer before closing.</td><td rowspan="9"></td></tr>
<tr><td>Joint marketing</td></tr>
<tr><td>Joint presentations (e.g. industry fairs)</td></tr>
<tr><td>Joint communications</td></tr>
<tr><td>Strategy/planning regarding customers</td></tr>
<tr><td>Strategy/planning regarding suppliers</td></tr>
<tr><td>Third party contract novation</td></tr>
<tr><td>Personnel Issues:
Secondments
Retention Strategies</td></tr>
<tr><td>IT Planning/Database Migration</td></tr>
<tr><td>Other</td><td></td><td></td></tr>
</table>

UNITED STATES

Logan Breed
(Hogan Lovells)

Part 1: Merger Control and the "Standstill Obligation"

1. **Please identify the relevant merger control legislation in your jurisdiction. Please provide a link to the relevant legislation (if possible, in English) and also indicate:**
   - **whether the merger control system is mandatory or voluntary,**
   - **the relevant authority, and**
   - **the duration of the review period.**

If the threshold requirements for filing are met and no exemption is available, filing with the US antitrust agencies (i.e. the Department of Justice Antitrust Division (**Antitrust Division** or **DOJ**) and the Federal Trade Commission (**FTC**)) under the Hart-Scott-Rodino (**HSR**) Act is mandatory. While there is no scheme for voluntary filings, parties to non-reportable transactions can bring their transaction to the attention of the agencies.

Upon filing, there is a 30-day waiting period (or 15-day waiting period in the case of a cash tender offer or a transfer in bankruptcy covered by 11 US section 363(b)). Parties can request early termination, which the agencies may grant at their discretion. The agencies may also issue a request for additional information (also known as a second request), which extends the waiting period to the 30th day (or 10th day in the event of a cash tender offer or a transfer in bankruptcy covered by 11 US section 363(b)) after the date at which the parties are in "substantial compliance" with the second request.

2. **Does the merger control system in your jurisdiction impose a "*standstill obligation*" – meaning, that the transaction cannot be implemented prior to completing the merger control process? (Please cite the relevant legislation.) Please also indicate the *legal scope* of the standstill obligation according to the relevant legislation (e.g. the parties to the transaction cannot effect a change of control, cannot take steps towards implementation, etc.).**

If a filing is necessary under the HSR Act, the proposed transaction cannot be consummated until all filings are completed and the applicable waiting periods have expired.[1] During this time, the parties cannot affect a change of control by taking steps to transfer beneficial ownership and must continue to operate independently in the ordinary course of business. In addition, the parties must take precautions to avoid "unreasonable" sharing of competitively sensitive

1 15 USC §18a.

information as part of the pre-merger negotiation, due-diligence, and integration processes.

3. **Have the relevant authorities in your jurisdiction issued internal or external guidelines concerning the scope of the standstill obligation, and/or their authority to enforce it? Please provide a copy/link of such guidance, if possible in English.**

The FTC recently posted a blog post in which it described pitfalls companies should avoid during the pre-merger review process.[2]

4. **Are there any exceptions to the standstill obligation – for example, through derogation or "carve out"? Please describe the circumstances in which this is possible. Please also describe the relevant process, e.g. do parties need to apply to the authority for a derogation from the standstill obligation? If so, how long is the approval process? If there are specific cases addressing these issues, please identify them.**

No. The Act does not permit parties to carve out portions of the transaction for closing prior to expiration or early termination of the waiting period.

5. **Does a public bid exception exist in your jurisdiction? (For example, under the EU Merger Regulation it is possible to acquire shares as part of a public bid, provided that the shares are not exercised until the acquisition is cleared by the Commission.) If such an exception exists in your jurisdiction, please describe how it is applied.**

The HSR rules do contain provisions that shorten the waiting period applicable to tender offers relative to the ordinary 30-day waiting period. As noted in Question 1, there is a 15-day waiting period in the case of a cash tender offer or a transfer in bankruptcy covered by 11 US section 363(b). If a second request is issued, the waiting period is extended to the 10th day after the parties have substantially complied with the request. All other aspects of the HSR Act are equally applicable to public and non-public transactions.

6. **What powers does the relevant authority have to investigate and enforce violations of the standstill obligation? Are dawn raids possible? What timing applies to investigation/enforcement proceedings?**

The Antitrust Division enforces the Sherman Act, 15 USC §§ 1–2, while the FTC is an independent administrative agency and has exclusive responsibility for enforcing the FTC Act, 15 USC §§ 41–58, and joint authority (with the Antitrust Division) over enforcement of the Clayton Act, 15 USC §§ 12–27. Although both agencies have jurisdiction to enforce the antitrust laws, any given merger or acquisition will be examined by only one of the two bodies. Which agency will concern itself with any particular transaction is decided by informal discussions between the two agencies and can often be predicted (but not with certainty) on the basis of the agency's relative familiarity with the industry or companies involved.

---

[2] Holly Vedova, Keitha Clopper and Clarke Edwards, "Avoiding antitrust pitfalls during pre-merger negotiations and due diligence" (*FTC* 20 March 2018) <https://www.ftc.gov/news-events/blogs/competition-matters/2018/03/avoiding-antitrust-pitfalls-during-pre-merger>.

The Antitrust Division and the FTC have the power to subpoena documents and information in a merger investigation. In addition, the agencies have the authority to seek an injunction in US federal court prohibiting completion of a proposed transaction.

In addition, if a transaction has been completed in violation of the HSR Act and is believed to violate the antitrust laws, the agencies may seek to unwind the transaction through an action in US federal district court. This would be more likely where the agency believes the acquisition also violated the substantive merger laws.

7. **What are the possible penalties for violating the standstill obligation? Are there criminal sanctions, including on individuals? Have these been applied in practice? Is there a difference in enforcement between transactions involving domestic companies and "foreign-to-foreign" transactions? Does the authority have the power to unwind transactions implemented in breach of the standstill obligation? If so, has the authority made use of that power in practice? If yes, please provide examples.**

Failure to comply with the HSR requirements can result in a fine of up to US$16,000 per day and the agencies may seek to unwind the transaction.

A transaction subject to the HSR Act may not close prior to the expiry or early termination of the applicable waiting period or periods. Failure to comply can result in a fine of up to US$42,530 per day (as adjusted) and the agencies may seek to unwind a transaction that has been consummated in violation of the HSR Act. The agencies can impose fines for failure to file and observe the waiting period.

There are several recent examples arising from a failure to file under the HSR Act. For instance, in August 2015, the FTC filed a complaint against Third Point LLC and three affiliated hedge funds (collectively, **Third Point**) relating to their failure to make an HSR filing and observe the waiting period when acquiring Yahoo! Inc (**Yahoo**) shares in 2011. The complaint alleged that the investment-only exemption was inapplicable because Third Point took certain actions inconsistent with passivity, such as contacting potential Yahoo board members and making statements about proposing directors for Yahoo. Third Point settled with the FTC and the FTC did not seek civil penalties because the violation was inadvertent and it was Third Point's first HSR violation.

In another case dealing with the investor-only exemption, in September 2015 Leucadia National Corporation (**Leucadia**) settled a complaint brought by the FTC. In that case, the FTC argued the investment-only exemption did not apply when, as a result of a transaction, Leucadia's ownership interest in Knight Capital Group, Inc converted into shares of a new entity (KCG Holdings) worth approximately US$173 million. The FTC argued that Leucadia should have made an HSR filing and observed the waiting period, because the investment-only exemption does not apply when an institutional investor acquires voting securities of the same type as any entity included within the acquiring person, and in this instance, both the acquiring and acquired persons were broker-dealers. This was Leucadia's second HSR violation, and it agreed to pay civil penalties of US$240,000.

In October 2015, Len Blavatnik, an investor, agreed to pay civil penalties of US$656,000, settling a complaint brought by the FTC for his failure to make an HSR filing relating to his August 2014 acquisition of TangoMe shares worth approximately US$228 million. Blavatnik previously violated the HSR Act in 2010, and did not consult HSR counsel prior to acquiring TangoMe's shares.

Merging parties may also be fined for "gun-jumping" – in other words, taking steps that have the effect of transferring beneficial ownership of the target business prior to the expiry or early termination of the applicable waiting period or periods.

In the most recent example of such an enforcement action, in November 2014, a US federal court ordered Flakeboard America Limited and SierraPine, both makers of MDF particleboard, to pay to the Antitrust Division fines of almost US$5 million for pre-closing actions that allegedly violated HSR gun-jumping and Sherman Act laws under a settlement agreement.

Previously, the Antitrust Division, in January 2010, fined Smithfield Foods and Premium Standard Farms for an alleged gun-jumping violation where Smithfield entered into a merger agreement with Premium Standard and reserved for itself the right to review certain contracts of Premium Standard. The Antitrust Division claimed that the parties violated the HSR Act when Premium Standard submitted three large, multi-year contracts to Smithfield for approval, alleging that this action was sufficient to show that the acquirer had taken "operational control" of the target prior to the expiry of the HSR Act waiting period. The parties agreed to pay a US$900,000 fine.

Unless an exemption applies, sanctions are applied in cases involving closing before clearance in foreign-to-foreign mergers in the same manner as the sanctions are applied to domestic transactions. For example, in 1997, Mahle GmbH (**Mahle**), a German piston manufacturer, and Metal Leve SA (**Metal Leve**), a Brazilian competitor, were each fined US$2.8 million for failure to file and observe the HSR waiting period prior to closing an acquisition by Mahle of 50.1% of Metal Leve. Both companies manufactured diesel engine parts through US subsidiaries.

There are no special remedy rules or practices applicable to foreign-to-foreign mergers. If the transaction gives rise to competitive issues in the United States, those issues must be resolved before the transaction can proceed.

8. How does the relevant authority typically learn of potential violations of the standstill obligation? Does the authority actively monitor the trade press?

The antitrust agencies have jurisdiction to investigate and challenge transactions that fall below the HSR Act notification thresholds, even after they are consummated. They have challenged many such transactions, in industries including pharmaceuticals, medical diagnostics, medical devices, chemical additives (oxidates), educational marketing databases, voting machines, software and food processing.

The agencies may learn of violations in the course of conducting its investigation of a reportable transaction. Violations may be discovered by the agency based on the information it has collected from the transacting parties or upon parties voluntarily notifying the agencies of potential gun-jumping issues. For example, in 2006 Flarion Technologies and Qualcomm Inc agreed to pay a $1.8 million penalty to the DOJ for gun-jumping violations. DOJ agreed to reduce the penalty from the statutory maximum because both companies voluntarily reported the "gun-jumping" to the DOJ and took measures to change their contract.

The antitrust agencies may also learn about potential violations through other means. The agencies are comprised of divisions that specialize in different industries. These divisions have developed numerous contacts with the industries in which they review transactions and actively monitor the trade press in their respective areas. The agencies may also learn about potential violations or changes in control from affected stakeholders and market participants themselves.

9. Please describe the relevant authority's enforcement of the standstill obligation. If there have been cases, please describe the specific conduct that was found to violate the standstill provision and the criteria applied by the relevant authority or court. Has the relevant authority considered the market impact of the conduct? (Please refer to the Annex.)

See Annex and the response to Question 7 above.

10. In cases involving alleged violations of the standstill obligation under the relevant merger control laws, has the relevant authority (or court) *also* considered the substantive antitrust laws? (Please refer to the Annex.)

Yes, US agencies may also consider the substantive antitrust laws while investigating an alleged violation of the standstill obligation. The *Qualcomm/Flarion* transaction described above is one example.

11. Is private enforcement of the standstill obligation possible?

Mergers and acquisitions can, under some circumstances, be challenged by private parties and by state attorneys general, but we are not aware of a case in which a private plaintiff has successfully brought an action for a violation of the standstill obligation.

12. Please describe the private law risks/consequences (i.e. contractual/validity consequences) for transactions that are subject to notification, but which are completed without notification/approval. Please identify any relevant cases and describe them.

The risk of a challenge by private parties has been reduced somewhat by court decisions requiring that such challengers demonstrate a threat that the private party challenger will be injured by the anticompetitive aspects of the transaction (rather than, for example, by the new firm's enhanced effectiveness as a competitor). In situations where a private party has standing to challenge a transaction, that party can seek the same remedies (including divestiture) that are available to the government, although a private party may be subject to certain equitable defenses (such as laches and "unclean hands"), which might protect a consummated transaction from attack.

13. Please describe policy and enforcement trends in your jurisdiction.

The most recent significant amendments to the HSR Rules were in 2005 when the FTC amended the rules regarding the application of the HSR Act to non-corporate entities (partnerships, LLCs etc.). Dollar thresholds in the HSR Act and the Rules are adjusted annually to reflect changes in the GNP. In July 2011, the FTC released significant amendments to the notification form, streamlining several items. The FTC more recently finalized some additional changes to the

HSR Rules, the most significant of which would apply to licensing transactions in the pharmaceutical industry.[3]

In 2013, the FTC formally adopted a change to its pre-merger rules which essentially codified the existing informal practice of withdrawing and refiling HSR notifications. The purpose of a "pull and refile" is to effectively restart the initial 30-calendar-day waiting period and allow the agencies additional time to complete a review of a transaction without being forced to issue a second request in order to obtain additional time. The new rule specifies that an acquirer can withdraw and refile a notification within the second business day of withdrawal without paying a new filing fee. While an acquirer can withdraw and refile multiple times, the proposals make clear that an acquirer can refile without paying a new fee only once.

In June 2016, the FTC announced an increase in the maximum civil penalties it may impose for violations of the HSR Act. The maximum civil penalty for HSR violations increased from a daily fine of US$16,000, to a much larger US$40,000 per day, which was most recently adjusted to US$42,530 in February 2019. These higher maximum civil fines apply to any penalties assessed after 1 August 2016, and to violations that predate the effective date. The agencies annually adjust for inflation their maximum civil penalty threshold every January.

As of 2016, rule changes allow for HSR filings to be submitted on DVD. The notification form and instructions were also updated in September 2016.

With regard to gun-jumping, in January 2014, the DOJ filed a complaint and settlement agreement against Flakeboard America Ltd and SierraPine alleging that after executing an asset-purchase agreement, under which Flakeboard proposed to acquire SierraPine's mills in Oregon and California, during the HSR waiting period, SierraPine closed one of its Oregon mills that competed with Flakeboard's mill. When the DOJ threatened to block the deal, the parties abandoned the transaction.

The DOJ alleged that SierraPine had no plans to close the mill prior to entering into the asset-purchase agreement with Flakeboard, but that days after announcing the transaction, a labor issue arose causing SierraPine to conclude that it would need to announce the closure of the mill sooner than it had originally planned or risk violating a closing condition under the agreement. The parties both understood that Flakeboard's refusal to waive the closing condition would cause SierraPine to close the mill prior to HSR clearance and regardless of whether the transaction ultimately closed. The parties worked together concerning the content and timing of the announcement of the mill's closure. They also worked together (including sharing competitively sensitive customer information) to transition the mill's customers to Flakeboard's competing mill.

The DOJ's complaint charged the parties with violations of the Sherman and HSR Acts, alleging their conduct "constituted an agreement between competitors to reduce output and allocate customers", a per se violation of section 1. Flakeboard

---

3 Refer to the FTC's website, <www.ftc.gov/enforcement/premerger-notification-program>, to confirm the currently applicable thresholds and for notice of any potential changes to rules.

agreed to disgorge the profits that it earned as a result and during the six months leading up to the settlement agreement – specifically $1.15 million. The DOJ said disgorgement was necessary because it would be impractical to order the closed mill to re-open in order to restore competition.

Further, the DOJ charged that the parties' coordination of the closing of Sierra-Pine's Oregon mill and joint actions to transition its customers to the Flakeboard mill during the HSR waiting period amounted to a violation of the HSR Act.

On 18 January 2017, the DOJ obtained a US$600,000 civil penalty from Duke Energy, a seller of wholesale electricity, for gun-jumping violations relating to Duke's acquisition of Osprey, an electricity generating plant in Florida. Duke agreed to purchase Osprey in August 2014. At the same time, the parties entered into a tolling agreement whereby Duke assumed control of operational responsibilities at Osprey and also retained any profit (or loss) from the operation of the plant. While similar tolling arrangements standing alone are not uncommon in the electric power generation industry, and the DOJ did not allege that the tolling agreement standing alone was a violation of the antitrust laws, the DOJ did allege that the use of the tolling agreement in conjunction with the purchase agreement was a gun-jumping violation, because it transferred beneficial control prior to HSR clearance. The DOJ obtained penalties from Duke for the 150-day period that the parties were non-compliant: from the effective time of the tolling agreement in October 2014 to the date that Duke received early termination of the HSR waiting period for the acquisition in February 2015.

Most recently, on 10 June 2019, DOJ announced a complaint and a settlement in connection with Canon Inc's acquisition of Toshiba Medical Systems Corp (**TSMC**), a subsidiary of Toshiba. Toshiba and Canon arranged for the creation of a special purpose company – MS Holding Corp (**MS Holding**) – and Toshiba created new classes of voting shares for TMSC and a single non-voting share with rights custom-made for Canon, and options convertible into ordinary shares. MS Holding then acquired the newly issued voting shares of TMSC for a nominal amount well below the HSR size of transaction threshold. Canon acquired both the non-voting shares and the convertible options – the acquisition of which is generally non-reportable under the HSR Act – for US$6.1 billion (the value of TMSC). Canon issued a press release regarding the share acquisition and acknowledging that the acquisition was intended "to make TMSC a Canon subsidiary."

The HSR Act's implementing regulations specifically prohibit the use of any "transaction(s) or other device(s) entered into or employed for the purpose of avoiding the obligation to comply with the requirements of the [HSR] act" (16 Code of Federal Regulations § 801.90). These are known as "devices for avoidance". When the agencies conclude that a transaction structure has been used as a device for avoidance, they determine whether the parties have an HSR reporting obligation by evaluating the substance of the transaction. In this case, the DOJ alleged that there was no independent business reason for the transaction structure because the transaction was intended to transfer complete ownership and control of TMSC from Toshiba to Canon. Therefore, Canon's acquisition of TMSC was subject to the HSR Act.

The final judgment imposed a US$5 million civil penalty, split evenly between Canon and Toshiba. Often, the DOJ and FTC impose penalties on the acquiring person only, but given the parties' intent to circumvent the HSR notification rules, the agencies instead sought penalties against both companies for most of the full amount that could have been levied – approximately US$6.4 million – and required each to institute an HSR Act compliance program, which must include, among other things, at least two hours of HSR training for all relevant employees.

Part 2: Substantive Antitrust Law in an M&A Context

1. **Please identify the relevant *substantive antitrust laws* in your jurisdiction that can potentially apply in an M&A context (e.g. for the EU, this would include Article 101 of the Treaty on the Functioning of the European Union). Please provide a link to the relevant legislation (if possible, in English).**

   Section 7 of the Clayton Act prohibits acquisitions of assets or stock where "the effect of such acquisition may be substantially to lessen competition, or to tend to create a monopoly". Transactions may also be challenged under section 1 or 2 of the Sherman Act as unreasonable restraints of trade or as attempts at monopolization. The FTC also has the authority under section 5 of the FTC Act to challenge a transaction as an "unfair method of competition". See also Part 1 for more information about the application of the HSR Act and its regulations.

2. **Do any guidelines exist in your jurisdiction concerning the application of the substantive antitrust laws in an M&A context – whether internal to the relevant authority, or external, formal or informal (e.g. speeches)? If so, please provide a copy/link to such guidance.**

   The DOJ and FTC recently released horizontal merger guidelines in 2010.[4] The non-horizontal merger guidelines were last released in 1984.[5] Recent speeches from the former Deputy Assistant Attorney General for Litigation of the DOJ Antitrust Division[6] and the current Director of the FTC's Bureau of Competition also provide guidance on how the agencies review vertical transactions.[7]

3. **As a general matter (not limited to M&A), how are the substantive antitrust laws enforced with respect to the exchange of competitively sensitive information between competing firms? Please also indicate the relevance of anti-competitive effects or intent in such enforcement.**

---

4 See DOJ and FTC, *Horizontal Merger Guidelines* (2010), available at <https://www.justice.gov/atr/horizontal-merger-guidelines-0>.

5 See DOJ and FTC, *Non-Horizontal Merger Guidelines* (1984), available at <https://www.justice.gov/atr/non-horizontal-merger-guidelines>.

6 See Jon Sallet, "The Interesting Case of the Vertical Merger" (ABA Fall Forum, 17 November 2016), available at <https://www.justice.gov/opa/speech/file/938236/download>.

7 See D Bruce Hoffman, "Vertical Merger Enforcement at the FTC," (Credit Suisse 2018 Washington Perspectives Conference, 10 January 2018), available at <https://www.ftc.gov/system/files/documents/public_statements/1304213/hoffman_vertical_merger_speech_final.pdf>.

See Part 1 and Annex.

4. Have there been any cases in your jurisdiction in which the substantive antitrust laws were enforced in an M&A context? Please describe/explain and cite any such cases. (See also Annex.)

See Annex.

5. Are the substantive antitrust laws more likely to apply at specific stages of the transaction – i.e. at an early stage, or prior to closing (or does it not make a difference)? Do companies face ongoing risk following the consummation (or failure) of their transaction for conduct that allegedly occurred pre-closing (pre-failure)?

The US antitrust laws apply throughout all stages of the transaction. See Part 1 and Annex. There is no statute of limitations, so companies do face ongoing risk following the consummation (or failure) of their transaction for conduct that allegedly occurred pre-closing (pre-failure).

6. Please explain how the relevant authority enforces (or could enforce) the substantive antitrust laws in an M&A context. How would the investigation occur, and what timing constraints would apply?

See Part 1 and Annex.

7. Is private enforcement of the substantive antitrust laws possible in an M&A context, and has it occurred?

Private parties may seek to challenge a merger or acquisition under sections 1 and 2 of the Sherman Act and section 7 of the Clayton Act. While less common than agency enforcement, such challenges have been brought. A recent example is *Steves & Sons Inc v Jeld-Wen Inc*,[8] in which the plaintiff alleges that the defendant's acquisition of a company that manufactures interior molded doorskins violated section 7 of the Clayton Act.

8. Could behavior subject to the substantive antitrust laws also be caught under the merger control rules/standstill obligation? (Please also refer to the Annex.)

See Part 1 and Annex.

9. Please describe the penalties for infringing the substantive antitrust laws. Please indicate whether these include criminal penalties, including individual criminal penalties. As a practical matter, how have these been applied in the context of an M&A transaction?

The agencies and private plaintiffs may sue under US antitrust laws for injunctive relief and may recover treble damages. The Sherman Act also allows the DOJ to pursue criminal sanctions. In addition, the FTC has standalone remedial authority to seek civil fines and injunctive relief for violations of section 5 of the FTC act. See also Part 1 and Annex.

10. Please describe policy and enforcement trends in your jurisdiction.

See Part 1 and Annex.

---

8 F Supp 3d 614 (ED Va 2018).

Matthew P Hendrickson, Rita Sinkfield Belin, Brian C Mohr, "The US FTC announces a consent settlement based on an application of the investment-only exemption to the Hart-Scott-Rodino Act's premerger notification requirements (Third Point)" 24 August 2015, e-Competitions Bulletin August 2015, Art. N° 75799

Andre P Barlow, "The US DOJ obtains $5 millions settlement for illegal pre-closing conducts (Flakeboard America/SierraPine)" 7 November 2014, e-Competitions Bulletin November 2014, Art. N° 70353

Clifford H Aronson, Matthew P Hendrickson, Kenneth B Schwartz, "The DOJ condemns pre-merger coordination requiring target company to sell factory (Flakeboard America/SierraPine)" 7 November 2014, e-Competitions Bulletin November 2014, Art. N° 70982

Ian G John, "The US DOJ requires disgorgement for gun-jumping violations in abandoned transaction (Flakeboard America/SierraPine)" 7 November 2014, e-Competitions Bulletin November 2014, Art. N° 73789

Jeffrey May, "The US DOJ reaches $5 millions settlement with companies after allegations of premerger coordination (Flakeboard America/SierraPine)" 7 November 2014, e-Competitions Bulletin November 2014, Art. N° 70008

Carl Sanchez, "The US DOJ imposes penalties for premerger "Gun Jumping" (Smithfield Foods/Premium Standard Farms)" 21 January 2010, e-Competitions Bulletin January 2010, Art. N° 74784

Steven C Sunshine, Ian G John, Neal R Stoll, "The US DoJ settles Hart-Scott-Rodino gun jumping charges stemming from buyer's pre-approval of target's purchasing contracts (Smithfield Foods/Premium Farms)" 21 January 2010, e-Competitions Bulletin January 2010, Art. N° 45539

J Bruce McDonald, Kathryn M Fenton, Bevin MB Newman, "The US DOJ imposes civil penalties for premerger 'Gun Jumping' (Smithfield Foods, Premium Standard Farms)" 21 January 2010, e-Competitions Bulletin January 2010, Art. N° 33748

Alec Y Chang, Neal R Stoll, "The US DoJ settles gun-jumping charges against communication technology companies (Qualcomm/Flarion)" 13 April 2006, e-Competitions Bulletin April 2006, Art. N° 45598

Jonathan Cheng, Vadim M Brusser, Alexis Brown-Reilly, "The US Department of Justice settles HSR Act violation case with record fine (ValueAct)" 12 July 2016, e-Competitions Bulletin July 2016, Art. N° 80223

Kelly Karapetyan, Beau W Buffier, "The US Department of Justice fines an activist investor for a record $11 million for violations of the HSR Act (ValueAct)" 12 July 2016, e-Competitions Bulletin July 2016, Art. N° 80289

Clifford H Aronson, Matthew P Hendrickson, Kenneth B Schwartz, "The US Department of Justice files a complaint against an activist investor before the US District Court for the Northern District of California for violations of the

Hart-Scott-Rodino Act's (ValueAct)" 4 April 2016, e-Competitions Bulletin April 2016, Art. N° 78989

Ian G John, Neal R Stoll, Sharis A Pozen, Karen Hoffman Lent, "The US FTC settles illegal information exchange allegations with hair restoration company (Bosley)" 8 April 2013, e-Competitions Bulletin April 2013, Art. N° 51648

James B Kobak Jr, Renee C Redman, "The US FTC collects significant penalties for violations of the pre-merger notification rules after clearing a merger in the market for electronic integratable drug information databases (Hearst/Medi-Span)" 15 October 2001, e-Competitions Bulletin October 2001, Art. N° 53265

Alec Y Chang, Neal R Stoll, "The US DoJ settles gun-jumping charges against communication technology companies (Qualcomm/Flarion)" 13 April 2006, e-Competitions Bulletin April 2006, Art. N° 45598

Jonathan Cheng, Vadim M Brusser, Alexis Brown-Reilly, "The US Department of Justice settles HSR Act violation case with record fine (ValueAct)" 12 July 2016, e-Competitions Bulletin July 2016, Art. N° 80223

Kelly Karapetyan, Beau W Buffier, "The US Department of Justice fines an activist investor for a record $11 million for violations of the HSR Act (ValueAct)" 12 July 2016, e-Competitions Bulletin July 2016, Art. N° 80289

Clifford H Aronson, Matthew P Hendrickson, Kenneth B Schwartz, "The US Department of Justice files a complaint against an activist investor before the US District Court for the Northern District of California for violations of the Hart-Scott-Rodino Act's (ValueAct)" 4 April 2016, e-Competitions Bulletin April 2016, Art. N° 78989

Ian G John, Neal R Stoll, Sharis A Pozen, Karen Hoffman Lent, "The US FTC settles illegal information exchange allegations with hair restoration company (Bosley)" 8 April 2013, e-Competitions Bulletin April 2013, Art. N° 51648

James B Kobak Jr, Renee C Redman, "The US FTC collects significant penalties for violations of the pre-merger notification rules after clearing a merger in the market for electronic integratable drug information databases (Hearst/Medi-Span)" 15 October 2001, e-Competitions Bulletin October 2001, Art. N° 53265

ANNEX

Table 1: Actual Enforcement of Specific Conduct under the Relevant Merger Control Rules and Substantive Antitrust Laws

Please identify whether the following type of conduct has been subject to investigation/enforcement in your jurisdiction, under the merger control laws or substantive antitrust laws. Please cite any such case(s) and provide a brief description in the table below.

Specific Conduct	Actual Enforcement under Merger Control Laws	Actual Enforcement under Substantive Antitrust Laws
Pre-signing due diligence	***US v Duke Energy and Calpine* (2014):** Prior to its HSR notification, the parties agreed to a "tolling agreement" which went into effect immediately upon signing and allegedly gave Duke beneficial ownership the Osprey power plant.	No
Post-signing/pre-approval due diligence	***US v Atlantic Richfield and Union Carbide* (1991)** – The DOJ alleged that provisions in the purchase agreement transferred beneficial ownership over assets of Union Carbide's subsidiary to that of Atlantic Richfield and that the parties failed to make HSR filings until the acquisition had been completed. ***US v Atlantic Richfield and UF Genetics* (1992)** – The DOJ alleged that UF Genetics acquired beneficial ownership of Richfield's ARCO Seed Company without filing an HSR form or observing the HSR waiting period.	No

Specific Conduct	Actual Enforcement under Merger Control Laws	Actual Enforcement under Substantive Antitrust Laws
Post-signing/pre-approval due diligence	***US v ValueAct* (2016)** – The DOJ alleged that ValueAct violated the HSR Act by purchasing voting shares in Baker Hughes and Halliburton while the proposed merger was under review by the DOJ; the DOJ also alleged that ValueAct attempted to discuss business strategies and influence corporate decision-making of executives at Baker Hughes and Halliburton while the transaction was still being reviewed.	No
Post-approval/pre-closing due diligence	No	***FTC v Chicago Bridge & Iron Company* (CB&I) *and Pitt-Des Moines Inc* (2008)** – Although the HSR waiting period expired, the FTC issued a civil investigative demand to the parties prior to closing and subsequently sued CB&I to divest Pitt's Construction and Water Divisions. ***US v Parker-Hannifin and CLARCOR* (2018)** – Although the HSR waiting period expired, the DOJ issued a civil investigative demand to the parties prior to closing and subsequently sued ▶

Specific Conduct	Actual Enforcement under Merger Control Laws	Actual Enforcement under Substantive Antitrust Laws
		Parker to divest its acquisition of CLARCOR's aviation fuel filtration division.
Use of "clean teams"	***In re Insilco Corp* (1998)** – The FTC alleged that Insilco, the buyer, violated s 5 of the FTC Act when it received competitively sensitive information from Helmut, including customer-specific price information, current and future pricing plans, competitive strategies and price formulas. ***In re Bosley and Aderans* (2013)** – The FTC alleged that the hair transplant services company repeatedly exchanged company-specific information about future product offerings, price floors, discounting practices and expansion plans. ***US v Flakeboard Am. Ltd and SierraPine* (2014)** – The DOJ alleged that SierraPine provided competitively sensitive information about customers to Flakeboard (including customers' names, types and purchase volumes).	No
Restrictions on the target in an M&A agreement, e.g. buyer approval required for: Investments above a certain level; New business above a certain level;	***United States v Computer Associates International, Inc* (2002)** – Merger agreement required buyer pre-approval for seller to offer customers discounts greater than 20% off list price.	No

Specific Conduct	Actual Enforcement under Merger Control Laws	Actual Enforcement under Substantive Antitrust Laws
Other obligations to consult/obtain approval from the buyer before closing.	***United States v Qualcomm and Flarion* (2006)** – The DOJ alleged Qualcomm exercised operational control over Flarion Technologies Inc by requiring the company to obtain consent on customer proposals, price discounts and quotations, licensing strategies and personnel decisions. ***United States v Smithfield Foods and Premium Standard Farms* (2010) –** The DOJ alleged Premium submitted each of its hog purchase agreements for approval by Smithfield irrespective of the contract's materiality while the HSR waiting period was still pending. ***United States v Duke Energy and Calpine Corporation* (2017) –** The parties entered into a tolling agreement under which Duke could exercise control over Calpine's Osprey facility, including its electricity output.	
Joint marketing	No	No
Joint presentations (e.g. industry fairs)	No	No
Joint communications	***In re Commonwealth Land Title Insurance Co* (1998)** – The FTC alleged that the companies prematurely relocated its operations and consolidated them with those of the target; in addition, the FTC alleged that the companies joined operations and specified that customers of both entities would receive the same prices, terms and conditions.	No

Specific Conduct	Actual Enforcement under Merger Control Laws	Actual Enforcement under Substantive Antitrust Laws
Strategy/planning regarding customers	***In re Torrington and Universal Bearings* (1991)** – Torrington (the buyer) alleged attempted to shift one of Universal's customers to itself during the HSR waiting period. ***United States v Titan Wheel International, Inc* (1996)** – Titan Wheel entered into an agreement to purchase a tire plant from Pirelli under which it was alleged to have taken beneficial control of Pirelli's customer and supplier lists. ***US v Gemstar-TV Guide International, Inc and TV Guide, Inc* (2003)** – The DOJ alleged that Gemstar and TV Guide agreed to stop competing for customers and jointly managed their interactive program guide business prior to the expiration of the HSR waiting period. ***US v Flakeboard Am Ltd and SierraPine* (2014)** – The DOJ alleged that the parties agreed on closing a particle mill during the HSR waiting period and coordinated in transferring SierraPine's customers to Flakeboard upon closure.	No
Strategy/planning regarding suppliers	***United States v Titan Wheel International, Inc* (1996)** – Titan Wheel entered into an agreement to purchase a tire plant from Pirelli under which it was alleged to have taken beneficial control of Pirelli's customer and supplier lists.	No

Specific Conduct	Actual Enforcement under Merger Control Laws	Actual Enforcement under Substantive Antitrust Laws
Third party contract novation	No	No
Personnel Issues: Secondments Retention Strategies	***United States v Input/Output, Inc and Laitram* (1999)** – Input/Output allegedly began to integrate its operations and personnel with those of Laitram's wholly-owned subsidiary DigiCOURSE prior to submitting HSR filings. ***United States v Titan Wheel International, Inc* (1996)** – Titan assumed critical management functions, including efforts to negotiate a key collective bargaining agreement for Pirelli's facility.	No
IT Planning/Database Migration	No	No
Other Failure to file and incomplete filings		***US v Automatic Data Processing* (1996) –** The DOJ obtained a US$2.97 million civil penalty for filing an incomplete premerger notification and required the company to divest the acquired assets. ***US v Sara Lee Corporation* (1996)** – The DOJ obtained a US$3.1 million civil penalty for a failure to file and the divesture of several bands of shoe care products.

Specific Conduct	Actual Enforcement under Merger Control Laws	Actual Enforcement under Substantive Antitrust Laws
		US v Mahle **(1997)** – The DOJ obtained the maximum civil penalty of US $5.6 million for the parties' intentional failure to file and required the divestiture of the acquired company's US piston business. ***US v Hearst Trust*** **(2001)** – The DOJ obtained a US$4 million civil penalty for filing an incomplete premerger notification and required the company to divest the acquired business.

Table 2: Hypothetical Enforcement of Specific Conduct under the Relevant Merger Control Rules and Substantive Antitrust Laws

For any conduct that is *not* the subject of actual enforcement (Table 1), please indicate in the Table below whether the conduct identified *could potentially* be enforced under the merger control laws and/or substantive antitrust laws.

Specific Conduct	Hypothetical Enforcement under Merger Control Laws	Hypothetical Enforcement under Substantive Antitrust Laws
Pre-signing due diligence		Yes
Post-signing/pre-approval due diligence		Yes
Post-approval/pre-closing due diligence		Yes
Use of "clean teams"		Yes

Specific Conduct	Hypothetical Enforcement under Merger Control Laws	Hypothetical Enforcement under Substantive Antitrust Laws
Restrictions on the target in an M&A agreement, e.g. buyer approval required for: Investments above a certain level; New business above a certain level; Other obligations to consult/obtain approval from the buyer before closing.		Yes
Joint marketing	Joint marketing efforts outside the ordinary course of business can violate gun-jumping rules where such activities allow the combining firms to coordinate business activities or represent to customers and/or suppliers that they are operating as a single entity.	Yes
Joint presentations (e.g. industry fairs)	Companies may continue to participate in trade associations and other industry gathering as they would in ordinary course, however, merging companies may not use such opportunities to coordinate business activities prior to closing.	No
Joint communications		No
Strategy/planning regarding customers		Yes
Strategy/planning regarding suppliers		Yes

Specific Conduct	Hypothetical Enforcement under Merger Control Laws	Hypothetical Enforcement under Substantive Antitrust Laws
Third party contract novation	While the parties may secure materiality commitments with respect to future activities while the transaction is pending, parties must continue to exercise independent control over their business operations as they would in ordinary course.	No
Personnel Issues: Secondments Retention Strategies		Yes
IT Planning/Database Migration	Assuming control over the IT operations or databases of the target prior to closing and during the notification period can fall foul of gun-jumping rules, particularly if such activities either (a) enable the buyer to remove the target as a competitor or customer/supplier, or (b) enable the buyer to access competitively sensitive information of the target.	No
Other		

BIOGRAPHIES

Sakshi Agarwal

Sakshi is a Senior Associate in the competition law practice of Trilegal based in Mumbai, India. She represents clients in contentious competition law matters and merger control notifications. She regularly represents clients across all fora, i.e., the CCI, DG, NCLAT, High Courts and the Hon'ble Supreme Court of India. She has acted for companies in complex antitrust litigation matters and assists Indian and multinational companies in relation to their compliance programs in India. She graduated from the West Bengal, National University of Juridical Sciences, Kolkata. She can be reached at sakshi.agarwal@trilegal.com.

Inbal Rosenblum Brand

Inbal Rosenblum-Brand is an advocate at M. Firon & Co and part of the antitrust and regulatory affairs department. She advises on both civil and criminal antitrust cases. Her practice includes notifications of mergers, advising clients and providing legal opinions in respect of all aspects of competition and antitrust law. Inbal received her law degree (LL.B.), and B.A. (Magna Cum Laude) in business administration, from Interdisciplinary Center Herzliya (IDC) in 2016.

Logan Breed

Logan Breed is a partner in the Washington office of Hogan Lovells. He concentrates his practice on antitrust clearance of mergers and acquisitions, antitrust litigation, and non-merger antitrust investigations. He also counsels clients on a wide variety of issues, including joint ventures and other strategic alliances between competitors, antitrust compliance, pricing, distribution, and distributor and dealer relations and consumer protection matters. Logan represents clients in matters before the US Federal Trade Commission, the Antitrust Division of the US Department of Justice, and various State Attorneys General. Logan has extensive experience in a wide variety of industries, including computer software and hardware, e-commerce, telecommunications, media and entertainment, defense, healthcare, and energy.

Neil Campbell

Neil Campbell is the Co-Chair of McMillan's Competition and International Trade Groups. His competition law experience includes over 300 merger clearances under the Competition Act and/or the Investment Canada Act, as well as representing companies in dozens of cartel investigations and related class actions. He is the Global Contributing Editor of Cartel Regulation (Lexology Getting the Deal Through series) and received the Dealmaker of the Year Award from Global Competition Review for his work on several high profile merger cases in 2016. Neil is a past co-chair of the IBA Antitrust Committee and is currently the co-chair of its Merger Working Group.

David Cardwell

David Cardwell is Counsel in the Antitrust and Competition Practice of Baker Botts' Brussels office. His practice focuses on UK and EU competition law, including a particular concentration on EU and international merger control laws, and UK competition law (both mergers and behavioural). Mr. Cardwell has represented clients in significant mergers and acquisitions across many industry areas, including the technology, pharmaceutical, media, automotive and heavy industry sectors. He has counseled clients in merger reviews before both the European Commission and national competition authorities, including cases involving advice on media plurality, regulated water industries and defense-related mergers.

Anisha Chand

Anisha Chand is a Partner in the competition law practice group of Khaitan & Co. in the Mumbai office. Prior to joining Khaitan & Co, Anisha was with Cyril Amarchand Mangaldas for a few years. She holds a law degree from the Government Law College, Mumbai. Anisha has been involved in advising domestic and multi-national companies on a full range of competition matters, including cartel enforcement, abuse of dominance, merger control, leniency and competition audit/compliance in diverse sectors including pharmaceutical, cement, e-commerce, radio taxis, sports, telecom, automobiles, media and entertainment, financial services, agro-chemicals, etc. Many of such matters have been seminal and precedent-setting, contributing significantly to the competition law jurisprudence in India. She has consistently been recognized as leading expert in competition law in India in Who's Who Legal.

Cecil Saehoon Chung

Cecil Saehoon Chung is a senior foreign counsel at Yulchon. As Vice-Chair of the Antitrust Practice Group and Head of the International Antitrust Team, Cecil handles all aspects of antitrust, consumer protection and trade regulation as well as litigation and counseling matters covering diverse industries, with a particular emphasis on international antitrust. Cecil has practiced law for more than thirty years, primarily focusing on antitrust, trade regulation, consumer protection, and intellectual property. In his antitrust practice, Cecil has handled numerous criminal grand jury investigations, civil class action cases, regulatory merger and non-merger investigation/litigation matters, and consumer protection matters. He also has extensive experience in handling intellectual property issues, both straightforward patent infringement litigation and licensing matters and also in the context of the antitrust and IP interface.

Yves Comtois

Yves Comtois is Legal Consultant with the Antitrust and Competition Practice of Baker Botts' Brussels office. With more than 25 years of experience in antitrust matters, Mr. Comtois has advised clients in high profile cases across a broad range of industries in all areas of competition law, including mergers and acquisitions, abuse of dominance and cartels. He was recently involved in the in-depth investigation of the Halliburton/Baker Hughes merger. Prior to working with Baker Botts, Mr. Comtois was a Partner for several years in the competition law group of McCarthy Tétrault in Montreal. He started off his career by practising competition law for three years with an international law firm in Brussels. Mr. Comtois graduated from the law faculty of McGill University in 1990 and received a diploma of specialised studies from the College of Europe in Bruges in 1991. He co-authored the first French-language textbook on Canadian competition law with his former Montreal colleagues Madeleine Renaud and Yves Bériault.

Eytan Epstein

Eytan Epstein is a senior partner at M. Firon & Co. He is an esteemed practitioner and is recognized as one of the national and international leaders in competition matters. Eytan practices corporate, M&A, commercial and trade law, and specializes in antitrust law. He has extensive experience dealing with competition issues before the Israeli Restrictive Practices Authority, and represents Israeli and foreign clients engaged in finance, telecommunications, energy, insurance, pharmaceuticals, retail and other industries. Eytan is the co-author of the book Competition Law in Israel issued in English in 2016, and has published numerous articles on antitrust and competition issues in Israel.

Sandhya Foster

Sandhya Foster is an Associate in the competition regulatory and trade department of Herbert Smith Freehills South Africa LLP based in Johannesburg with experience in mergers and prohibited practices in South Africa and other African jurisdictions. Sandhya is an admitted attorney in South Africa. She holds a Business Science degree (honours in law) and LLB from the University of Cape Town as well as a Certificate in Competition Law from the University of Witwatersrand.

Marcos Pajolla Garrido

Associate of the Competition Law Practice Group at Pinheiro Neto Advogados. LL.B. from the São Paulo University (2007). Specialization degree in competition law from the Getúlio Vargas Foundation (2009). LL.M. in corporate and commercial law from the London School of Economics and Political Science (2015). Foreign associate at the competition law practice of Bredin Prat, Brussels (2016).

Gönenç Gürkaynak

Gönenç Gürkaynak is a founding partner of ELIG Gürkaynak Attorneys-at-Law, where he heads the competition law and regulatory department. He has unparalleled experience in Turkish competition law counseling issues with more than 20 years of competition law experience, starting with the establishment of the Turkish Competition Authority. Every year, Gönenç represents multinational companies and large domestic clients in more than 35 written and oral defences in investigations of the Turkish Competition Authority, about 15 antitrust appeal cases in the high administrative court, and over 85 merger clearances of the Turkish Competition Authority. He graduated from Ankara University, Faculty of Law in 1997 and received his LL.M. degree from Harvard Law School. He was called to the Istanbul Bar in 1998 and is qualified to practice in Istanbul, New York, Brussels and England and Wales (currently a non-practising Solicitor). He has published more than 150 articles in English and Turkish by various international and local publishers, and also holds teaching positions at undergraduate and graduate levels at two universities, and gives lectures in other universities in Turkey.

Andrea Hamilton

Andrea Hamilton is a partner at McDermott Will & Emery in Brussels. Drawing on experience from both sides of the Atlantic, Andrea focuses her practice on the EU and national aspects of merger control investigations as well as non-merger conduct investigations and antitrust litigation and the creation and implementation of antitrust compliance programs. She advises on and coordinates the antitrust aspects of complex, international transactions and global investigations and counsels clients on important strategic issues. Andrea's industry experience includes aerospace and defense, chemicals, pharmaceuticals, life sciences, financial services, consumer products and media and entertainment, among others. She was recognized by GCR as one of the 40 leading private practitioners in the world under the age of 40. Andrea has also been recognized by the Legal500 and was recently named by Who's Who Legal as one of the three most highly regarded partners in Europe in its Future Leaders category.

Michael Han

Michael Han is a partner at Fangda Partners in Beijing. He has twelve years' experience in advising clients on all aspects of Chinese competition law, covering a broad range of industry sectors including chemicals, consumer products and retail, energy and natural resources, financial institutions, healthcare, infrastructure and transport and private equity. Michael also worked as an official with MOFTEC (now the Ministry of Commerce, or MOFCOM). Michael is able to offer clients advice drawn from rich experience as both a regulator in China and as a practitioner. In addition to his understanding and knowledge of MOFCOM, Michael has extensive experience in dealing with the two anti-monopoly enforcement agencies that regulate the conduct rules under the Anti-Monopoly Law: the National Development & Reform Commission (NDRC) and the State Administration for Industry and Commerce (SAIC).

Etsuko Hara

Etsuko Hara is a partner at Anderson Mori & Tomotsune and an associate professor at the University of Tokyo Graduate Schools for Law and Politics. She has broad experience in the area of antitrust, including international cartel cases, multi-jurisdictional merger filings as well as distribution arrangements, franchising, and strategic alliances. She handles various inbound and outbound cross border transactions, especially in the form of direct investment, joint ventures, and distribution, license and franchise agreements.

Catriona Hatton

Catriona Hatton is the partner in charge of Baker Botts' Brussels office and co-chair of the firm's global antitrust and competition practice. With more than 25 years of experience practicing EU law in Brussels, Catriona advises on EU and national law aspects of international mergers and has represented clients in some of the largest most complex deals in the market. She has also represented clients in antitrust complaints to, and investigations by, the European Commission and numerous national competition authorities. Her practice includes advising on compliance with the competition rules in a wide range of commercial agreements, the conduct of antitrust audits and the design and implementation of compliance programs. Catriona has represented clients in such sectors as chemicals, oilfield services, pharmaceuticals, financial services, media and entertainment, transport, and energy. Catriona is co-chair of the International Bar Association's Merger Working Group, is recommended in Chambers Global and Europe, and has been named by Who's Who Legal as one of the Top 12 Global Elite Thought Leaders in Competition.

Kristin Heilborn

Kristin Heilborn is a Senior Associate in Roschier's EU & Competition practice, advising clients in a variety of competition law matters, including high-stakes cartel and dominance investigations, transactions and multi-jurisdictional merger filings as well as self-assessments, compliance and distribution.

Kristin's experience covers a wide range of industry sectors, such as energy, basic industry, insurance, media and retail.

Kristian Hugmark

Kristian Hugmark is Head of Roschier's EU & Competition practice in Sweden. Kristian practices all areas of competition law and state aid in Sweden and in the EU, across all industries. He is also experienced in regulatory matters, in particular related to the transport and telecom industries. Before joining Roschier in 2015, Kristian was based in Brussels for 13 years, working both for the European Commission and in private practice.

Niko Hukkinen

Niko Hukkinen is a Helsinki-based partner at Frontia Attorneys at Law specialized in EU & competition, green economy & energy and M&A. He has extensive experience especially in M&A-related competition law, dominance matters, horizontal and vertical cooperation between undertakings, state aid and public procurement. Niko regularly acts for industrial and private equity clients in complex merger control analyses and processes both before the EU institutions as well as domestic instances, including the coordination of multi-jurisdictional filings globally. Niko's experience also includes cases related to the abuse of dominant market position, self-assessment of distribution, cooperation and JV agreements as well as compliance policies in, for example, the energy, forestry, health care, pharmaceuticals, aviation, retail and food industries. In addition to the above, Niko has been involved in matters in the growing green economy and energy sector, such as related to electric cars, wind and wave power, waste management, chemicals and nuclear power.

Arshad (Paku) Khan

Arshad (Paku) Khan is Executive Director of Khaitan & Co's Competition/Antitrust team. He is a highly experienced competition lawyer with nearly 230 years of experience with key advisory roles in all aspects of Indian, EU, Irish, and US competition/antitrust law, including merger control, cartel, and abuse of dominance cases. He is a certified mediator with considerable competition law litigation experience and is a qualified solicitor/lawyer in multiple jurisdictions in Europe and the United States. Paku has played lead roles in high-profile merger, cartels, dominance, and state aid cases before the European Commission, the Irish Competition Authority, the Competition Commission of India, and other regulatory bodies and has considerable experience in senior positions in private practice, in-house, and government roles focusing on competition/antitrust, regulatory law, M&A, securities exchange practice, and technology law.

David Mamane

David Mamane is a Partner and head of Schellenberg Wittmer's Competition Group in Zurich. He advises in proceedings before the Swiss Competition Commission, is experienced in Swiss and European competition law and has broad experience in national and multi-jurisdictional merger control procedures, cartel and abuse of dominance investigations, dawn raids, internal investigations, compliance, and leniency procedures

Mazor Matzkevich

Mazor Matzkevich is a partner at M. Firon & Co., heading the competition, antitrust and regulatory affairs department, subsequent to its merger with Epstein and Co., where Ms. Matzkevich headed the antitrust practice since 2010. Ms. Matzkevich's practice focuses on all aspects of antitrust including class actions and criminal litigation and the evolving segments of the Concentration and the Food laws. Ms. Matzkevich has extensive experience in representing corporations vis-à-vis the Israeli Competition Authority, including through complicated mergers' review and global merger notifications. After her admission to the Israeli Bar, Ms. Matzkevich joined the Israeli Competition Authority in 1998, and led the Authority's criminal practice until 2002. In 2002 Mazor was admitted to the New York State Bar, and soon after joined the U.S. Federal Trade Commission's North East Regional Office as a staff attorney. During her six years tenure at the Federal Trade Commission, Ms. Matzkevich practiced both antitrust and was the lead counsel or co-counsel of merger and non-merger cases involving various industries, including high-tech, retail, pharmaceuticals, agro-chemistry, energy, hospitals, and food. Ms. Matzkevich has an LL.B and LL.M degrees from the Hebrew University.

Jean Meijer

Jean Meijer is a competition partner based in Herbert Smith Freehills' Johannesburg office with over 20 years of experience. She works with clients on all aspects of competition law, including merger control, cartel and other prohibited practice investigations, exemption applications and competition compliance. She has knowledge of the competition laws of many African countries and regularly assists clients with multi-jurisdictional African mergers.

Alastair Mordaunt

Alastair Mordaunt is a partner at Freshfields Bruckhaus Deringer, based in Hong Kong, where he co-heads the firm's competition practice in Asia. His practice covers advising clients on competition law matters across Asia, including in relation to merger control, foreign investment regulations and antitrust enforcement. Alastair has worked with Freshfields in the London, Brussels and Washington DC offices. His career also includes four years at the UK's competition authority, the Office of Fair Trading (2007-2011), where he was Director of its Mergers Group and then Director of a dedicated competition enforcement team.

Miranda Noble

Miranda Noble is a partner at MinterEllison. She is known for providing clients with clear, pragmatic and responsive advice to assist them in navigating Australia's competition and consumer laws to ensure they achieve their objectives and manage risk. She has deep expertise in complex competition issues in domestic and global M&A transactions, both through the Australian Competition and Consumer Commission's informal clearance process and in merger authorisation applications and associated litigation before the Australian Competition Tribunal and Federal Court.

Jens Munk Plum

Jens Munk Plum is a partner at Kromann Reumert in Copenhagen. He is experienced in all aspects of competition law, particularly abuse of dominance, including discount schemes, prices and refusal to supply. Jens also has extensive experience in mergers, and has special knowledge within the telecommunications, finance, retail and industry sectors. He represented EY in the gun jumping case before the ECJ. Drawing on his in-depth knowledge of Danish and international case law and the competition authorities' practices and procedures, Jens provides solution-oriented advice and is able to quickly understand his clients' businesses. Jens has conducted several landmark cases before the Danish Competition Council and the Danish Competition Appeals Tribunal, and has also handled criminal competition cases.

Amilcar Peredo

Amilcar Peredo is a partner at Basham, Ringe y Correa in Mexico. He has broad experience representing national and international clients in all areas of competition law, including pre-merger filings before the Competition Commission, investigations for cartel cases and abuse of dominance, leniency applications, compliance programs and general advice on competition matters. In 2004 published one of the few books on Mexican antitrust law called (in English) "Economic Competition: Theory and Practice" which is used as a text in many Mexican universities. He obtained his law degree at the Universidad Nacional Autonoma de Mexico in 1996.He also obtained a masters degree at the Georgetown University Law Center, specializing in antitrust law.

Paul Schoff

Paul Schoff is a partner at MinterEllison. He specialises in advising on risks from the access and restrictive trade practices provisions of Australia's Competition & Consumer Act, including misuse of market power and price fixing. He manages risk for his clients from regulatory investigations, defends enforcement action under competition and securities laws, as well as achieves competition clearance for major mergers. His specialties include risk & regulatory, antitrust, competition law, cartels, communications regulation, securities regulation, executive accountability frameworks.

Christian Steinle

Christian Steinle is a partner at Gleiss Lutz in Stuttgart and Brussels. He has considerable experience in European and international antitrust law. He focuses on merger control and cartel cases as well as private antitrust litigation, online and distribution antitrust law, antitrust compliance programmes and internal investigations. He co-heads Gleiss Lutz's interdisciplinary Compliance & Investigations focus group and is member of the IBA Merger Working Group. Christian studied in Tübingen, Fribourg (Switzerland), Bonn and Speyer. He has been a partner at Gleiss Lutz since 2008. In 2004 he was seconded as in-house counsel to a multinational group where he specialised in international antitrust litigation.

Didier Théophile

Didier Théophile is a partner at Darrois Villey Maillot Brochier. He is the founder and head of the firm's antitrust and competition law practice. His practice covers all aspects of competition law from counseling to litigation, including matters of merger control, non-merger conduct, and state aid. He regularly represents clients before French and European competition authorities and has significant experience in large cross-border transactions and high-profile antitrust litigation and private enforcement actions. He is also particularly recognized for his antitrust law expertise in regulated sectors, such as media and telecom. Didier teaches competition law at Strasbourg University. A former Non-Governmental Advisor for the French competition authority to the International Competition Network, Didier Théophile is the President of the association of lawyers specializing in competition law in France.

Anastasia Usova

Anastasia Usova is a counsel and Head of the Antitrust practice of Redcliffe Partners with more than 10 years of experience in competition law at leading law firms in Ukraine and Belgium. She focuses on complex antitrust matters, such as abuse of dominance, cartels, commercial and pricing practices, and distribution agreements. Anastasia also assists clients with merger notifications in Ukraine and has experience in the coordination of multijurisdictional merger filings in the CIS and the EU. In addition, Anastasia deals with the unfair competition issues, such as misleading advertising and unauthorised use of trademarks. Anastasia is recognized among Next generation lawyers in Competition by Legal 500 and recommended among leading practitioners in Competition/ Antitrust Law in Ukraine by The Best Lawyers.

Amalie Wijesundera

Amalie Wijesundera is a Senior Associate in Schellenberg Wittmer's Competition as well as Information and Communication Technology Groups in Zurich. She graduated from the University of Berne and prior to joining Schellenberg Wittmer worked as a Scientific Collaborator at the Competition Commission of Switzerland.

Atsushi Yamada

Atsushi Yamada is a partner at Anderson Mori & Tomotsune focusing on competition law. Prior to joining Anderson Mori & Tomotsune, he has worked at the Tokyo office of a US law firm and a local Japanese firm after serving as a judge at the Tokyo District Court as well as other courts. With such background, Mr. Yamada has extensive experience in litigation and general corporate matters. His competition law practice covers a broad area including assisting clients in investigations by competition authorities (cartels/dominance/unfair trade practices), representation in courts and tribunals challenging decisions made by competition authorities, follow-on civil litigation, and merger filings. He also provides advice relating to structuring new businesses and compliance. His clients include both multinational and Japanese companies in various industries, such as information technology, pharmaceutical, manufacturing, construction, transportation, financial institutions and trading houses.

Cristianne Zarzur

Cristianne Saccab Zarzur is a partner at Pinheiro Neto Advogados. She is a permanent board member of the Brazilian Institute of Competition and Consumer Relations, having previously been its president (from 2014 to 2015), vice president (from 2012 to 2013), director of legal affairs (from 2010 to 2011) and a counsellor (from 2006 to 2009). She graduated in law from the Universidade Presbiteriana Mackenzie, Brazil in 1995 and specialised in law and fundamentals of the economy for lawyers at the Fundação Getúlio Vargas – Escola de Administração de Empresas de São Paulo, Brazil in 2002. She also worked as a foreign associate at Howrey LLC in 2000/2001.

Concurrences
Competition Laws Review

Concurrences Review

Concurrences is a print and online quarterly peer reviewed journal dedicated to EU and national competitions laws. It has been launched in 2004 as the flagship of the Institute of Competition Law in order to provide a forum for academics, practitioners and enforcers. The Institute's influence and expertise has garnered interviews with such figures as Christine Lagarde, Bill Kovacic, François Hollande and Margarethe Vestager.

CONTENTS

More than 15,000 articles, print and/or online. Quarterly issues provide current coverage with contributions from the EU or national or foreign countries thanks to more than 1,200 authors in Europe and abroad. Approximately 25 % of the contributions are published in English, 75 % in French, as the official language of the General Court of justice of the EU; all contributions have English abstracts.

FORMAT

In order to balance academic contributions with opinions or legal practice notes, Concurrences provides its insight and analysis in a number of formats:

- Forewords: Opinions by leading academics or enforcers
- Interviews: Interviews of antitrust experts
- On-Topics: 4 to 6 short papers on hot issues
- Law & Economics: Short papers written by economists for a legal audience
- Articles: Long academic papers
- Case Summaries: Case commentary on EU and French case law
- Legal Practice: Short papers for in-house counsels
- International: Medium size papers on international policies
- Books Review: Summaries of recent antitrust books
- Articles Review: Summaries of leading articles published in 45 antitrust journals

BOARDS

The Scientific Committee is headed by Laurence Idot, Professor at Panthéon Assas University. The International Committee is headed by Frederic Jenny, OECD Competition Comitteee Chairman. Boards members include Bruno Lasserre, Mario Monti, Howard Shelanski, Richard Whish, Wouter Wils, etc.

ONLINE VERSION

Concurrences website provides all articles published since its inception, in addition to selected articles published online only in the electronic supplement.

WRITE FOR CONCURRENCES

Concurrences welcome spontaneous contributions. Except in rare circumstances, the journal accepts only unpublished articles, whatever the form and nature of the contribution. The Editorial Board checks the form of the proposals, and then submits these to the Scientific Committee. Selection of the papers is conditional to a peer review by at least two members of the Committee. Within a month, the Committee assesses whether the draft article can be published and notifies the author.

e-Competitions
Antitrust Case Laws e-Bulletin

e-Competitions Bulletin

CASE LAW DATABASE

e-Competitions is the only online resource that provides consistent coverage of antitrust cases from 55 jurisdictions, organized into a searchable database structure. e-Competitions concentrates on cases summaries taking into account that in the context of a continuing growing number of sources there is a need for factual information, i.e., case law.

- 10,000 case summaries
- 3,500 authors
- 55 countries covered
- 26,500 subscribers

SOPHISTICATED EDITORIAL AND IT ENRICHMENT

e-Competitions is structured as a database. The editors make a sophisticated technical and legal work on all articles by tagging these with key words, drafting abstracts and writing html code to increase Google ranking. There is a team of antitrust lawyers – PhD and judges clerks - and a team of IT experts. e-Competitions makes comparative law possible. Thanks to this expert editorial work, it is possible to search and compare cases.

PRESTIGIOUS BOARDS

e-Competitions draws upon highly distinguished editors, all leading experts in national or international antitrust. Advisory Board Members include: Sir Christopher Bellamy, Ioanis Lianos (UCL), Eleanor Fox (NYU), Damien Géradin (Tilburg University), Barry Hawk (Fordham University) Fred Jenny (OECD), Jacqueline Riffault-Silk (Cour de cassation), Wouter Wils (DG COMP), etc.

LEADING PARTNERS

- Association of European Competition Law Judges: The AECLJ is a forum for judges of national Courts specializing in antitrust case law. Members timely feed e-Competitions with just released cases.
- Academics partners: Antitrust research centres from leading universities write regularly in e-Competitions: University College London, King's College London, Queen Mary University, etc.
- Law firms: Global law firms and antitrust niche firms write detailed cases summaries specifically for e-Competitions: Allen & Overy, DLA Piper, Jones Day, Norton Rose Fulbright, Skadden Arps, White & Case, etc.

INSTITUTE of
Competition Law
Antitrust databases and resources

The Institute of Competition Law

The Institute of Competition Law is a publishing company, founded in 2004 by Dr. Nicolas Charbit, based in Paris and New-York. The Institute cultivates scholarship and discussion about antitrust issues though publications and conferences. Each publication and event is supervised by editorial boards and scientific or steering committees to ensure independence, objectivity, and academic rigor. Thanks to this management, the Institute has become one of the few think tanks in Europe to have significant influence on antitrust policies.

AIM

The Institute focuses government, business and academic attention on a broad range of subjects which concern competition laws, regulations and related economics.

BOARDS

To maintain its unique focus, the Institute relies upon highly distinguished editors, all leading experts in national or international antitrust: Bill Kovacic, Mario Monti, Eleanor Fox, Barry Hawk, Laurence Idot, Fred Jenny, etc.

AUTHORS

3,800 authors, from 55 jurisdictions.

PARTNERS

- Universities: University College London, King's College London, Queen Mary University, Paris Sorbonne Panthéon-Assas, etc.
- Law firms: Allen & Overy, Cleary Gottlieb Steen & Hamilton, DLA Piper, Hogan Lovells, Jones Day, Norton Rose Fulbright, Skadden Arps, White & Case, etc.

EVENTS

More than 350 events since 2004 in Brussels, London, New York, Paris, Singapore and Washington, DC.

ONLINE VERSION

Concurrences website provides all articles published since its inception.

PUBLICATIONS

The Institute publishes Concurrences Journal, a print and online quarterly peer-reviewed journal dedicated to EU and national competitions laws. e-Competitions is a bi-monthly antitrust news bulletin covering 55 countries. The e-Competitions database contains over 12,000 case summaries from 2,600 authors.

Concurrences+
ANTITRUST LAW PORTAL

15 years of archives 25,000 articles

4 DATABASES

Concurrences Review:
Access to latest issue and archives

- 25,000 articles from 2004 to the present
- European and national doctrine and case law

e-Competitions Bulletin:
Access to latest issue and archives

- 10,000 case summaries from 1911 to the present
- Case law of 55 jurisdictions

Conferences:
Access to the documentation of all Concurrences events

- 300 conferences (New York, Washington DC, Brussels, Paris, London, Hong Kong)
- 250 PowerPoint presentations, proceedings and syntheses
- 450 videos
- Verbatim reports (in progress)

e-Books:
Access to all Concurrences books

- 27 e-Books available
- 5 forthcoming
- PDF version

NEW

New search engine:
Optimized results to save time

- Search results sorted by date, jurisdiction, keyword, economic sector, author, etc.

New modes of access:
IP address recognition

- No need to enter codes: immediate access
- No need to change codes when your team changes: offers increased security and saves time

Mobility:

- Responsive design: site optimized for tablets and smartphones

www.ingramcontent.com/pod-product-compliance
Lightning Source LLC
LaVergne TN
LVHW051048210926
848486LV00001B/45
9781939007100